N STUDIES INFORMATION GUIDE SERIES

Donald Koster, Professor of English, Adelphi University,
lew York

ies:

ICAN LITERATURE AND CULTURE SINCE WORLD WAR II—
*les D. Peavy**

ARCHITECTURE AND ART—*Edited by David M. Sokol*

FOLKLORE—*Edited by Richard M. Dorson**

HUMOR AND HUMORISTS—*Edited by M. Thomas Inge**

LANGUAGE AND LITERATURE—*Edited by Henry Wasser**

MUSIC—*Edited by Barbara Hampton**

POPULAR CULTURE—*Edited by Marshall W. Fishwick*
*drum**

CAN PRESIDENCY—*Edited by Kenneth E. Davison**

RELIGION AND PHILOSOPHY—*Edited by Ernest R. Sandeen**

STUDIES—*Edited by David W. Marcell**

OGY OF THE AMERICAS—*Edited by Thomas C. Greaves**

IN AMERICA—*Edited by Richard G. Durnin**

RICAN JEWISH LITERATURE—*Edited by Ira Bruce Nadel**

OF AMERICA—*Edited by Charles Mark*

AMERICA—*Edited by Virginia R. Terris**

s is part of the

ORMATION GUIDE LIBRARY

nsists of a number of separate series of guides covering
he social sciences, humanities, and current affairs.

Paul Wasserman, Professor and former Dean, School of
formation Services, University of Maryland

HISTORY
UNITED
OF AM

The above ser
GALE INF

The Library c
major areas in

General Editor
Library and In

HISTORY OF THE UNITED STATES OF AMERICA

A GUIDE TO INFORMATION SOURCES

Volume 3 in the American Studies Information Guide Series

Ernest Cassara

Professor of History
George Mason University
Fairfax, Virginia

Gale Research Company
Book Tower, Detroit, Michigan 48226

Library of Congress Cataloging in Publication Data

Cassara, Ernest, 1925-
  History of the United States of America.

  (American studies information guide series; v. 3) (Gale information
guide library)
  Includes index.
  1. United States--History--Bibliography. I. Title.
Z1236.C33 [E178]   016.973   73-17551
ISBN 0-8103-1266-2

VITA

Ernest Cassara is professor of history and former chairman of the department at George Mason University, Fairfax, Virginia. He is a graduate of Tufts University and received his Ph.D. from Boston University. He has taught at Tufts; Albert Schweitzer College, Churwalden, the Grisons, Switzerland, where he served as director of the college; and at Goddard College, where he also served as dean. He was visiting professor of history at the University of Munich, under the Fulbright-Hays program, in the academic year 1975-76. He is author of ENLIGHTENMENT IN AMERICA.

CONTENTS

Contents

Contents

Contents

Contents

Contents

Contents

FOREWORD

Basic to the broad range of American studies is American history, the record of America's past as set down both by those actively involved in its making and by those who have devoted their professional lives to its observation and analysis. Despite the relatively short span of this record, its scope and complexity are staggering.

To comb this tremendous field in order to produce a reliable and useful guide to study and research is a task that makes the adjective "formidable" seem a gross understatement. I believe, however, that Professor Cassara has succeeded beyond expectation in doing exactly that. My reading of his manuscript has left me with a feeling of admiration for the skill, the objectivity, and the sense of balance he has employed in the painstaking job of selecting and annotating the approximately two thousand items that comprise his bibliographical listing.

Beyond his achievement in judicious selection is that of his unusually fine organization of his manifold materials. The reader will, I think, find it remarkably easy to use Professor Cassara's guide in picking his way through the tangled growth of America's history. A reference volume can have few greater virtues.

Donald N. Koster
Series Editor

ACKNOWLEDGMENTS

I have enjoyed the facilities and the helpfulness of the staffs of the following libraries in the preparation of this book, and it is a pleasure to acknowledge my debt to them: the Fenwick Library, George Mason University; the Widener Library, Harvard University; the Library of Congress; the New York Public Library (especially Reference Room 315A, American History); and the Alderman Library, the University of Virginia.

Special words of appreciation are due my graduate students at George Mason University, who have influenced the selection of books and what I have had to say about them; my colleagues on the faculty, who have given words of encouragement and sage advice; the Committee on Educational Aid and Faculty Research, for a grant which made it possible for me to spend time at more distant libraries; and to May L. Thompson, Doris N. Suttlehan, and Barbara S. Cooper, who typed the manuscript and who doubtless thought the stream of annotations would never end.

Greenwood, Maine

INTRODUCTION

A. ON THE CHOICE OF BOOKS

More than once during the preparation of this guide the author has had occasion to recall the story of the Maine potato farmer at harvest time sitting among piles of spuds and sorting them for market in small, medium, and large sizes. A visitor, after observing the process for a time, asked him if he did not get bored working at a job like that hour after hour. On the contrary, said the farmer, it was not a boring job but a very difficult one because it required so much thought. "Thought?" asked the incredulous visitor. "Yes," replied the farmer. "You have to make so many choices."

There are literally thousands of works on American history from which to choose. It has been very difficult to separate out the two thousand or so included in this annotated bibliography. Naturally, not all will agree with the choice that has been made. On the whole, however, the books included are those which have received recognition for making valuable contributions to our understanding of the American past. Most were published in the past generation, but an effort has been made to include older works that have achieved a lasting place in historical literature. Because of space considerations, a deliberate decision was made early in the selection process to exclude journal articles, no matter how worthy, and to concentrate on books. Actually many articles do appear as selections in anthologies that will be found under various topics.

It is hoped that this guide will prove useful to the layman who enjoys reading history as well as to students seeking guidance in research projects and to librarians trying to be helpful. Since historians argue among themselves--as do members of other disciplines--an attempt has been made to include a spectrum of interpretations. It is important that the existence of varieties of interpretation be recognized by layman and student alike. Only in rare instances, however, have schools of thought been labelled as such in the annotations.

The selection is made up of a mixture of narrative histories and monographs. Most can be labelled as scholarly, but there is a good sprinkling of so-called popular books that make for enjoyable reading. To have eliminated the latter completely would have given a distorted view of what literature is available.

This is not to say, however, that this author considers the scholarly works included dull!

The American past is too rich a field to be left solely to historians. Thus, the reader will find here a liberal number of books by literary critics, economists, political scientists, sociologists, social psychologists, journalists, and others. This is especially true of the sections devoted to the period since World War II, where many of the works listed are by persons who are not historians. This is as it should be, since historians must patiently wait the passage of time before subjecting events to their evaluation. What is included in these latter sections can be looked on as the raw material of history. In using it--as Carl Becker would have put it--Everyman is his own historian.

Included for most time periods is a generous selection of biographies, autobiographies, and the collected writings of prominent individuals. These lists, far from complete, are meant to be suggestive of the rich literature available. Extensive lists of such works may be found in many of the reference works included in part I, especially in the excellent new edition of the HARVARD GUIDE TO AMERICAN HISTORY. (See entry no. 48 below.)

A word, possibly of apology, should be said about the problems of annotation. It is difficult, not to say foolhardy, to summarize a book in a few lines. In many cases, I have attempted to give an indication of a book's argument and point of view, though in the case of long, complex works, this approach has generally been avoided. It is hoped, in any case, that no serious distortions have crept in.

B. HOW TO USE THIS GUIDE

The first chapter of this guide (1) is devoted to information about reference materials, research facilities, journals, and other matters a reader will find useful in carrying through a research project.

The second chapter (2) lists works that cover the full span of American history or substantial portions of it. These works, which are both general and topical in nature, provide background on a given subject.

The remaining chapters of the guide (3-9) are arranged to follow the chronology of American history. Included in these sections are specialized works which go into detail on particular events.

For each time period, topical headings have been given. Some of these vary from period to period. Witchcraft and prohibition, for instance, have not been constant issues in American life, whereas government and politics have.

It is suggested that in carrying out a research project, the reader refer to these chapters of the guide:

1. Reference works for particular events and persons

2. Comprehensive works for background

3-9. The appropriate sections of the chronology for books dealing with the topics*

Index. Comprehensive listings, especially for topics that span time periods

*Most of the books listed in this guide include bibliographies of their own. Therefore, no special mention of this has been made in the annotations.

Chapter 1

AIDS TO RESEARCH

A. REFERENCE WORKS

1. Comprehensive

1 COMPTON'S ENCYCLOPEDIA AND FACT-INDEX. 24 vols. Chicago:
F.E. Compton, 1971. Illus.

> Articles for a popular audience, profusely illustrated.
> Formerly entitled COMPTON'S PICTURED ENCYCLO-
> PEDIA (1922, 1924, 1928-38) and COMPTON'S PIC-
> TURED ENCYCLOPEDIA AND FACT-INDEX (1940-42,
> 1944-45, 1947-68).

2 THE ENCYCLOPEDIA AMERICANA. International ed. 30 vols. New
York: Americana Corp., 1975. Illus.

> A standard reference work of use to historians for handy
> reference. Successor to ENCYCLOPAEDIA AMERICANA
> (1829-58) and THE AMERICANA (1907-12).

3 THE NEW ENCYCLOPAEDIA BRITANNICA. 15th ed. 30 vols. Chicago:
Encyclopaedia Britannica, 1974. Illus.

> The new edition has been radically rearranged. It is
> divided into sections, one of which attempts to integrate
> various fields of knowledge into a comprehensible whole.
> Volume 1: PROPAEDIA: OUTLINE OF KNOWLEDGE
> AND GUIDE TO BRITANNICA; volumes 2-11: MICRO-
> PAEDIA: READY REFERENCE AND INDEX; volumes 12-
> 30: MACROPAEDIA: KNOWLEDGE IN DEPTH.

2. Historical

a. GENERAL

4 Cole, Donald B. HANDBOOK OF AMERICAN HISTORY. New York:

Harcourt, Brace & World, 1968. 350 p. Maps, tables. Paperbound.

> A book that can be used for reference or general read-
> ing. Cole has divided American history into the tradi-
> tional periods and has listed events by date, with expla-
> nations of their importance. He includes brief biograph-
> ical summaries of significant persons within each time
> frame.

5   CONCISE DICTIONARY OF AMERICAN HISTORY. Edited by Wayne
Andrews. New York: Charles Scribner's Sons, 1962. 1,164 p.

> A condensation of James Truslow Adams. DICTIONARY
> OF AMERICAN HISTORY, q.v., no. 6.

6   DICTIONARY OF AMERICAN HISTORY. Edited by James Truslow Adams.
2d ed., rev. 7 vols., including index and supplement. New York:
Charles Scribner's Sons, 1940, 1961 [supplement].

> The most reliable dictionary available, edited by a
> leading scholar. The articles are full and informative.

7   ENCYCLOPEDIA OF AMERICAN HISTORY. Edited by Stephen P. Elliott.
Guilford, Conn.: Dushkin Publishing Group, 1973. 413 p. Illus.,
ports., maps, charts.

> Articles were contributed by a group of noted scholars.
> The book includes many portraits and other illustrations
> in an attractive format. Also included is a bibliography
> of recent works in American history, arranged by period.

8   HARPER'S ENCYCLOPEDIA OF UNITED STATES HISTORY. Edited by
Benson John Lossing. 10 vols. New York: Harper & Brothers, 1901.

> An older work of continuing value because of the stand-
> ing of the scholars who contributed to it. They include
> John Fiske, Woodrow Wilson, Alfred T. Mahan, and
> Moses Coit Tyler.

9   Hurwitz, Howard L. AN ENCYCLOPEDIC DICTIONARY OF AMERICAN
HISTORY. New York: Washington Square Press, 1968. 894 p.

> For quick reference. Includes brief listings of persons,
> places, and explanations of events.

10   Johnson, Thomas H., ed. THE OXFORD COMPANION TO AMERICAN
HISTORY. New York: Oxford University Press, 1966. 912 p.

> In consultation with historian Harvey W. Wish, Johnson
> has written a useful reference work. The encyclopedic
> entries are informative and make enjoyable reading.
> This virtue is probably due to the fact that Johnson is
> a literary scholar.

11   Morris, Richard B., ed. ENCYCLOPEDIA OF AMERICAN HISTORY.
      Enl. and updated. New York: Harper & Row, 1970. 864 p. Illus.,
      maps.

      Morris arranges events in a basic political chronology.
      In addition, he provides chronologies of developments
      in economic, social, intellectual, and cultural spheres
      and biographies of 400 famous individuals.

12   THE STATISTICAL HISTORY OF THE UNITED STATES FROM COLONIAL
      TIMES TO THE PRESENT. Stamford, Conn.: Fairfield Publishers, 1965;
      distributed by Horizon Press, New York. 1,015 p. Illus., tables.

      Combines HISTORICAL STATISTICS OF THE UNITED
      STATES, COLONIAL TIMES TO 1957 (1960) and the
      Continuation to 1962 and Revisions (1965). The editors
      have accomplished the task by the interleaving of the
      volumes. Statistics on all aspects of American life are
      to be found here, including population and migration,
      economics (industry, labor, agriculture, and trade),
      transportation and communication, elections and politics,
      etc.

13   WEBSTER'S GUIDE TO AMERICAN HISTORY: A CHRONOLOGICAL,
      GEOGRAPHICAL, AND BIOGRAPHICAL SURVEY AND COMPENDIUM.
      Edited by Charles Van Doren and Robert McHenry. Springfield, Mass.:
      Merriam Co., 1971. 1,441 p. Illus., ports., maps, tables, cartoons.

      A useful reference guide. The first part of the work is
      made up of a chronological table of events from 1492 to
      1969, accompanied by apt quotations from leading
      figures in each period. The remaining part of the book
      is devoted to maps and tables which deal with a variety
      of topics, political and cultural, followed by over 1,000
      biographies of prominent figures.

b. TOPICAL

14   Bergman, Peter M., ed. THE CHRONOLOGICAL HISTORY OF THE
      NEGRO IN AMERICA. New York: Harper & Row, 1969. 698 p.

      A year-by-year listing of developments, from 1492 to
      1968. Bergman also includes a brief "bibliography of
      bibliographies."

15   Boatner, Mark Mayo III. THE CIVIL WAR DICTIONARY. New York:
      David McKay, 1959. 990 p. Illus., maps, diagrams.

      Contains entries on individuals (about 2,000 biographical

sketches), companies, battles, etc. Boatner, a former army officer, defines military terms in a manner helpful to the layman. The maps and diagrams complement the text.

16 _____. ENCYCLOPEDIA OF THE AMERICAN REVOLUTION. New York: David McKay, 1966. 1,308 p. Maps.

A useful reference work by a military man. Includes critiques and comments on the battles. Maps give clear indications of military movements.

17 Filler, Louis. A DICTIONARY OF AMERICAN SOCIAL REFORM. New York: Philosophical Library, 1963. 859 p.

Much more comprehensive than the title implies. Includes hundreds of entries on social movements, reformers, and events--many of them beyond the scope of what would usually be classed under social reform. Lucid, concise definitions.

18 Greene, Evarts B., and Harrington, Virginia D. AMERICAN POPULA-TION BEFORE THE FEDERAL CENSUS OF 1790. 1932. Reprint. Gloucester, Mass.: Peter Smith, 1966. 228 p.

Compiles figures from various sources, such as the records of the states, to give a picture of population and its distribution in America before the first census was taken by the new federal government in 1790.

19 Hodge, Frederick Webb, ed. HANDBOOK OF AMERICAN INDIANS NORTH OF MEXICO. 2 vols. 1905. Reprint. New York: Pageant Books, 1959. Illus.

A massive encyclopedia of Indian life, originally issued by the Smithsonian Institution's Bureau of American Ethnology.

20 INTERNATIONAL LIBRARY OF NEGRO LIFE AND HISTORY. Edited by Charles H. Wesley et al. 10 vols. New York: Publishers Co., 1967-68. Illus., ports.

The volumes in the collection were written or edited by experts in various fields and include historical and cultural themes. Well illustrated.

c. BIOGRAPHICAL

i. General

21 CONCISE DICTIONARY OF AMERICAN BIOGRAPHY. Edited by Joseph G.E. Hopkins et al. New York: Charles Scribner's Sons, 1964. 1,283 p.

A condensation of the DICTIONARY OF AMERICAN BIOGRAPHY, q.v., no. 22.

22   DICTIONARY OF AMERICAN BIOGRAPHY. Edited by Allen Johnson et al. 21 vols., 3 supplements. New York: Charles Scribner's Sons, 1928- .

The standard reference work of American biography. The entries, which are very full, were written by well-known scholars. The editors have included only persons who are deceased. Supplementary volumes are published from time to time; the third supplement brings the work to 1945. For quick reference, a condensation of the main work is available in the CONCISE DICTIONARY OF AMERICAN BIOGRAPHY, q.v., no. 21.

23   THE NATIONAL CYCLOPAEDIA OF AMERICAN BIOGRAPHY: BEING THE HISTORY OF THE UNITED STATES ILLUSTRATED IN THE LIVES OF THE FOUNDERS, BUILDERS, AND DEFENDERS OF THE REPUBLIC, AND OF THE MEN AND WOMEN WHO ARE DOING THE WORK AND MOULDING THE THOUGHT OF THE PRESENT TIME. Edited "by Distinguished Biographers . . . ." 53 vols. and 12 supplements to date. Clifton, N.J.: James T. White Co., 1892- . Ports.

An older work which has been supplemented periodically with new volumes. Portraits of the subjects are included.

24   WHO'S WHO IN AMERICA, 1976-1977. 39th ed. 2 vols. Chicago: Marquis, 1976.

The most authoritative reference work on prominent Americans. Brief entries give factual information.

25   WHO WAS WHO IN AMERICA. 6 vols. Chicago: Marquis, 1942- .

Biographies of prominent Americans who are deceased. Five numbered volumes (1-5) provide entries on individuals from 1896 to 1973. An unnumbered volume (rev. ed., 1967) gives biographies from 1607 to 1896.

ii. Topical

26   BIOGRAPHICAL DIRECTORY OF THE UNITED STATES EXECUTIVE BRANCH, 1774-1971. Edited by Robert Sobel. Westport, Conn.: Greenwood Press, 1971. 501 p.

Brief biographies of presidents, vice presidents, and cabinet members. Presidents of the Continental Congress are included.

27   CONTEMPORARY AUTHORS: A BIO-BIBLIOGRAPHICAL GUIDE TO CUR-
      RENT AUTHORS AND THEIR WORKS. Edited by Clare D. Kinsman. 64
      vols. to date. Detroit: Gale Research Co., 1962- . Biannual.

      Biographical listings of use to the student of recent his-
      tory. Volumes 1-24 have been revised and updated.

28   DIRECTORY OF AMERICAN SCHOLARS. 6th ed. Vol. 1: HISTORY.
      New York: Bowker, 1974. 772 p.

      A work compiled with the cooperation of the Council of
      Learned Societies. Includes brief biographical entries
      on practicing historians and a geographic index.

29   NOTABLE AMERICAN WOMEN, 1607-1950. Edited by Edward T. James
      et al. 3 vols. Cambridge, Mass.: Harvard University Press, 1971.

      An attempt to rectify the inequities of earlier biogra-
      phical reference works which tend to ignore all but the
      most famous women. The selections, which are full and
      informative, were written by scholars who specialize in
      the history of the various fields represented by women
      covered.

30   U.S. Congress. House. BIOGRAPHICAL DIRECTORY OF THE AMERICAN
      CONGRESS, 1774-1961. 85th Cong., 2d sess. House Document no.
      442. Washington, D.C.: Government Printing Office, 1961. 1,863 p.
      Illus.

      Brief biographical sketches of all persons who have
      served in the American Congresses. Included are those
      in the Continental Congress, 1774-88, and the Congress
      under the Constitution to the year 1961.

31   U.S. Department of the Interior. BIOGRAPHICAL AND HISTORICAL
      INDEX OF AMERICAN INDIANS AND PERSONS INVOLVED IN INDIAN
      AFFAIRS. 8 vols. Boston: G.K. Hall, 1966.

      A massive collection of information. Includes bibliog-
      raphy.

32   WHO'S WHO OF AMERICAN WOMEN, 1974-1975. 8th ed. Chicago:
      Marquis, 1973.

      Cites prominent women in American society.

3. Related Fields

33   DICTIONARY OF THE SOCIAL SCIENCES. Edited by Julius Gould and
      William L. Kolb. New York: Free Press of Glencoe, 1964. 777 p.

      Articles written by British Commonwealth and American

scholars and published under the auspices of UNESCO
to promote a uniform terminology in the social sciences.

34   THE ENCYCLOPEDIA OF PHILOSOPHY.   Edited by Paul Edwards et al.
8 vols. in 4.   1967.   Reprint.   New York: Macmillan, 1972.

Articles by leading scholars of philosophy, political
science, history, and other fields, on individuals, philosophical ideas and systems, etc. Each article includes
a bibliography.

35   Hart, James D.   THE OXFORD COMPANION TO AMERICAN LITERA-
TURE.   4th ed.   New York: Oxford University Press, 1965.   1,004 p.
Table.

A reference work containing brief entries on authors,
books, periodicals, literary genres, cultural institutions,
philosophical concepts, etc. Excellent for handy reference is the "Chronological Index," a table which gives
literary developments in parallel columns with political
and social developments.

36   INTERNATIONAL ENCYCLOPEDIA OF THE SOCIAL SCIENCES.   Edited
by David L. Sills.   17 vols.   New York: Macmillan, 1968.   Illus.

Successor to the ENCYCLOPEDIA OF THE SOCIAL
SCIENCES. Lengthy articles by recognized scholars,
with bibliographies appended. The final volume includes
a directory of contributors and an index.

37   Jones, Howard Mumford, and Ludwig, Richard M.   GUIDE TO AMERICAN
LITERATURE AND ITS BACKGROUNDS SINCE 1890.   4th ed., rev. and
enl.   Cambridge, Mass.: Harvard University Press, 1972.   278 p.

Gives lists of books on general history and background
of the period covered and provides lists of significant
authors and bibliography on various literary trends.

B. ATLASES

38   THE AMERICAN HERITAGE PICTORIAL ATLAS OF UNITED STATES HIS-
TORY.   Edited by Hilde Heun Kagan.   New York: American Heritage
Publishing Co.; distributed by McGraw-Hill Book Co., 1966.   424 p.
Illus., maps.

Maps in full color with accompanying commentary, from
prehistoric America to the venture into space. Of particular note are the portfolios of pictorial maps: Battles
of the Revolution, City Views, Battles of the Civil War,
National Parks of the United States.

39   ATLAS OF AMERICAN HISTORY. Edited by James Truslow Adams and
      R.V. Coleman. New York: Charles Scribner's Sons, 1943. 360 p.
      Maps.

      A historical atlas with 147 maps arranged chronologically.
      Includes maps of roads, canals, railroads, military cam-
      paigns, forts. Designed as a supplement to the DIC-
      TIONARY OF AMERICAN HISTORY, q.v., no. 6.

40   Esposito, Vincent J., ed. THE WEST POINT ATLAS OF AMERICAN
      WARS. 2 vols. New York: Praeger, 1959. Maps, tables.

      This extensive work provides commentary and maps of
      actions in major engagements in the wars fought by the
      United States. Volume 1: 1689-1900; volume 2: 1900-
      1953.

41   Lord, Clifford L., and Lord, Elizabeth H. HISTORICAL ATLAS OF THE
      UNITED STATES. Rev. ed. 1953. Reprint. New York: Johnson Re-
      print Corp., 1969. 253 p. Illus., maps.

      The period covered is 1486-1950. Maps are topogra-
      phical, demographical, ecological, political, social,
      etc.

42   Shepherd, William R. HISTORICAL ATLAS. 9th ed., rev. 1964. Re-
      print (with further revisions). New York: Barnes & Noble, 1973. 379
      p. Maps, tables.

      An authoritative atlas of world history which includes
      maps and tables on developments in the United States.

43   U.S. Department of the Interior. Geological Survey. THE NATIONAL
      ATLAS OF THE UNITED STATES OF AMERICA. Washington, D.C.: Gov-
      ernment Printing Office, 1970. 430 p. Maps.

      A splendid collection of maps with explanations of pro-
      cedures used in creating them. Sections: general re-
      ference maps; special subject maps; physical (landforms,
      geophysical forces, geology, marine features, soils, cli-
      mate, water); economic (fishing and forestry, mineral
      and energy resources, manufacturing, business, transpor-
      tation); socio-cultural; administrative (congressional dis-
      tricts, etc.); mapping and charting; world. The history
      section includes maps of prehistoric sites; Indian tribes,
      cultures, and languages; discovery of North America;
      exploration and settlement; territorial growth; battle
      sites; election results; historic landmarks; geographic
      expeditions.

C. BIBLIOGRAPHIES

1. General

44 American Bibliographical Center. AMERICA: HISTORY AND LIFE: A GUIDE TO PERIODICAL LITERATURE. Santa Barbara, Calif.: Clio Press, 1964-   .

> A quarterly index of periodical literature from 1964, with precis of individual articles. A five-year index, 1964-69, was published in 1971.

45 Beers, Henry P. BIBLIOGRAPHIES IN AMERICAN HISTORY: GUIDE TO MATERIALS FOR RESEARCH. 2d ed. New York: H.W. Wilson, 1942. 503 p.

> Includes bibliographies of published and manuscript materials to the end of 1941. Categories include general research aids, period and topical listings (such specialized fields as diplomatic, economic, education, social, cultural).

46 Cohen, Hennig, ed. ARTICLES IN AMERICAN STUDIES, 1954-1968: A CUMULATION OF THE ANNUAL BIBLIOGRAPHIES FROM "AMERICAN QUARTERLY." 2 vols. Ann Arbor, Mich.: Pierian Press, 1972.

> Bibliographies of articles reprinted as they appeared, year by year, in the AMERICAN QUARTERLY of the American Studies Association. Brief annotations. Volume 2 includes indices of authors and personal names. Volume 1: 1954-63; volume 2: 1964-68. These bibliographies were edited successively for the ASA by Donald N. Koster and Myron H. Luke.

47 GUIDE TO HISTORICAL LITERATURE. Edited for the American Historical Association by George F. Howe et al. New York: Macmillan, 1961. 997 p.

> An annotated bibliography which deals with history generally but has an excellent section on the United States.

48 HARVARD GUIDE TO AMERICAN HISTORY. Edited by Frank Freidel and Richard K. Showman. 2 vols. Rev. ed. Cambridge, Mass.: Harvard University Press, 1974.

> A standard research guide in a newly revised edition. Sections deal with research, writing, editing documents, aids to research, etc. The bulk of the work is devoted to extensive bibliographies arranged chronologically and topically, with a section on biographical writings.

49 HISTORY: REVIEWS OF NEW BOOKS. Washington: Heldref Publications, 1971- .

  Issued monthly, ten times a year. A section of each issue is devoted to works in American history. Books are reviewed within a few months of publication.

50 REVIEWS IN AMERICAN HISTORY. Westport, Conn.: Redgrave Information Resources, 1973- .

  A quarterly publication made up of essay reviews of recent works in American history. The reviewers are well-known historians.

51 U.S. Library of Congress. A GUIDE TO THE STUDY OF THE UNITED STATES OF AMERICA: REPRESENTATIVE BOOKS REFLECTING THE DEVELOPMENT OF AMERICAN LIFE AND THOUGHT. Edited by Roy P. Basler et al. Washington, D.C.: Government Printing Office, 1960. 1,208 p.

  Sections of the work, which contains 6,487 annotated entries, range from literature on political events to various aspects of social life and culture. Topical arrangement.

52 Winchell, Constance M. GUIDE TO REFERENCE BOOKS. 8th ed. Chicago: American Library Association, 1967. 762 p.

  Annotated entries. Includes a section on U.S. history which lists guides, bibliographies, indices, manuscripts and archives, regions, historical societies, dictionaries and handbooks, general histories, source books, and atlases. Three supplements, by Eugene P. Sheehy, were published for 1965-66, 1967-68, 1969-70.

53 WRITINGS ON AMERICAN HISTORY. Washington, D.C.: American Historical Association, 1904- .

  An annual annotated compilation of historical works. Currently running several years behind, it has reached 1960. Index for the years 1902-40 was published by the Association in 1956.

54 WRITINGS ON AMERICAN HISTORY, 1973-74: A SUBJECT BIBLIOGRAPHY OF ARTICLES. Edited by James J. Dougherty et al. Washington, D.C.: American Historical Association, 1974. 276 p.

  First of a new series. Listings are reprinted from the AMERICAN HISTORICAL REVIEW and cover the period June 1973-June 1974. Arranged geographically and topically. No annotations.

2. Topical

55 Bemis, Samuel Flagg, and Griffin, Grace G. GUIDE TO THE DIPLO-
MATIC HISTORY OF THE UNITED STATES, 1775-1921. Washington,
D.C.: Government Printing Office, 1935. 996 p.

> An annotated guide by diplomatic historians of note.
> It is arranged chronologically and topically.

56 Cordasco, Francesco, and LaGumina, Salvatore. ITALIANS IN THE
UNITED STATES: A BIBLIOGRAPHY OF REPORTS, TEXTS, CRITICAL
STUDIES AND RELATED MATERIALS. New York: Oriole Editions, 1972.
153 p.

> Contains 1,462 items, including novels such as Mario
> Puzo's THE GODFATHER (1969). Some are annotated.

57 Dumond, Dwight L. A BIBLIOGRAPHY OF ANTISLAVERY IN AMERICA.
Ann Arbor: University of Michigan Press, 1961. 119 p.

> A definitive bibliography of the primary sources. Du-
> mond has included the significant writings of those who
> took part in the great campaign.

58 Hasse, Adelaide R. MATERIALS FOR A BIBLIOGRAPHY OF THE PUBLIC
ARCHIVES OF THE THIRTEEN ORIGINAL STATES: COVERING THE
COLONIAL PERIOD AND STATE PERIOD TO 1789. 1906. Reprint.
New York: Argonaut Press, 1966. 339 p.

> A state-by-state listing of archival holdings. Originally
> published as volume 2 of the ANNUAL REPORT OF THE
> AMERICAN HISTORICAL ASSOCIATION for 1906.

59 INDEX TO LITERATURE ON THE AMERICAN INDIAN. San Francisco:
Indian Historian Press, 1972- .

> An annual bibliography listing books and periodical
> articles for the year, starting with 1970. The 1972
> edition includes a list of native American publications.

60 Kaplan, Louis, et al. A BIBLIOGRAPHY OF AMERICAN AUTOBIOG-
RAPHIES. Madison: University of Wisconsin Press, 1961. 384 p.

> Brief descriptions of the authors and of contents of the
> volumes. 6,377 entries.

61 Nevins, Allan, et al., eds. CIVIL WAR BOOKS: A CRITICAL BIB-
LIOGRAPHY. 2 vols. Baton Rouge: Louisiana State University Press,
1967-69.

> Sponsored by the U.S. Civil War Centennial Commission.

Annotations are grouped under such headings as political, military, biographical, Negro. Nevins's collaborators were James I. Robertson, Jr., and Bell I.
Wiley.

62   Smith, James W., and Jamison, A. Leland, eds. RELIGION IN AMERI-
CAN LIFE. 4 vols. Princeton, N.J.: Princeton University Press, 1961.

The first two volumes contain essays by leading scholars
on various aspects of religion in American society. The
final volumes consist of a running commentary by Nelson
Burr on historical developments: A Critical Bibliography
of Religion in America. Volume 3: Part 1--Bibliogra-
phical Guides: General Surveys and Histories; Part 2--
Evolution of American Religion. Volume 4: Part 3--
Religion and Society; Part 4--Religion in the Arts and
Literature, Religion and the Arts; Part 5--Intellectual
History, Theology, Philosophy, and Science, American
Theology.

63   Trask, David F., et al. A BIBLIOGRAPHY OF UNITED STATES-LATIN
AMERICAN RELATIONS SINCE 1810: A SELECTED LIST OF ELEVEN
THOUSAND PUBLISHED REFERENCES. Lincoln: University of Nebraska
Press, 1968. 472 p.

Not annotated, but the editors explain their basis for
selection of the items included.

64   U.S. Library of Congress. THE NEGRO IN THE UNITED STATES: A
SELECTED BIBLIOGRAPHY. Edited by Dorothy B. Porter. Washington,
D.C.: Government Printing Office, 1970. 325 p.

Includes 1,781 entries with Library of Congress call
numbers, compiled by the librarian of the Negro Collection at Howard University.

65   Wynar, Lubomyr R. AMERICAN POLITICAL PARTIES: A SELECTIVE
GUIDE TO PARTIES AND MOVEMENTS OF THE 20th CENTURY. Little-
ton, Colo.: Libraries Unlimited, 1969. 427 p.

Includes 3,095 entries, with introductions to major
categories. Some individual listings are annotated,
especially of reference works.

3. Series

The American Historical Association, Washington, D.C., publishes a continuing
series of pamphlets of bibliographical essays by leading scholars. Those in the
U.S. series are listed below by author, with date of publication in parentheses.

66   Berwick, Keith B. THE FEDERAL AGE, 1789-1829 (1961). 42 p.

67   Blum, Albert B. A HISTORY OF THE AMERICAN LABOR MOVEMENT (1972). 41 p.

68   Bridges, Hal. CIVIL WAR AND RECONSTRUCTION. 2d ed. (1962). 25 p.

69   Carter, Harvey L. FAR WESTERN FRONTIERS (1972). 64 p.

70   DeConde, Alexander. NEW INTERPRETATIONS IN AMERICAN FOREIGN POLICY. 2d ed. (1961). 43 p.

71   Elkins, Stanley, and McKitrick, Eric. THE FOUNDING FATHERS: YOUNG MEN OF THE REVOLUTION (1962). 30 p.

72   Fite, Gilbert C. AMERICAN AGRICULTURE AND FARM POLICY SINCE 1900 (1964). 30 p.

73   Freidel, Frank. THE NEW DEAL IN HISTORICAL PERSPECTIVE. 2d ed. (1965). 25 p.

74   Galambos, Louis. AMERICAN BUSINESS HISTORY (1967). 34 p.

75   Gaustad, Edwin S. RELIGION IN AMERICA: HISTORY AND HISTO-RIOGRAPHY (1973). 59 p.

76   Grantham, Dewey W., Jr. CONTEMPORARY AMERICAN HISTORY: THE UNITED STATES SINCE 1945 (1975). 46 p.

77   Greene, Jack P. THE REAPPRAISAL OF THE AMERICAN REVOLUTION IN RECENT HISTORICAL LITERATURE (1967). 84 p.

78   Hagan, William T. THE INDIAN IN AMERICAN HISTORY (1971). 34 p.

79   Harlan, Louis R. THE NEGRO IN AMERICAN HISTORY (1965). 29 p.

80   Hicks, John D. NORMALCY AND REACTION, 1921-1933: AN AGE OF DISILLUSIONMENT (1960). 23 p.

81   May, Ernest R. AMERICAN INTERVENTION: 1917 AND 1941. 2d ed. (1969). 28 p.

82   Morgan, Edmund S. THE AMERICAN REVOLUTION: A REVIEW OF CHANGING INTERPRETATIONS (1958). 22 p.

83   Mowry, George E. THE PROGRESSIVE ERA, 1900-20: THE REFORM PERSUASION (1972). 39 p.

84   Scott, Franklin D. THE PEOPLING OF AMERICA: PERSPECTIVES ON IMMIGRATION (1972). 75 p.

85   Sellers, Charles Grier. JACKSONIAN DEMOCRACY (1958). 20 p.

86   Singletary, Otis A., and Bailey, Kenneth K. THE SOUTH IN AMERICAN HISTORY. 2d ed. (1965). 31 p.

87   Stevens, Harry R. THE MIDDLE WEST. 2d ed. (1965). 28 p.

88   Stover, John F. TRANSPORTATION IN AMERICAN HISTORY (1970). 40 p.

89   Wright, Louis B. NEW INTERPRETATIONS OF AMERICAN COLONIAL HISTORY. 3d ed. (1969). 32 p.

The Goldentree Bibliographies in American History, under the general editorship of Arthur S. Link, is a series in progress. Each volume is a select bibliography of books and articles (organized topically but without annotations), compiled by a recognized scholar. The series, available in hard cover and paperback, was originated by Appleton-Century-Crofts and is being continued by the AHM Publishing Corp., Northbrook, Illinois. The volumes available to date are listed below according to author, with date of publication in parentheses.

90   Bremner, Robert H. AMERICAN SOCIAL HISTORY SINCE 1860 (1971). 144 p.

91   Burr, Nelson R. RELIGION IN AMERICAN LIFE (1971). 192 p.

92   De Santis, Vincent P. THE GILDED AGE, 1877-1896 (1973). 168 p.

93   Donald, David. THE NATION IN CRISIS, 1861-1877 (1969). 112 p.

94   Fehrenbacher, Don E. MANIFEST DESTINY AND THE COMING OF THE CIVIL WAR (1970). 144 p.

95   Ferguson, E. James. CONFEDERATION, CONSTITUTION, AND EARLY NATIONAL PERIOD, 1781-1815 (1975). 168 p.

96   Fowler, Wilton B. AMERICAN DIPLOMATIC HISTORY SINCE 1890
      (1975). 176 p.

97   Greene, Jack P. THE AMERICAN COLONIES IN THE EIGHTEENTH
      CENTURY, 1689-1763 (1969). 160 p.

98   Grob, Gerald N. AMERICAN SOCIAL HISTORY BEFORE 1860 (1970).
      160 p.

99   Herbst, Jurgen. THE HISTORY OF AMERICAN EDUCATION (1973). 172
      p.

100   Kirkland, Edward C. AMERICAN ECONOMIC HISTORY SINCE 1860
      (1971). 96 p.

101   Link, Arthur S., and Leary, William M., Jr. THE PROGRESSIVE ERA
      AND THE GREAT WAR, 1896-1920 (1969). 96 p.

102   Shy, John. THE AMERICAN REVOLUTION (1973). 152 p.

103   Taylor, George Rogers. AMERICAN ECONOMIC HISTORY BEFORE 1860
      (1969). 128 p.

104   Vaughan, Alden T. THE AMERICAN COLONIES IN THE SEVENTEENTH
      CENTURY (1971). 144 p.

D. ARCHIVES AND LIBRARIES

The National Archives and Records Service in Washington, D.C., a division of
the General Services Administration, has the care of government documents and
records of historical value. The following publication is indispensable to the
person planning to use this repository:

105   U.S. National Archives and Records Service, General Services Adminis-
      tration. GUIDE TO THE NATIONAL ARCHIVES OF THE UNITED STATES.
      Washington, D.C.: Government Printing Office, 1974. 909 p.

          A guide that describes the history and function of each
          agency and lists records available. (In 1970, records
          totaled nearly one million cubic feet.) The guide is
          divided as follows: 1. U.S. Government--General; 2.
          Records of the Legislative Branch; 3. Records of the
          Judicial Branch; 4. Records of the Executive Branch
          (also includes independent agencies); 5. Records of,
          or Relating to, Other Governments (District of Columbia,
          Confederate records, Imperial Russian government records,

Virgin Islands, Spanish governors of Puerto Rico, Foreign
records seized, 1941-   ); and 6. Other Holdings.

106   FEDERAL RECORDS CENTERS.   These regional centers of the National
Archives contain the records of the federal district courts and other papers of
interest in a given region.   They are located in Atlanta, Boston, Chicago,
Denver, Forth Worth, Kansas City, Los Angeles, New York, Philadelphia, San
Francisco, Seattle, and Washington.

An unfortunate trend has allowed the dispersal of the records of administrations
since the late 1920s in presidential libraries across the country.   Thus far, the
following have been established:

107   HERBERT HOOVER LIBRARY, West Branch, Iowa.

108   FRANKLIN D. ROOSEVELT LIBRARY, Hyde Park, New York.

109   HARRY S. TRUMAN LIBRARY, Independence, Missouri.

110   DWIGHT D. EISENHOWER LIBRARY, Abilene, Kansas.

111   LYNDON B. JOHNSON LIBRARY, Austin, Texas.

112   JOHN F. KENNEDY LIBRARY.

At this writing a permanent location for the Kennedy
Library has not been chosen.   Work goes forward, however, with the task of gathering the materials that will
be deposited there.

These libraries hold not only the papers and memorabilia of the presidents, but
of those persons who served in their respective administrations.   Individuals wish-
ing to use the various archives and libraries listed above would do well to make
arrangements by mail to insure access to the materials sought.   Generally, re-
strictions are placed only on sensitive materials having to do with defense or
foreign policy.   Calendars of holdings are available on request.

Too numerous to list here are the archives maintained by individual state governments and the collections of historical societies, publicly and privately financed,
which are found throughout the country.   The following guides give locations
and brief descriptions of holdings.

113   DIRECTORY OF HISTORICAL SOCIETIES AND AGENCIES IN THE UNITED
STATES AND CANADA, 1973-1974.   Edited by Donna McDonald.   Nashville, Tenn.:   American Association for State and Local History, 1972.
378 p.   Illus.

Lists societies in each city, arranged by states. Gives brief descriptions of collections.

114   DIRECTORY OF SPECIAL LIBRARIES AND INFORMATION CENTERS. Edited by Margaret Labash Young et al. 3d ed. 3 vols. Detroit: Gale Research Co., 1974.

A listing useful to the historian because it contains brief descriptions of the holdings of the various historical societies and organizations in the United States, as well as information on other private and governmental holdings of use in historical research, and the names of the leading personnel with whom contact can be made. A supplement is issued periodically.

115   U.S. National Historical Publications Commission. GUIDE TO ARCHIVES AND MANUSCRIPTS IN THE UNITED STATES. Edited by Philip M. Hamer. New Haven, Conn.: Yale University Press, 1961. 798 p.

A state-by-state listing of archives and their manuscript collections. Includes names of directors of the institutions.

Illuminating discussions of public and private archives and libraries, the facilities and services they provide, and the problems they face, are found in the following:

116   Jones, H.G. THE RECORDS OF A NATION: THEIR MANAGEMENT, PRESERVATION, AND USE. New York: Atheneum, 1969. 326 p. Illus., facsim.

117   Whitehill, Walter Muir. INDEPENDENT HISTORICAL SOCIETIES: AN ENQUIRY INTO THEIR RESEARCH AND PUBLICATION FUNCTIONS AND THEIR FINANCIAL FUTURE. Boston: Boston Athenaeum; distributed by Harvard University Press, 1962. 611 p.

E. MICROFILM AND TAPE COLLECTIONS

1. Microfilm Collections

Recent technological developments have made it possible to reproduce manuscripts, documents, and printed works by microphotography. Massive collections have been recorded on microfilm, microfiche, and microcards that occupy little space and make it possible for interested persons to use collections many miles away from the originals. And, of course, complete runs of newspapers, such as the NEW YORK TIMES, have become available in this form. By now, hundreds of collections have been reproduced. The following publications, issued annually, may be consulted for materials available.

118 GUIDE TO MICROFORMS IN PRINT. Edited by Albert James Diaz.
Washington, D.C.: NCR-Microcard Editions, 1961- .

119 SUBJECT GUIDE TO MICROFORMS IN PRINT. Edited by Albert James
Diaz. Washington, D.C.: NCR-Microcard Editions, 1962/63- .

A notable collection of rare works, of particular interest to the historian, is
now available in microcard form, a product of a subsidiary company of ENCY-
CLOPAEDIA BRITANNICA:

120 THE MICROBOOK LIBRARY OF AMERICAN CIVILIZATION. Chicago:
Library Resources, 1971.

> This important addition to the expanding list of micro-
> fiche collections includes books, pamphlets, and periodi-
> cals from the colonial period to the outbreak of World
> War I. History, belle-lettres, travel, and many other
> categories are represented in this collection, which totals
> approximately 19,000 works, many very rare. Cata-
> logued according to the Library of Congress system with
> directories by author, title, and subject, with a fourth
> volume devoted to a Biblio-Guide Index.

2. Tape and Oral History

The tape recorder has made possible the development of the field of oral history,
a program to record reminiscences of participants in noteworthy events. Since
much of what is put on tape would not have been recorded otherwise, the historian is offered a new source of material. Some have complained that much
trivia is included in oral history recordings; yet, oral history often provides
nuances not found in written documents.

Many oral history projects are now in progress. The first notable project was
begun at Columbia University by Allan Nevins in 1948. The interviews in this
important collection are available in written transcripts and are catalogued in:

121 Columbia University. Oral History Research Office. THE ORAL HISTORY
COLLECTION OF COLUMBIA UNIVERSITY. New York: 1960. 111 p.

122 _____. SUPPLEMENT. New York: 1962. 50 p.

The guides listed below provide information on projects underway and the techniques and uses of oral history.

123 Baum, Willa K. ORAL HISTORY FOR THE LOCAL HISTORICAL SOCIETY.
Stockton: Conference of California Historical Societies, 1969. 44 p.
Illus.

124 Dixon, Elizabeth I., and Mink, James V. ORAL HISTORY AT ARROW-
HEAD: PROCEEDINGS. First National Colloquium on Oral History.
Los Angeles: Oral History Association, 1967. 135 p.

125 Shumway, Gary L. ORAL HISTORY IN THE UNITED STATES: A DIREC-
TORY. New York: Oral History Association, 1971. 120 p.

126 Waserman, Manfred J., ed. BIBLIOGRAPHY ON ORAL HISTORY. New
York: Oral History Association, 1971. 48 p.

F. PERIODICALS

The journals in categories 1 and 2 below are of particular use to persons interested in American history. Those listed in categories 3 and 4 occasionally carry
articles bearing on American historical themes. The following information is
provided: title, frequency of publication, publisher.

1. Journals of American History

a. GENERAL

127 AMERICAN HERITAGE. Bimonthly. American Heritage Publishing Co.

128 JOURNAL OF AMERICAN HISTORY. Quarterly. Organization of American Historians.

129 PERSPECTIVES IN AMERICAN HISTORY. Annual. Charles Warren Center for Studies in American History, Harvard University.

130 PROLOGUE: JOURNAL OF THE NATIONAL ARCHIVES. Quarterly.
National Archives and Records Service of the General Services Administration, United States.

b. TOPICAL

131 AMERICAN JEWISH ARCHIVES. Semiannual. Hebrew Union College,
Jewish Institute of Religion.

132 AMERICAN JEWISH HISTORICAL QUARTERLY. Quarterly. American
Jewish Historical Society.

133 AMERICAN WEST. Bimonthly. American West Publishing Co.

134 CIVIL WAR HISTORY: A JOURNAL OF THE MIDDLE PERIOD. Quarter-

ly. Kent State University Press.

135 HISTORIC PRESERVATION. Quarterly. National Trust for Historic Preservation.

136 HISTORY NEWS. Monthly. American Association for State and Local History.

137 JOURNAL OF CHURCH AND STATE. Three issues yearly. J.M. Dawson Studies in Church and State, Baylor University.

138 JOURNAL OF NEGRO HISTORY. Quarterly. Association for the Study of Negro Life and History.

139 JOURNAL OF SOUTHERN HISTORY. Quarterly. Southern Historical Association.

140 LABOR HISTORY. Quarterly. Tamiment Institute.

141 PACIFIC HISTORICAL REVIEW. Quarterly. Pacific Coast Branch, American Historical Association.

142 PROCEEDINGS OF THE AMERICAN ANTIQUARIAN SOCIETY. Semi-annual. American Antiquarian Society.

143 WESTERN HISTORICAL QUARTERLY. Quarterly. Western History Association and Utah State University.

144 WILLIAM AND MARY QUARTERLY. Quarterly. Institute of Early American History and Culture, College of William and Mary.

2. Interdisciplinary Journals of American Studies

a. GENERAL

145 AMERICAN QUARTERLY. Quarterly. American Studies Association and the University of Pennsylvania.

146 AMERICAN STUDIES. Occasional. Midcontinent American Studies Association, the University of Kansas, and the University of Missouri at Kansas City.

147 AMERIKASTUDIEN/AMERICAN STUDIES. Formerly JAHRBUCH FUR AMERIKASTUDIEN. Semiannual. Deutsche Gesellschaft fur Amerikastudien.

148 CANADIAN REVIEW OF AMERICAN STUDIES. Semiannual. Canadian Association for American Studies.

149 INDIAN JOURNAL OF AMERICAN STUDIES. Semiannual. American Studies Research Centre, Hyderabad.

150 JOURNAL OF AMERICAN STUDIES. Three issues yearly. British Association for American Studies and the Cambridge University Press.

b. TOPICAL

151 AFRO-AMERICAN STUDIES: AN INTERDISCIPLINARY JOURNAL. Quarterly. Gordon and Breach, Science Publishers, New York.

152 EARLY AMERICAN LITERATURE. Three issues yearly. Modern Language Association's Early American Literature Group.

153 JOURNAL OF POPULAR CULTURE. Quarterly. Popular Culture Association, Popular Literature Section of the Modern Language Association of America, and the Popular Culture Section of the Midwest Modern Language Association.

154 NEW ENGLAND QUARTERLY: A HISTORICAL REVIEW OF NEW ENGLAND LIFE AND LETTERS. Quarterly. Colonial Society of Massachusetts and the New England Quarterly.

3. Other Historical Journals

a. GENERAL

155 AMERICAN HISTORICAL REVIEW. Quarterly. American Historical Association.

156 HISTORIAN. Quarterly. Phi Alpha Theta, International Honor Society in History.

157 HISTORY TODAY. Monthly. History Today, London, England.

158 JOURNAL OF INTERDISCIPLINARY HISTORY. Quarterly. MIT School of Humanities and Social Science.

159 JOURNAL OF SOCIAL HISTORY. Quarterly. Rutgers University.

160 JOURNAL OF THE HISTORY OF IDEAS. Quarterly. City University of New York.

b. TOPICAL

161 AGRICULTURAL HISTORY. Quarterly. Agricultural History Society and the University of California Press.

162 AMERICAN JOURNAL OF LEGAL HISTORY. Quarterly. American Society for Legal History.

163 AMERICAN LITERATURE: A JOURNAL OF LITERARY HISTORY, CRITICISM, AND BIBLIOGRAPHY. Quarterly. Duke University Press.

164 AMERICAN NEPTUNE: A QUARTERLY JOURNAL OF MARITIME HISTORY. Quarterly. Peabody Museum of Salem.

165 BUSINESS HISTORY REVIEW. Quarterly. Harvard Graduate School of Business Administration.

166 CATHOLIC HISTORICAL REVIEW. Quarterly. American Catholic Historical Association.

167 CHURCH HISTORY. Quarterly. American Society of Church History.

168 HISTORY AND THEORY: STUDIES IN THE PHILOSOPHY OF HISTORY. Occasional. Wesleyan University Press.

169 HISTORY OF EDUCATION QUARTERLY. Quarterly. History of Education Society.

170 HISTORY OF POLITICAL ECONOMY. Quarterly. Duke University Press.

171 HUNTINGTON LIBRARY QUARTERLY: A JOURNAL FOR THE HISTORY AND INTERPRETATION OF ENGLISH AND AMERICAN CIVILIZATION. Quarterly. Huntington Library.

172 ISIS: INTERNATIONAL REVIEW DEVOTED TO THE HISTORY OF SCIENCE AND ITS CULTURAL INFLUENCES. Five issues yearly. History of Science Society.

173 JOURNAL OF ECONOMIC HISTORY. Quarterly. Economic History Association.

174 JOURNAL OF FOREST HISTORY. Quarterly. Forest History Foundation.

175 JOURNAL OF LIBRARY HISTORY, PHILOSOPHY AND COMPARATIVE LIBRARIANSHIP. Quarterly. School of Library Science, Florida State University.

176 JOURNAL OF THE HISTORY OF PHILOSOPHY. Quarterly. Journal of the History of Philosophy.

177 JOURNAL OF THE HISTORY OF THE BEHAVIORAL SCIENCES. Quarterly. Clinical Psychology Publishing Co., Brandon, Vermont.

178 PROCEEDINGS OF THE AMERICAN PHILOSOPHICAL SOCIETY HELD AT PHILADELPHIA FOR PROMOTING USEFUL KNOWLEDGE. Bimonthly. American Philosophical Society.

179 TECHNOLOGY AND CULTURE. Quarterly. Society for the History of Technology.

4. Journals in Related Fields

180 AMERICAN ANTHROPOLOGIST. Quarterly. American Anthropological Association.

181 AMERICAN ANTIQUITY: JOURNAL OF THE SOCIETY FOR AMERICAN ARCHAEOLOGY. Quarterly. Society for American Archaeology.

182 AMERICAN ARCHIVIST. Quarterly. Society of American Archivists.

183 AMERICAN ECONOMIC REVIEW. Quarterly. American Economic Association.

184 AMERICAN JOURNAL OF ECONOMICS AND SOCIOLOGY. Quarterly. American Journal of Economics and Sociology.

185 AMERICAN JOURNAL OF INTERNATIONAL LAW. Five issues yearly. American Society of International Law.

186 AMERICAN JOURNAL OF SOCIOLOGY. Bimonthly. University of Chicago.

187 AMERICAN POLITICAL SCIENCE REVIEW. Quarterly. American Political Science Association.

188 AMERICAN SOCIOLOGICAL REVIEW. Bimonthly. American Sociological Association.

189 AMERICAN SOCIOLOGIST. Quarterly. American Sociological Association.

190 ANNALS OF THE AMERICAN ACADEMY OF POLITICAL AND SOCIAL SCIENCE. Bimonthly. American Academy of Political and Social Science.

191 ANNALS OF THE ASSOCIATION OF AMERICAN GEOGRAPHERS. Quarterly. Association of American Geographers.

192 CLA JOURNAL. Quarterly. College Language Association (specializing in black literature).

193 DEMOGRAPHY. Quarterly. Population Association of America.

194 ECONOMIC GEOGRAPHY. Quarterly. Clark University.

195 ETHNOHISTORY. Quarterly. American Society for Ethnohistory. Formerly the Ohio Valley Historical Indian Conference.

196 EXPLORATIONS IN ECONOMIC HISTORY. Quarterly. Formerly EXPLORATIONS IN ENTREPRENEURIAL HISTORY. Kent State University Press.

197 FOREIGN AFFAIRS. Quarterly. Council on Foreign Relations.

198 GEOGRAPHICAL REVIEW. Quarterly. American Geographical Society.

199 JOURNAL OF AMERICAN FOLKLORE. Quarterly. American Folklore Society.

200 JOURNAL OF ECONOMIC LITERATURE. Quarterly. American Economic Association.

201 JOURNAL OF POLITICAL ECONOMY. Bimonthly. University of Chicago Press.

202 JOURNAL OF POLITICS. Quarterly. Southern Political Science Association.

203 MILITARY AFFAIRS. Quarterly. American Military Institute.

204 PAPERS OF THE BIBLIOGRAPHICAL SOCIETY OF AMERICA. Quarterly. Bibliographical Society of America.

205 PMLA: PUBLICATIONS OF THE MODERN LANGUAGE ASSOCIATION OF AMERICA. Six issues yearly. Modern Language Association.

206 POLITICAL SCIENCE QUARTERLY. Quarterly. Academy of Political Science.

207 REVIEW OF POLITICS. Quarterly. University of Notre Dame.

208 SOUTHERN FOLKLORE QUARTERLY: A PUBLICATION DEVOTED TO THE HISTORICAL AND DESCRIPTIVE STUDY OF FOLKLORE AND TO THE DISCUSSION OF FOLK MATERIAL AS A LIVING TRADITION. Quarterly. South Atlantic Modern Language Association and the University of Florida.

Chapter 2

COMPREHENSIVE HISTORIES

A. GENERAL

209 ALBUM OF AMERICAN HISTORY. Edited by James Truslow Adams. 2d
rev. ed. 6 vols. New York: Charles Scribner's Sons, 1969. Illus.

> A massive collection of pictures, with brief commen-
> taries, from various periods of American history, 1492–
> 1968. Useful in achieving an understanding of clothing,
> life styles, etc.

210 Barck, Oscar Theodore, Jr., and Blake, Nelson Manfred. SINCE 1900:
A HISTORY OF THE UNITED STATES IN OUR OWN TIMES. 4th ed.
New York: Macmillan, 1965. 974 p. Illus., ports., maps.

> A standard text on events of the twentieth century. A
> political chronology dominates, but much cultural mate-
> rial is included. Written with verve.

211 Beard, Charles A., and Beard, Mary R. THE MAKING OF AMERICAN
CIVILIZATION. New York: Macmillan, 1937. 990 p. Illus., front.,
plates, maps.

> A comprehensive text by notable historians dealing with
> political, economic, intellectual, and social develop-
> ment. Designed primarily for younger readers.

212 Bernstein, Barton J., ed. TOWARDS A NEW PAST: DISSENTING ES-
SAYS IN AMERICAN HISTORY. New York: Pantheon, 1968. 380 p.

> An attempt by a group of "new left" historians to shake
> up the field of historical scholarship and the "consensus
> school" that has dominated it since World War II. The
> contributors insist that there has been much more conflict
> in American history than the past generation of historians
> was willing to admit. Contributors include the editor
> himself, Eugene Genovese, Christopher Lasch, Michael
> Lebowitz, Jesse Lemisch, Staughton Lynd, and Stephan

Thernstrom. Topics run the gamut from early America
to the present.

213 Boorstin, Daniel J. THE AMERICANS. 3 vols. New York: Random
House, 1958-73.

A provocative work on the emergence of the American
character which minimizes the significance of thought.
The author believes that Americans have been, from
the beginning, more concerned with action than with
theory. The third volume puts particular stress on technological accomplishments and raises questions about the
quality of life in modern America. Volume 1: The Colonial Experience; volume 2: The National Experience;
volume 3: The Democratic Experience.

214 Channing, Edward. A HISTORY OF THE UNITED STATES. 6 vols.
1905-25. Reprint. New York: Macmillan, 1949. Illus., maps.

A standard history. Channing was noted for his objective, impartial approach. Volume 1: THE PLANTING
OF A NATION IN THE NEW WORLD, 1000-1660;
volume 2: A CENTURY OF COLONIAL HISTORY,
1660-1760; volume 3: THE AMERICAN REVOLUTION,
1761-1789; volume 4: FEDERALISTS AND REPUBLI-
CANS, 1789-1815; volume 5: THE PERIOD OF TRAN-
SITION, 1815-1848; volume 6: THE WAR FOR SOUTH-
ERN INDEPENDENCE.

215 Commager, Henry Steele, ed. DOCUMENTS OF AMERICAN HISTORY.
9th ed. New York: Appleton-Century-Crofts, 1973. 838 p.

A selection of documents from early America to 1973.
Commager includes the most important passages and pref-
aces each item with an explanation of its significance.

216 Degler, Carl N. OUT OF OUR PAST: THE FORCES THAT SHAPED
MODERN AMERICA. Rev. ed. New York: Harper & Row, 1970. 566
p.

Interprets the past in the light of the interests of the
present. Therefore, while the book is strong in showing
how the United States came to be as it is, it inevitably
neglects many significant events and personalities of the
past.

217 Garraty, John A. THE AMERICAN NATION: A HISTORY OF THE
UNITED STATES. New York: Harper & Row, 1968. 920 p. Illus.,
ports., maps, facsims.

A well-thought-out and well-written survey, enriched by

portfolios of illustrations by AMERICAN HERITAGE.
Garraty takes into account and evaluates recent scholarship.

218 _____. INTERPRETING AMERICAN HISTORY: CONVERSATIONS WITH
HISTORIANS. 2 vols. New York: Macmillan, 1970. Ports. Paperbound.

Transcripts of tape-recorded conversations with historians
who are experts in various phases of U.S. history. Garraty draws them out on their own works, controversies
over interpretation, and other matters. Twenty-nine discussions are included.

219 Garraty, John A., and Divine, Robert A., eds. TWENTIETH-CENTURY
AMERICA: CONTEMPORARY DOCUMENTS AND OPINIONS. Boston:
Little, Brown, 1968. 698 p. Paperbound.

A collection that includes statements from persons as
separated in time and mood as Mark Twain and Senator
J. William Fulbright. The editors have grouped the
material under the following categories: Imperialism and
World Power, The Progressive Era, The First World War,
The Twenties, The Age of the Great Depression, From
Isolation to World Leadership, Domestic Problems since
1945, The Cold War. They provide a headnote to each
selection.

220 Handlin, Oscar. THE AMERICANS: A NEW HISTORY OF THE PEOPLE
OF THE UNITED STATES. Boston: Little, Brown, 1963. 434 p. Illus.

This book grew out of Handlin's interest in immigration,
looked at in context of the overall development of the
United States. He dwells less on political and more on
economic and cultural matters. Less factual than impressionistic.

221 Hicks, John D., et al. THE AMERICAN NATION: A HISTORY OF THE
UNITED STATES FROM 1865 TO THE PRESENT. 5th ed. Boston: Houghton Mifflin, 1971. 841 p. Illus., ports., maps, tables.

Hicks's well-known text, enlarged and brought up to
date with the collaboration of George E. Mowry and
Robert E. Burke. The first half of the survey is entitled
THE FEDERAL UNION, q.v., no. 222.

222 _____. THE FEDERAL UNION: A HISTORY OF THE UNITED
STATES TO 1877. 5th ed. Boston: Houghton Mifflin, 1970. 800 p.
Illus., ports., maps, facsims., tables.

The well-known text by Hicks, brought up to date in

collaboration with George E. Mowry and Robert E.
Burke. Ranges from the discovery of America through
the Civil War. The second half of the survey is entitled THE AMERICAN NATION, q.v., no. 221.

223 Hildreth, Richard. HISTORY OF THE UNITED STATES OF AMERICA.
Rev. ed. 6 vols. 1880. Reprint. New York: Augustus M. Kelley,
1969.

Hildreth, an attorney, newspaper editor, and reformer,
also wrote a work on banking and an antislavery novel.
This history features social and intellectual developments
as well as the usual political framework and is a classic
of nineteenth-century historiography. Volumes 1 and
2: COLONIAL, 1497-1773; volume 3: REVOLUTION-
ARY, 1773-1789; volume 4: ADMINISTRATION OF
WASHINGTON, 1789-1797; volume 5: JOHN ADAMS
AND JEFFERSON; volume 6: MADISON AND MON-
ROE.

224 McMaster, John Bach. A HISTORY OF THE PEOPLE OF THE UNITED
STATES, FROM THE REVOLUTION TO THE CIVIL WAR. 8 vols. New
York: Appleton, 1883-1913. Maps, plans.

A history crammed with colorful detail by a leading
historian of the late nineteenth and early twentieth centuries. McMaster attributes a unique nature to the
American "genius."

225 Morison, Samuel Eliot, et al. THE GROWTH OF THE AMERICAN RE-
PUBLIC. 6th ed. 2 vols. New York: Oxford University Press, 1969.
Illus., fronts., ports., plates, maps, tables.

A famous, very readable text, brought up to date by
Morison, his partner, Henry Steele Commager, and a
new member of the team, William E. Leuchtenburg, who
contributes material on the most recent period.

226 Rhodes, James F. HISTORY OF THE UNITED STATES FROM THE COM-
PROMISE OF 1850 TO THE FINAL RESTORATION OF HOME RULE AT
THE SOUTH IN 1877. 8 vols. New York: Macmillan, 1910-19. Illus.,
maps.

Rhodes began publication of his history in 1888. The
first seven volumes are still the most detailed for the
period 1850-77. He then decided to extend his account
in an eighth volume covering the period from Hayes to
McKinley, 1877-96.

227 Sullivan, Mark. OUR TIMES, 1900-1925. 6 vols. 1926-35. Reprint.
New York: Charles Scribner's Sons, 1971-72. Illus., ports., maps,

facsims., music.

> Educated in the law, Sullivan turned to journalism for
> a career. This work conveys the excitement of a par-
> ticipant in the times described. The six volumes, co-
> piously illustrated, deal with the major political and
> social issues of the day. Volume 1: THE TURN OF
> THE CENTURY, 1900-1904; volume 2: AMERICA
> FINDING HERSELF; volume 3: PRE-WAR AMERICA;
> volume 4: THE WAR BEGINS, 1909-1914; volume 5:
> OVER HERE, 1914-1918; volume 6: THE TWENTIES.

228 Wiebe, Robert H. THE SEARCH FOR ORDER, 1877-1920. New York:
Hill & Wang, 1967. 347 p.

> The survey of the years from Hayes to Harding, which
> were years of great change. Much detail is included
> in a well-written analysis of the contending forces in
> American life.

229 Williams, William Appleman. THE CONTOURS OF AMERICAN HISTORY.
1961. Reprint. Chicago: Quadrangle Books, 1966. 519 p. Paperbound.

> An iconoclastic discussion of the meaning of American
> history. Williams, believing the study of history is "a
> way of learning," concludes his review of the past
> with the conviction that Americans "have the chance
> to create the first truly democratic socialism in the
> world." This edition contains a new foreword by the
> author.

B. TOPICAL

1. Agriculture

230 Benedict, Murray R. FARM POLICIES OF THE UNITED STATES, 1790-
1950: A STUDY OF THEIR ORIGINS AND DEVELOPMENT. New York:
Twentieth Century Fund, 1953. 564 p.

> This history includes manifold aspects of farming--ownership
> of land, conservation policies, farm supports, tenant
> farming, tariffs, transportation, and much more. Designed
> for the general reader.

231 Bidwell, Percy W., and Falconer, John I. HISTORY OF AGRICULTURE
IN THE NORTHERN UNITED STATES, 1620-1860. 1925. Reprint. New
York: Peter Smith, 1941. 524 p. Illus., plates, maps., diagrs.

> A cooperative effort of a number of scholars, originally

published by the Carnegie Institution, Washington, D.C.
The work is divided as follows: Agriculture in the Earliest Settlements; Rural Economy in the Eighteenth Century; Expansion and Progress, 1800-40; Period of Transformation. The book is in narrative form but it is very
useful for reference also.

232 Gates, Paul W. THE FARMER'S AGE: AGRICULTURE, 1815-1860. New
York: Holt, Rinehart & Winston, 1960. 478 p. Illus., maps, facsims.,
tables.

Covers a period during which great technological innovations were being made. Gates deals with northern and
southern farming, public land policy, types of crops,
living conditions of the farmer and the hired hand, and
much more.

233 Gray, Lewis C. HISTORY OF AGRICULTURE IN THE SOUTHERN UNI-
TED STATES TO 1860. 2 vols. 1933. Reprint. New York: Augustus
M. Kelley, 1973.

Originally published as a report of the Carnegie Institution of Washington, this is a massive study ranging from
the colonial period to the eve of the Civil War. Gray
deals with both the plantation system and the small farm
and thoroughly explores crops, livestock, technological
developments, labor (slave and free), and the socio-
economic aspects of agriculture.

234 Saloutos, Theodore. FARMER MOVEMENTS IN THE SOUTH, 1865-1933.
1960. Reprint. Lincoln: University of Nebraska Press, 1964. 363 p.
Paperbound.

In this study of reform movements in southern agriculture
from the close of the Civil War to the beginning of the
New Deal, Saloutos deals with such groups as the Grange,
the Farmers' Alliance, and the Populists, discussing leaders and programs presented for the improvement of the
farmer's lot.

235 Saloutos, Theodore, and Hicks, John D. AGRICULTURAL DISCONTENT
IN THE MIDDLE WEST, 1900-1939. Madison: University of Wisconsin
Press, 1951. 590 p.

American agriculture went through great changes in the
years covered. It was hit by inflation in World War I
and severely shaken by the Great Depression. The authors show how the farmers finally organized and began
using their political power.

236 Stedman, Murray S., Jr., and Stedman, Susan W. DISCONTENT AT

THE POLLS: A STUDY OF FARMER AND LABOR PARTIES, 1827-1948.
1950. Reprint. New York: Russell & Russell, 1967. 200 p. Illus.

Attempts to show how farmer and labor parties have
dramatized issues and grievances that the established
political parties ignored.

2. American Characteristics

237 Arieli, Yehoshua. INDIVIDUALISM AND NATIONALISM IN AMERICAN
IDEOLOGY. Cambridge, Mass.: Harvard University Press, 1964. 455
p.

An Israeli scholar's analysis of forces and ideas feeding
into American ideology. Arieli uses concepts drawn
from European social scientists, particularly Mannheim;
he believes that American nationalism stems from individualism and democracy.

238 Baldwin, Leland D. THE MEANING OF AMERICA: ESSAYS TOWARD
AN UNDERSTANDING OF THE AMERICAN SPIRIT. Pittsburgh: University of Pittsburgh Press, 1955. 319 p. Illus.

A collection of sixteen short essays. Among other things,
Baldwin attempts to explain American political and economic practices by examining U.S. history.

239 Brogan, D.W. THE AMERICAN CHARACTER. 1944. Reprint. New
York: Alfred A. Knopf, 1950. 189 p.

Written for Englishmen in an attempt to explain certain
aspects of the American's outlook on his history and
present-day life. Brogan, who was an expert on American and French history at Cambridge University, writes
with wit about the foibles as well as the more flattering
aspects of the American character.

240 Burlingame, Roger. THE AMERICAN CONSCIENCE. New York: Alfred
A. Knopf, 1957. 444 p.

A study of American moral attitudes, intended for a
popular audience. Burlingame sees a pervasive Puritanism in American attitudes through the years. He illustrates his theme with many lively examples.

241 Burns, Edward M. THE AMERICAN IDEAL OF MISSION: CONCEPTS OF
NATIONAL PURPOSE AND DESTINY. New Brunswick, N.J.: Rutgers
University Press, 1957. 398 p. Illus., front.

Examines the "sense of mission" which the author believes
has been a constant factor in American history. He

traces it and its various transmutations from the Puritans
of the seventeenth century to the welfare state of the
twentieth.

242   Joseph, Franz M., ed. AS OTHERS SEE US: THE UNITED STATES
       THROUGH FOREIGN EYES. Princeton, N.J.: Princeton University Press,
       1959. 368 p.

       Continues the old tradition of gathering comment by
       foreigners about the United States. The editor, who
       believes there is such a thing as a national character,
       has included essays by twenty persons, including Ray-
       mond Aron and Denis Brogan, on their impressions of
       America.

243   Kammen, Michael. PEOPLE OF PARADOX: AN INQUIRY CONCERN-
       ING THE ORIGINS OF AMERICAN CIVILIZATION. New York: Alfred
       A. Knopf, 1972. 316 p. Illus.

       An analysis by a noted colonial historian of the "con-
       trapuntal" themes that run through the American cultural
       experience from the early period to the present. Kam-
       men sees the origins of American civilization in the
       hundred years dating from 1660, a period in which some
       of the European preconceptions of the colonists remained
       intact while others underwent change under the impact
       of the environment of the New World. The author
       believes this explains apparent contradictions in Ameri-
       can attitudes through the intervening years.

244   Potter, David M. PEOPLE OF PLENTY: ECONOMIC ABUNDANCE AND
       THE AMERICAN CHARACTER. Chicago: University of Chicago Press,
       1954. 245 p. Illus.

       In original form, the Charles R. Walgreen Foundation
       Lectures at the University of Chicago. Potter believes
       America's economic abundance has had a decided psy-
       chological impact on the character of its people. He
       brings to bear on his theme the tools of the behavioral
       and social sciences as well as of history.

245   Weinberg, Albert K. MANIFEST DESTINY: A STUDY OF NATIONALIST
       EXPANSIONISM IN AMERICAN HISTORY. Baltimore: Johns Hopkins
       Press, 1935. 572 p.

       A study of the rhetoric used by American leaders to
       justify territorial acquisition, starting with Louisiana
       and Florida and ending with the Spanish-American War.
       Weinberg looks more at the moral arguments given and
       less at possible economic motivations.

246 Weiss, Richard. THE AMERICAN MYTH OF SUCCESS: FROM HORATIO
ALGER TO NORMAN VINCENT PEALE. New York: Basic Books, 1969.
276 p.

> Weiss surveys American literature over a hundred-year
> period to trace the evolution of the American idea of
> success. He examines books on how to succeed in
> business, self-help books, inspirational guides, etc.

3. The Arts

247 Andrews, Wayne. ARCHITECTURE, AMBITION AND AMERICANS. 1955.
Reprint. New York: Free Press of Glencoe, 1964. 319 p. Illus.

> A survey of American building styles, from the beginnings
> to mid-twentieth century, stressing the artistic aspects
> of architecture. Andrews deals also with the architects,
> and their customers as well, with a critical eye.

248 Atkinson, Brooks. BROADWAY. New York: Macmillan, 1970. 484 p.
Illus., ports.

> This drama critic's exuberant history of the New York
> theatre goes into all aspects of play production. Atkin-
> son discusses the great plays and actors up to 1950,
> with a postscript that briefly carries the history to
> 1970.

249 Burchard, John E., and Bush-Brown, Albert. THE ARCHITECTURE OF
AMERICA: A SOCIAL AND CULTURAL HISTORY. Boston: Little, Brown,
1961. 595 p. Illus.

> The authors deal with the years 1600 to 1960, with
> greater concentration on the period since the 1880s,
> relating architecture to social and intellectual con-
> cerns. Helpful illustrations are integrated with a well-
> written narrative.

250 Cowell, Henry, ed. AMERICAN COMPOSERS ON AMERICAN MUSIC:
A SYMPOSIUM. 1933. Reprint. New York: Frederick Ungar, 1962.
240 p. Music.

> A collection on "creative music in America." Among
> the participants are George Gershwin and Charles Ives.
> This edition has a new introduction by the editor.

251 Craven, Wayne. SCULPTURE IN AMERICA. New York: Crowell, 1968.
742 p. Illus.

> A full history that analyzes the work of individual sculp-
> tors but also sets their work in the context of develop-

ments in the arts. Craven covers the entire gamut from the woodcarvers and stonecutters of the colonial period to present-day sculptors, relating artistic developments to social trends.

252 Goodrich, Lloyd. THREE CENTURIES OF AMERICAN ART. New York: Praeger, 1966. 145 p. Illus.

A pictorial survey with commentary by the director of the Whitney Museum, based on the 1966 exposition, "Art of the United States, 1670-1966."

253 Hitchcock, H. Wiley. MUSIC IN THE UNITED STATES: A HISTORICAL INTRODUCTION. Englewood Cliffs, N.J.: Prentice-Hall, 1969. 270 p. Illus., music.

A survey of music from that of the symphony orchestra to the popular song. Hitchcock makes an effort to relate musical developments to broader cultural themes, but his accent is on music.

254 Jacobs, Lewis. THE RISE OF THE AMERICAN FILM: A CRITICAL HISTORY, WITH AN ESSAY: EXPERIMENTAL CINEMA IN AMERICA, 1921-1947. New York: Teachers College Press, 1968. 663 p. Illus.

To his original work published in 1939, which traced the history of motion pictures from 1896, the author has added an extended essay on developments in experimental film. Based on extensive documentation, the book covers the cinema as art and as industry, and also deals with the impact it has had on society. Richly illustrated with scenes from notable films.

255 Larkin, Oliver W. ART AND LIFE IN AMERICA. Rev. ed. New York: Holt, Rinehart and Winston, 1960. 576 p. Illus.

A full survey of American art from the early colonial limners to present-day artists. Larkin relates artistic developments to the social life of the people. Excellent illustrations in color and black and white.

256 Meserve, Walter J. AN OUTLINE HISTORY OF AMERICAN DRAMA. Totowa, N.J.: Littlefield, Adams, 1965. 392 p. Paperbound.

This concise history deals with the development of the stage from colonial times to mid-twentieth century. Meserve discusses the leading dramatists and analyzes their most important plays. Poetic and musical productions are included.

257 Nye, Russel B. THE UNEMBARRASSED MUSE: THE POPULAR ARTS IN

AMERICA. New York: Dial Press, 1970. 497 p. Illus., ports., facsims.

This colorful history of the popular arts touches on everything, including country music. Profusely illustrated with materials that add much to the text.

4. Black Americans

258 Aptheker, Herbert, ed. A DOCUMENTARY HISTORY OF THE NEGRO PEOPLE IN THE UNITED STATES. 1951. Reprint. New York: Citadel Press, 1969. 960 p.

Covers the years 1661-1910. Aptheker includes material, written by blacks, from periodicals of various kinds, letters, pamphlets, etc., with introductory comments. He stresses the black man's struggle for equality. The preface is by W.E.B. Du Bois.

259 _____. A DOCUMENTARY HISTORY OF THE NEGRO PEOPLE IN THE UNITED STATES, 1910-1932. New York: Citadel Press, 1973. 745 p.

A sequel to the earlier DOCUMENTARY HISTORY, q.v., no. 258. The documents included in this volume cover a great variety of events, personalities, and topics: the back-to-Africa movement of Marcus Garvey; reactions to the Ku Klux Klan, lynching, segregation; the trade union movement; the emergence of W.E.B. Du Bois.

260 Blaustein, Albert P., and Zangrando, Robert L., eds. CIVIL RIGHTS AND THE AMERICAN NEGRO: A DOCUMENTARY HISTORY. New York: Trident Press, 1968. 686 p.

Includes materials dating from Jamestown, 1619, to the racial riots of the 1960s. The editors accent legal opinions, but such friends of the black man as Charles Sumner and W.E.B. Du Bois are also represented.

261 Franklin, John Hope. FROM SLAVERY TO FREEDOM: A HISTORY OF NEGRO AMERICANS. 3d ed. New York: Alfred A. Knopf, 1967. 751 p. Illus., ports.

A comprehensive history by a leading black historian. This is a full account, dealing with struggle, accomplishment, and failure in the political and social realms. Franklin maintains an objective stance even as he recounts examples of gross injustice.

262 Jordan, Winthrop D. WHITE OVER BLACK: AMERICAN ATTITUDES TOWARD THE NEGRO, 1550-1812. Chapel Hill: University of North Carolina Press, 1968. 671 p. Map.

Traces the attitudes of whites toward the black man from

the mid-sixteenth century to 1812. Jordan, therefore, provides information on English attitudes the colonists brought with them to the New World. He surveys the introduction of slavery in the West Indies and on the North American continent. This detailed history also deals with such matters as English attitudes to the color black, sexual relationships between whites and blacks, and white attitudes on the question of the humanity of the black.

263   Mannix, Daniel P., and Cowley, Malcolm. BLACK CARGOES: A HISTORY OF THE ATLANTIC SLAVE TRADE, 1518-1865. New York: Viking Press, 1962. 306 p. Illus.

This account deals with the capture and enslavement of blacks in Africa and their sale to slave traders who brought them to the New World. The horrors of the Middle Passage are vividly portrayed, as are the other aspects of the trade.

264   Meier, August, and Rudwick, Elliott M., eds. THE MAKING OF BLACK AMERICA: ESSAYS IN NEGRO LIFE & HISTORY. 2 vols. in 1. New York: Atheneum, 1969.

A comprehensive compilation of articles dealing with the black throughout American history. The editors accent what blacks have done, rather than what whites have done about blacks, and include the work of political and behavioral scientists as well as historians. Topics range from origins in Africa to recent militancy and the ghetto. Volume 1: THE ORIGINS OF BLACK AMERICANS; volume 2: THE BLACK COMMUNITY IN MODERN AMERICA.

265   Miller, Loren. THE PETITIONERS: THE STORY OF THE SUPREME COURT OF THE UNITED STATES AND THE NEGRO. New York: Pantheon, 1966. 476 p.

By a California jurist, a son of a slave. Miller's legal history covers the years 1789 to 1965, discussing the court's dealings with the black both as slave and as freedman. Miller tells the story with objectivity and a certain amount of humor.

266   Quarles, Benjamin. THE NEGRO IN THE MAKING OF AMERICA. New York: Collier Books, 1964. 288 p. Paperbound.

A general review of the history of the black man in America. Quarles covers the transportation of slaves to the New World; the black's life as slave and as freedman; the Civil War, Reconstruction, and subsequent dis-

illusionment; and the gain in civil rights in the twentieth
century.

5. Business and Economics

267   Bruchey, Stuart W. THE ROOTS OF AMERICAN ECONOMIC GROWTH,
1607-1861: AN ESSAY IN SOCIAL CAUSATION. New York: Harper &
Row, 1965. 252 p.

> Bruchey isolates factors that resulted in economic growth
> up to the Civil War and also discusses problems of
> methodology and literature in the field. He considers
> the Protestant ethic and the relationships of economics
> to politics and technological advancement.

268   Bunke, Harvey C. A PRIMER ON AMERICAN ECONOMIC HISTORY.
New York: Random House, 1969. 188 p.

> Within a very small compass, a survey of American eco-
> nomic development. The author examines the proposi-
> tion, which he thinks is basic to Americans, that reason
> and will "can construct a felicitous society of free and
> noble men."

269   Chandler, Alfred D., Jr. STRATEGY AND STRUCTURE: CHAPTERS IN
THE HISTORY OF INDUSTRIAL ENTERPRISE. Cambridge, Mass.: MIT
Press, 1962. 477 p. Diagrs.

> Stresses the importance of administrative organization in
> business success. Chandler examines the history of the
> corporate structure of almost one hundred of the largest
> twentieth-century business enterprises, giving special
> attention to DuPont, General Motors, Standard Oil of
> New Jersey, and Sears-Roebuck.

270   Clark, Victor S. HISTORY OF MANUFACTURES IN THE UNITED STATES.
3 vols. New York: McGraw-Hill Book Co., 1929. Plates, maps,
tables, diagrs.

> The study was sponsored by the Carnegie Institution of
> Washington and deals with the whole sweep of the his-
> tory of manufacturing from 1607 to 1928. Clark analyzes
> business organization, labor, marketing, finances, tech-
> nology, etc.

271   Cochran, Thomas C. THE AMERICAN BUSINESS SYSTEM: A HISTORICAL
PERSPECTIVE, 1900-1955. 1957. Reprint. New York: Harper & Row,
1962. 234 p. Paperbound.

> Integrates the history of business with social history,
> economics, and the history of technology. Cochran's

objective is to provide an overview that will create for
the reader an understanding of how such events as the
crash of 1929 fit into the pattern of twentieth-century
development.

272 Dodd, Edwin M. AMERICAN BUSINESS CORPORATIONS UNTIL 1860,
WITH SPECIAL REFERENCE TO MASSACHUSETTS. Cambridge, Mass.:
Harvard University Press, 1954. 524 p. Illus.

The development of statutes applying to business in
Massachusetts from 1780 to 1860. Dodd, an expert in
corporation law, looks at what happened in the legislature and the courts at both the national and state
levels.

273 Dorfman, Joseph. THE ECONOMIC MIND IN AMERICAN CIVILIZA-
TION. 5 vols. New York: Viking Press, 1946-59.

A full history of the subject, giving the views of government, business, and labor, as well as the theories of
economists in each period. Volumes 1 and 2: 1606-
1865; volume 3: 1865-1918; volumes 4 and 5: 1918-
1933.

274 Faulkner, Harold U. AMERICAN ECONOMIC HISTORY. 8th ed. New
York: Harper & Brothers, 1960. 843 p. Illus., maps, charts, graphs.

A standard text. Faulkner covers the geography of the
United States and discusses economic development from
the colonial period to the present.

275 Friedman, Milton, and Schwartz, Anna J. A MONETARY HISTORY OF
THE UNITED STATES, 1867-1960. Princeton, N.J.: Princeton University Press, 1963. 884 p. Tables, diagrs.

A detailed and complex history of the money supply
and how it affects, and is affected by, economic trends,
from the close of the Civil War.

276 Goodrich, Carter. GOVERNMENT PROMOTION OF AMERICAN CANALS
AND RAILROADS, 1800-1890. New York: Columbia University Press,
1960. 392 p. Map.

An economist's evaluation of the efforts of government
and private capital to develop the internal transportation of the United States.

277 _____, ed. THE GOVERNMENT AND THE ECONOMY, 1783-1861.
Indianapolis: Bobbs-Merrill, 1967. 586 p.

A collection of primary materials with an introductory

essay by the editor. The pieces deal with government
promotion of such enterprises as transportation, western
settlement, manufactures, commerce, corporations. Also
covers money and credit, tariffs, and labor--slave and
free.

278 Hacker, Louis M. COURSE OF AMERICAN ECONOMIC GROWTH AND
DEVELOPMENT. New York: Wiley, 1970. 408 p.

This economic history follows the usual chronology of
American history but goes far beyond simple economics
to demonstrate how political, military, social, intellectual, religious, and moral movements have had their
impact on U.S. development.

279 _____. THE TRIUMPH OF AMERICAN CAPITALISM: THE DEVELOP-
MENT OF FORCES IN AMERICAN HISTORY TO THE END OF THE NINE-
TEENTH CENTURY. 1940. Reprint. New York: Columbia University
Press, 1946. 470 p.

Stresses economic determinants in American history.
Hacker divides the book into two sections, the first
dealing with the development of mercantile capitalism
in the Revolutionary period, the second with the emergence of industrial capitalism in the Civil War.

280 Hammond, Bray. BANKS AND POLITICS IN AMERICA, FROM THE RE-
VOLUTION TO THE CIVIL WAR. Princeton, N.J.: Princeton University Press, 1957. 782 p.

A study of banks, bankers, monetary policies, and business, from the early period to the Civil War. Hammond
takes exception to the prevailing notion that agrarian
America was overwhelmingly against debt and paper
money. He believes the rapid economic growth of the
United States indicates just the opposite tendency.

281 Hartz, Louis. ECONOMIC POLICY AND DEMOCRATIC THOUGHT:
PENNSYLVANIA, 1776-1860. Cambridge, Mass.: Harvard University
Press, 1948. 381 p. Maps, diagrs.

This case study of economic policy shows that, in the
period covered, Pennsylvania government was heavily
involved in business and industry. The shift to a laissez-
faire approach came toward the end of the period.

282 Hutchins, John G.B. THE AMERICAN MARITIME INDUSTRIES AND PUB-
LIC POLICY, 1789-1914: AN ECONOMIC HISTORY. 1941. Reprint.
New York: Russell & Russell, 1969. 648 p.

The economic aspects of the merchant marine. The

author covers shipping, shipbuilding, financial considerations, and governmental policy.

283 Jones, Peter d'A. THE CONSUMER SOCIETY: A HISTORY OF AMERICAN CAPITALISM. Baltimore: Penguin Books, 1965. 407 p. Paperbound.

This expanded version of Jones's earlier book, AMERICA'S WEALTH (New York: Macmillan, 1963), covers the entire period from the colonial era to the present. A useful introduction to the subject with much detail.

284 Kirkland, Edward C. A HISTORY OF AMERICAN ECONOMIC LIFE. 4th ed. New York: Appleton-Century-Crofts, 1969. 636 p.

A full survey, from the colonial period to the reconversion following the Second World War. Pays particular attention to the interaction of government and business.

285 Letwin, William, ed. A DOCUMENTARY HISTORY OF AMERICAN ECONOMIC POLICY SINCE 1789. Rev. and enl. ed. New York: W.W. Norton, 1972. 514 p.

Covers the years 1789 to 1961. Documents are grouped under these headings: Tariffs, Internal Improvements, Corporation Law, Central Banking, Regulation of Railroads, Antitrust Policy, Monetary Policy, Conservation, Income Taxation, Immigration Policy, Agricultural Price Supports, The National Recovery Administration, Regulation of the Financial Market, Full Employment Policy, Foreign Aid. The editor supplies an extensive introduction to the collection and introductions to each section.

286 Shannon, Fred A. AMERICA'S ECONOMIC GROWTH. 3d ed. New York: Macmillan, 1951. 1,007 p. Maps.

Originally published in 1934 as ECONOMIC HISTORY OF THE PEOPLE OF THE UNITED STATES, this text has been revised and brought up to date several times. Devotes more space to industrialization than to the earlier periods.

287 Smith, Walter B., and Cole, Arthur H. FLUCTUATIONS IN AMERICAN BUSINESS, 1790-1860. 1935. Reprint. New York: Russell & Russell, 1969. 219 p. Illus., tables.

Amasses a great deal of economic, statistical material to illustrate what was happening to American business in the period. Valuable tables.

288 Sobel, Robert. PANIC ON WALL STREET: A HISTORY OF AMERICA'S FINANCIAL DISASTERS. New York: Macmillan, 1968. 469 p.

Panics, recessions, and depressions from 1792 to 1962. Sobel categorizes the types of trouble Wall Street has had and differentiates between them in order to illustrate his conviction that generalizations are inappropriate and misleading.

289 Studenski, Paul, and Krooss, Herman E. FINANCIAL HISTORY OF THE UNITED STATES: FISCAL, MONETARY, BANKING AND TARIFF, IN-CLUDING FINANCIAL ADMINISTRATION AND STATE AND LOCAL FINANCE. 2d ed. New York: McGraw-Hill Book Co., 1963. 605 p. Tables.

A textbook that systematically treats fiscal matters--federal, state, and local--from the colonial period to 1950. The authors deal with monetary, banking, and foreign trade policies and show how these are inter-related.

290 Ware, Caroline F. THE EARLY NEW ENGLAND COTTON MANUFAC-TURE: A STUDY IN INDUSTRIAL BEGINNINGS. 1931. Reprint. New York: Russell & Russell, 1966. 349 p. Illus.

Using the records of a few dozen early manufacturers, as well as other source materials, the author traces the development of the cotton industry from 1790 to the eve of the Civil War. Her narrative includes much anec-dotal material.

6. Communication

291 Barnouw, Erik. A HISTORY OF BROADCASTING IN THE UNITED STATES. 3 vols. New York: Oxford University Press, 1966-70. Illus., ports.

A comprehensive history by one who has been involved in the development of the medium. Volume 1: A TOWER OF BABEL, TO 1933; volume 2: THE GOLDEN WEB, 1933-1953; volume 3: THE IMAGE EMPIRE, FROM 1953.

292 Bleyer, Willard G. MAIN CURRENTS IN THE HISTORY OF AMERICAN JOURNALISM. 1927. Reprint. New York: DaCapo Press, 1973. 474 p. Illus., front., facsims.

A history of the development of the newspaper, dealing with editors and their products--good, bad, and indiffer-ent--from the colonial period, with its English back-ground, to the twentieth century.

293   Mott, Frank L. AMERICAN JOURNALISM: A HISTORY, 1690-1960.
3d ed. New York: Macmillan, 1962. 915 p. Illus., ports., plates,
facsims.

A comprehensive work designed as a narrative history,
with some features of a reference work. Mott begins
the history with the early newspapers of New England in
1690 and carries it to 1960 and the electronic media.

294   _____. A HISTORY OF AMERICAN MAGAZINES. 5 vols. Cambridge,
Mass.: Harvard University Press, 1930-68. Illus., ports., plates, facsims.

This exhaustive history deals with every type of magazine in every period of American history, from serious,
scholarly journals to professional and business organs
to mass circulation sports and recreation magazines.
Each volume includes supplements that tell the history
of prominent magazines in each period. Volume 1:
1741-1850; volume 2: 1850-1865; volume 3: 1864-
1885; volume 4: 1885-1905; volume 5: SKETCHES OF
21 MAGAZINES, 1905-1930.

7. Conservation

295   Nash, Roderick. WILDERNESS AND THE AMERICAN MIND. Rev. ed.
New Haven, Conn.: Yale University Press, 1973. 318 p. Illus.

An exploration of American thought on the meaning of
the wilderness from the time the Puritans first confronted
it to that of recent legislative attempts to save its last
vestiges. Thoreau, Muir, Pinchot, and many more play
an important part in these pages.

296   Robbins, Roy M. OUR LANDED HERITAGE: THE PUBLIC DOMAIN,
1776-1936. 1942. Reprint. New York: Peter Smith, 1950. 460 p.
Illus., maps.

A study of governmental policy in the distribution of
lands in the West. He discusses the various land acts
passed by Congress and their consequences for the people
who actually occupied the territories.

8. Diplomacy

297   Allen, H.C. GREAT BRITAIN AND THE UNITED STATES: A HISTORY
OF ANGLO-AMERICAN RELATIONS (1783-1952). New York: St.
Martin's Press, 1955. 1,024 p. Maps.

The work of an English professor of American history, the
book conveys a broad sympathy for English-speaking na-

tions on both sides of the Atlantic. Although Allen
concentrates his attention on political and economic
relations, he does not neglect the larger cultural relations.

298 Bailey, Thomas A. A DIPLOMATIC HISTORY OF THE AMERICAN PEOPLE.
8th ed. New York: Appleton-Century-Crofts, 1969. 1,055 p. Illus.,
maps.

A general survey of the field by a leading scholar.
Bailey writes with wit in a relaxed style and conveys
pungent insights into the nature of American diplomacy.

299 _____. THE MAN IN THE STREET: THE IMPACT OF AMERICAN PUB-
LIC OPINION ON FOREIGN POLICY. New York: Macmillan, 1948.
344 p.

An attempt to determine to what extent public opinion
influences the making of American foreign policy.
Bailey covers the period from the Revolution to the
twentieth century. The bulk of the book deals with
this century, since the author is able to make use of
public opinion polls.

300 Bemis, Samuel Flagg. A DIPLOMATIC HISTORY OF THE UNITED STATES.
4th ed. New York: Henry Holt, 1955. 1,018 p. Illus.

A comprehensive survey of American diplomatic practice
from the beginnings of the nation, by a notable scholar
in the field. He covers internal national developments
as they are related to foreign relations.

301 _____. THE LATIN AMERICAN POLICY OF THE UNITED STATES: AN
HISTORICAL INTERPRETATION. 1943. Reprint. New York: W.W.
Norton, 1967. 484 p. Illus., maps, diagr. Paperbound.

A very full, learned discussion of U.S. involvement
with the other nations of the hemisphere to the south.
Bemis covers the years between 1776 and the time of
writing.

302 Bemis, Samuel Flagg, et al., eds. THE AMERICAN SECRETARIES OF
STATE AND THEIR DIPLOMACY. 18 vols. to date. 1928- . Reprint.
Vols. 1-10. New York: Pageant Book Co., 1958. Vols. 11-18. New
York: Cooper Square, 1963- .

A joint effort by scholars of diplomacy to supply full
accounts of the heads of American foreign policy from
Robert R. Livingston, secretary of foreign affairs for the
Continental Congress (1781-83), to Christian A. Herter,
who served as secretary of state under President Dwight

D. Eisenhower from 1959 to 1961. Extensive appendices
supply the texts of treaties.

303 Blumenthal, Henry. FRANCE AND THE UNITED STATES: THEIR DIPLO-
MATIC RELATIONS, 1789-1914. Chapel Hill: University of North
Carolina Press, 1970. 326 p. Table.

A survey of the relations of the two nations, concentrating on the years since 1871. The author makes use of
French and American archives. He interprets U.S.
policy as designed to stem the influence of France
while establishing the United States as a world power.
Blumenthal holds that French policy, on the other hand,
while seeking to restrain the spread of American influence, contained an element of admiration for an old
ally.

304 _____. A REAPPRAISAL OF FRANCO-AMERICAN RELATIONS, 1830-
1871. Chapel Hill: University of North Carolina Press, 1959. 269 p.
Tables.

The high points of the relations of the two countries in
a period that saw revolutions and the Franco-Prussian
War. The relationship was not as cordial as has been
supposed.

305 DeConde, Alexander. A HISTORY OF AMERICAN FOREIGN POLICY.
2d ed. New York: Charles Scribner's Sons, 1971. 998 p. Illus.,
ports., maps, plans.

A detailed examination of the nation's foreign relations,
from the beginning to the present, by a leading expert
in the field.

306 _____, ed. ISOLATION AND SECURITY: IDEAS AND INTERESTS IN
TWENTIETH-CENTURY AMERICAN FOREIGN POLICY. Durham, N.C.:
Duke University Press, 1957. 215 p.

Essays that grew out of an interdisciplinary seminar at
Duke University, 1956, sponsored by the Social Science
Research Council. The contributors--R.N. Current, J.S.
Vinson, R.H. Ferrell, W.R. Allen, W.L. Neumann,
K.W. Thompson, and the editor--deal with such topics
as collective security, military force and foreign policy,
isolationism, and the peace movement.

307 Dulles, Foster Rhea. AMERICA'S RISE TO WORLD POWER, 1898-1954.
New York: Harper & Brothers, 1955. 314 p. Illus.

Starting with the Spanish-American War, Dulles describes
the rise of the United States to the status of a world

power. A readable survey with breadth rather than depth. Dulles tends to slight America's dealings with its neighbors in the Western Hemisphere.

308 _____. PRELUDE TO WORLD POWER: AMERICAN DIPLOMATIC HISTORY, 1860-1900. New York: Macmillan, 1965. 246 p.

A history of the growing aspiration in the United States to achieve the status of a world power, which was reflected in the strengthening of America's war-making capability and in a growing contentiousness that almost resulted in war with Chile and did result in one with Spain over Cuba and the Philippines.

309 Ferrell, Robert H. AMERICAN DIPLOMACY: A HISTORY. Rev. ed. New York: W.W. Norton, 1969. 944 p. Illus., ports., maps, tables.

Designed as a college textbook, the work provides an overview of American foreign policy from the Revolution to the present day. Ferrell divides the book into chapters following standard periodization.

310 Kennan, George F. AMERICAN DIPLOMACY, 1900-1950. Chicago: University of Chicago Press, 1953. 163 p.

The Charles R. Walgreen Lectures at the University of Chicago, in which a professional diplomat examines trends in American foreign policy. Kennan believes that it has been much too idealistic. He also chastises the forces that have led to isolationism.

311 Leopold, Richard W. THE GROWTH OF AMERICAN FOREIGN POLICY: A HISTORY. New York: Alfred A. Knopf, 1962. 899 p. Maps.

Although he covers the entire span of American history, Leopold treats the earlier periods briefly and concentrates on the years since 1889. He surveys conflicting interpretations along the way and includes sketches of the personalities responsible for policy formulation.

312 Logan, John A. NO TRANSFER: AN AMERICAN SECURITY PRINCIPLE. New Haven, Conn.: Yale University Press, 1961. 439 p. Maps.

A study of the Monroe Doctrine. Logan insists that American refusal to recognize possible new European claims to territory in the New World is the most consistent element in U.S. foreign policy.

313 Neumann, William L. AMERICA ENCOUNTERS JAPAN: FROM PERRY TO MACARTHUR. Baltimore: Johns Hopkins Press, 1963. 361 p.

This critical history does not concern itself with the ins

and outs of diplomacy but rather with the ideas and
attitudes of Americans toward Japan over a hundred-year
period. Neumann is critical of American leaders, especially of Franklin D. Roosevelt.

314 Osgood, Robert E. IDEALS AND SELF-INTEREST IN AMERICAN FOREIGN
RELATIONS: THE GREAT TRANSFORMATION OF THE TWENTIETH CEN-
TURY. 1953. Reprint. Chicago: University of Chicago Press, 1964.
503 p. Paperbound.

Covers the years from the Spanish-American War to
World War II, delineating the rationale behind American
actions. Osgood finds that some of America's foreign
policy has resulted from idealistic disinterestedness and
some from the most definite self-interest.

315 Pratt, Julius W. A HISTORY OF UNITED STATES FOREIGN POLICY.
3d ed. Englewood Cliffs, N.J.: Prentice-Hall, 1972. 640 p. Maps.

This standard text considers the aims and "tools" of
foreign policy and systematically treats it through the
years from the Revolution to the presidency of Richard
M. Nixon.

316 U.S. Department of State. TREATIES AND OTHER INTERNATIONAL
AGREEMENTS OF THE UNITED STATES OF AMERICA, 1776-1949. Edited
by Charles I. Bevins. 10 vols. to date. Washington, D.C.: Government Printing Office, 1961- .

The complete text of multilateral agreements to which
the United States has been a party, along with bilateral
agreements between the United States and other nations,
arranged alphabetically from Afghanistan to Peru.

317 Williams, William Appleman. AMERICAN-RUSSIAN RELATIONS, 1781-
1947. 1952. Reprint. New York: Octagon Books, 1971. 367 p.

Approaches the subject more from the American side of
the relationship, although Williams is not particularly
happy with the U.S. record.

9. Education

318 Cremin, Lawrence A. THE TRANSFORMATION OF THE SCHOOL: PRO-
GRESSIVISM IN AMERICAN EDUCATION, 1876-1957. New York: Alfred
A. Knopf, 1961. 427 p.

The first detailed history of the rise of progressive education, this work traces the influence of the ideas of
its proponents, and its eventual decline. Cremin places
his history in the context of national developments,

writing with insight and felicity.

319 Cubberly, Ellwood P. PUBLIC EDUCATION IN THE UNITED STATES:
A STUDY AND INTERPRETATION OF AMERICAN EDUCATIONAL HIS-
TORY. Rev. and enl. ed. Boston: Houghton Mifflin, 1934. 810 p.
Illus., ports., plates, maps, tables, diagrs.

Directed at beginners in the field. Cubberly traces the
development of schools in the United States from the
early years of the nation, devoting more space to the
period following the Civil War. He discusses modern
teaching techniques and stresses the need for practical
education.

320 Curti, Merle. SOCIAL IDEAS OF AMERICAN EDUCATORS. 1935. Reprint. Totowa, N.J.: Littlefield, Adams, 1968. 667 p.

Examines the social thought of a group of influential
educational leaders: Horace Mann, Henry Barnard,
Booker T. Washington, William James, John Dewey,
and several others. Curti's analysis makes it obvious
that there is a gulf between aspiration and reality.

321 Edwards, Newton, and Richey, Herman G. THE SCHOOL IN THE
AMERICAN SOCIAL ORDER. 2d ed. Boston: Houghton Mifflin, 1963.
694 p. Illus.

The authors place the school in the context of political,
intellectual, and social developments in each period,
also showing the effects of economics and governmental
attitudes. Among the many topics covered are tax support, relations with the churches, and the movement
for compulsory education. A fair amount of space is
devoted to the recent period.

322 Elson, Ruth M. GUARDIANS OF TRADITION: AMERICAN SCHOOL-
BOOKS OF THE NINETEENTH CENTURY. Lincoln: University of Nebraska Press, 1964. 437 p. Illus.

A study based on hundreds of textbooks that molded the
minds of young Americans in the elementary schools of
the nineteenth century. The author discusses what the
children were taught about God, nature, man, politics,
their country, race, and much else.

323 Hofstadter, Richard, and Metzger, Walter P. THE DEVELOPMENT OF
ACADEMIC FREEDOM IN THE UNITED STATES. New York: Columbia
University Press, 1955. 543 p.

Academic freedom is examined first in "the Age of the
College" and then in "the Age of the University." The

authors deal primarily with the freedom of faculty members, although they do touch on student rights when
they run parallel to those of the faculty.

324 Hofstadter, Richard, and Smith, Wilson, eds. AMERICAN HIGHER EDU-
CATION, A DOCUMENTARY HISTORY. 2 vols. Chicago: University
of Chicago Press, 1961.

Covers the years from the founding of Harvard in 1636
to 1948. The editors arrange the documents chronologically and supply an introduction to each period and
headnotes to the selections; a comprehensive collection.

325 Rudolph, Frederick. THE AMERICAN COLLEGE AND UNIVERSITY: A
HISTORY. New York: Alfred A. Knopf, 1962. 568 p.

The development of American institutions of higher learning from colonial times to mid-twentieth century. Rudolph relates his educational history to political and
social developments of each period with which he deals.

326 Veysey, Laurence R. THE EMERGENCE OF THE AMERICAN UNIVERSITY.
Chicago: University of Chicago Press, 1965. 519 p.

Deals with higher education in the years 1865 to 1910.
Veysey evaluates contending curricula and points of
view. The first section of the book deals with ideas,
the second with administrative structure.

10. Feminism

327 Flexner, Eleanor. CENTURY OF STRUGGLE: THE WOMAN'S RIGHTS
MOVEMENT IN THE UNITED STATES. 1959. Reprint. New York:
Atheneum, 1968. 398 p. Illus. Paperbound.

Discusses the place of women in the United States and
the various campaigns to improve their lot, culminating
in the passage of the suffrage amendment to the Constitution in 1920. The determined campaigners come alive
in these pages, with their strengths and weaknesses made
obvious.

328 Kraditor, Aileen S., ed. UP FROM THE PEDESTAL: SELECTED WRITINGS
IN THE HISTORY OF AMERICAN FEMINISM. Chicago: Quadrangle
Books, 1968. 372 p.

Documents dating from 1642 to 1966. Kraditor has
chosen excerpts from speeches, articles, reports, letters,
etc., in order to illuminate the issues that have involved notable women in the struggle for an equal place
in society; she has provided an informative introduction.

329 Lerner, Gerda, ed. BLACK WOMEN IN WHITE AMERICA: A DOCU-
MENTARY HISTORY. New York: Pantheon, 1972. 666 p.

A selection of works, most by black women, covering
the years from the 1830s to about 1970. Lerner has
taken excerpts from all types of materials--letters, newspapers and periodicals, speeches--to illustrate the struggle the black woman has carried on. She provides informative introductions to the sections of the book.

330 O'Neill, William L. EVERYONE WAS BRAVE: THE RISE AND FALL OF
FEMINISM IN AMERICA. Chicago: Quadrangle Books, 1969. 380 p.

The supposed triumph of the women's movement in gaining suffrage in 1920 was really the beginning of its
decline, according to O'Neill. The author traces
events leading to that victory and delineates the disillusionment that set in after when women discovered
their lot was not essentially different from what it had
been before. Later chapters deal with such matters as
the "feminine mystique."

331 Scott, Anne Fior. THE SOUTHERN LADY, FROM PEDESTAL TO POLI-
TICS, 1830-1930. Chicago: University of Chicago Press, 1970. 247 p.

An attempt to remove the myth surrounding womanhood
in the South. The author examines her subject in the
ante-bellum period and during the Civil War, but especially since that conflict, in the context of her involvement in missionary and reform activities. She
depends not only on documentary evidence in the usual
sense but makes full, imaginative use of literature as
well.

332 Sinclair, Andrew. THE BETTER HALF: THE EMANCIPATION OF AMERI-
CAN WOMEN. New York: Harper & Row, 1965. 430 p. Illus.,
ports.

The novelist and historian recounts the struggle of women
for a place equal with men in American society and especially for the attainment of suffrage.

11. Government and Politics

333 Binkley, Wilfred E. AMERICAN POLITICAL PARTIES: THEIR NATURAL
HISTORY. 4th ed., enl. New York: Alfred A. Knopf, 1963. 486 p.

Combines scholarship with practical political knowledge.
Binkley traces, with wit as well as objectivity, various
interests that have coalesced into political parties, from
the beginning to the present.

334   Burns, James MacGregor. PRESIDENTIAL GOVERNMENT: CRUCIBLE
       OF LEADERSHIP. Boston: Houghton Mifflin, 1966. 384 p.

       Sets up a model of the ideal, strong presidency and
       then determines which figures, from George Washington
       to Lyndon Johnson, fit it. Burns believes only the
       president can clearly set and execute national policy.

335   Chambers, William N., and Burnham, Walter Dean, eds. THE AMERICAN
       PARTY SYSTEMS: STAGES OF POLITICAL DEVELOPMENT. New York:
       Oxford University Press, 1967. 332 p. Illus.

       Papers from the Conference on American Political Party
       Development, 1966, held at Washington University, St.
       Louis; arranged chronologically from the 1790s to the
       present. Contributors include members of various disci-
       plines, including Paul Goodman, Richard McCormick,
       and the editors.

336   Ekirch, Arthur A., Jr. THE DECLINE OF AMERICAN LIBERALISM. New
       York: Longmans, Green, 1955. 444 p.

       A discussion of American politics from the Revolution to
       the 1950s. Ekirch sees a progressive departure from
       classical liberalism and is pessimistic in his evaluation
       of present and future possibilities.

337   Galloway, George B. HISTORY OF THE HOUSE OF REPRESENTATIVES.
       New York: Crowell, 1962. 346 p. Ports., tables, diagrs.

       The history of how "the people's house" was devised
       originally and how it developed through the years.
       Galloway, who served on the staff of Congress for
       many years, is in a unique position to observe the
       strong and weak points of House structure and its re-
       lations with the Senate, the executive, and the Supreme
       Court.

338   Guttmann, Allen. THE CONSERVATIVE TRADITION IN AMERICA. New
       York: Oxford University Press, 1967. 222 p.

       Guttmann contends that the conservative tradition in
       America has not, on the whole, been expressed politi-
       cally, but rather in other areas. He looks at literature,
       the military, and religion in this exposition, and he
       holds that conservatism cropped up as a political move-
       ment in the South where it was necessary to justify
       slavery.

339   Hartz, Louis. THE LIBERAL TRADITION IN AMERICA: AN INTERPRE-
       TATION OF AMERICAN POLITICAL THOUGHT SINCE THE REVOLUTION.

New York: Harcourt, Brace, 1955. 329 p.

A study of American political tradition with a particular point of view. Hartz is less concerned with individual spokesmen than with representative ideas, although he indulges from time to time in psychological analysis.

340 Hofstadter, Richard. THE AMERICAN POLITICAL TRADITION AND THE MEN WHO MADE IT. 1948. Reprint. New York: Alfred A. Knopf, 1973. 440 p.

A series of essays analyzing American politics and major individuals, from the founding fathers to Franklin Roosevelt. Hofstadter punctures some myths along the way, with rapier wit.

341 _____. THE IDEA OF A PARTY SYSTEM: THE RISE OF LEGITIMATE OPPOSITION IN THE UNITED STATES, 1780-1840. Berkeley and Los Angeles: University of California Press, 1969. 293 p.

The Jefferson Memorial Lectures at the University of California at Berkeley. Elucidates the process by which the nation's early leaders gave up their aversion to political parties and began developing the party system, using English ideas of party as a basis of comparison.

342 _____. THE PARANOID STYLE IN AMERICAN POLITICS, AND OTHER ESSAYS. New York: Alfred A. Knopf, 1965. 328 p.

Although in this collection Hofstadter asserts that paranoia is not a monopoly of the right wing, he attributes it to various groups in American history that have held to the conspiracy theory, such as the McCarthyites and Birchites.

343 Hyman, Harold M. TO TRY MEN'S SOULS: LOYALTY TESTS IN AMERICAN HISTORY. Berkeley and Los Angeles: University of California Press, 1959. 414 p. Illus.

Written when the issue of loyalty oaths was prominent, Hyman's work shows that such oaths have been part of American life since 1609 and that they have been re-emphasized in times of crisis. He accumulates much documentation and holds that such tests are useless.

344 Johnson, Walter. 1600 PENNSYLVANIA AVENUE: PRESIDENTS AND THE PEOPLE, 1929-1959. Boston: Little, Brown, 1960. 390 p.

A study of presidential leadership, dealing with Hoover, F.D. Roosevelt, Truman, and Eisenhower. Johnson places these presidents in the context of world developments and evaluates their effectiveness in the office he considers essential to the perpetuation of democracy.

345 Key, V.O., Jr. THE RESPONSIBLE ELECTORATE: RATIONALITY IN PRESIDENTIAL VOTING, 1936-1960. Cambridge, Mass.: Harvard University Press, 1966. 179 p. Port.

Voting patterns are analyzed, from the elections of F.D. Roosevelt to Kennedy. Key marshalls statistics to demonstrate his belief that the electorate judged candidates on the basis of policy issues. Upon Key's death the book was finished by Milton C. Cummings, Jr.

346 Lipset, Seymour M., and Raab, Earl. THE POLITICS OF UNREASON: RIGHT-WING EXTREMISM IN AMERICA, 1790-1970. New York: Harper & Row, 1970. 581 p.

Discusses movements which, from the early days of the republic to the present, have sought to deny rights to ideological opponents. The Know-Nothing party and Ku Klux Klan inevitably come in for much discussion, as do the McCarthyites, the John Birch Society, and the movement to make George Wallace president. The authors differentiate between the supporters of such movements.

347 Lott, Davis N., ed. THE PRESIDENTS SPEAK: THE INAUGURAL ADDRESSES OF THE AMERICAN PRESIDENTS FROM WASHINGTON TO NIXON. 3d ed. New York: Holt, Rinehart and Winston, 1969. 319 p. Illus.

The editor includes explanatory notes on each address. Other material includes lists of the presidents and vice presidents, the Declaration of Independence, the Articles of Confederation, and the Constitution.

348 Mayer, George H. THE REPUBLICAN PARTY, 1854-1966. 2d ed. New York: Oxford University Press, 1967. 615 p. Paperbound.

A history of the party, from its halting beginning as a third force in American politics in the years immediately preceding the election of Lincoln to the mid-term election of 1966. Mayer examines platforms, personalities, and the performance of the party when in power.

349 Nagel, Paul C. ONE NATION INDIVISIBLE: THE UNION IN AMERICAN THOUGHT, 1776-1861. New York: Oxford University Press, 1964. 335 p.

The term "Union" was used in several senses from the

time of the Revolution to the Civil War. Nagel analyzes the different uses of the word, the emotional
images conveyed, and how they affected the emerging
sense of nationalism. He quotes generously from the
sources.

350   Porter, Kirk H., and Johnson, Donald Bruce, eds. NATIONAL PARTY
PLATFORMS. Urbana: University of Illinois Press, 1970. 779 p.

Includes platforms of the various American political
parties from the first "true platform" of the Democrats
in 1840 through the presidential campaign of 1968.

351   Roseboom, Eugene H. A HISTORY OF PRESIDENTIAL ELECTIONS, FROM
GEORGE WASHINGTON TO RICHARD NIXON. 3d ed. New York:
Macmillan, 1970. 648 p.

A survey of the quadrennial struggle for the presidential
nomination and election. Roseboom also deals with
each administration so that continuity between elections
can be considered and issues in each succeeding election can be made intelligible.

352   Rossiter, Clinton L. THE AMERICAN PRESIDENCY. 2d ed. 1960. Reprint. New York: Time, 1963. 346 p.

In their original form, the Charles R. Walgreen Foundation Lectures at the University of Chicago, 1956. Rossiter examines the office and the men who have filled
it, provisions for the presidency in the Constitution,
the power of the presidency and attempts to restrict it.
He believes it to be "one of the few truly successful
government institutions ever created."

353   _____. CONSERVATISM IN AMERICA: THE THANKLESS PERSUASION.
2d ed., rev. New York: Alfred A. Knopf, 1962. 306 p.

Rossiter sets conservatism in a historical context, drawing on English history and on American colonial developments from the time of Cotton Mather; he concludes
with a suggested program for modern conservatives.

354   Schlesinger, Arthur M., Jr., et al., eds. HISTORY OF AMERICAN
PRESIDENTIAL ELECTIONS, 1789-1968. 4 vols. New York: Chelsea
House and McGraw-Hill, 1971.

Covers presidential elections from Washington to Nixon;
authorities provide essays and a selection of pertinent
documents on each campaign.

355   Williamson, Chilton. AMERICAN SUFFRAGE: FROM PROPERTY TO

DEMOCRACY, 1760-1860. Princeton, N.J.: Princeton University Press, 1960. 306 p.

A study of the transition from suffrage based on property ownership to universal male suffrage, which Williamson attempts to show was largely accomplished before the rise of the Jacksonians. His findings refute Turner's thesis, since broader male suffrage originated in the East rather than the West.

356 Wiltse, Charles M. THE JEFFERSONIAN TRADITION IN AMERICAN DEMOCRACY. 1935. Reprint. New York: Hill and Wang, 1960. 273 p.

A systematic presentation of Jefferson's political principles and how they have since been embodied in the American experience. The first part of the book is based largely on Jefferson's papers.

12. Immigration

357 Billington, Ray A. THE PROTESTANT CRUSADE, 1800-1860. 1938. Reprint. Chicago: Quadrangle Books, 1964. 526 p. Paperbound.

A history of the reaction of "native Americans" to the influx of immigrants. Billington impartially examines the fears of the nativists that they would be engulfed by illiteracy, crime, corruption, and Roman Catholicism, and the organizations they formed to resist such developments. He traces the emergence of the Know-Nothing party. Many of the fears of the nativists materialized, so many of them, in fact, that Billington believes much of their propaganda was unnecessary since Americans could see for themselves the resultant transformation of the cities.

358 Divine, Robert A. AMERICAN IMMIGRATION POLICY, 1924-1952. New Haven, Conn.: Yale University Press, 1957. 228 p. Tables.

Examines legislation passed in 1924 that restricted immigration to the United States, as well as the ideas of opponents of such legislation. Divine attempts to show the consequences of the 1924 legislation on immigration in the social, economic, and other spheres.

359 Handlin, Oscar. RACE AND NATIONALITY IN AMERICAN LIFE. Boston: Little, Brown, 1957. 300 p.

An examination of the sources of racism, dealing with discrimination felt by various immigrant groups and the blacks. Handlin looks at the economic system, sex,

the family, and many other aspects, in seeking the
springs of racist attitudes.

360 Hansen, Marcus Lee. ATLANTIC MIGRATION, 1607-1860: A HISTORY
OF THE CONTINUING SETTLEMENT OF AMERICA. 1940. Reprint.
New York: Harper & Row, 1964. 408 p. Front., plates. Paperbound.

Deals with the many factors in the Old World that
prompted migration to the New: economic changes,
political and religious oppression, and the appealing
pictures painted by emigrant agents. Latin America
and the United States were in competition for the immigrant, the former seeming for awhile to hold more
promise to the European. The great migration was made
possible by the improved system of transportation. Hansen's work is enriched by the inclusion of eyewitness
accounts.

361 _____. THE IMMIGRANT IN AMERICAN HISTORY. Cambridge, Mass.:
Harvard University Press, 1940. 241 p.

This collection of nine essays gives an overview of the
role of the immigrant; written by a scholar who had
delved deeply into the primary materials.

362 Higham, John. STRANGERS IN THE LAND: PATTERNS OF AMERICAN
NATIVISM, 1860-1925. Rev. ed. New York: Atheneum, 1966. 440
p. Illus., ports. Paperbound.

A study of the reception the immigrant received from
"native" Americans. Higham concludes his study with
an appraisal of the effects of the Immigration Act of 1924,
which severely restricted movement from certain parts of
the world to the United States.

363 Jones, Maldwyn A. AMERICAN IMMIGRATION. Chicago: University
of Chicago Press, 1960. 359 p. Illus.

This general account of immigration to the United States
describes Old World backgrounds, acculturation of immigrant groups, and their interaction. Jones spells out
the important part played by the newcomer in several
areas of American life--economic, social, and political.
The immigrant's presence influenced the movement west
and sectional strife and had an important impact on the
development of American foreign policy. The author
examines the successive waves of immigration from the
colonial period to the twentieth century.

364 Taylor, Philip A.M. THE DISTANT MAGNET: EUROPEAN EMIGRATION
TO THE U.S.A. New York: Harper & Row, 1971. 338 p. Illus.,

front., ports., maps., diagrs., cartoons.

Describes the migration of thirty-five million people to the United States from 1830 to 1930. This is a general treatment dealing with immigrants from both northwest and southeast Europe. Taylor follows them from their native habitats across the ocean, by sail and steam, to their new environments in America. The book is made more useful by an excellent collection of pictures, maps, and diagrams.

365   Wittke, Carl F. WE WHO BUILT AMERICA. Rev. ed. Cleveland: Press of Case Western Reserve, 1964. 568 p.

A detailed, systematic history of immigration from the colonial period on. Wittke deals with each national group in turn, including in his survey a review of the cultural baggage--art, music, etc.--the immigrants brought with them, as well as their contributions in these cultural fields and in the professions, business, and labor. The reactions of the nativists, the Know-Nothings, and the Ku Klux Klan, and the passage of legislation to restrict immigration are dealt with as well.

13. Indians

366   THE AMERICAN HERITAGE BOOK OF INDIANS. Edited by Alvin M. Josephy, Jr. New York: American Heritage Publishing Co., distributed by Simon & Schuster, 1961. Illus.

The lives of the Indians of Peru, and Central and North America, from prehistory to the late nineteenth century; the book concentrates on their fate since the coming of Europeans. The narrative is by William Brandon.

367   Debo, Angie. A HISTORY OF THE INDIANS OF THE UNITED STATES. Norman: University of Oklahoma Press, 1970. 413 p. Illus., ports., map.

Survey of the history of the American Indians from the coming of the white man to the mid-twentieth century. The author, a noted specialist, devotes much space to the impact whites have had on Indian civilization.

368   Driver, Harold E. INDIANS OF NORTH AMERICA. 2d rev. ed. Chicago: University of Chicago Press, 1969. 649 p. Illus., maps.

The anthropology of the American Indian, covering all aspects of his life; includes helpful illustrations.

369 Josephy, Alvin M., Jr. THE INDIAN HERITAGE OF AMERICA. New York: Alfred A. Knopf, 1971. 413 p. Illus., ports., maps, facsims.

A general survey of the Indian tribes of America, written for a general audience. A sympathetic account with many informative illustrations.

370 Swanton, John R. THE INDIAN TRIBES OF NORTH AMERICA. Smithsonian Institution Bureau of American Ethnology Bulletin 145. Washington, D.C.: Government Printing Office, 1952. 726 p. Illus.

A state-by-state consideration of the history and way of life of the tribes. Swanton also includes the Indians of Canada, the West Indies, Mexico, and Central America.

371 Underhill, Ruth Murray. RED MAN'S AMERICA: A HISTORY OF THE INDIANS IN THE UNITED STATES. Chicago: University of Chicago Press, 1953. 410 p. Illus., maps.

The American Indian from his origins in prehistory to the 1950s, by a specialist in Indian culture.

372 _____. RED MAN'S RELIGION: BELIEFS AND PRACTICES OF THE INDIANS NORTH OF MEXICO. Chicago: University of Chicago Press, 1965. 311 p. Illus.

The development of various aspects of Indian life--history, agriculture, war, etc.--as they have affected and have been affected by his religion.

373 Vogel, Virgil J. AMERICAN INDIAN MEDICINE. Norman: University of Oklahoma Press, 1970. 603 p. Illus.

Deals with Indian theories of disease, shamanistic practices, therapeutic methods, and the influence of Indian medicine on folk medicine of the white man.

374 Washburn, Wilcomb E. RED MAN'S LAND, WHITE MAN'S LAW: A STUDY OF THE PAST AND PRESENT STATUS OF THE AMERICAN INDI-AN. New York: Charles Scribner's Sons, 1971. 288 p. Facsim.

An examination of how the Indian got to be where he is today. Washburn includes sections on the Indian's legal status, problems of land ownership, his education, and various treaty rights. He is critical of the management of the Bureau of Indian Affairs.

375 Wissler, Clark. INDIANS OF THE UNITED STATES. Rev. ed. Garden City, N.Y.: Doubleday, 1966. 336 p. Ports., plates, map.

A survey of the Indian tribes and their ways of life. The book, originally published in 1940, has been revised by Lucy Wales Kluckhohn.

14. Intellectual and Social Life

376 Barker, Charles A. AMERICAN CONVICTIONS: CYCLES OF PUBLIC
THOUGHT, 1600-1850. Philadelphia: Lippincott, 1970. 632 p. Illus.

> A survey of major thought patterns in America to the
> eve of the Civil War. Barker attempts to interrelate
> governmental developments, religious, economic and
> social thought.

377 Blau, Joseph L. MEN AND MOVEMENTS IN AMERICAN PHILOSOPHY.
New York: Prentice-Hall, 1952. 414 p.

> A survey of the development of intellectual history,
> dealing with such major movements as transcendentalism,
> idealism, realism, pragmatism, and naturalism, and
> major figures from Edwards to Emerson and James to
> Dewey. Blau clarifies the issues at stake in each
> successive movement.

378 Bryan, William Alfred. GEORGE WASHINGTON IN AMERICAN LITERA-
TURE, 1775-1865. New York: Columbia University Press, 1952. 292 p.
Port.

> The treatment of the Washington legend in historical
> and other types of literature: biography, fiction, oratory,
> and verse. Bryan includes many illustrative quotations.

379 Commager, Henry Steele. THE AMERICAN MIND: AN INTERPRETATION
OF AMERICAN THOUGHT AND CHARACTER SINCE THE 1880s. New
Haven, Conn.: Yale University Press, 1950. 485 p. Front.

> Picks up the story where Vernon L. Parrington's MAIN
> CURRENTS IN AMERICAN THOUGHT, q.v., no. 389,
> broke off. Commager sees the 1880s as a great water-
> shed of American thought in the twentieth century. It
> is fitting that he give prominent place to such figures
> as William James. A rich book with, at times, cutting
> analyses.

380 Conkin, Paul K. PURITANS AND PRAGMATISTS: EIGHT EMINENT
AMERICAN THINKERS. New York: Dodd, Mead, 1968. 506 p. Paperbound.

> The author sees striking similarities if not causal con-
> nections in the thought of the Puritans and pragmatists
> he includes in this collection. The substantial essays
> deal with Jonathan Edwards, Benjamin Franklin, John
> Adams, Ralph Waldo Emerson, Charles S. Peirce, William

James, John Dewey, and George Santayana, who he believes are among the most important thinkers in American history.

381 Curti, Merle. THE GROWTH OF AMERICAN THOUGHT. 3d. New York: Harper & Row, 1964. 959 p. Illus., ports., facsims.

The development of ideas in America is put in a social context by the dean of American intellectual historians. From the Christian heritage the colonists had in common, Curti traces the manifold changes that have taken place to the present. A prime book for American intellectual history.

382 Furnas, J.C. THE AMERICANS: A SOCIAL HISTORY OF THE UNITED STATES, 1587-1914. New York: G.P. Putnam's Sons, 1969. 1,015 p. Illus.

A huge sprawling collection of facts concerning the social lives of Americans. Furnas's popular approach is entertaining. He does not attempt to impose a thesis on his material.

383 Gabriel, Ralph H. THE COURSE OF AMERICAN DEMOCRATIC THOUGHT. 2d ed. New York: Ronald Press, 1956. 522 p.

The intellectual history traces the "American democratic faith" from mid-nineteenth to mid-twentieth century in its various mutations from Emerson and Thoreau, through the Civil War, Social Darwinism, and two world wars.

384 Hofstadter, Richard. ANTI-INTELLECTUALISM IN AMERICAN LIFE. New York: Alfred A. Knopf, 1963. 447 p.

Hofstadter hops, skips, and jumps through American history, dealing with such occurrences as the Great Awakening, the revivalism of Billy Graham, trends in education, and American business attitudes, pointing up the betrayal of the intellect throughout. This is not, however, a sweeping condemnation, for Hofstadter seeks the good points in his subjects.

385 Jones, Howard Mumford. THE AGE OF ENERGY: VARIETIES OF AMERICAN EXPERIENCE, 1865-1915. New York: Viking Press, 1971. 564 p. Illus.

In this intellectual history, Jones has sought a unifying concept to attach to a diverse and complex period. The result is revealed in the title of the volume. His analysis deals with many figures, movements, and sections of the country.

386   Lasch, Christopher. THE NEW RADICALISM IN AMERICA, 1889-1963: THE INTELLECTUAL AS A SOCIAL TYPE. New York: Alfred A. Knopf, 1965. 380 p.

     A selection of "radicals," ranging from Jane Addams to Norman Mailer, are subjected to psychological as well as literary analysis.

387   Miller, Perry. LIFE OF THE MIND IN AMERICA: FROM THE REVOLUTION TO THE CIVIL WAR. New York: Harcourt, Brace & World, 1965. 349 p.

     Miller died before he could complete this volume. Though a fragment, it is rich with the insights he brought to his other studies of the American literature and intellect.

388   Nevins, Allan, ed. AMERICAN SOCIAL HISTORY AS RECORDED BY BRITISH TRAVELERS. 1923. Reprint. New York: Augustus M. Kelley, 1969. 586 p.

     Excerpts from the travel accounts of Britons who visited the United States from 1789 to 1922. The book is divided into four periods with Nevins providing an introduction to each. The comments on American life by these visitors were sometimes friendly and positive; however, the more negative comments received most of the attention. Nevins provides a good balance. Among the more well-known visitors represented are Frances Trollope, Captain Basil Hall, Harriet Martineau, Captain Marryat, Charles Dickens, Anthony Trollope, Charles Lyell, Herbert Spencer, Matthew Arnold, and James Bryce.

389   Parrington, Vernon L. MAIN CURRENTS IN AMERICAN THOUGHT: AN INTERPRETATION OF AMERICAN LITERATURE FROM THE BEGINNINGS TO 1920. 3 vols. New York: Harcourt, Brace, 1927-30.

     Probably the most influential history of the development of American thought. Parrington unabashedly adopted a Jeffersonian agrarian tone, which permeates the work; but despite this, he had a large sympathy for men like John Winthrop. Volume 1: THE COLONIAL MIND, 1620-1800; volume 2: THE ROMANTIC REVOLUTION IN AMERICA, 1800-1860; volume 3: THE BEGINNINGS OF CRITICAL REALISM IN AMERICA, 1860-1920. The third volume remained unfinished at Parrington's death but was published because of its inherent interest.

390   Persons, Stow. AMERICAN MINDS: A HISTORY OF IDEAS. New York: Henry Holt, 1958. 480 p.

     Persons analyzes successive thought patterns in the Ameri-

can experience; he presents the Puritan mind, the mind
of the Enlightenment, and so on, but makes no attempt
to trace the transition from one to the next or to com-
pare them. Each intellectual portrait is skillfully drawn,
however, and provides a good beginning point for research.

391 Peterson, Merrill D. THE JEFFERSONIAN IMAGE IN THE AMERICAN
MIND. New York: Oxford University Press, 1960. 558 p.

Peterson has made a thorough study of the sources and
demonstrates the continuing power of Jefferson and his
ideas to stir the intellect and the emotions in every
period of U.S. history.

392 Schneider, Herbert W. A HISTORY OF AMERICAN PHILOSOPHY. 2d
ed. New York: Columbia University Press, 1963. 590 p.

A systematic exposition of American thought from the
Puritans to modern times. Schneider deals sympathetically with the major figures and relates their intellectual activity to political and social developments.

393 Shryock, Richard H. MEDICINE AND SOCIETY IN AMERICA, 1660-
1860. New York: New York University Press, 1960. 182 p.

Originally the Anson G. Phelps Lectures on Early American History for 1959 at New York University. Shryock
places medical developments in the broad context of
social life and also deals with the evolution of the
medical profession.

394 Tyler, Alice Felt. FREEDOM'S FERMENT: PHASES OF AMERICAN SO-
CIAL HISTORY TO 1860. 1944. Reprint. Freeport, N.Y.: Books for
Libraries Press, 1970. 619 p. Illus., ports., plates, plans.

A review of the multifold utopian and humanitarian ventures in the first half of the nineteenth century. In the
first part of the book, the author sets forth the thought
and experiences of the transcendentalists, millenarians,
spiritualists, Mormons, religious Communists, Shakers,
and the utopian socialists. Many of these sought to
separate themselves from the society of their day. The
second part of the book is devoted to those who sought
to transform society through campaigns for education,
penal reform, temperance, peace, the rights of women,
and abolition of slavery. The book is based on both
primary and secondary sources and contains illustrations
that illuminate the subjects included.

395 White, Morton. SCIENCE AND SENTIMENT IN AMERICA: PHILOSO-

PHICAL THOUGHT FROM JONATHAN EDWARDS TO JOHN DEWEY. New York: Oxford University Press, 1972. 366 p.

> The relationship of philosophy and science. White believes that the questions raised by modern science have forced the philosopher to deal with man's life and civilization, at least until recent years. He illumines the thought of American philosophers over a two-hundred-year period.

396 Wish, Harvey. SOCIETY AND THOUGHT IN EARLY AMERICA: A SOCIAL AND INTELLECTUAL HISTORY OF THE AMERICAN PEOPLE THROUGH 1865. 2d ed. New York: David McKay, 1962. 624 p. Illus., ports.

> Links phases of American thought and social life to representative men in each period and section (e.g., Roger Williams in New England, William Fitzhugh in Virginia). This approach, however, does not prevent Wish from delving into a full range of topics from the beginning of the American settlements to the conclusion of the Civil War.

397 _____. SOCIETY AND THOUGHT IN MODERN AMERICA: A SOCIAL AND INTELLECTUAL HISTORY OF THE AMERICAN PEOPLE FROM 1865. 2d ed. New York: David McKay, 1962. 656 p. Illus., ports.

> As in his earlier work, SOCIETY AND THOUGHT IN EARLY AMERICA, q.v., no. 396, Wish hinges developments in a particular period to the lives of notable individuals. By relating their careers to contemporary occurrences he elucidates social and intellectual themes of the time.

15. Labor

398 Brooks, Thomas R. TOIL AND TROUBLE: A HISTORY OF AMERICAN LABOR. 2d ed., rev. and enl. New York: Delacorte, 1971. 431 p.

> Surveys American labor from the colonial period to the twentieth century. Brooks concludes the work with a discussion of present-day labor problems. He believes the development of welfare benefits within the corporate structure has slowed recognition by society as a whole of its social obligations. The foreword is by A.H. Raskin.

399 Commons, John R., et al. HISTORY OF LABOR IN THE UNITED STATES. 4 vols. 1918-35. Reprint. New York: Macmillan, 1940.

> The standard work in the field. The authors believe that American labor, on the whole, rejected radicalism

and accepted a capitalist framework because of the
promise of betterment which seemed possible of achievement.

400   Dulles, Foster Rhea. LABOR IN AMERICA: A HISTORY. 3d ed. New
York: Crowell, 1966. 448 p.

The history of labor from colonial times to the 1960s.
The book pays more attention to the nineteenth and
twentieth century developments, such as the rise of the
Knights of Labor, the AFL, and the CIO.

401   Morris, James O. CONFLICT WITHIN THE AFL: A STUDY OF CRAFT
VERSUS INDUSTRIAL UNIONISM, 1901-1938. Ithaca, N.Y.: Cornell
University Press, 1958. 328 p.

The struggle between the two types of unionism and the
consequent emergence of the CIO and its battles with
the AFL. A study that tilts in favor of industrial unionism.

402   Pelling, Henry. AMERICAN LABOR. Chicago: University of Chicago
Press, 1960. 247 p. Illus.

A British scholar looks at labor conditions and the rise
of labor unions in the various periods from the colonial
period to the late 1950s. A great deal of detail is
included in brief compass.

403   Rayback, Joseph G. A HISTORY OF AMERICAN LABOR. New York:
Macmillan, 1959. 459 p.

A survey from the colonial period to the present, with
concentration on the period from 1890, when American
industry was rapidly transformed by the machine. Rayback puts the laboring man in the context of developments in the political and social spheres, as well as in
that of industry.

404   Taft, Philip. ORGANIZED LABOR IN AMERICAN HISTORY. New York:
Harper & Row, 1964. 839 p.

A general history of the trade union movement from the
Civil War to World War I. The work is thorough and
well organized. Taft compares the Knights of Labor to
company unions and makes it clear that government in-
hibited organization of labor until the policy changed
under the New Deal.

16. Law and Constitution

405   Brant, Irving. THE BILL OF RIGHTS: ITS ORIGIN AND MEANING. Indianapolis: Bobbs-Merrill, 1965. 573 p.

Brant claims that more than sixty rights are protected by the Constitution and the first ten amendments; he enumerates them and shows their origins in English and American colonial experience and discusses present-day court interpretations.

406   Chafee, Zechariah. FREE SPEECH IN THE UNITED STATES. 1941. Reprint. Cambridge, Mass.: Harvard University Press, 1954. 650 p.

A weighing of the guarantee of freedom of speech in the First Amendment against various legislative attempts to limit it in the twentieth century. Chafee examines various controversial cases--such as those having to do with a supposed Communist menace--interpreting rulings of the Supreme Court. A basic book on the subject.

407   Corwin, Edward S. THE CONSTITUTION AND WHAT IT MEANS TO-DAY. 13th ed., rev. by Harold W. Chase and Craig R. Ducat. Princeton, N.J.: Princeton University Press, 1973. 619 p.

A systematic discussion of the provisions of the Constitution as they have been modified in practice. Corwin takes up in turn the powers of Congress, the executive, the judiciary, and other basic elements, and then analyzes the amending power and specific amendments from the Bill of Rights on down.

408   Friedman, Lawrence M. A HISTORY OF AMERICAN LAW. New York: Simon and Schuster, 1973. 656 p.

A general history of the development of the law and legal profession from the colonial period to the twentieth century. Friedman traces its roots in English law and its development in the New World.

409   Green, Fletcher M. CONSTITUTIONAL DEVELOPMENT IN THE SOUTH ATLANTIC STATES, 1776-1860: A STUDY IN THE EVOLUTION OF DEMOCRACY. 1930. Reprint. New York: DaCapo Press, 1971. 342 p.

Green's study of Maryland, Virginia, North Carolina, South Carolina, and Georgia sets forth the elements from English colonial experience that went into the original constitutions of these states and traces successive constitutional changes to the eve of the Civil War.

410 Haines, Charles G. THE ROLE OF THE SUPREME COURT IN AMERICAN GOVERNMENT AND POLITICS. 2 vols. 1944-57. Reprint. New York: DaCapo Press, 1973.

> Originally published as two separate volumes; the second was completed by Foster H. Sherwood, who sought to maintain Haines's interpretation. The work summarizes significant cases and illustrates how the personal attitudes and political views of the justices affected their rulings and consequent constitutional development. Volume 1: 1789-1835; volume 2: 1835-1864.

411 Howe, Mark DeWolfe, ed. READINGS IN AMERICAN LEGAL HISTORY. 1949. Reprint. New York: DaCapo Press, 1971. 538 p.

> A book originally devised for a course at Harvard. Howe selected some problems that have persisted in American legal history and provided excerpts from the pertinent cases.

412 Kelly, Alfred H., and Harbison, Winfred A. THE AMERICAN CONSTITUTION: ITS ORIGINS AND DEVELOPMENT. 4th ed. New York: W.W. Norton, 1970. 1,229 p. Tables.

> The American Constitution from its background in English and colonial practices to the present day, presented for readers with no technical background. Appendices give the texts of the Articles of Confederation and the Constitution.

413 Konvitz, Milton R., ed. BILL OF RIGHTS READER: LEADING CONSTITUTIONAL CASES. 4th ed., rev. and enl. Ithaca, N.Y.: Cornell University Press, 1968. 1,222 p.

> Konvitz has included the Bill of Rights and those sections on rights in the original Constitution, following them with the texts of court cases through the 1960s. He also includes selections from the opinions of justices of the Supreme Court, with introductions to each.

414 McCloskey, Robert G. THE AMERICAN SUPREME COURT. Chicago: University of Chicago Press, 1960. 270 p.

> McCloskey narrates the contribution of the Supreme Court to the development of the Constitution illustrating with particular, notable cases. He takes the position that the Court indulges in law making, a role not assigned it by the Constitution.

415 Mason, Alpheus T. THE SUPREME COURT FROM TAFT TO WARREN. Rev. ed. Baton Rouge: Louisiana State University Press, 1968. 308 p.

Mason pays most attention to the question of judicial
review of legislation; he includes much biographical
and philosophical data.

416 Murphy, Paul L. THE CONSTITUTION IN CRISIS TIMES, 1918-1969.
New York: Harper & Row, 1972. 588 p. Illus.

This history concentrates on the Supreme Court, although
the author inevitably shows the impact that the other
branches of government, particularly the executive, have
had on constitutional development. A combination of
philosophy, legal argument, and the interplay of some-
times clashing personalities.

417 Schwartz, Bernard, ed. THE BILL OF RIGHTS: A DOCUMENTARY HIS-
TORY. 2 vols. New York: Chelsea House, 1971.

The origin and history of the Bill of Rights, with documents relating to its background in English history and
its development in the United States. Schwartz provides
commentary that places each document in context and
provides insight into its meaning.

418 Sutherland, Arthur E. CONSTITUTIONALISM IN AMERICA: ORIGIN
AND EVOLUTION OF ITS FUNDAMENTAL IDEAS. New York: Blaisdell,
1965. 633 p.

A study of leading principles of American constitutionalism from Magna Charta to the present, by a notable
constitutional scholar. Sutherland is particularly concerned with such matters as the idea of written law,
majority rule, minority rights, equality, and the balanc-
ing of governmental power. He gives generous excerpts
from original documents.

419 Swindler, William F. COURT AND CONSTITUTION IN THE TWENTIETH
CENTURY. 2 vols. Indianapolis: Bobbs-Merrill, 1969-70.

Swindler describes major crises that have resulted in new
departures in constitutional interpretation. Appendices
include digests of landmark cases and biographical
sketches of justices of the Supreme Court. Volume 1:
THE OLD LEGALITY, 1889-1932; volume 2: THE NEW
LEGALITY, 1932-1968.

420 Warren, Charles. THE SUPREME COURT IN UNITED STATES HISTORY.
Rev. ed. 2 vols. 1926. Reprint. Boston: Little, Brown, 1937. Fronts.,
ports., plates.

Traces the history of the Court from 1789 to the First
World War. Warren describes its decisions in the context

of political events and gives contemporary reactions to
them.

17. Literature

421 Bone, Robert A. THE NEGRO NOVEL IN AMERICA. Rev. ed. New
Haven, Conn.: Yale University Press, 1965. 299 p.

Covers the years since 1890. Bone deals with both
aesthetic values and the social background in his analysis. He traces the emergence of the black novel from
years of relative neglect to years of recognition and
probes the societal pressures on the black writer in a
white-dominated society.

422 Cunliffe, Marcus. THE LITERATURE OF THE UNITED STATES. Baltimore:
Penguin Books, 1959. 394 p. Paperbound.

A British scholar's exposition of the main themes in
American literary history, with a consideration of its
leading figures, from the colonial period to the present.

423 Howard, Leon. LITERATURE AND THE AMERICAN TRADITION. Garden City, N.Y.: Doubleday, 1960. 354 p.

Searches for "an American tradition" in literature.
Howard thinks he has found it in the concern for the
individual and faith in his ability. He analyzes the
sweep of American literature with this in mind.

424 Kazin, Alfred. ON NATIVE GROUNDS: AN INTERPRETATION OF
MODERN AMERICAN PROSE LITERATURE. New York: Reynal & Hitchcock, 1942. 554 p.

An evaluation of American literature since 1890 by a
noted critic. Kazin writes with sympathetic understanding of the authors included but at the same time
sets high standards by which they should be judged.

425 Martin, Jay. HARVESTS OF CHANGE: AMERICAN LITERATURE, 1865-
1914. Englewood Cliffs, N.J. Prentice-Hall, 1967. 382 p.

A discussion of leading writers of the period: James,
Howells, Crane, Norris, Dreiser, Mark Twain, Bellamy,
Henry Adams, Emily Dickinson, and more. Martin
places them in their social setting and gives a critical
evaluation of their work.

426 Mencken, H.L. THE AMERICAN LANGUAGE. Abridged by Raven I.
McDavid, Jr. New York: Alfred A. Knopf, 1967. 926 p.

This one-volume abridgment captures the spirit of the original, q.v., no. 427.

427 _____. THE AMERICAN LANGUAGE: AN INQUIRY INTO THE DEVELOPMENT OF ENGLISH IN THE UNITED STATES. 4th ed. 2 vols. New York: Alfred A. Knopf, 1949.

The noted critic's masterful study of American English and how it differs from the mother tongue. The book is, in effect, a series of essays on American usage in Mencken's pungent, witty, biting style.

428 Rideout, Walter B. THE RADICAL NOVEL IN THE UNITED STATES, 1900-1954: SOME INTERRELATIONS OF LITERATURE AND SOCIETY. Cambridge, Mass.: Harvard University Press, 1956. 339 p.

A survey of the response of American novelists to economic and social ills and their critique of society under the influence of socialist and Communist movements. Among those included are Jack London, Upton Sinclair, Waldo Frank, Josephine Herbst, and James G. Farrell.

429 Spiller, Robert E., et al., eds. LITERARY HISTORY OF THE UNITED STATES. 3d ed., rev. 2 vols. 1963. Reprint. New York: Macmillan, 1969. Table.

A critical history and bibliography, the joint effort of fifty-seven literary scholars. American literature in each period is described and analyzed in this authoritative work. Volume 1: HISTORY; volume 2: BIBLIOGRAPHY.

18. The Military

430 Cunliffe, Marcus. SOLDIERS & CIVILIANS: THE MARTIAL SPIRIT IN AMERICA, 1775-1865. Boston: Little, Brown, 1968. 499 p. Illus.

The growth of the military tradition from the Revolution to the Civil War. Cunliffe puts his history in a large framework, relating purely military matters to what was happening to the society at large. His evaluation of military personalities is penetrating.

431 Millis, Walter, ed. AMERICAN MILITARY THOUGHT. Indianapolis: Bobbs-Merrill, 1966. 608 p.

This source book includes documents ranging from Benjamin Franklin's call for a voluntary militia in 1747 to Secretary of Defense Robert S. McNamara's policy in the 1960s. Millis provides an extended introduction that places the documents in historical context, and headnotes to each selection.

432 Sprout, Harold H., and Sprout, Margaret. THE RISE OF AMERICAN NAVAL POWER, 1776-1918. 1939. Reprint. Princeton, N.J.: Princeton University Press, 1967. 404 p. Paperbound.

Concentrates on American naval policy as it relates to politics, foreign affairs, and public opinion. The Sprouts are not concerned with the operational details of the fleets but rather with the role sea power has played in American imperialism and in war.

19. Recreation

433 Dulles, Foster Rhea. AMERICA LEARNS TO PLAY: A HISTORY OF POPULAR RECREATION, 1607-1940. New York: Appleton-Century, 1940. 458 p. Illus., front., plates, facsims.

A serious scholarly consideration with touches of humor befitting the subject. Dulles looks at the manifold forms of recreation, from those of the aristocracy to those of the common people of the mining town, from the horse to the automobile and airplane.

434 Ezell, John S. FORTUNE'S MERRY WHEEL: THE LOTTERY IN AMERICA. Cambridge, Mass.: Harvard University Press, 1960. 339 p. Facsims., tables.

Lotteries were an accepted means of raising money for causes, worthy and otherwise, through much of the nation's history. Ezell covers the years from the colonial period to the late nineteenth century, giving a mass of detail about lotteries' origins, prevalence, and decline.

20. Religion

435 Ahlstrom, Sidney E. A RELIGIOUS HISTORY OF THE AMERICAN PEOPLE. New Haven, Conn.: Yale University Press, 1972. 1,158 p.

The author differs from previous historians of religion in America by devoting one fourth of his book to Catholic, Jewish, and other elements of religious diversity, even though he asserts that the United States has been dominated by a Puritan Protestant ideology from colonial days to the 1960s. He views these "countervailing" groups as responsible for the development of a pluralistic nation.

436 Blau, Joseph L., and Baron, Salo W., eds. JEWS OF THE UNITED
STATES, 1790-1840: A DOCUMENTARY HISTORY. 3 vols. New York:
Columbia University Press, 1963.

> This collection of materials illustrates the involvement
> of Jews in American affairs from the beginnings of the
> nation. The documents include religious provisions of
> the state constitutions, communications between Jewish
> leaders and well-known statesmen, a will manumitting
> slaves, public documents, private letters, etc. The
> editors provide a general introduction and introductions
> to the sections.

437 Cross, Whitney R. THE BURNED-OVER DISTRICT: THE SOCIAL AND
INTELLECTUAL HISTORY OF ENTHUSIASTIC RELIGION IN WESTERN
NEW YORK, 1800-1850. Ithaca, N.Y.: Cornell University Press, 1950.
396 p. Maps.

> Western New York was swept by recurring waves of
> revivalism in the period covered. Cross relates this
> phenomenon to political, economic, and social develop-
> ments, without minimizing the importance of the reli-
> gious beliefs of his subjects.

438 McLoughlin, William G. MODERN REVIVALISM: FROM CHARLES GRAN-
DISON FINNEY TO BILLY GRAHAM. New York: Ronald Press, 1959.
551 p.

> A social and intellectual study of three phases of reli-
> gious revival in recent times, represented by the careers
> of Finney, Billy Sunday, Dwight L. Moody, and Graham.
> McLoughlin writes the biographies of these men but also
> relates the themes of revivalism to those of American
> history generally--progress, individualism, perfectibility,
> and nationalism.

439 Maynard, Theodore. THE STORY OF AMERICAN CATHOLICISM. New
York: Macmillan, 1960. 712 p.

> A survey of the development of Roman Catholicism in
> the New World from the age of discovery and the Span-
> ish and French missions to the 1920s, with a summary
> of the Catholic "cultural contribution" and "corporate
> vision." Maynard expresses his own views, often in
> the first person. An appendix lists the archdiocesan
> and diocesan sees.

440 Olmstead, Clifton E. HISTORY OF RELIGION IN THE UNITED STATES.
Englewood Cliffs, N.J.: Prentice-Hall, 1960. 640 p. Maps.

> A history of religious belief and church and sectarian
> organizations, from their sources in Europe to their adap-

tation to the New World. Olmstead gives an objective
view of the evolution of belief from the early period to
the mid-twentieth century.

441 Pfeffer, Leo. CHURCH, STATE, AND FREEDOM. Boston: Beacon Press,
1953. 692 p.

Examines the American concept of separation of church
and state, comparing it with practices in other nations.
Pfeffer gives the historical background of separation,
deals with state intervention in church affairs and vice
versa, and devotes several chapters to religion and the
public schools.

442 Schappes, Morris U. A DOCUMENTARY HISTORY OF THE JEWS IN
THE UNITED STATES, 1654-1875. 3d ed. New York: Schocken Books,
1971. 790 p.

A collection of original sources by individuals and
groups prominent in the shaping of the Jewish communities of the United States.

443 Smith, H. Shelton, et al. AMERICAN CHRISTIANITY: AN HISTORICAL
INTERPRETATION WITH REPRESENTATIVE DOCUMENTS. 2 vols. New
York: Charles Scribner's Sons, 1960-63. Illus., ports., facsims.

The authors alternate their summaries and interpretations
with selections from contemporary documents. An excellent selection of materials and illustrations. Volume
1: 1607-1820; volume 2: 1820-1960.

Smith, James W., and Jamison, A. Leland, eds. RELIGION IN AMERI-
CAN LIFE. See no. 62.

444 Stokes, Anson Phelps. CHURCH AND STATE IN THE UNITED STATES.
3 vols. New York: Harper & Brothers, 1950.

The first thorough, comprehensive history of the development of separation of church and state, methodically
treating each period of the nation's history. Stokes
quotes generously from the original documents.

445 Stokes, Anson Phelps, and Pfeffer, Leo. CHURCH AND STATE IN THE
UNITED STATES. Rev. ed. New York: Harper & Row, 1964. 672 p.

An abridged and revised version of the three-volume
original by Stokes, q.v., no. 444. Pfeffer has brought
the work up to the 1960s.

446 Sweet, William Warren. THE STORY OF RELIGION IN AMERICA. Rev.

and enl. ed. New York: Harper & Brothers, 1950. 504 p.

An authoritative survey of the churches and sectarian groups from the colonial period to the mid-twentieth century. Sweet is objective in his presentation and relates religion to political, intellectual, and social developments.

447   Weisberger, Bernard A.   THEY GATHERED AT THE RIVER: THE STORY OF THE GREAT REVIVALISTS AND THEIR IMPACT UPON RELIGION IN AMERICA.   Boston: Little, Brown, 1958.   360 p.   Illus., ports.

Deals with the preachers who made careers of traveling about attempting to stir up, or "revive" religious groups in the nineteenth century. Weisberger tells of the famous ones--Lyman Beecher, Charles G. Finney, Dwight L. Moody, and Billy Sunday--as well as of many lesser known. He discusses the schisms caused in churches by revivalist activities, the scandals caused by some of them, the hysteria that often accompanied their meetings, and the other effects they had on Protestantism.

21. Science and Technology

448   THE AMERICAN HERITAGE HISTORY OF FLIGHT.   Edited by Alvin M. Josephy, Jr.   New York: American Heritage Publishing Co.; distributed by Simon & Schuster, 1962.   416 p.   Illus., ports.

A richly illustrated history of the development of air travel. The narrative is by Arthur Gordon, with two chapters contributed by Marvin W. McFarland.

449   Burlingame, Roger.   THE MARCH OF THE IRON MEN: A SOCIAL HISTORY OF UNION THROUGH INVENTION.   1938.   Reprint.   New York: Grosset & Dunlap, 1960.   516 p.   Illus., maps.

Places great weight on American progress through invention. Burlingame imaginatively demonstrates the impact of printing, the railroad, the telegraph, and many other technological developments on the quality of life.

450   Oliver, John W.   HISTORY OF AMERICAN TECHNOLOGY.   New York: Ronald Press, 1956.   676 p.

A comprehensive survey from colonial days to the utilization of the atom. The author interprets America as a predominantly technological society and seeks to prove his thesis by showing how technology bears on every area of its life.

451   Singer, Charles, et al., eds.   A HISTORY OF TECHNOLOGY.   5 vols.

Oxford, Eng.: Clarendon Press, 1954-58. Illus., ports., maps.

This major work spans the centuries from ancient times to 1900, with some consideration of American developments in the context of western history as a whole.

22. Urban Life

452 Friedman, Lawrence M. GOVERNMENT AND SLUM HOUSING: A CENTURY OF FRUSTRATION. Chicago: Rand McNally, 1968. 206 p.

A study of lower class and slum housing. Friedman begins his consideration of government action with the 1867 New York tenement house law. Although he believes the efforts of government in slum clearance have been much less than adequate, he is optimistic that effective action can be taken.

453 Green, Constance M. THE RISE OF URBAN AMERICA. New York: Harper & Row, 1965. 208 p.

A brief, general survey of the development of cities, from the seaports of colonial America to the metropolises of the 1960s. A well-written, detailed book, with occasional flashes of humor.

454 Jackson, Kenneth T., and Schultz, Stanley K., eds. CITIES IN AMERICAN HISTORY. New York: Alfred A. Knopf, 1972. 522 p. Illus., maps, tables.

A collection of articles by notable scholars, with introductions to each section by the editors. The materials are grouped under these headings: The City in American History; Cities in the New World, 1607-1800; Cities in an Expanding Nation, 1780-1865; Immigration, Migration, and Mobility, 1865-1920; the Recurrent Urban Crisis; Bosses, Machines, and Urban Reform; Dilemmas of Metropolitan America.

455 Scully, Vincent J. AMERICAN ARCHITECTURE AND URBANISM. New York: Praeger, 1969. 275 p. Illus., maps, plans.

This historical survey considers the man-made environment, that is the urban area, from that of the Pueblo Indians to the problems of urban blight in the mid-twentieth century. Scully believes today's architectural style stems from American restlessness. A scholarly consideration with a full set of illustrations.

456 Tunnard, Christopher, and Reed, Henry H. AMERICAN SKYLINE: THE GROWTH AND FORM OF OUR CITIES AND TOWNS. Boston: Hough-

ton Mifflin, 1955. 302 p. Illus.

A discussion of city planning and architecture in an historical context. The authors believe the "regional city" to be an inevitable development as suburban sprawl continues to occur. Drawings by John Cohen.

Chapter 3

EARLY AMERICA, TO 1789

A. EUROPEAN EXPANSION INTO THE NEW WORLD

1. General

See also relevant portions of general works in 3,B,1.

457 Abbott, Wilbur C. THE EXPANSION OF EUROPE: A SOCIAL AND POLITICAL HISTORY OF THE MODERN WORLD, 1415-1789. Rev. ed. 2 vols. in 1. New York: Henry Holt, 1929. Illus., front., ports., plates, maps.

> This older work places the settlement and development of colonies in the New World in the context of the expansion of the nations of the Old. Abbott deals with social and intellectual as well as political and economic matters.

458 Brebner, John B. THE EXPLORERS OF NORTH AMERICA, 1492-1806. New York: Macmillan, 1933. 518 p. Maps.

> A colorful account based largely on original sources. Brebner explores the motivations of the many curious and brave men who gradually pieced together a picture of the continent, traces their routes, and evaluates their accomplishments.

459 Cassidy, Vincent H. THE SEA AROUND THEM: THE ATLANTIC OCEAN, A.D. 1250. Baton Rouge: Louisiana State University Press, 1968. 219 p. Illus.

> Deals with a period much earlier than that of the beginning of settlement in the New World, but provides much information on European attitudes and knowledge of the sea from Greek and Roman times to the mid-thirteenth century. Includes discussion of ships, cartography, and navigational aids.

460 Debenham, Frank. DISCOVERY AND EXPLORATION: AN ATLAS-
HISTORY OF MAN'S WANDERINGS. Garden City, N.Y.: Doubleday,
1960. 272 p. Illus., ports., maps.

Deals with exploration and discovery on a world-wide
scale through the centuries; puts the discovery and exploration of America in a larger context.

461 De Voto, Bernard. THE COURSE OF EMPIRE. Boston: Houghton Mifflin,
1952. 664 p. Maps.

Deals with the first three centuries of exploration of
America, ending with the early 1880s. DeVoto looks
at the lay of the land, the conception the explorers
had of it, its exploration, and the struggle of four
empires to claim it. A rich, colorful presentation.

462 Dorn, Walter L. COMPETITION FOR EMPIRE, 1740-1763. 1940. Reprint. New York: Harper & Row, 1963. 436 p. Illus., ports., maps.
Paperbound.

A study of Anglo-French rivalry in a period of transition
from feudalism to a competitive, industrial society. A
topical rather than chronological approach. Thorough
analyses of the Seven Years' War and other contests are
included.

463 Elliott, J.H. THE OLD WORLD AND THE NEW, 1492-1650. New York:
Cambridge University Press, 1970. 128 p.

An English historian's account of European thinking
concerning the New World, originally delivered as
lectures at Queen's University, Belfast. Elliott deals
with the political, economic, and intellectual consequences of the discovery in lucid and elegant prose.

464 Morison, Samuel Eliot. THE EUROPEAN DISCOVERY OF AMERICA. 2
vols. New York: Oxford University Press, 1971-74. Illus., ports.,
plates, maps, facsims.

A vivid account by a historian who knows the sea well.
Morison makes extensive use of the original accounts
by participants in the great exploration; he writes with
wit and verve. Volume 1: THE NORTHERN VOYAGES,
A.D. 500-1600; volume 2: THE SOUTHERN VOYAGES,
A.D. 1492-1616.

465 Nowell, Charles E. THE GREAT DISCOVERIES AND THE FIRST COLON-
IAL EMPIRES. Ithaca, N.Y.: Cornell University Press, 1954. 164 p.
Maps. Paperbound.

This introductory survey pictures the European setting

and considers, respectively, the Portuguese, Spanish, French, Dutch, and English empires.

466 O'Gorman, Edmundo. THE INVENTION OF AMERICA: AN INQUIRY INTO THE HISTORICAL NATURE OF THE NEW WORLD AND THE MEANING OF ITS HISTORY. Bloomington: Indiana University Press, 1961. 177 p. Illus., maps.

Based on a series of lectures delivered at Indiana University. O'Gorman, a Mexican historian, traces the development of the myth of the New World in the thinking of Europeans.

467 Sauer, Carl Ortwin. SIXTEENTH-CENTURY NORTH AMERICA: THE LAND AND THE PEOPLE AS SEEN BY THE EUROPEANS. Berkeley and Los Angeles: University of California Press, 1971. 331 p. Illus., maps.

An account by a leading geographer of European reactions to the New World and its peoples in the period before colonial settlements began. Much of the volume is based on original accounts by explorers.

468 Viereck, Philip, ed. THE NEW LAND: DISCOVERY, EXPLORATION, AND EARLY SETTLEMENT OF NORTHEASTERN UNITED STATES, FROM EARLIEST VOYAGES TO 1621, TOLD IN THE WORDS OF THE EXPLORERS THEMSELVES. New York: John Day, 1967. 254 p. Illus., maps, facsims.

These first-hand accounts are linked together by commentary by the editor. Viereck has selected material from letters, journals, logbooks, and publications of the explorers. Adding to understanding the primary materials are reproductions of maps used by the explorers.

469 Wright, Louis B. GOLD, GLORY, AND THE GOSPEL: THE ADVENTUROUS LIVES AND TIMES OF THE RENAISSANCE EXPLORERS. New York: Atheneum, 1970. 378 p. Maps.

Wright deals with motivations and accomplishments of Columbus, daGama, Magellan, and many others, asserting that, given the nature of their age, there was nothing inconsistent in their desire to find gold and at the same time to make converts to Christianity.

2. Topical

470 Boxer, C.R. THE DUTCH SEABORNE EMPIRE, 1600-1800. New York: Alfred A. Knopf, 1965. 352 p. Ports., plates, map.

With the use of much statistical material from Dutch and

other sources, Boxer traces the rise and decline of the Netherlands' imperial venture. The little nation became, within a short period after achieving independence from Spain, the most advanced naval and trading nation in the world. Dutch racial attitudes, squabbling among the states, and external factors, Boxer believes, led to the country's decline.

471 Bridenbaugh, Carl. VEXED AND TROUBLED ENGLISHMEN, 1590-1642. New York: Oxford University Press, 1968. 506 p.

A study of English habits and outlook on life in the early years of colonization, which the author believes will contribute to an understanding of the mental baggage the colonists brought to the New World. Bridenbaugh not only used local English court records, other manuscripts, and printed materials, but also visited the places and homes of many of the first settlers of America in order to recreate the lives they led in their original abodes.

472 Eccles, W.J. FRANCE IN AMERICA. New York: Harper & Row, 1972. 309 p. Illus., map.

Surveys the development of French Canada from the beginnings to 1783, dealing with cultural as well as political themes. The author also traces developments in the West Indies and Louisiana.

473 Gibson, Charles. SPAIN IN AMERICA. New York: Harper & Row, 1966. 253 p. Illus., ports., maps.

An interpretive history dealing with all aspects of the Spanish experience in America: exploration, colonization, relation to Indians, competition with other European powers, etc. Also enlightening are Gibson's discussion of the role of the church in America and the economic and social distinctions that developed among the settlers.

474 Gipson, Lawrence H. THE BRITISH EMPIRE BEFORE THE AMERICAN RE-VOLUTION. 15 vols. New York: Alfred A. Knopf, 1936-70. Maps.

Valuable for its detailed examination of political developments in the various sections of the British Empire up until the American Declaration of Independence in 1776. Volume 13 contains a useful summary of the entire effort.

475 Horgan, Paul. CONQUISTADORS IN NORTH AMERICAN HISTORY. 1936. Reprint. Greenwich, Conn.: Fawcett, 1969. 240 p. Paperbound.

This colorful account begins with the voyage of Columbus and traces the establishment of Spanish colonies in the Northern Hemisphere under the leadership of Conquistadors DeVaca, Ponce de Leon, Vargas, Cortez, and their successors.

476 Morison, Samuel Eliot. ADMIRAL OF THE OCEAN SEA: A LIFE OF CHRISTOPHER COLUMBUS. 2 vols. Boston: Little, Brown, 1942. Illus., plates, maps, tables, diagrs.

In preparation for this work, Morison and cohorts from Harvard followed the same routes taken by Columbus, sailing in vessels comparable to those used by the great navigator. The result is a scholarly narrative written with great force and color.

477 Notestein, Wallace. THE ENGLISH PEOPLE ON THE EVE OF COLONIZATION, 1603-1630. New York: Harper & Brothers, 1954. 319 p. Illus., ports., maps.

A detailed history of English politics and social life in the reigns of the Stuart monarchs, James I and Charles I, by a specialist in the period. Reveals those aspects of English life and thought that inevitably affected the outlook of the first English settlers of the New World.

478 Parkman, Francis. FRANCE AND ENGLAND IN NORTH AMERICA. 9 vols. 1865-92. Reprint. New York: Frederick Ungar, 1965. Illus., ports., maps.

Parkman produced his magnum opus between the years 1865 and 1892. His intimate knowledge of the sources and his flowing prose style made him the leading American historian of his time. Volume 1: PIONEERS OF FRANCE IN THE NEW WORLD; volume 2: THE JESUITS IN NORTH AMERICA IN THE SEVENTEENTH CENTURY; volume 3: LASALLE AND THE DISCOVERY OF THE GREAT WEST; volume 4: THE OLD REGIME IN CANADA; volume 5: COUNT FRONTENAC AND NEW FRANCE UNDER LOUIS XIV; volumes 6 and 7: A HALF-CENTURY OF CONFLICT; volumes 8 and 9: MONTCALM AND WOLFE.

479 _____. THE PARKMAN READER: FROM THE WORKS OF FRANCIS PARKMAN. Edited by Samuel Eliot Morison. Boston: Little, Brown, 1955. 548 p. Port., maps.

This thoughtful selection from the voluminous writings of the nineteenth-century historian displays the most colorful and readable passages from FRANCE AND ENGLAND IN NORTH AMERICA, q.v., no. 478.

480 Parry, J.H. THE SPANISH SEABORNE EMPIRE. New York: Alfred A. Knopf, 1966. 416 p. Illus., maps, facsims.

>   Covers the establishment of the Spanish colonies in America and their relationship to the parent country from the late fifteenth century to the beginning of the nineteenth. Parry deals with many aspects of Spanish life and culture as it adapted to the new environment and clearly reveals the less-than-humane practices of the conquistadors.

481 Prescott, William Hickling. HISTORY OF THE CONQUEST OF MEXICO, AND HISTORY OF THE CONQUEST OF PERU. New York: Modern Library, 1936. 1,324 p. Illus., maps.

>   Two major works of nineteenth-century romantic historiography. Prescott's accent is on the actions of great men; he deals little with other factors in this marvel of prose style. The first work originally appeared in 1843, the second in 1847.

482 Rowse, A.L. THE ELIZABETHANS AND AMERICA. New York: Harper & Brothers, 1959. 221 p. Illus.

>   Originally delivered as the Trevelyan Lectures at the University of Cambridge. Rowse deals with those who had a great interest in America--Queen Elizabeth, Drake, Hakluyt, Raleigh, among others--and what they did about it. Detailed but entertaining.

B. THE ENGLISH COLONIES

1. General

See also relevant works in 3,A.

483 THE AMERICAN HERITAGE HISTORY OF THE THIRTEEN COLONIES. Edited by Michael Blow. New York: American Heritage Publishing Co.; distributed by Simon & Schuster, 1967. 384 p. Illus., ports., maps, facsims.

>   Traces the development of the various colonies. The text was written for a popular audience by Louis B. Wright, and the copious illustrations show views of the ports of New England, the plantations of the South, and many other aspects of American life and culture.

484 Andrews, Charles M. COLONIAL FOLKWAYS: A CHRONICLE OF AMERICAN LIFE IN THE REIGN OF THE GEORGES. New Haven, Conn.:

Yale University Press, 1919. 265 p. Front., ports., plates.

A social history of the American settlements in the late colonial period. A rounded picture of everyday life in the northern, middle, and southern colonies.

485 _____. THE COLONIAL PERIOD OF AMERICAN HISTORY. 4 vols. 1934-38. Reprint. New Haven, Conn.: Yale University Press, 1964. Paperbound.

A standard history. In the first three volumes the author systematically reviews developments in each of the colonies and sections; the fourth volume he devotes to England's commercial and colonial policy. Andrews's writing lacks color and drama, but he includes a wealth of information and his evaluations are judicious.

486 Bancroft, George. HISTORY OF THE UNITED STATES OF AMERICA FROM THE DISCOVERY OF THE CONTINENT. 6 vols. 1885. Reprint. New York: Kennikat Press, 1967.

A classic of U.S. historiography of the nineteenth century by a Unitarian minister turned politician, diplomat, and historian. Bancroft interprets American history under the influence of transcendentalism and Jacksonian democracy. This is a reprint of the author's final revision. Valuable reading both for content and mood. Volume 1: THE UNITED STATES OF AMERICA AS COLONIES; volume 2: HISTORY OF THE COLONIZATION OF THE UNITED STATES OF AMERICA; volumes 3-5: THE AMERICAN REVOLUTION; volume 6: THE FORMATION OF THE AMERICAN CONSTITUTION.

487 _____. HISTORY OF THE UNITED STATES OF AMERICA FROM THE DISCOVERY OF THE CONTINENT. Edited by Russel B. Nye. Chicago: University of Chicago Press, 1966. 412 p. Port., map.

An abridgment of the original six-volume work, q.v., no. 486.

488 Barbour, Philip L. THE THREE WORLDS OF CAPTAIN JOHN SMITH. Boston: Houghton Mifflin, 1964. 572 p. Illus., ports., maps, geneal. tables.

Smith had many adventures in Eastern Europe and the Near East before he succumbed to the lure of the New World. Barbour, in dealing with these aspects of his career, as well as with his experience in Virginia, provides a good picture of the adventurer and an adventurous age.

Boorstin, Daniel J. THE AMERICANS. Vol. 1. See no. 213.

489 Bridenbaugh, Carl. CITIES IN THE WILDERNESS: THE FIRST CENTURY
OF URBAN LIFE IN AMERICA, 1625-1742. 2d ed. 1955. Reprint.
New York: Capricorn Books, 1964. 512 p. Paperbound.

An examination of the development of the towns of
colonial America as centers of population and trade
and as perpetuators of the culture of Europe. Bridenbaugh concentrates on four aspects: the physical nature
of the settlements, their economic development, their
social life, and how they confronted resultant urban
problems. Filled with detail.

490 Hawke, David Freeman. THE COLONIAL EXPERIENCE. Indianapolis:
Bobbs-Merrill, 1966. 794 p. Illus., ports., maps, facsims.

This textbook systematically surveys American colonial
developments, after a review of the age of discovery
and the European background. Hawke carries the history to the writing of the Constitution.

491 Kavenaugh, W. Keith, ed. FOUNDATIONS OF COLONIAL AMERICA:
A DOCUMENTARY HISTORY. 3 vols. New York: Chelsea House and
R.R. Bowker, 1973. Tables.

The editor brings together in each volume the charters
and other public documents of each of the colonies,
devoting a volume to each section of the seaboard.
Topics include government at all levels, trade, land
grants, church affairs, individual moral behavior, etc.
Volume 1: NORTHERN COLONIES; volume 2: MID-
DLE ATLANTIC COLONIES; volume 3: SOUTHERN
COLONIES.

492 Kraus, Michael. THE ATLANTIC CIVILIZATION: EIGHTEENTH-CEN-
TURY ORIGINS. Ithaca, N.Y.: Cornell University Press, 1949. 345 p.

A rich analysis of the interaction of Britain and her
colonies in many aspects of cultural life: religion,
social life, science, humanitarianism, and the arts.

493 Miller, John C. THE FIRST FRONTIER: LIFE IN COLONIAL AMERICA.
New York: Delacorte Press, 1966. 288 p.

Though designed for younger readers, this is a useful
summary of social life in the colonial period for more
advanced readers. Miller deals with religion, housing,
food, dress, recreation, and many other facets of life
in the New World.

494 Nettels, Curtis P. THE ROOTS OF AMERICAN CIVILIZATION: A
HISTORY OF AMERICAN COLONIAL LIFE. 2d ed. New York: Appleton-
Century-Crofts, 1963. 748 p. Illus., maps.

> The colonial years through the Revolution. Nettels
> devotes a substantial amount of space to the European
> background before treating the development of the
> colonies in the New World. He locates the roots of
> many American attitudes in the early period.

495 Osgood, Herbert L. THE AMERICAN COLONIES IN THE EIGHTEENTH
CENTURY. 4 vols. 1924–25. Reprint. Gloucester, Mass.: Peter
Smith, 1958.

> A continuation of the author's AMERICAN COLONIES
> IN THE SEVENTEENTH CENTURY, q.v., no. 496,
> again concentrating on the institutional aspects of the
> history. Volume 1 of this edition includes a foreword
> on Osgood by Arthur M. Schlesinger.

496 _____. THE AMERICAN COLONIES IN THE SEVENTEENTH CENTURY.
3 vols. 1904–7. Reprint. Gloucester, Mass.: Peter Smith, 1957.

> This detailed history by a member of the objective
> school of historians explores all aspects of governmental
> and judicial provisions in the American colonies. Vol-
> umes 1 and 2: THE CHARTERED COLONIES, BEGIN-
> NINGS OF SELF-GOVERNMENT; volume 3: IMPERIAL
> CONTROL. BEGINNINGS OF THE SYSTEM OF ROYAL
> PROVINCES.

497 Pomfret, John E. FOUNDING THE AMERICAN COLONIES, 1583–1660.
New York: Harper & Row, 1970. 397 p. Illus., ports., maps.

> A history of colonization, stressing the failures as well
> as the successes. Pomfret methodically traces the peo-
> pling of the seaboard and the various efforts to establish
> stable governments and societies.

498 Savelle, Max, and Wax, Darold D. HISTORY OF COLONIAL AMERICA.
3d ed. Hinsdale, Ill.: Dryden Press, 1973. 860 p. Illus., maps.

> A thorough, standard text, recently revised. Originally
> published as THE FOUNDATIONS OF AMERICAN CI-
> VILIZATION (1942).

499 Sutherland, Stella H. POPULATION DISTRIBUTION IN COLONIAL
AMERICA. 1936. Reprint. New York: AMS Press, 1966. 385 p.
Maps.

> Using tax lists, militia rolls, and whatever census reports
> were available, the author has compiled a useful popu-

lation summary of the colonies in pre-Revolutionary days. The maps provide a graphic picture of population distribution.

500   Ver Steeg, Clarence L. THE FORMATIVE YEARS: 1607-1763. New York: Hill and Wang, 1964. 342 p. Illus., maps.

A discussion of the development of the colonies. Ver Steeg sketches them in their distinctiveness but also shows in what ways they were similar.

501   Wertenbaker, Thomas Jefferson. THE FIRST AMERICANS, 1607-1690. 1927. Reprint. Chicago: Quadrangle Books, 1971. 378 p. Illus., ports., plates, map, facsims. Paperbound.

Points up the great similarities among the early colonists, north and south, as they confronted the wilderness. Their interests diverged gradually. By the close of the seventeenth century, Wertenbaker believes, the Americans had developed their own unique culture.

502   Wright, Louis B. THE ATLANTIC FRONTIER: COLONIAL AMERICAN CIVILIZATION, 1607-1763. 1947. Reprint. Ithaca, N.Y.: Cornell University Press, 1959. 383 p. Plates, maps.

Concentrates on the social development of the northern, middle Atlantic and southern colonies from the beginnings to the eve of difficulty with the mother country. Wright indicates the emergence of distinctly American interests that led to the Revolutionary mentality.

2. Regional

a. THE SOUTH

503   Beverley, Robert. THE HISTORY AND PRESENT STATE OF VIRGINIA. Edited by Louis B. Wright. 1947. Reprint. Charlottesville: University Press of Virginia, 1968. 401 p. Illus.

A reprinting of the work of a Virginia planter and politician, first published in 1705 and revised in 1722. Beverley wrote with candor and humor of the strengths and weaknesses of his fellow planters and their habits, and of the neighboring Indians. In the introduction to this edition Wright describes Beverley's life and the writing of the history. The illustrations are from the original edition.

504   Bridenbaugh, Carl. MYTHS AND REALITIES: SOCIETIES OF THE CO-LONIAL SOUTH. 1952. Reprint. New York: Atheneum, 1962. 222 p. Paperbound.

Originally delivered as a series of lectures at the
Louisiana State University. Drawing heavily on original
sources, and stressing social and intellectual themes,
the author deals successively with the Chesapeake area,
the Carolinas, and the back settlements in the eighteenth century.

505　Crane, Verner W. THE SOUTHERN FRONTIER, 1670-1732. 1929. Reprint. Ann Arbor: University of Michigan Press, 1956. 412 p.

Deals with the struggle over the land between South
Carolina and the Spanish settlements to the South. An
important part of the contest was for control of trade
with the Indians.

506　Craven, Wesley Frank. THE SOUTHERN COLONIES IN THE SEVEN-
TEENTH CENTURY, 1607-1689. Baton Rouge: Louisiana State University Press, 1949. 470 p. Illus., maps, facsims.

The first volume of a multivolume HISTORY OF THE
SOUTH, written by a group of distinguished historians.
Craven places the settlement of Virginia, Maryland,
and the Carolinas in the larger context of the Atlantic
world, and traces their political and economic development.

507　Morton, Richard L. COLONIAL VIRGINIA. 2 vols. Chapel Hill: University of North Carolina Press, 1960. Illus., ports., maps, facsims.

This chronological account runs from the beginnings of
the Virginia Colony to 1763; it is written with grace
and quiet humor. Morton accents political developments. Volume 1: THE TIDEWATER PERIOD, 1607-
1710; volume 2: WESTWARD EXPANSION AND PRE-
LUDE TO REVOLUTION.

508　Mullin, Gerald W. FLIGHT AND REBELLION: SLAVE RESISTANCE IN
EIGHTEENTH-CENTURY VIRGINIA. New York: Oxford University Press,
1972. 219 p. Maps, tables.

Using newspaper accounts as an important source of evidence, Mullin attempts to demonstrate that there was
constant resistance by slaves in Virginia in the eighteenth
century. He includes an investigation of Gabriel's
Insurrection, one of the famous outbreaks of rebellion.
Mullin seeks to overturn the stereotype of slave docility.

509　Wertenbaker, Thomas Jefferson. THE OLD SOUTH: THE FOUNDING
OF AMERICAN CIVILIZATION. 1942. Reprint. New York: Cooper

Square, 1963. 378 p. Illus., plans, facsims.

Stresses cultural themes, rather than political history.
Wertenbaker considers in turn the settlements of Virginia, Maryland, the Carolinas, and the movement into
the Appalachians. He attempts to show how the various
nationalities and language groups contributed to the
creation of a southern civilization.

510 _____. THE PLANTERS OF COLONIAL VIRGINIA. 1922. Reprint.
New York: Russell & Russell, 1959. 260 p.

This carefully documented work shows that early in the
plantation's history social and economic differentiation
became marked. Wertenbaker discusses the emerging
classes and gives attention also to the indentured servants who came to the colony.

511 Willison, George F. BEHOLD VIRGINIA, THE FIFTH CROWN: BEING
THE TRIALS, ADVENTURES, AND DISASTERS OF THE FIRST FAMILIES
OF VIRGINIA, THE RISE OF THE GRANDEES, AND THE EVENTUAL
TRIUMPH OF THE COMMON AND UNCOMMON SORT IN THE REVO-
LUTION. New York: Harcourt, Brace, 1951. 433 p. Maps.

With many rich quotations from the original sources,
Willison tells the story of the settlement and development of Virginia with drama and wit. He recounts in
detail the many trials and setbacks the colony suffered.

b. MIDDLE COLONIES

512 Bonomi, Patricia U. A FACTIOUS PEOPLE: POLITICS AND SOCIETY
IN COLONIAL NEW YORK. New York: Columbia University Press,
1971. 355 p. Illus., map, table.

A scholarly interpretation of New York's turbulent early
history. Bonomi concentrates on political developments
between 1689 and 1770 but necessarily deals with social,
economic, and religious developments where they bear
on the issues at hand. Offers new interpretations.

513 Bronner, Edwin B. WILLIAM PENN'S "HOLY EXPERIMENT": THE FOUND-
ING OF PENNSYLVANIA, 1681-1701. New York: Temple University
Publications; distributed by Columbia University Press, 1962. 306 p.

A political history, but one which introduces social and,
in this case, necessarily, religious detail. Bronner
describes the early years of the Quaker colony and attempts to relate the belief and actions of the Friends
to political developments.

514 Colden, Cadwallader. HISTORY OF THE FIVE INDIAN NATIONS OF CANADA, WHICH ARE DEPENDENT ON THE PROVINCE OF NEW YORK IN AMERICA, AND ARE THE BARRIER BETWEEN THE ENGLISH AND FRENCH IN THAT PART OF THE WORLD. 1747. Reprint. Toronto: Coles Publishing Co., 1972. 304 p.

> Colden, royal official in New York and leading figure of the American Enlightenment, recounts the history and ways of living of the Indian tribes he thought could be cultivated to act as a buffer between the English-speaking colony and the French of Canada. The original edition was published in 1727. This is a facsimile of the 1747 London edition.

515 Wertenbaker, Thomas Jefferson. THE FOUNDING OF AMERICAN CIVILIZATION: THE MIDDLE COLONIES. 1938. Reprint. New York: Cooper Square, 1963. 377 p.

> Stresses cultural rather than political elements of the diverse Middle Colonies: Dutch settlements of New Netherland, the Quaker and German groups in Pennsylvania, and the Puritans in New Jersey. Includes a consideration of social customs and arts and architecture.

c. NEW ENGLAND

516 Adams, James Truslow. THE FOUNDING OF NEW ENGLAND. 1921. Reprint. Boston: Little, Brown, n.d. 498 p. Paperbound.

> This interpretation gives an important place to economic factors in the settling of New England, Adams believing that too much stress has been given the religious motivation. A thorough discussion of the Puritan cultural heritage, the geography of the new settlement, and political and social views.

517 Bradford, William. HISTORY OF PLYMOUTH PLANTATION, 1606-1646. Edited by William T. Davis, 1908. Reprint. New York: Barnes & Noble, 1959. 455 p. Map, facsims.

> Bradford was governor of Plymouth during most of its early years. His account, which is rich in information on religion, government, economics, and social life, is the first classic in American history, a work of strength, beauty, and pathos. This edition reproduces the spelling of the original manuscript.

518 _____. OF PLYMOUTH PLANTATION, 1620-1647. Edited by Samuel Eliot Morison. New York: Alfred A. Knopf, 1952. 506 p. Maps.

> A version of the HISTORY, q.v., no. 517, with moder-

nized spelling and orthography, and an excellent introduction by the editor.

519 Demos, John. A LITTLE COMMONWEALTH: FAMILY LIFE IN PLY-
MOUTH COLONY. New York: Oxford University Press, 1970. 201
p. Illus., tables.

With the help of the records and artifacts that have
survived, Demos examines the family life of the Plymouth colony in the seventeenth century. He applies
modern psychological interpretation to the relationships
of family members and to their interactions with neighbors and compares the Separatist family with the American family of the twentieth century. Complements
Edmund Morgan, THE PURITAN FAMILY, q.v., no.
566.

520 Jones, Mary Jeanne Anderson. CONGREGATIONAL COMMONWEALTH:
CONNECTICUT, 1636-1662. Middletown, Conn.: Wesleyan University
Press, 1968. 233 p. Illus., map.

Connecticut was an offshoot of Puritan Massachusetts,
its inhabitants migrating in 1636 for reasons of faith
and land. The author has made a thorough study of
the sources in search of the intellectual, religious,
and economic motivations for the establishment of the
colony and its governmental arrangements. Selection
of documents included in appendices.

521 Langdon, George D., Jr. PILGRIM COLONY: A HISTORY OF NEW
PLYMOUTH, 1620-1691. New Haven, Conn.: Yale University Press,
1966. 266 p. Map.

Traces developments in the Separatist colony from its
beginnings to the year it was merged by the British
government with the Massachusetts Bay Colony. Langdon
deals with the religious aspirations of the founders,
the fanning out of the population into new towns
beyond Plymouth, the coming of religious dissenters,
and, of course, the Indians.

522 Lockridge, Kenneth A. A NEW ENGLAND TOWN: THE FIRST HUN-
DRED YEARS: DEDHAM, MASSACHUSETTS, 1636-1736. New York:
W.W. Norton, 1970. 208 p. Maps, tables.

The application of demographic techniques to an early
Puritan community. Lockridge traces its evolution over
a hundred-year period and thus provides a valuable case
study in colonial history.

523 Morgan, Edmund S. VISIBLE SAINTS: THE HISTORY OF A PURITAN

IDEA. Ithaca, N.Y.: Cornell University Press, 1963. 159 p.

A brief but significant exposition explaining the relation of the theological notion of the sainthood of the elect in New England to state policy and other aspects of Puritan life. Morgan believes the idea of visible saint-hood emerged in the New World rather than in the Old.

524 Morton, Thomas. THE NEW ENGLISH CANAAN. Edited by Charles Francis Adams, Jr. 1883. Reprint. New York: Burt Franklin, 1966. 390 p.

Morton's riotously funny version of his running quarrel with the Plymouth and Massachusetts Bay colonies and his expulsion from his outpost at Merrymount. The Puritans saw his drunken revelries with cohorts and Indian consorts, and especially his sale of guns and powder to the Indians, as threats to their communities. Morton, asserting his rights as an Englishman, sought to give the Puritans a "bad press" in this book, published first in Amsterdam in 1637.

525 Perry, Ralph Barton. PURITANISM AND DEMOCRACY. New York: Vanguard Press, 1944. 704 p.

A philosophical analysis of the contributions of both Puritanism and democracy to American society. Perry believes these were the elements most important in the American view of life and way of doing things. A comprehensive and systematic work.

526 Simpson, Alan. PURITANISM IN OLD AND NEW ENGLAND. 1955. Reprint. Chicago. University of Chicago Press, 1961. 126 p. Paper-bound.

Originally a series of lectures delivered at the University of Chicago, these essays illumine Puritan practice in the Old and New Worlds in the light of their beliefs. Simpson writes with a light touch, accenting the Puritan intellect and literature.

527 Vaughan, Alden T. NEW ENGLAND FRONTIER: PURITANS AND INDI-ANS, 1620-1675. Boston: Little, Brown, 1965. 446 p. Illus., maps.

Gives a more optimistic picture of relations between the two groups than has been customary. Vaughan attempts to prove that some Indians welcomed the white man as an ally against their own enemies. By the close of the time span he covers, however, most Indians were gone from New England and the white man had control of the land.

528 Wertenbaker, Thomas Jefferson. THE PURITAN OLIGARCHY: THE FOUNDING OF AMERICAN CIVILIZATION. 1947. Reprint. New York: Charles Scribner's Sons, 1970. 373 p. Illus., ports. Paperbound.

Ranked as a classic study of Puritanism. Wertenbaker gives an overview of Puritanism in America, tracing its roots back to East Anglia and taking the story forward through the alteration of the Massachusetts Bay Charter following the Glorious Revolution. Wertenbaker devotes considerable space to the cultural dimensions of Puritanism as well as to its political fortunes.

529 Willison, George F. SAINTS AND STRANGERS. New York: Reynal & Hitchcock, 1945. 526 p. Front.

A colorful and stirring account of the Separatist settlement of Plymouth Colony, after its many misadventures in the Old World. The Pilgrims ("Saints") brought with them men and women who did not share their religious aspirations ("Strangers"). Willison traces the developments in the colony until it was merged with Massachusetts in 1691, giving many rich quotations from the original sources.

530 Winthrop, John. WINTHROP'S JOURNAL: HISTORY OF NEW ENGLAND, SIXTEEN THIRTY TO SIXTEEN FORTY-NINE. Edited by James K. Hosmer. 2 vols. 1908. Reprint. New York: Barnes & Noble, 1959.

The journal kept by the governor and prime mover of the Massachusetts Bay Colony. Provides insight into Puritan attitudes as well as an account of political and social developments in the formative years.

531 Zuckerman, Michael. PEACEABLE KINGDOMS: NEW ENGLAND TOWNS IN THE EIGHTEENTH CENTURY. New York: Alfred A. Knopf, 1970. 344 p.

Zuckerman argues that the town meeting was the instrument for reaching consensus in the town, leaving little room for individualism or dissent. He has studied the records of a selection of Massachusetts towns and believes that, although individualism may be part of American rhetoric, the majoritarianism insisted upon in these communities has had a formative influence on the American outlook.

3. Topical

a. BUSINESS AND ECONOMICS

532 Bailyn, Bernard. THE NEW ENGLAND MERCHANTS IN THE SEVEN-

TEENTH CENTURY. New York: Harper & Brothers, 1955. 257 p.
Illus., maps, geneal. table.

Deals with the beginnings of economic life in New
England, especially Massachusetts, with the rise of fur
trading, fishing, rudimentary industry, trade, and commerce. Bailyn traces the rise of merchant families and
their growing influence in the total life of the community. An excellent combination of social and economic
history.

533 Bond, Beverley W., Jr. THE QUIT-RENT SYSTEM IN THE AMERICAN
COLONIES. 1919. Reprint. Gloucester, Mass.: Peter Smith, 1965.
492 p.

The quitrent was a carry-over from feudal times and was
a widespread practice in America. Bond traces the
development of the practice in Europe and examines
its implementation in the various types of colonies in
the New World--corporate, proprietary, and royal.
Includes an introduction by the noted colonial historian,
Charles M. Andrews.

534 Bridenbaugh, Carl. THE COLONIAL CRAFTSMAN. 1950. Reprint.
Chicago: University of Chicago Press, 1961. 224 p. Illus.

Pictures the life of the craftsman in both town and
country, concentrating more on human details than
on his product. Bridenbaugh shows how the trades
developed and the part they played in the coming of
the Revolution. The illustrations of the work and
products of the craftsmen are from the famous French
ENCYCLOPEDIE.

535 Bruchey, Stuart W., ed. THE COLONIAL MERCHANT: SOURCES AND
READINGS. New York: Harcourt, Brace & World, 1966. 208 p.
Facsims., tables.

Primary materials from the period, along with introductions and statistical tables on colonial population and
commerce. Topics dealt with are: English Mercantilism
and the Navigation Acts, the Puritan Economic Ethic,
the Southern Staple Trade, and the Merchants of the
Middle and Northern Colonies.

536 Davis, Joseph S. ESSAYS IN THE EARLIER HISTORY OF AMERICAN
CORPORATIONS. 2 vols. 1917. Reprint. New York: Russell &
Russell, 1965. Illus.

The work is made up of several studies of corporations
and business leaders in America prior to 1800. Davis
has used diaries, letters, record books, newspapers, and
many other primary sources.

537 Tolles, Frederick B. MEETING HOUSE AND COUNTING HOUSE: THE QUAKER MERCHANTS OF COLONIAL PHILADELPHIA, 1682-1763. 1948. Reprint. New York: W.W. Norton, 1963. 306 p. Illus. Paperbound.

Tolles believes much of the worldly success of the Friends in Philadelphia was the result of their religious practice. His account is lightened by a quiet humor.

538 Weeden, William B. ECONOMIC AND SOCIAL HISTORY OF NEW ENGLAND, 1620-1789. 2 vols. 1890. Reprint. New York: Hillary House, 1963.

A basic work that deals with many aspects of economic life. Among the many topics are the economic use of wampum, agriculture, fishing, the fur trade, homespun industries, travel and communication, and the social consequences of these activities. Weeden deals also with such representative figures as Samuel Sewall, Peter Faneuil, Jonathan Edwards, and Benjamin Franklin.

b. DIPLOMACY

539 Savelle, Max. THE ORIGINS OF AMERICAN DIPLOMACY: THE INTERNATIONAL HISTORY OF ANGLOAMERICA, 1492-1763. New York: Macmillan, 1967. 637 p. Maps.

A thorough analysis of diplomatic history from the discovery by Columbus to the Peace of Paris, which handed over New France to the British. Savelle goes into the most detail in his coverage of diplomatic machinations in Europe, but he does devote some space to the diplomacy carried on in America among the colonial settlements.

c. EDUCATION

540 Bailyn, Bernard. EDUCATION IN THE FORMING OF AMERICAN SOCIETY: NEEDS AND OPPORTUNITIES FOR STUDY. Chapel Hill: University of North Carolina Press, 1960. 147 p.

A brief but provocative treatment. Bailyn sees the school in Puritan society as an institution that supplemented the child's education, which was carried on in the home, church, etc.

541 Cremin, Lawrence A. AMERICAN EDUCATION: THE COLONIAL EXPERIENCE, 1607-1783. New York: Harper & Row, 1970. 702 p.

A full work by a leading historian of American education.

While dealing with schools in the various colonies, the author interprets education much more broadly as a product of the student's life in his community.

542   Middlekauff, Robert. ANCIENTS AND AXIOMS: SECONDARY EDUCATION IN EIGHTEENTH-CENTURY NEW ENGLAND. New Haven, Conn.: Yale University Press, 1963. 218 p.

Concentrates primarily on the school as an institution and the efforts of the towns to finance it, only touching on social implications. Middlekauff traces the process by which the grammar school, dominated by a Greek and Latin curriculum, gave up the final two years of a boy's secondary education to the academy, which introduced him to vocational and commercial subjects as well.

543   Morison, Samuel Eliot. HARVARD COLLEGE IN THE SEVENTEENTH CENTURY. 2 vols. Cambridge, Mass.: Harvard University Press, 1936. Illus., front., ports., plates, maps, plans, facsims.

A rich record of higher education in the Puritan commonwealth. Morison, writes with wit and humor whether dealing with curriculum, theological controversy, or student pranks. Based on European university as well as Harvard archives.

d. THE GLORIOUS REVOLUTION

544   Hall, Michael G., et al. THE GLORIOUS REVOLUTION IN AMERICA: DOCUMENTS ON THE COLONIAL CRISIS OF 1689. Chapel Hill: University of North Carolina Press, 1964. 231 p. Maps. Paperbound.

The editors supply a brief introduction to the volume and to each chapter of documents. The collection ranges from official reports to excerpts from diaries.

545   Lovejoy, David S. THE GLORIOUS REVOLUTION IN AMERICA. New York: Harper & Row, 1972. 396 p.

A study of the outbreak of trouble in the American colonies at the time of the departure of James II from the British throne and the accession of William and Mary. The author develops the significance of American grievances as a part of the continuing struggle of the colonists for their constitutional rights in the empire.

e. GOVERNMENT AND POLITICS

546   Bailyn, Bernard. THE ORIGINS OF AMERICAN POLITICS. New York:

Alfred A. Knopf, 1968. 173 p.

Developed from lectures delivered at Brown University,
these essays deal with the structure of colonial politics.
Bailyn believes that the British heritage of the American
colonists underwent a transformation as a result of their
experience on the frontier of the New World.

547 Barnes, Viola F. THE DOMINION OF NEW ENGLAND: A STUDY IN
BRITISH COLONIAL POLICY. 1923. Reprint. New York: Frederick
Ungar, 1960. 303 p.

Traces the fortunes of the dominion created out of seven
northern provinces and placed under the governorship of
Sir Edmund Andros in 1686. The ill-fated dominion,
after experiencing much turmoil in the colonists' rebellious response to Andros and British policy, came to an
end with the Glorious Revolution in 1689.

548 Beer, George Louis. THE OLD COLONIAL SYSTEM, 1660-1754. 2 vols.
New York: Macmillan, 1913.

A sequel to the author's ORIGINS OF THE BRITISH
COLONIAL SYSTEM, 1578-1660, q.v., no. 549. A
study of colonial policy and its implementation. Beer
deals with developments in each of the British possessions
in the New World and with such topics as economics
and the slave trade.

549 _____. THE ORIGINS OF THE BRITISH COLONIAL SYSTEM, 1578-
1660. 1908. Reprint. New York: Macmillan, 1922. 446 p.

Deals with the development of British colonial policy
under the Tudors, Stuarts, and the Commonwealth, based
on documentation from British Archives. Beer goes into
great detail on administrative workings but also deals
with such social matters as the spreading use of tobacco
and Stuart attempts to regulate it.

550 Clarke, Mary P. PARLIAMENTARY PRIVILEGE IN THE AMERICAN CO-
LONIES. New Haven, Conn.: Yale University Press, 1943. 314 p.

Traces the efforts of the assemblies in the American
colonies to attain greater authority over their own affairs from the first one, established in Virginia in 1619, to
those at the end of the Revolution in 1783. Clarke provides
English parliamentary background and then details the
workings of the assemblies and the success of their efforts on the American continent and in the islands.

551 Dickerson, Oliver M. AMERICAN COLONIAL GOVERNMENT, 1696-
1765: A STUDY OF THE BRITISH BOARD OF TRADE IN ITS RELATIONS

TO THE AMERICAN COLONIES, POLITICAL, INDUSTRIAL, ADMINIS-
TRATIVE. 1912. Reprint. New York: Russell & Russell, 1962. 390
p. Illus., front., facsims.

An early analysis of colonial policy of the British government, concerning itself particularly with the Board of
Trade but also explaining the involvement of other
governmental departments.

552 Greene, Jack P. THE QUEST FOR POWER: THE LOWER HOUSES OF
ASSEMBLY IN THE SOUTHERN ROYAL COLONIES, 1689-1776. Chapel
Hill: University of North Carolina Press, 1963. 539 p. Tables.

Covers the assemblies in Virginia, North Carolina,
South Carolina, and Georgia, concentrating on their
debates of constitutional questions from the accession
of William and Mary to the outbreak of the Revolution.
Appendices include lists of royal governors, speakers,
and leaders in the lower houses of the assemblies.

553 Labaree, Leonard W. ROYAL GOVERNMENT IN AMERICA: A STUDY
OF THE BRITISH COLONIAL SYSTEM BEFORE 1783. 1930. Reprint.
New York: Frederick Ungar, 1964. 491 p.

Using the office of the royal governor as a vehicle,
Labaree explores British colonial policy and authority
and how it was implemented, to the close of the Revolution. His painstaking study inevitably deals with
the attitudes of the colonial assemblies and their contests with the representatives of the crown in America.
Thoroughly documented.

554 _____, ed. ROYAL INSTRUCTIONS TO BRITISH COLONIAL GOVER-
NORS, 1670-1776. 2 vols. 1935. Reprint. New York: Octagon
Books, 1967.

Following up his earlier work, ROYAL GOVERNMENT
IN AMERICA, q.v., no. 553, Labaree here presents a
comprehensive collection of the instructions given royal
governors on their appointment and during their tenure
in office. He includes those of the West Indies, the
colonies on the mainland, Nova Scotia, and Newfound-
land. Other features include a list of the governors
and the dates of their service.

555 Sosin, Jack M. WHITEHALL AND THE WILDERNESS: THE MIDDLE
WEST IN BRITISH COLONIAL POLICY, 1760-1775. Lincoln: University
of Nebraska Press, 1961. 318 p. Maps.

A study of British governmental policy on the American
interior from the Seven Years' War to the eve of the
American Revolution.

556   Sydnor, Charles S. GENTLEMEN FREEHOLDERS: POLITICAL PRACTICES IN WASHINGTON'S VIRGINIA. Chapel Hill: University of North Carolina Press, 1952. 189 p.

> Analyzes the aristocracy of Virginia and how it carried on the affairs of the colony.

f. INTELLECTUAL AND SOCIAL LIFE

557   de Crevecoeur, J. Hector St. John. LETTERS FROM AN AMERICAN FARMER; AND SKETCHES OF EIGHTEENTH-CENTURY AMERICA: MORE LETTERS FROM AN AMERICAN FARMER. New York: New American Library, 1963. 477 p. Paperbound.

> Essays in the form of letters by the Frenchman who migrated to Canada, served under Montcalm in the French and Indian War, and then became a naturalized American citizen in 1765. He married an American and settled on a farm in Orange County, New York. These essays include the famous "What is an American?" and give warm, vivid descriptions of life in America. This edition includes a foreword by Albert E. Stone.

558   Gummere, Richard M. THE AMERICAN COLONIAL MIND AND THE CLASSICAL TRADITION: ESSAYS IN COMPARATIVE CULTURE. Cambridge, Mass.: Harvard University Press, 1963. 241 p.

> A classicist's study of the influence of the literature of Greece and Rome on the thinking of leading figures of the colonial period, including William Byrd, Samuel Sewall, James Logan, and Benjamin Franklin. He concludes that men such as Adams and Jefferson were steeped in the classical tradition and were constantly influenced by it in their thoughts and actions.

559   Hofstadter, Richard. AMERICA AT 1750: A SOCIAL PORTRAIT. New York: Alfred A. Knopf, 1971. 322 p.

> Although a specialist in the recent period of U.S. history, Hofstadter at the time of his death was engaged in writing a projected three-volume work which would have traced American political fortunes from 1750 to the present. This book contains his unfinished effort in that direction. It provides insight into such topics as the Great Awakening, slavery, and the middle-class make-up of America.

560   Jones, Howard Mumford. O STRANGE NEW WORLD: AMERICAN CULTURE: THE FORMATIVE YEARS. New York: Viking Press, 1964. 478 p. Illus., facsim.

> An examination of how Old World ways fared in the

New. Jones sees the settlers as bringing the heritage
of the Renaissance with them; he traces the impact the
physical surroundings and the development of such ideas
as republicanism had on the culture and learning of
Europe.

561   Miller, Perry. ERRAND INTO THE WILDERNESS. 1956. Reprint. New
York: Harper & Row, 1964. 254 p. Paperbound.

A collection of shorter pieces by the leading scholar
of Puritan thought in America. The topics range from
the sense of Puritan mission and the essentials of its
thought to Jonathan Edwards and the Great Awakening,
and the transition to Emersonian transcendentalism.

562   _____. THE NEW ENGLAND MIND. 2 vols. 1939-53. Reprint.
Boston: Beacon Press, 1961. Front. Paperbound.

Two profound volumes of American intellectual history.
Miller concentrates on the public pronouncements of
the leaders of the Massachusetts Bay Colony and in the
first volume pieces together a complex of ideas dominated by "Augustinian piety." The second volume carries
the story through and beyond the "Half-Way Covenant"
to the stirrings of the Age of Reason, tracing the interplay of events and the intellect. Volume 1: THE
SEVENTEENTH CENTURY; volume 2: FROM COLONY
TO PROVINCE.

563   _____. ORTHODOXY IN MASSACHUSETTS, 1630-1650. 1933. Reprint. Boston: Beacon Press, 1959. 346 p. Paperbound.

In this forerunner of his NEW ENGLAND MIND, q.v.,
no. 562, Miller traces the intellectual indebtedness of
the Puritans to Old World theologians who were, he
believes, the source of the idea of "non-separating
congregationalism" in church government.

564   _____, ed. THE AMERICAN PURITANS: THEIR PROSE AND POETRY.
Garden City, N.Y.: Doubleday, 1956. 360 p. Maps. Paperbound.

Based on the earlier anthology which he edited with
Thomas Johnson, THE PURITANS, q.v., no. 565,
Miller has put into smaller compass the essentials of
Puritanism in the words of its exponents. He has
included figures not represented in the original.

565   Miller, Perry, and Johnson, Thomas, eds. THE PURITANS: A SOURCE
BOOK OF THEIR WRITINGS. 2 vols. 1938. Reprint. New York:
Harper & Row, 1969. Illus., fronts., port., maps, facsims. Paperbound.

Excerpts from the writings of leading figures in Puritan

New England, arranged so as to present their thought
on various topics: history, the state and society, manners
and customs, literature, education, science, and theology. A lengthy introduction by the editors gives an
excellent exposition of the Puritan view of life.

566 Morgan, Edmund S. THE PURITAN FAMILY. Rev. ed. New York: Harper & Row, 1966. 206 p. Paperbound.

Places the family life of the New England Puritans into
the context of their theology and the life of the state.
Morgan's exposition of the responsibility of husband and
wife to each other and to their children and servants
illuminates the meaning of the Puritan experience.

567 Morison, Samuel Eliot. THE INTELLECTUAL LIFE OF COLONIAL NEW
ENGLAND. 2d ed. 1956. Reprint. Ithaca, N.Y.: Cornell University Press, 1960. 288 p.

In this revised version of the book originally published
in 1935 as NEW ENGLAND PRONAOS, Morison surveys various aspects of New England intellectual life
and the means devised for its perpetuation: literature
(prose and poetry), printing, libraries, grammar schools,
etc., and states that the tone of society improved
rather than deteriorated. Lucid, enjoyable reading.

Parrington, Vernon L. MAIN CURRENTS IN AMERICAN THOUGHT.
Vol. 1. See no. 389.

568 Schneider, Herbert W. THE PURITAN MIND. 1930. Reprint. Ann
Arbor: University of Michigan Press, 1964. 271 p. Paperbound.

A philosopher's review of the main tenets of Puritanism
and how they were implemented in society. Schneider
believes that republicanism grew out of controversies
over how the churches should be governed. He carries
his analysis well into the eighteenth century, discussing
the Great Awakening and Benjamin Franklin as a secu-
larized Puritan.

569 Wertenbaker, Thomas Jefferson. THE GOLDEN AGE OF COLONIAL
CULTURE. 2d rev. ed. New York: New York University Press, 1949.
171 p.

The title refers to the mid-eighteenth century. In these
chapters, originally delivered as a series of lectures,
Wertenbaker considers the social life of Boston, New
York, Philadelphia, Annapolis, Williamsburg, and
Charleston, which he evaluates as rich and sophisticated
compared to that of the back country.

570 Wright, Louis B. THE CULTURAL LIFE OF THE AMERICAN COLONIES, 1607-1763. New York: Harper & Row, 1957. 304 p. Illus., ports., map.

> Covers the years from the early seventeenth century to the eve of the troubles with Britain. The author deals with education, science, books and libraries, the press and communication, and a multitude of other cultural manifestations, providing many facts and figures. A useful synthesis.

571 _____. THE FIRST GENTLEMEN OF VIRGINIA: INTELLECTUAL QUALITIES OF THE EARLY COLONIAL RULING CLASS. 1940. Reprint. Charlottesville: University Press of Virginia, 1964. 384 p. Paperbound.

> A somewhat idealized portrait. Wright attempts to show that Virginia had a true aristocracy, even if a home-grown one. His examples include, among others, William Byrd, Robert Beverley, and William Fitzhugh. He describes the contents of Virginia libraries to show their intellectual concerns.

g. LABOR

572 Jernegan, Marcus W. LABORING AND DEPENDENT CLASSES IN COLONIAL AMERICA, 1607-1783. 1931. Reprint. New York: Frederick Ungar, 1965. 256 p.

> A discussion of the lot of indentured servants and slaves from the beginnings of settlement to the conclusion of the Revolution, with concentration on New England and the South. Jernegan investigates provisions for the relief of the poor and for public education and deals with psychological as well as the physical conditions of persons in these levels of society.

573 Morris, Richard B. GOVERNMENT AND LABOR IN EARLY AMERICA. New York: Columbia University Press, 1946. 573 p.

> Covers the first two centuries of the American experience. Morris has made a detailed study of government legal records to discover policies and practices regarding free and indentured labor in twenty-five jurisdictions. He deals with, among other things, wage control and employment conditions in both land and maritime ventures.

574 Smith, Abbot E. COLONISTS IN BONDAGE: WHITE SERVITUDE AND CONVICT LABOR IN AMERICA, 1607-1776. 1947. Reprint. Gloucester, Mass.: Peter Smith, 1964. 443 p.

> A compilation of statistical information drawn from many

types of contemporary records. The work is arranged in
three sections: The Trade in Servants, Penal Transportation, The Servant in the Plantations.

h. LITERATURE

575 Murdock, Kenneth. LITERATURE AND THEOLOGY IN COLONIAL NEW
ENGLAND. 1949. Reprint. New York: Harper & Row, 1963. 249 p.
Paperbound.

Examines the Puritan "plain style" and other characteristics of their writing as manifestations of their theological outlook. Murdock discusses their histories,
diaries, and poetry in particular detail.

576 Tyler, Moses Coit. HISTORY OF AMERICAN LITERATURE, 1607-1765.
New York: Collier Books, 1962. 541 p. Paperbound.

A product of scholarship in the second half of the nineteenth century, Tyler's analysis has stood the test of
time. This work on literary history, published in 1878-
79 in two volumes, is still widely consulted. He deals
with the thought and style of the leading figures and
relates their careers to developments in their time.

577 Ziff, Larzer, ed. THE LITERATURE OF AMERICA: COLONIAL PERIOD.
New York: McGraw-Hill Book Co., 1970. 662 p.

A large anthology of primary materials designed to present the best of colonial literature and "to represent
those aspects of the culture that were of greatest consequence in shaping the character of American literature." Ziff supplies a general introduction and brief
introductions to the sections. The collection is divided
into four parts: An America of the Mind: Exploration
and Initial Settlement; Puritanism; the Cultures of
Eighteenth-Century America; Toward a National Culture.

j. RELIGION

578 Mather, Cotton. BONIFACIUS: AN ESSAY UPON THE GOOD. Edited
by David Levin. Cambridge, Mass.: Harvard University Press, 1966.
214 p. Facsim.

A valuable primary source. Mather, a leading divine
of the third generation, sets forth the duties of magis-
trates, businessmen, clergymen, and other members of
society, in the Puritan commonwealth. A book which
Benjamin Franklin claimed as a major influence on his
life. Originally published in 1710, the volume includes

an appendix on Indian Christianity and an advertisement
for BIBLIA AMERICANA. Levin's introduction includes
an examination of Mather's thought.

579 _____. MAGNALIA CHRISTI AMERICANA: OR, THE ECCLESIASTICAL
HISTORY OF NEW ENGLAND FROM ITS FIRST PLANTING IN THE YEAR
1620 UNTO THE YEAR OF OUR LORD 1698, IN SEVEN BOOKS. 2
vols. 1853-55. Reprint. New York: Russell & Russell, 1967.

Mather's church history heaps praise on the early heroes
of New England and laments the heresy of such as Roger
Williams. The author fully displays his great learning
in a text studded with historical and literary allusions.
Originally published in 1702, this edition includes
translations of Mather's quotations from the Hebrew,
Greek, and Latin.

580 Pope, Robert G. THE HALF-WAY COVENANT: CHURCH MEMBERSHIP
IN PURITAN NEW ENGLAND. Princeton, N.J.: Princeton University
Press, 1969. 332 p. Tables.

Pope brings to his narrative of the relaxation of earlier
standards of membership in the Puritan churches insight
provided by the disciplines of demography, anthropology,
and sociology. He examined records of churches in
Massachusetts and Connecticut for his study.

581 Sweet, William Warren. RELIGION IN COLONIAL AMERICA. 1942.
Reprint. New York: Cooper Square, 1965. 380 p.

A thorough discussion of the various established churches
in the colonies and the challenge of sects and dissenters
to their authority. Sweet maintains a balance in his
account between religious, social, and economic developments.

i. The Antinomian Controversy

582 Battis, Emery J. SAINTS AND SECTARIES: ANNE HUTCHINSON AND
THE ANTINOMIAN CONTROVERSY IN THE MASSACHUSETTS BAY
COLONY. Chapel Hill: University of North Carolina Press, 1962.
394 p. Port., maps.

A full discussion of the turmoil that swept Massachusetts
Bay Colony as a result of the attempt of the leaders to
silence Anne Hutchinson and her followers when they
threatened to upset the stable order of the community
by stressing a covenant of grace. Battis documents the
story and offers psychoanalytical interpretations of Mis-
tress Hutchinson's actions.

583   Hall, David D., ed. THE ANTINOMIAN CONTROVERSY, 1636-1638. Middletown, Conn.: Wesleyan University Press, 1968. 455 p.

A collection of materials relating to the controversy that arose over Anne Hutchinson when she challenged the religious leadership of the Massachusetts Bay Colony.

ii. The Great Awakening

584   Gaustad, Edwin S. THE GREAT AWAKENING IN NEW ENGLAND. 1957. Reprint. Chicago: Quadrangle Books, 1968. 185 p. Paperbound.

Deals with the upsurge of religious emotion in New England between 1740 and 1743, tracing the divisive debates between proponents, such as Jonathan Edwards, and the opponents, such as Charles Chauncy. Gaustad interprets the Awakening as a religiosocial phenomenon. He concludes with an analysis of its influence on later American religious history.

585   Gewehr, Wesley M. THE GREAT AWAKENING IN VIRGINIA, 1740-1790. 1930. Reprint. Gloucester, Mass.: Peter Smith, 1965. 300 p. Ports., maps.

Traces the spread of the Awakening from New England and the Middle Colonies into Virginia. Gewehr successively deals with the movement among the Presbyterians, the Baptists, and the Methodists, and goes on to show its ramifications in social and political life. On the whole, a sympathetic treatment.

586   Heimert, Alan. RELIGION AND THE AMERICAN MIND: FROM THE GREAT AWAKENING TO THE REVOLUTION. Cambridge, Mass.: Harvard University Press, 1966. 682 p.

Examines religious thinking in the colonies between 1740 and 1776 in an attempt to show that Jonathan Edwards and his followers and other evangelical Christians contributed more to the preparation of "the American mind" for Revolution than did the liberals, Christian and Deist, as has been thought. Biographical glossary included.

587   Heimert, Alan, and Miller, Perry, eds. THE GREAT AWAKENING: DOCUMENTS ILLUSTRATING THE CRISIS AND ITS CONSEQUENCES. Indianapolis: Bobbs-Merrill, 1967. 733 p. Paperbound.

A collection giving generous excerpts from writings of the Awakening with editorial introductions to each. Heimert provides an extensive introduction to the collection, in which he sets forth the issues at stake in the

controversy. Among the many figures included are
Jonathan Edwards, George Whitefield, Gilbert Tennent,
Charles Chauncy, and Jonathan Mayhew.

588   Maxson, Charles H. THE GREAT AWAKENING IN THE MIDDLE COLO-
NIES. 1920. Reprint. Gloucester, Mass.: Peter Smith, 1958. 165 p.

On the whole, a sympathetic treatment of the Awakening whose democratic features Maxson believes were
responsible for undermining the established churches in
New England. Concentrates on the role of George
Whitefield and developments in the Dutch Reformed
and Presbyterian churches in the Middle Colonies.

k. SCIENCE AND TECHNOLOGY

589   Cohen, I. Bernard. FRANKLIN AND NEWTON: AN INQUIRY INTO
SPECULATIVE EXPERIMENTAL SCIENCE AND FRANKLIN'S WORK IN
ELECTRICITY AS AN EXAMPLE THEREOF. Philadelphia: American
Philosophical Society, 1956. 683 p. Illus., ports.

An examination of Benjamin Franklin's scientific knowledge and accomplishments. Cohen, a historian of
science, compares Franklin with Newton and concludes
that the former was not well grounded in scientific
theory. Paradoxically, this may have furthered his
famous accomplishments, since he was willing to venture
into areas a more accomplished theoretician probably
would have avoided.

590   Hindle, Brooke. THE PURSUIT OF SCIENCE IN REVOLUTIONARY AMERI-
CA, 1735-1789. Chapel Hill: University of North Carolina Press, 1956.
421 p. Illus., ports.

A detailed and well-informed history of science in the
period of the Enlightenment. Hindle deals with the
development of the various branches of science and
provides revealing sketches of the contributions of men
in the several colonies, many of whom took an active
part in the political events of the period.

Shryock, Richard H. MEDICINE AND SOCIETY IN AMERICA, 1660-1860.
See no. 393.

591   Stearns, Raymond P. SCIENCE IN THE BRITISH COLONIES OF AMERI-
CA. Urbana: University of Illinois Press, 1970. 780 p. Illus., ports.,
facsims.

Traces in great detail the development of the sciences
in the British American colonies, from the beginning to

the eve of the Revolution. Stearns has drawn heavily from the records of the Royal Society for the Promotion of Natural Knowledge and demonstrates that the Americans were part of an international community of scientists. He examines carefully and fully the contributions of individuals in the various colonies.

I. WARFARE

592 Hamilton, Edward P. THE FRENCH AND INDIAN WARS: THE STORY OF BATTLES AND FORTS IN THE WILDERNESS. Garden City, N.Y.: Doubleday, 1962. 330 p. Illus., maps.

This account of the battles between the British colonists and their opponents includes helpful descriptions of the terrain, modes of travel, instruments of war, and many other details.

593 Leach, Douglas E. ARMS FOR EMPIRE: A MILITARY HISTORY OF THE BRITISH COLONIES IN NORTH AMERICA, 1607-1763. New York: Macmillan, 1973. 579 p. Maps.

Leach covers the period from the first British settlements in America to the year French Canada became part of the empire. His is a colorful and often witty narrative dealing with such matters as how the militias were organized and performed, how British and American military strategy evolved, the various conflicts such as Bacon's Rebellion, the Indian wars, and much more.

594 _____. FLINTLOCK AND TOMAHAWK: NEW ENGLAND IN KING PHILIP'S WAR. 1958. Reprint. New York: W.W. Norton, 1966. 314 p. Ports., maps.

Concentrates on military developments of the war of 1675-76, when the chief of the Wampanoags determined to rid New England of the white man. Leach also explores the social and intellectual repercussions of the terror that gripped the communities.

595 Peckham, Howard H. THE COLONIAL WARS, 1689-1762. Chicago: University of Chicago Press, 1964. 248 p. Illus., ports., maps.

Relates the struggle among the French, English, and Spanish empires to happenings in the colonies. Peckham gives vivid accounts of such trying contests as the French and Indian War and believes that the colonists came to a greater recognition of the need for military cooperation among themselves.

596 Washburn, Wilcomb E. THE GOVERNOR AND THE REBEL: A HISTORY

OF BACON'S REBELLION IN VIRGINIA. Chapel Hill: University of North Carolina Press, 1957. 263 p. Port., maps, facsim.

Washburn believes the older view of Bacon as a hero of the frontier democracy to be wrong. In this history, Bacon emerges as a demagogue in 1676, and Governor Berkeley as a hero.

m. WITCHCRAFT

597 Burr, George Lincoln, ed. NARRATIVES OF THE WITCHCRAFT CASES, 1648-1706. 1914. Reprint. New York: Barnes & Noble, 1959. 485 p. Facsims.

A compilation of source materials with introductions to each selection by the editor. He includes such important items as Increase Mather's REMARKABLE PROVIDENCES, Cotton Mather's MEMORABLE PROVIDENCES and WONDERS OF THE INVISIBLE WORLD, and the attack on the Mathers by Robert Calef, MORE WONDERS OF THE INVISIBLE WORLD.

598 Hansen, Chadwick. WITCHCRAFT AT SALEM. New York: George Braziller, 1969. 267 p.

An examination of the witchcraft hysteria that broke out at Salem in the Massachusetts Bay Colony in 1692. Opposing the traditional view, Hansen seeks to demonstrate that witchcraft was practiced at Salem and that reactions were the result of fear, not fraudulence. The author brings modern psychological theory to bear in his analysis.

599 Kittredge, George Lyman. WITCHCRAFT IN OLD AND NEW ENGLAND. 1929. Reprint. New York: Russell & Russell, 1956. 641 p.

This classic study of witchcraft examines the primary sources on both sides of the Atlantic in great detail; it provides an essential starting point for a study of this topic.

600 Starkey, Marion. THE DEVIL IN MASSACHUSETTS: A MODERN INQUIRY INTO THE SALEM WITCH TRIALS. New York: Alfred A. Knopf, 1949. 328 p.

A colorful and skillful recounting of the witchcraft delusion that swept Salem, Massachusetts in 1692. The author attributes the beginning of the hysteria to the overactive imaginations of young girls, fed by the stories told by a slave woman from the West Indies. She traces the fate of the various victims of the hysteria

and the actions of clerical and lay leaders in response
to it.

4. Prominent Individuals

See also the section on Prominent Individuals, 3,C,4.

GENERAL

601　Morison, Samuel Eliot. BUILDERS OF THE BAY COLONY. Rev. and
　　enl. ed. Boston: Houghton Mifflin, 1962. 418 p. Illus., front., ports.

> A series of biographies which, in the original edition
> of 1930, helped create a new, sympathetic attitude
> toward the Puritan founders. Following sketches of
> precursors Richard Hakluyt and Captain John Smith and
> troublemaker Thomas Morton of Merrymount, Morison
> deals with such prominent men as John Winthrop (Sr.
> and Jr.), Thomas Shepard, John Hull, Henry Dunster,
> Nathaniel Ward, Robert Child, John Eliot, William Pyn-
> chon, and the poetess Anne Bradstreet.

JOHN COTTON

602　Ziff, Larzer. THE CAREER OF JOHN COTTON: PURITANISM AND
　　THE AMERICAN EXPERIENCE. Princeton, N.J.: Princeton University
　　Press, 1962. 280 p.

> A modern account of the leading theologian of the
> Massachusetts Bay Colony. Primarily an intellectual
> history, to a great extent based on Cotton's sermons,
> but with strong biographical elements. Ziff includes
> a thorough consideration of Cotton's part in the antino-
> mian controversy that drove Anne Hutchinson from the
> Bay Colony and of his debate with Roger Williams over
> freedom of conscience.

JONATHAN EDWARDS

603　Miller, Perry. JONATHAN EDWARDS. 1949. Reprint. New York:
　　Meridian Books, 1959. 340 p. Paperbound.

> Miller alternates between the external occurrences in
> Edwards' life and the development of his thought. In-
> evitably, much of the book is devoted to the Great
> Awakening and its aftermath. A difficult but rewarding
> work.

604　Winslow, Ola E. JONATHAN EDWARDS, 1703-1758: A BIOGRAPHY.

1940. Reprint. New York: Octagon Books, 1973. 418 p. Illus.

A scholarly work, but one that stresses the human aspects of Edwards's career and misfortunes rather than
his theological ruminations and the controversy they
led to.

THE MATHERS

605 Middlekauff, Robert. THE MATHERS: THREE GENERATIONS OF PURI-
TAN INTELLECTUALS, 1596-1728. New York: Oxford University Press,
1971. 452 p.

This biographical study of the "Mather Dynasty" (Richard,
Increase, Cotton) is also an intellectual history of the
period. Another contribution to the rehabilitation of
Cotton Mather in American history.

606 Wendell, Barrett. COTTON MATHER: THE PURITAN PRIEST. New
York: Harcourt, Brace & World, 1963. 288 p. Paperbound.

The sympathetic account of Mather draws heavily on
his diary to demonstrate his self-questioning, tortured
soul. First published in 1891.

POCAHONTAS

607 Barbour, Philip L. POCAHONTAS AND HER WORLD: A CHRONICLE
OF AMERICA'S FIRST SETTLEMENT IN WHICH IS RELATED THE STORY
OF THE INDIANS AND THE ENGLISHMEN, PARTICULARLY CAPTAIN
JOHN SMITH, CAPTAIN SAMUEL ARGALL, AND MASTER JOHN ROLFE.
Boston: Houghton Mifflin, 1970. 340 p. Illus., ports., maps.

Using the life of Pocahontas as a vehicle, Barbour
reveals much about the early Virginia colony and the
struggle for authority and wealth. Little is known of
the Indian princess, but more about the leading figures
at Jamestown, her father Chief Powhaton, her husband
John Rolfe, and Captains Smith and Argall. A lively
narrative.

SAMUEL SEWALL

608 Strandness, T.B. SAMUEL SEWALL: A PURITAN PORTRAIT. East Lansing: Michigan State University Press, 1967. 250 p. Map.

Strandness systematically discusses each aspect of the
multifold career of the New England Puritan businessman and jurist. He makes good use of Sewall's DIARY,
q.v., no. 609, in recreating his life and surroundings.

609 Thomas, M. Halsey, ed. THE DIARY OF SAMUEL SEWALL. 2 vols. New York: Farrar, Straus and Giroux, 1973. Illus., fronts., ports., facsims.

> The personal and state affairs of the prominent second generation merchant and jurist of the Massachusetts Bay Colony are revealed in detail in one of the most famous diaries to survive. A mine of information concerning Puritan attitudes on all aspects of life. Includes much pathos and (unintentional) humor. This edition contains full notes by the editor, a chronology, Sewall's anti-slavery tract, THE SELLING OF JOSEPH, genealogical appendix, and other items.

610 Winslow, Ola E. SAMUEL SEWALL OF BOSTON: New York: Macmillan, 1964. 243 p. Illus., front., facsims.

> The work sees Judge Sewall as a transition figure from the Puritan to the Yankee, and provides much background for an understanding of the man and the age in which he lived.

611 Wish, Harvey, ed. THE DIARY OF SAMUEL SEWALL. New York: G.P. Putnam's Sons, 1967. 189 p.

> An abridged version of the famous diary with a useful introduction by the editor. The complete diary has been edited in a new edition by M. Halsey Thomas, q.v., no. 609.

ROGER WILLIAMS

612 Miller, Perry. ROGER WILLIAMS: HIS CONTRIBUTION TO THE AMERICAN TRADITION. 1953. Reprint. New York: Atheneum, 1962. 269 p. Paperbound.

> Miller places the more important works of Williams in a lengthy, running commentary of his own. Because of the great difficulty in understanding the original texts, he has given a modern version (spelling, punctuation, etc.). Among Williams's writings included are A KEY INTO THE LANGUAGE OF AMERICA, THE BLOODY TENENT OF PERSECUTION FOR CAUSE OF CONSCIENCE, THE BLOODY TENENT YET MORE BLOODY, THE HIRELING MINISTRY NONE OF CHRISTS, and GEORGE FOX DIGG'D OUT OF HIS BURROWES, as well as various of his letters.

613 Morgan, Edmund S. ROGER WILLIAMS: THE CHURCH AND THE STATE. New York: Harcourt, Brace & World, 1967. 170 p.

> It was Williams's thinking on the relationship of church

and state that got him into trouble and led to his banish-
ment from the Massachusetts Bay Colony. Morgan follows
the development of Williams's thought, guiding the reader through the maze of theological argumentation.

614   Williams, Roger. THE COMPLETE WRITINGS OF ROGER WILLIAMS.
       7 vols. 1866-74 (vols. 1-6). Reprint. New York: Russell & Russell, 1963.

       The original Narragansett edition is reprinted in volumes
       1-6; volume 7 is a new publication, edited by Perry
       Miller, which contains an essay by him on Williams,
       as well as tracts not included in the Narragansett edi-
       tion. Among the contents: THE BLOUDY TENANT OF
       PERSECUTION, THE BLOUDY TENANT YET MORE
       BLOODY [sic], GEORGE FOX DIGG'D OUT OF HIS
       BURROWES.

615   Winslow, Ola E. MASTER ROGER WILLIAMS: A BIOGRAPHY. New
       York: Macmillan, 1957. 328 p. Illus.

       A scholarly, well-written biography that presents both
       the man and his ideas in a skillful blend.

THE WINTHROPS

616   Dunn, Richard S. PURITANS AND YANKEES: THE WINTHROP DYNAS-
       TY OF NEW ENGLAND, 1630-1717. 1962. Reprint. New York:
       W.W. Norton, 1971. 386 p. Ports., map.

       Using primary sources, the author sets forth the influ-
       ence of three generations of Winthrops, starting with
       John, the governor of the Massachusetts Bay Colony.
       These men played a large role in fashioning the future
       of both Massachusetts and Connecticut and their influ-
       ence on history has been great.

617   Morgan, Edmund S. THE PURITAN DILEMMA: THE STORY OF JOHN
       WINTHROP. Boston: Little, Brown, 1958. 238 p.

       A short, sympathetic account of the life of the first
       governor of the Massachusetts Bay Colony. Morgan,
       basing his study on the original sources, weaves together
       biography and public developments of the Puritan Com-
       monwealth.

C. REVOLUTION AND CONSTITUTIONS

1. The Revolution

a. GENERAL

618   Alden, John R. A HISTORY OF THE AMERICAN REVOLUTION. New

York: Alfred A. Knopf, 1969. 564 p. Illus., ports., maps.

A review of the military aspects of the war, supplemented by a consideration of social and political developments. Alden's treatment of Washington is balanced; the general is superior to his contemporaries but
definitely a more fallible human being than the figure
presented by many historians.

619 THE AMERICAN HERITAGE BOOK OF THE REVOLUTION. Edited by
Richard M. Ketchum. 1958. Reprint. New York: American Heritage
Publishing Co., 1971. 384 p. Illus., ports., plates, maps.

This beautifully illustrated work with a scholarly narrative provides an understanding of the Americans and
their social milieu in the Revolutionary period.

620 Andrews, Charles M. THE COLONIAL BACKGROUND OF THE AMERI-
CAN REVOLUTION: FOUR ESSAYS IN AMERICAN COLONIAL HIS-
TORY. Rev. ed. New Haven, Conn.: Yale University Press, 1931.
230 p.

Concentrates on the interdependence of the colonies and
the mother country in order to shed light on British
mercantile policy of the eighteenth century and the
controversies that arose over it.

Bancroft, George. HISTORY OF THE UNITED STATES OF AMERICA.
Vols. 3-5. See no. 486.

621 Beloff, Max, ed. THE DEBATE ON THE AMERICAN REVOLUTION,
1761-1783: A SOURCEBOOK. 1949. Reprint. New York: Harper &
Row, 1965. 309 p. Paperbound.

This collection includes British as well as American
documents.

622 Commager, Henry Steele, and Morris, Richard B., eds. THE SPIRIT OF
SEVENTY-SIX: THE STORY OF THE AMERICAN REVOLUTION AS TOLD
BY PARTICIPANTS. 1958. Reprint. New York: Harper & Row, 1967.
1,400 p. Illus., ports., maps, facsim.

A massive collection of original materials. The editors
include excerpts from diaries, letters, newspapers, official documents, British and American, and from many
other sources.

623 Gipson, Lawrence H. THE COMING OF THE REVOLUTION, 1763-1775.
New York: Harper & Brothers, 1954. 301 p. Illus., ports., maps.

Gipson uses the vast wealth of information gathered for

his multi-volume BRITISH EMPIRE BEFORE THE AMERI-
CAN REVOLUTION, q.v., no. 474, in this reevalua-
tion of the Revolution. He takes the same broad,
imperial view when dealing with the grievances of the
Americans.

624   Jensen, Merrill. THE FOUNDING OF A NATION: A HISTORY OF
THE AMERICAN REVOLUTION, 1763-1776. New York: Oxford University Press, 1968. 748 p.

Attempts to prove the thesis of John Adams and Benjamin
Rush that the American Revolution occurred in the hearts
and minds of the people. Jensen gives the political
history of the crucial years between the end of the
Seven Years' War and the vote in the Second Continental Congress for independence, showing through an
analysis of newspapers, pamphlets, and other sources
how the sentiment for separation developed.

625   _____, ed. TRACTS OF THE AMERICAN REVOLUTION, 1763-1776.
Indianapolis: Bobbs-Merrill, 1967. 572 p.

Influential pamphlets in the dispute with Britain, including generous excerpts from the writings of James Otis,
Daniel Dulany, Richard Bland, John Dickinson et al.,
with introduction by the editor.

626   Knollenberg, Bernhard. ORIGIN OF THE AMERICAN REVOLUTION,
1759-1766. New York: Macmillan, 1960. 494 p.

This history concludes that the American colonists had
true grievances against the British government and were
not just imagining them. Knollenberg, building his
case on the original records, details a series of acts
against the Americans from 1759 on which, combined
with mismanagement and corruption, stimulated the
colonists to rebel.

627   McDonald, Forrest. E PLURIBUS UNUM: THE FORMATION OF THE
AMERICAN REPUBLIC, 1776-1790. Boston: Houghton Mifflin, 1965.
341 p.

McDonald traces the turbulent years of the Revolution
and the development of the American national government, giving a full treatment of the men who contended
with the issue of state sovereignty versus a strong central
government.

628   Mackesy, Piers. THE WAR FOR AMERICA, 1776-1783. Cambridge,
Mass.: Harvard University Press, 1964. 585 p. Illus., ports., maps.

A military history of the Revolution as it was seen by the

British. Mackesy shows that the Crown's ministers considered the war a global one and were as concerned for the future of the West Indies as for that of the thirteen colonies. The study is based on British sources.

629 Miller, John C. ORIGINS OF THE AMERICAN REVOLUTION. Boston: Little, Brown, 1943. 533 p. Illus., ports.

A scholarly account of events from the beginning of the reign of George III to the Declaration of Independence. Miller believes the Revolution was the result of legitimate grievances on the part of the Americans, deliberately setting aside the argument for economic determinism. Includes vivid sketches of leaders on both sides of the Atlantic.

630 _____. TRIUMPH OF FREEDOM, 1775-1783. Boston: Little, Brown, 1948. 734 p. Maps.

A general treatment of the Revolution covering political, diplomatic, economic, and social, as well as military events. Miller interprets the struggle as one for freedom, although he includes the less flattering aspects: citizen lethargy, money-grubbing merchant suppliers of the forces, the unheroic among the soldiery.

631 Mitchell, Broadus. THE PRICE OF INDEPENDENCE: A REALISTIC VIEW OF THE AMERICAN REVOLUTION. New York: Oxford University Press, 1974. 374 p.

Concentrates on the less heroic aspects of the Revolution. Not all were brave, willing to sacrifice, and devoted to independence. Mitchell attempts to balance the more glamorous accounts with much evidence of personal greed, governmental incompetence, and so on. A healthy corrective to the standard accounts.

632 Morgan, Edmund S. THE BIRTH OF THE REPUBLIC, 1763-1789. Chicago: University of Chicago Press, 1956. 176 p.

This readable, popular account takes cognizance of the various possible interpretations of the events covered. An excellent, brief introduction to the period.

633 Morris, Richard B. THE AMERICAN REVOLUTION RECONSIDERED. New York: Harper & Row, 1967. 189 p.

A series of four essays on the Revolution and its consequences in world history. Morris believes that the Revolution, far from being conservative as often pictured, was as much a movement for social reform as for politi-

cal independence. The effects of the Revolution, he
believes, are still being felt in revolutionary struggles
in our time.

634   Palmer, R.R. THE AGE OF THE DEMOCRATIC REVOLUTION: A POLI-
TICAL HISTORY OF EUROPE AND AMERICA, 1760-1800. 2 vols. Princeton, N.J.: Princeton University Press, 1959-64. Maps.

This brilliant, detailed study of the "age of revolution"
places events in America in the context of what was
transpiring in Europe. Volume 1: THE CHALLENGE;
volume 2: THE STRUGGLE.

635   Trevelyan, George Otto. THE AMERICAN REVOLUTION. Edited by
Richard B. Morris. New York: David McKay, 1964. 605 p.

An abridged version of a colorful Whiggish history of
the Revolution published by the famous English historian
in six volumes between 1899 and 1914. Trevelyan took
a severe view of George III and the North ministry,
interpreting their actions as attempts to restrict the
constitutional liberties of the Americans and the English
as well. This abridgment eliminates much of the military action described in the original.

636   Wood, Gordon S. THE CREATION OF THE AMERICAN REPUBLIC, 1776-
1787. Chapel Hill: University of North Carolina Press, 1969. 667 p.

A detailed examination of the ideas that justified the
Revolution and the creation of an independent American
government. Wood bases his study to a great extent
on pamphlet and periodical literature of the eighteenth
century and discusses the major problems with which
the Americans had to contend: the philosophy of natural
rights, the idea of equality, the basis for suffrage, the
authority of government, etc.

637   Wright, Esmond, ed. CAUSES AND CONSEQUENCES OF THE AMERICAN
REVOLUTION. 1943. Reprint. Chicago: Quadrangle Books, 1964. 316
p. Paperbound.

A collection of articles by noted American and British
historians discussing various approaches to the Revolution.
The editor provides a lengthy essay as an introduction
to the problems discussed. Among those included:
Charles M. Andrews, Lawrence Henry Gipson, Arthur
M. Schlesinger, Edmund S. Morgan, Lewis B. Namier,
Richard B. Morris.

b. REGIONAL

638   Adams, James Truslow. REVOLUTIONARY NEW ENGLAND, 1691-1776.

Boston: Atlantic Monthly Press, 1923. 483 p. Illus., front., port., plates, facsims.

> Traces through a fairly long period of time, the growth of grievances that culminated in revolution. Adams' treatment is comprehensive and scholarly in this sequel to his FOUNDING OF NEW ENGLAND, q.v., no. 516.

639   Alden, John R. THE SOUTH IN THE REVOLUTION, 1763-1789. Baton Rouge: Louisiana State University Press, 1957. 458 p. Illus., ports., maps.

> The South's role in the Revolution, from the Peace of Paris to the formation of the new government under the Constitution, is treated fully and in readable fashion. This is a volume in the cooperative effort, A HISTORY OF THE SOUTH.

c. TOPICAL

i. Black Americans

640   Quarles, Benjamin. THE NEGRO IN THE AMERICAN REVOLUTION. 1961. Reprint. New York: W.W. Norton, 1973. 244 p. Front. Paperbound.

> An investigation of the part the blacks played as combatants and as laborers and servants among the support forces in the armies of both the British and Americans. Quarles sets forth many individual cases and makes use of general statistics.

ii. Business and Economics

641   East, Robert A. BUSINESS ENTERPRISE IN THE AMERICAN REVOLU-TIONARY ERA. 1938. Reprint. New York: AMS Press, 1969. 387 p.

> A comprehensive study of the forces, unleashed by the Revolution, which led to the emergence of a capitalist group in the new nation.

642   Schlesinger, Arthur M. THE COLONIAL MERCHANTS AND THE AMERI-CAN REVOLUTION. 1917. Reprint. New York: Atheneum, 1968. 647 p. Paperbound.

> Economics played an important role in the controversies leading to the Revolution. This study reveals attitudes and actions of the colonial merchants in the years 1763 to 1776: their initial opposition to the trade policies of

Great Britain, their part in the nonintercourse agreements, and their reactions to the upsurge of Revolutionary violence.

iii. Declaration of Independence

643 Becker, Carl L. THE DECLARATION OF INDEPENDENCE: A STUDY IN
THE HISTORY OF POLITICAL IDEAS. 1922. Reprint. New York: Vintage Books, n.d. 310 p. Paperbound.

With the subtlety and wit that characterized all of his writing, Becker examines the work of another great stylist,
Thomas Jefferson, and traces the various stages through
which the Declaration went and how it fared at the hands
of the final editorial committee, the Continental Congress.

644 Hawke, David Freeman. A TRANSACTION OF FREE MEN: THE BIRTH
AND COURSE OF THE DECLARATION OF INDEPENDENCE. New York:
Charles Scribner's Sons, 1964. 282 p.

Concentrates on the relationship of John Adams and
Thomas Jefferson and their contribution to independence.
Hawke gives an exposition of the development of their
thought leading up to the Second Continental Congress.
He surmises that Jefferson intended the Declaration of
Independence to speak to the future, giving it a mean-
ing his contemporaries could not comprehend.

iv. Diplomacy

645 Bemis, Samuel Flagg. THE DIPLOMACY OF THE AMERICAN REVOLU-
TION. 3d ed. 1957. Reprint. Bloomington: Indiana University Press,
1960. 305 p.

The development of American diplomacy from the defeat
of France in the Seven Years' War, 1763, through the
Treaty of Paris which ended the Revolution in 1783.
Bemis pictures the colonies as pawns in an international
struggle. The achievement of the Americans was that
they could gain support from France in their struggle
with Britain without cost to themselves. This study is
based on primary material in the archives of France,
England, Spain, and the Netherlands.

646 Morris, Richard B. THE PEACEMAKERS: THE GREAT POWERS AND
AMERICAN INDEPENDENCE. New York: Harper & Row, 1965. 590
p. Illus., ports., maps, facsims.

Follows the intricate diplomatic doings that resulted in
the Treaty of Paris of 1783 and the end of the Revolu-

tion. The American commissioners, Franklin, Adams,
and Jay, inevitably come in for much comment, but
so do their French and British counterparts. A well-
documented account of the personalities and the issues
involved.

647 Stinchcombe, William C. THE AMERICAN REVOLUTION AND THE
FRENCH ALLIANCE. Syracuse, N.Y.: Syracuse University Press, 1969.
244 p. Ports.

Reinforces the traditional opinion that the United States
was assured of success in its fight for independence when
it sought and achieved an alliance with France. Stinchcombe's treatment of public attitudes in America concerning the French and their aid is particularly detailed.

v. Government and Politics

648 Bailyn, Bernard. THE IDEOLOGICAL ORIGINS OF THE AMERICAN RE-
VOLUTION. Cambridge, Mass.: Harvard University Press, 1967. 348
p.

Originally appeared as the introduction to PAMPHLETS
OF THE AMERICAN REVOLUTION, 1750-1776, q.v.,
no. 649. Bailyn has here expanded his analysis of the
ideas and arguments that appear in the pamphlets. He
traces the origin of the Revolutionary ideology to classical antiquity, English common law, rationalism of the
Enlightenment, Puritanism, and English opposition theory.
Its development, he believes, was stimulated by the
conviction that there was a conspiracy to deprive the
colonists of their rights.

649 _____, ed. PAMPHLETS OF THE AMERICAN REVOLUTION, 1750-1776.
1 vol. to date. Cambridge, Mass.: Harvard University Press, 1965- .

The first of a projected series of volumes which will re-
print outstanding pamphlets of the Revolution. Bailyn
has written an extended introduction and headnotes to
each selection. Included are pamphlets by Jonathan
Mayhew, John Aplin, Richard Bland, Thomas Fitch,
James Otis, Oxenbridge Thacher, Stephen Hopkins,
Martin Howard, Jr., Benjamin Church, Daniel Dulany,
John Dickinson, and a number of anonymous pamphlets.

650 Burnett, Edmund C. THE CONTINENTAL CONGRESS. 1941. Reprint.
New York: W.W. Norton, 1964. 769 p.

Burnett puts the Congress at the center of events of the
Revolution and the Confederation period, when there
was no executive in the U.S. government. The

policies and day-to-day activities of the Congress are
detailed, with heavy stress given the actual words of
members.

651   _____, ed. LETTERS OF MEMBERS OF THE CONTINENTAL CONGRESS.
8 vols. 1921-36. Reprint. Gloucester, Mass.: Peter Smith, 1963.

Provides a valuable insight into the minds of members
of the Congress as it gravitated to the conclusion that
independence was a necessity. The clash of personalities and the day-to-day workings of the Congress are
also revealed. Letters run from 29 August 1774 to 25
July 1789.

652 Dickerson, Oliver M. THE NAVIGATION ACTS AND THE AMERICAN
REVOLUTION. Philadelphia: University of Pennsylvania Press, 1951.
358 p.

Takes the position that the Navigation and Trade Acts
were sources of little friction and had been accepted
by most Americans involved with no complaint. The
real trouble began when the British government attempted
to tighten up enforcement and, in addition, sought new
revenue by imposing taxes within the colonies. Dickerson made use of British Treasury materials for the first
time.

653 Douglass, Elisha P. REBELS AND DEMOCRATS: THE STRUGGLE FOR
EQUAL POLITICAL RIGHTS AND MAJORITY RULE DURING THE AMERI-
CAN REVOLUTION. 1955. Reprint. Chicago: Quadrangle Books,
1965. 383 p. Paperbound.

Douglass sees democratic sentiment arising out of the
struggle for independence and an attempt on the part
of conservatives ("Whigs") to thwart it.

654 Ferguson, E. James. THE POWER OF THE PURSE: A HISTORY OF
AMERICAN PUBLIC FINANCE, 1776-1790. Chapel Hill: University of
North Carolina Press, 1961. 358 p.

The author uses archival material and statistics in an
effort to revise some old presuppositions concerning
public finance in the period. He covers the financing
of the Revolution and the relations between the Confederation government and the states in the aftermath.

655 Labaree, Benjamin Woods. THE BOSTON TEA PARTY. New York: Oxford University Press, 1964. 355 p. Map.

Using the Tea Party as a jumping-off place for an
analysis of the forces leading to the Revolution, Labaree

examines the incident in great detail, believing that it
was quite important as a stimulant to rebellion.

656 Labaree, Leonard W. CONSERVATISM IN EARLY AMERICAN HISTORY.
1948. Reprint. Ithaca, N.Y.: Cornell University Press, 1968. 182 p.

> In a series of lectures that provides a sampling of im-
> portant conservative thinkers and their contribution to
> American colonial history, Labaree gives the thoughts
> of Cadwallader Colden, Thomas Hutchinson, Landon
> Carter, Jonathan Boucher, and William Worthington,
> among others, on government, society, religion, and
> education. Many conservatives agreed with the liberals
> that Britain was wrong in imposing taxes on the Ameri-
> cans, but they drew the line at civil disobedience and
> violence.

657 Morgan, Edmund S., ed. PROLOGUE TO REVOLUTION: SOURCES AND
DOCUMENTS ON THE STAMP ACT CRISIS, 1764-1766. Chapel Hill:
University of North Carolina Press, 1959. 174 p. Front. Paperbound.

> Documents included deal with the Sugar Act, the Stamp
> Act, the colonial assemblies, the American and British
> press, the rebellion, and the repeal of the Act. The
> editor introduces each section.

658 Morgan, Edmund S., and Morgan, Helen M. THE STAMP ACT CRISIS:
PROLOGUE TO REVOLUTION. Chapel Hill: University of North Carolina Press, 1953. 320 p.

> A lively account of the crisis of 1764-65. The Morgans
> cover the main points of the dispute between the colonies
> and Britain and give insight into the feelings of the main
> characters in the confrontation.

659 Mullett, Charles F. FUNDAMENTAL LAW AND THE AMERICAN REVO-
LUTION, 1760-1776. 1933. Reprint. New York: Octagon Books,
1966. 216 p.

> An examination of the eighteenth century understanding
> of natural law by the English and American authors most
> widely quoted, and an exposition of how the concept
> was adapted to the argument of the colonists on such
> subjects as natural and civil rights, taxation, equality,
> and legislation.

660 Rossiter, Clinton. SEEDTIME OF THE REPUBLIC: THE ORIGIN OF THE
AMERICAN TRADITION OF POLITICAL LIBERTY. New York: Harcourt,
Brace, 1953. 572 p.

> A comprehensive examination of the development of

American political liberty. Rossiter discusses the major
political, economic, and religious forces working toward
freedom, traces the contributions of six significant leaders
(Thomas Hooker, Roger Williams, John Wise, Jonathan
Mayhew, Richard Bland, and Benjamin Franklin), and
examines important writings advocating the rights of
man and the formalization of that idea in a frame of
government.

661 Ubbelohde, Carl. THE VICE-ADMIRALTY COURTS AND THE AMERICAN
REVOLUTION. Chapel Hill: University of North Carolina Press, 1960.
242 p.

Describes the policies and procedures of the courts and
the types of cases that came before them. The controversies stemming from the courts' practices fed the fires
of Revolution. Ubbelohde begins his account in 1763
and carries it to the outbreak of the war.

vi. Intellectual and Social Life

662 Boorstin, Daniel J. THE LOST WORLD OF THOMAS JEFFERSON. 1948.
Reprint. Boston: Beacon Press, 1960. 317 p. Paperbound.

An attempt to re-create the "Jeffersonian Circle" of
intellectuals whose interaction helped determine the
direction of the Enlightenment in America. The circle
included David Rittenhouse, Dr. Benjamin Rush, Benjamin Smith Barton, Joseph Priestley, Charles Wilson
Peale, and Thomas Paine. Boorstin provides an overview of the intellectual world of Jefferson and his
friends and then examines their views on such topics
as God, nature, equality, government, toleration,
education, and materialism.

663 Colbourn, H. Trevor. THE LAMP OF EXPERIENCE: WHIG HISTORY AND
THE INTELLECTUAL ORIGINS OF THE AMERICAN REVOLUTION. Chapel
Hill: University of North Carolina Press, 1965. 255 p.

A study of the English historical writings that influenced
the generation of Revolutionary Americans. Colbourn
analyzes the Whig theory of history, reviews the works
of its exemplars, and indicates the ways in which it
influenced the Americans in their argument against the
mother country. He includes catalogues of these works
in private colleges and public collections, to indicate
how widely read these works were.

664 Granger, Bruce I. POLITICAL SATIRE IN THE AMERICAN REVOLUTION,
1763-1783. 1960. Reprint. New York: Russell & Russell, 1971. 328 p.

A literary scholar's analysis. He gives background on
the literary scene and then deals with satirical responses
to the Stamp Act and other crises, the British government, the Continental Congress, the British and American armies, the loyalists, etc.

665   Greene, Evarts B. THE REVOLUTIONARY GENERATION, 1763-1790.
1943. Reprint. Chicago: Quadrangle Books, 1971. 500 p. Paperbound.

A comprehensive history of the period, going much
beyond the political and military spheres to include
social, intellectual, religious, economic, and other
aspects of American life.

Gummere, R.M. THE AMERICAN COLONIAL MIND AND THE CLAS-
SICAL TRADITION. See no. 558.

666   Jameson, J. Franklin. THE AMERICAN REVOLUTION CONSIDERED AS
A SOCIAL MOVEMENT. 1926. Reprint. Boston: Beacon Press, 1956.
117 p. Paperbound.

This brief but seminal work attempts to demonstrate that
Revolutionary attitudes went much beyond the political
sphere and permeated cultural and social aspects of
American life. Originally delivered in lecture form.

667   Jefferson, Thomas. NOTES ON THE STATE OF VIRGINIA. Edited by
William Peden. 1954. Reprint. New York: W.W. Norton, 1972. 342
p. Illus., map. Paperbound.

A leading work expressing the ideas and attitudes of
the American Enlightenment, in an edition that includes
informative notes. Jefferson wrote this book in response
to the inquiries of a French diplomat. He discusses the
ecology and demography of Virginia and comments on
the mores of its people. A good source for his ideas
on government, education, science, religion, and
slavery as it affected both the black and white man.

668   Koch, Adrienne, ed. THE AMERICAN ENLIGHTENMENT: THE SHAPING
OF THE AMERICAN EXPERIMENT AND A FREE SOCIETY. New York:
George Braziller, 1965. 669 p.

An anthology of the writings of five giants of the Enlightenment in America: Benjamin Franklin, John Adams,
Thomas Jefferson, James Madison, Alexander Hamilton.
Koch provides an over-all introduction, and introductions to the writings of each figure, as well as excerpts
that give a keen insight into their private and public
lives.

669 Main, Jackson Turner. THE SOCIAL STRUCTURE OF REVOLUTIONARY
AMERICA. Princeton, N.J.: Princeton University Press, 1965. 338 p.

Covering the period between 1763 and 1788, the author
investigates class structure from an economic and social
point of view. He gives examples of upward mobility
on the part of men who began at the bottom of both
economic and social ladders, using acquisition of property as his measure. Although calling this a tentative
study, he concludes that there was a long-term tendency
toward greater inequality.

670 Savelle, Max. SEEDS OF LIBERTY: THE GENESIS OF THE AMERICAN
MIND. 1948. Reprint. Seattle: University of Washington Press, 1965.
635 p. Illus., ports., maps, music, facsims.

This extended discussion of the cultural and intellectual
life of Americans in the eighteenth century, with flash-
backs to earlier periods, covers all areas. A chapter on
music, written by Cyclone Covey, is included.

671 Schlesinger, Arthur M. THE BIRTH OF A NATION: A PORTRAIT OF
THE AMERICAN PEOPLE ON THE EVE OF INDEPENDENCE. New York:
Alfred A. Knopf, 1968. 277 p.

Attempts to determine the interrelationships of social,
intellectual, economic, religious, artistic, and recrea-
tional aspects of American life in the century and a
half preceding the Revolution. Written for a popular
audience.

672 _____. PRELUDE TO INDEPENDENCE: THE NEWSPAPER WAR ON
BRITAIN, 1764-1776. New York: Alfred A. Knopf, 1958. 343 p.

The press did much to stir up the passions of Americans
against the British government. Schlesinger analyzes
the newspaper war, giving many examples of the type
of rhetoric used. He does not, however, consider the
pamphlet warfare, which was also quite influential. He
provides appendices on newspaper circulation, paper
manufacturing and the taxes levied on it, and other
pertinent matters.

673 Tyler, Moses Coit. THE LITERARY HISTORY OF THE AMERICAN RE-
VOLUTION. 2 vols. in 1. 1897. Reprint. New York: Burt Franklin,
1970.

A pioneer study of the literature of the Revolutionary
period which has not been superseded. Tyler sympathetically but critically examines many leaders of the day.
He believes that literature reflects the attitudes of a

period even as it helps form them. Covers the period
from 1763 to 1783.

vii. Loyalists

674　Brown, Wallace. THE GOOD AMERICANS: THE LOYALISTS IN THE
AMERICAN REVOLUTION. New York: William Morrow, 1969. 313 p.

> A study of the motivations and actions of those who
> remained faithful to the British government during and
> after the American Revolution. The author deals with
> the fate of the Tories both at the hands of their fellow
> Americans who became revolutionaries and those of the
> British government.

675　Nelson, William H. THE AMERICAN TORY. New York: Oxford University Press, 1961. 194 p.

> Deals with the conflict of the Tories with their fellow
> Americans. Nelson believes they failed to make their
> points effectively because they were not organized,
> failed as propagandists, and concerned themselves with
> problems of administrative rather than constitutional re-
> form. Men such as Thomas Hutchinson and Joseph Gal-
> loway, who are discussed at length, could not compete
> with the capable leaders of the patriots. The removal
> of the Tories to England and other parts of the empire
> deprived America of an "organic conservatism" which
> did not reappear.

676　Norton, Mary Beth. THE BRITISH-AMERICANS: THE LOYALIST EXILES
IN ENGLAND, 1774-1789. Boston: Little, Brown, 1972. 333 p.

> A study of the Tories who chose to migrate and live in
> England (about 7,000 of them) rather than remain in an
> independent United States. Norton deals with the at-
> titude of the British government toward these loyal sons.
> They were not received with cordiality and were not
> consulted on American problems; they encountered finan-
> cial problems when the war lasted longer than they
> expected and then, when it was lost, had to adapt to
> life in their new environment.

677　Oliver, Peter. PETER OLIVER'S ORIGIN AND PROGRESS OF THE
AMERICAN REVOLUTION: A TORY VIEW. Edited by Douglass Adair
and John A. Schutz. San Marino, Calif.: Huntington Library, 1961.
194 p. Port.

> Oliver, the Massachusetts iron manufacturer and jurist
> who could not accept the Revolution, moved to Halifax,
> Nova Scotia, and then settled in Britain. Living on a
> pension from the government, he put down his account

of events in America. An emotional, biased account, but valuable as a demonstration of the state of mind of some Tories.

678 Smith, Paul H. LOYALISTS AND REDCOATS: A STUDY IN BRITISH REVOLUTIONARY POLICY. Chapel Hill: University of North Carolina Press, 1964. 211 p.

Deals with British attempts to use the American Tories in the prosecution of the Revolutionary War. Although the government under Lord North vacillated on use of the Loyalists in the armed forces, increasing reluctance to send more British troops to the colonies spurred the desire to do so. Smith believes that Britain's failure to provide guidance and leadership to the Tories hampered the war effort.

viii. Religion

679 Allen, Ethan. REASON THE ONLY ORACLE OF MAN. Edited by John Pell. New York: Scholars' Facsimiles & Reprints, 1940. 566 p.

A facsimile reprint of the 1784 work on Deism which scandalized orthodox Christians. Probably a joint work by Allen and Dr. Thomas Young. The witty attacks on Christianity and superstition are balanced by an attempt to construct a "compendious system" of natural religion. Pell provides an editorial introduction and appends Allen's sequel to the work. The book provides an excellent example of the thinking of the Deists.

680 Baldwin, Alice M. THE NEW ENGLAND CLERGY AND THE AMERICAN REVOLUTION. Durham, N.C.: Duke University Press, 1928. 235 p.

Examines the influence of the preachments of the New England clergy, especially the Congregationalists and Presbyterians, on the climate that led to the Revolution. Baldwin judges their influence to have been great, to a large extent because their theological and ecclesiastical preoccupations so closely paralleled the issues that became prominent in the period of contention.

681 Bridenbaugh, Carl. MITRE AND SCEPTRE: TRANSATLANTIC FAITHS, IDEAS, PERSONALITIES AND POLITICS, 1689-1775. New York: Oxford University Press, 1962. 368 p. Illus.

Asserts that religion was central to the argument between the mother country and the American colonies, since the period was more an age of faith than of reason. The attempt to introduce the English bishopric in America was one of the causes celebres of the time and stirred

violent emotions. The relation between church and
state was, therefore, an essential consideration in the
events leading to the Revolution.

682   Koch, G. Adolf. REPUBLICAN RELIGION: THE AMERICAN REVOLU-
TION AND THE CULT OF REASON. 1933. Reprint. Gloucester, Mass.:
Peter Smith, 1964. 350 p. Front.

An attempt to rehabilitate Deism and free thought in
the Revolutionary period, which Koch believes were
neglected or denounced because historians tended to
be clergymen. He deals with Ethan Allen, Elihu Palmer, Thomas Paine, and "respectable Deists," among
others.

683   Morais, Herbert M. DEISM IN EIGHTEENTH-CENTURY AMERICA. 1934.
Reprint. New York: Russell & Russell, 1960. 203 p.

A comprehensive look at the religion of the Enlightenment. Morais finds deistic elements in the thoughts on
nature of the late Puritan Cotton Mather and traces the
rise of natural religion and its challenge to Christianity
in the persons of Ethan Allen, Thomas Paine, Elihu
Palmer, and many others.

ix. Science and Technology

See works listed under Science and Technology, 3,B,3,j.

x. Urban Life

684   Bridenbaugh, Carl. CITIES IN REVOLT: URBAN LIFE IN AMERICA,
1743-1776. 1955. Reprint. New York: Capricorn Books, 1964. 466
p. Illus., ports., map, facsims. Paperbound.

This history of urban life stresses developments in Boston,
Newport, New York, Philadelphia, and Charleston during
both war and peace. Bridenbaugh describes the physical
characteristics of these urban centers, their economic
life and commerce, and various aspects of their cultural
lives: music, art, science, and philanthropy.

685   Bridenbaugh, Carl, and Bridenbaugh, Jessica. REBELS AND GENTLE-
MEN: PHILADELPHIA IN THE AGE OF FRANKLIN. 1942. Reprint.
New York: Oxford University Press, 1965. 413 p. Illus., front.,
ports., maps.

Philadelphia became, during the Age of Franklin, the
second most important city in the British Empire. While
not minimizing Franklin's great contribution to his adopted

city, the Bridenbaughs trace in rich detail the contributions of many others, prominent and obscure, to the
development of its cultural life.

xi. Warfare

686   Alden, John R. THE AMERICAN REVOLUTION, 1775-1783. New York:
Harper & Row, 1954. 294 p. Illus., maps.

A history devoted to a large extent to the military
operations of the Revolution. Alden draws on recent
research by British and American scholars and includes
maps of the crucial battles.

687   Higginbotham, Don. THE WAR OF AMERICAN INDEPENDENCE: MILI-
TARY ATTITUDES, POLICIES, AND PRACTICE, 1763-1789. New York:
Macmillan, 1971. 509 p. Illus., maps.

A history that stresses civilian control of the military.
Higginbotham sets out in detail the efforts of the Congress to maintain its authority over military leaders and
forces, stressing policy matters rather than battlefield
operations.

688   Peckham, Howard H. THE WAR FOR INDEPENDENCE: A MILITARY
HISTORY. Chicago: University of Chicago Press, 1958. 226 p.

Stressing military operations, Peckham concludes that
the Americans won the war despite great odds against
such an accomplishment. They lacked unity; the Congress lacked power; the officers lacked experience.
But bumbling British leadership was no match for the
determination of the American leaders to control their
own destiny.

689   Rice, Howard C., Jr., and Brown, Anne S.K., trans. and eds. THE
AMERICAN CAMPAIGNS OF ROCHAMBEAU'S ARMY, 1780, 1781, 1783.
2 vols. Princeton, N.J.: Princeton University Press, 1972. Illus.,
maps.

Primary material, handsomely presented. These descriptions of the inhabitants and topography of the American
colonies, with detailed maps, by three French officers
(Clermont-Crevecoeur, Verger, and Berthier) assigned to
aid in the American Revolution are useful in attaining
a contemporary view of the Americans and their social
and natural environment on the eve of independence.

2. The Constitutions

a. ARTICLES OF CONFEDERATION

690 Jensen, Merrill. THE ARTICLES OF CONFEDERATION: AN INTERPRE-
TATION OF THE SOCIAL-CONSTITUTIONAL HISTORY OF THE AMERI-
CAN REVOLUTION, 1774-1781. 1940. Reprint. Madison: University
of Wisconsin Press, 1966. 309 p. Paperbound.

> Jensen places the development of the first constitution of
> the United States in the context of Revolutionary develop-
> ments in the various states, traces the internal discontent
> that led to the war and the Declaration of Independence,
> and shows how the provisions of the Articles evolved from
> the interests of the thirteen states.

691 _____. THE NEW NATION: A HISTORY OF THE UNITED STATES
DURING THE CONFEDERATION, 1781-1789. 1950. Reprint. New
York: Vintage Books, n.d. 464 p. Paperbound.

> This work examines the traditional view that the United
> States lived through a "critical period" in the years it
> was governed under the Articles of Confederation. Jen-
> sen discovers many positive accomplishments under a
> constitution which was deliberately designed to maintain
> the sovereignty of the individual states. The confedera-
> tion, he maintains, achieved a fair measure of economic
> and political well-being for the people.

692 McDonald, Forrest, and McDonald, Helen Shapiro, eds. CONFEDERA-
TION AND CONSTITUTION, 1781-1789. Columbia: University of South
Carolina Press, 1968. 230 p.

> The editors have brought together documents, official
> and private correspondence, speeches, essays, and other
> materials, to convey contemporary attitudes toward the
> government under the Articles of Confederation (the lack
> of power of the Congress is accented), and the develop-
> ment of interest in strengthening it under the new Con-
> stitution.

b. CONSTITUTIONAL CONVENTION, 1787

693 Beard, Charles A. AN ECONOMIC INTERPRETATION OF THE CONSTI-
TUTION OF THE UNITED STATES. 1913. Reprint. New York: Free
Press, 1965. 352 p. Paperbound.

> A controversial work which is still being debated.
> Beard, although admitting that he was working with
> quite limited sources, interpreted the Constitution as

the work of men who were guided by their own economic interests; he holds that the greater mass of the people were kept from having their views represented by the restrictive, property-based suffrage provisions of the time.

694   Bowen, Catherine Drinker. MIRACLE AT PHILADELPHIA: THE STORY OF THE CONSTITUTIONAL CONVENTION, MAY TO SEPTEMBER, 1787. Boston: Little, Brown, 1966. 365 p. Illus., ports.

Summarizes the issues involved in the Convention, giving in readable, popular style a day-to-day account of the debates, and characterizations of the participants.

695   Brown, Robert E. CHARLES BEARD AND THE CONSTITUTION: A CRITICAL ANALYSIS OF "AN ECONOMIC INTERPRETATION OF THE CONSTITUTION." 1956. Reprint. New York: W.W. Norton, 1965. 219 p. Paperbound.

In this severe stricture on Charles Beard and his ECONOMIC INTERPRETATION OF THE CONSTITUTION, q.v., no. 693, Brown shows that Beard's evidence was incomplete and that he drew unwarranted conclusions from it. The author retraces Beard's procedure and refutes him at every turn.

696   Farrand, Max. THE FRAMING OF THE CONSTITUTION OF THE UNITED STATES. 1913. Reprint. New Haven, Conn.: Yale University Press, 1967. 293 p. Paperbound.

In relatively brief compass, Farrand describes the gathering of notables at the Constitutional Convention and the course of the debates. His character sketches are useful for understanding the contending interests represented.

697   _____, ed. THE RECORDS OF THE FEDERAL CONVENTION OF 1787. 3 vols. 1911. Reprint. New Haven, Conn.: Yale University Press, 1966.

Brings together the scattered sources on what transpired at the Convention in Philadelphia that produced the Constitution. Farrand provides a day-by-day account of the proceedings, using the notes made by various participants. Also included are the Virginia, New Jersey, and other plans presented at the Convention, as well as correspondence of participants and observers of the momentous gathering.

698   McDonald, Forrest. WE THE PEOPLE: THE ECONOMIC ORIGINS OF THE CONSTITUTION. Chicago: University of Chicago Press, 1958. 446 p.

A detailed refutation of Charles Beard's influential work, AN ECONOMIC INTERPRETATION OF THE CONSTITUTION OF THE UNITED STATES, q.v., no. 693. McDonald condemns the superficiality of the surveys Beard made of the economic holdings of the delegates to the Constitutional Convention, and the defects in his methodology. He demonstrates that Beard's generalizations were, therefore, invalid.

699 Madison, James. NOTES OF DEBATES IN THE FEDERAL CONVENTION OF 1787. Athens: Ohio University Press, 1966. 682 p.

Although one of the most active participants in the debates that resulted in the Constitution, Madison kept the fullest set of notes of the day-to-day activities of the convention. This edition includes an introduction by Adrienne Koch which provides information on Madison's original notations and his later treatment of them. Unfortunately, no index is included.

700 Rossiter, Clinton. 1787: THE GRAND CONVENTION. New York: Macmillan, 1966. 443 p. Illus., ports.

A thorough analysis of the events leading to the Constitutional Convention and of the proceedings of that body. Rossiter treats the Convention as a "case study" in democratic politics and a splendid example of decision making in the process of bargaining. Rossiter sees the Convention, which chose among various options, as an example of man's ability to control history to some extent.

701 Schuyler, Robert L. THE CONSTITUTION OF THE UNITED STATES: AN HISTORICAL SURVEY OF ITS FORMATION. New York: Macmillan, 1923. 220 p.

Originally delivered as lectures at Cambridge University and the London School of Economics. Schuyler presents an analysis of the Articles of Confederation and the Constitution, attempting to demonstrate how they grew out of American experience.

702 U.S. House. DOCUMENTS ILLUSTRATIVE OF THE FORMATION OF THE UNION OF THE AMERICAN STATES. Edited by Charles C. Tansill. 69th Cong., 1st sess. House Document no. 398. Washington, D.C.: Government Printing Office, 1927. 1,125 p.

A useful compilation of materials relating to the Constitutional Convention of 1787. The Farrand edition, q.v., no. 697, is superior in that it provides cross references and other scholarly aids.

703 Van Doren, Carl C. THE GREAT REHEARSAL: THE STORY OF THE
MAKING AND RATIFYING OF THE CONSTITUTION OF THE UNITED
STATES. New York: Viking Press, 1948. 348 p. Illus., ports.

Interprets the Constitutional Convention as the forerunner
of the writing of a constitution for a world government.
Van Doren does not, however, impose this thesis on
the history he relates. He discusses the plans for a
new government submitted by contending groups and
explores the arguments of the "federalists" and "anti-
federalists."

704 Warren, Charles. THE MAKING OF THE CONSTITUTION. 1928. Reprint. New York: Barnes & Noble, 1967. 844 p.

A day-by-day account of the Constitutional Convention.
Warren, a leading constitutional scholar, explains the
proceedings and also quotes liberally from letters of
the participants, newspaper accounts, etc.

c. THE DEBATE ON RATIFICATION

705 Borden, Morton, ed. THE ANTIFEDERALIST PAPERS. East Lansing:
Michigan State University Press, 1965. 272 p.

This imaginative collection brings together counteressays
to those in THE FEDERALIST, q.v., no. 707. Borden
has collected materials that appeared in the newspapers
in 1787-88, from the pens of those who opposed adoption of the Constitution and has arranged them to cor-
respond to the topics dealt with in the Hamilton-Madison-
Jay collection. A useful contribution to an understanding of the issues in debate.

706 Elliott, Jonathan, ed. THE DEBATES IN THE SEVERAL STATE CON-
VENTIONS ON THE ADOPTION OF THE FEDERAL CONSTITUTION AS
RECOMMENDED BY THE GENERAL CONVENTION AT PHILADELPHIA
IN 1787. 2d ed. 5 vols. 1888-96. Reprint. New York: Burt Frank-
lin, 1968.

Materials gathered from the ratifying conventions and
also from the debate in the surrounding communities,
including pamphlets and newspapers.

707 Hamilton, Alexander, et al. THE FEDERALIST. Edited by Jacob E.
Cooke. Middletown, Conn.: Wesleyan University Press, 1961. 702 p.

Newspaper essays advocating the adoption of the Constitution of 1787 by three prominent politicians of the

day: Alexander Hamilton, James Madison, and John Jay.
The editor provides a text as close as possible to the
original and indicates changes made by the authors in
later editions. He also discusses problems of authorship,
since the originals were signed with the nom de plume
"Publius" and it is not known for certain who wrote
certain of the installments.

708 Lewis, John D., ed. ANTI-FEDERALISTS VERSUS FEDERALISTS: SELECT-
ED DOCUMENTS. San Francisco: Chandler Publishing Co., 1967. 434
p.

Documents are grouped under the following headings:
Minority Reports from the Philadelphia Convention,
General Defenses of the Constitution, Debate Over
the Ratification: Anti-Federalist Arguments, Defense
of the Constitution by the Federalist. An extensive
editorial introduction is included.

709 Main, Jackson Turner. THE ANTI-FEDERALISTS: CRITICS OF THE CON-
STITUTION, 1781-1788. Chapel Hill: University of North Carolina Press,
1961. 323 p.

This examination of the arguments of those who opposed
adoption of the Constitution of 1787 analyzes the debates that took place in the state ratifying conventions
in order to isolate the main themes running through the
argument. Objection to a strong national government
emerges as an important point which was shared both
by those who sought more democracy as well as those
who opposed such a development. Main reckons that
the majority of the people opposed the Constitution.

710 Rutland, Robert A. THE ORDEAL OF THE CONSTITUTION: THE ANTI-
FEDERALISTS AND THE RATIFICATION STRUGGLE OF 1787-1788. Norman: University of Oklahoma Press, 1966. 342 p. Ports., facsims.

Examines the contest over the adoption of the Constitution. The author believes the opposition of the anti-
federalists stemmed from their concern for the protection
of civil liberties and that their lack of organization and
a constructive alternative led to their failure.

d. THE BILL OF RIGHTS

711 Levy, Leonard W. ORIGINS OF THE FIFTH AMENDMENT: THE RIGHT
AGAINST SELF-INCRIMINATION. New York: Oxford University Press,
1968. 573 p.

A history of the origin of the right against self-incrimination. Levy shows that it was a well-known principle

in English law before it was written into the Bill of
Rights. He traces it back to the thirteenth century and
shows how the principle was applied, or not applied,
in specific cases through the centuries.

712 _____, ed. FREEDOM OF THE PRESS FROM ZENGER TO JEFFERSON:
EARLY AMERICAN LIBERTARIAN THEORIES. Indianapolis: Bobbs-Merrill,
1966. 494 p.

A collection of primary materials from the 1730s to the
early 1800s, dealing with sedition, libel, and other
problems confronted by the press in a free society.
Levy has written an extensive introduction to the collection as a whole and brief introductions to each group
of documents.

713 Miller, Helen Hill. THE CASE FOR LIBERTY. Chapel Hill: University
of North Carolina Press, 1965. 270 p. Illus., ports., facsims.

An examination of the legal precedents for the American
Bill of Rights. The author has selected important court
cases and has set them in the context of the philosophical and political theory of the time.

714 Rutland, Robert A. THE BIRTH OF THE BILL OF RIGHTS, 1776-1791.
Chapel Hill: University of North Carolina Press, 1955. 349 p.

Traces the development of the concept of rights from
English beginnings to the ratification of the Bill of
Rights as amendments to the Constitution in 1791. Rut-
land stresses the importance of George Mason's "Virginia
Declaration of Rights" as an inspiration and guide.

3. The States

715 Brown, Robert E. MIDDLE-CLASS DEMOCRACY AND THE REVOLUTION
IN MASSACHUSETTS, 1691-1780. 1955. Reprint. New York: Russell
& Russell, 1968. 467 p.

An attempt to demonstrate that land ownership and the
franchise were much more prevalent than has been generally assumed. Thus, Brown believes, the Bay State
fought in the Revolution to preserve democracy rather
than to achieve it.

716 Brown, Robert E., and Brown, B. Katherine. VIRGINIA, 1705-1786:
DEMOCRACY OR ARISTOCRACY? East Lansing: Michigan State University Press, 1964. 333 p. Map.

Attempts to demonstrate that Virginia was not in the
control of an aristocracy, but rather had strong demo-

cratic elements. The authors have made extensive use
of archival materials in their effort to overthrow the
traditional view.

717 Brunhouse, Robert L. THE COUNTER-REVOLUTION IN PENNSYLVANIA,
1776-1790. 1942. Reprint. New York: Octagon Books, 1971. 376
p. Maps, tables.

Pennsylvania was to adopt one of the most radical of
state constitutions in the Revolution. Brunhouse traces
the rise of the radical party, its brief reign, and the
"counter-revolution" which overthrew it and established
the conservatives in power.

718 Main, Jackson Turner. POLITICAL PARTIES BEFORE THE CONSTITUTION.
Chapel Hill: University of North Carolina Press, 1973. 501 p. Illus.,
maps, tables.

The application of quantitative techniques, with the use
of a computer, to determine the voting patterns within
the legislatures of the American states, from the outbreak of the Revolution to the eve of the adoption of
the Constitution. The author uses maps and tables to
help convey the significance of his findings.

719 _____. THE SOVEREIGN STATES, 1775-1783. New York: New View-
points, 1973. 502 p. Map.

In this narrative of developments in the thirteen original
states during the course of the Revolutionary War, Main
treats distinctive local issues but relates them to the
problems confronting the new United States as a whole
as it struggled for independence.

720 _____. THE UPPER HOUSE IN REVOLUTIONARY AMERICA, 1763-1788.
Madison: University of Wisconsin Press, 1967. 333 p.

An analysis of the membership of the councils or senates
of the various colonies/states. Main, using quantitative
methods and depending on legal records, genealogies,
newspapers, etc., constructs generalizations about the
make-up and the actions of the upper houses.

721 Nevins, Allan. THE AMERICAN STATES DURING AND AFTER THE RE-
VOLUTION, 1775-1789. 1924. Reprint. New York: Augustus M.
Kelley, 1969. 746 p. Ports.

Nevins deals with political and economic developments
in each of the thirteen states and sets these into a
framework that encompasses the continent. This remains
the most detailed account available.

722 Patterson, Stephen E. POLITICAL PARTIES IN REVOLUTIONARY MASSA-CHUSETTS. Madison: University of Wisconsin Press, 1973. 310 p. Maps, tables.

> An attempt to demonstrate that political parties were
> formed in the Bay State during the course of the Revo-
> lution, even though it was then the style to decry such
> a development. The author uses the controversies over
> the writing of the constitutions of 1778 and 1780 to
> demonstrate his point.

723 Pole, J.R. POLITICAL REPRESENTATION IN ENGLAND AND THE ORIGINS OF THE AMERICAN REPUBLIC. New York: St. Martin's Press, 1966. 623 p.

> Pole deals with ideas on parliamentary representation
> in Britain and then traces constitutional developments in
> the United States in the Revolutionary period, giving
> particular attention to Virginia, Massachusetts, and
> Pennsylvania.

724 Selsam, J. Paul. THE PENNSYLVANIA CONSTITUTION OF 1776: A STUDY IN REVOLUTIONARY DEMOCRACY. 1936. Reprint. New York: DaCapo Press, 1971. 290 p.

> The Pennsylvania Constitution of 1776 was considered
> the most radically democratic of the constitutions of
> the former colonies. Selsam describes its origins, the
> great controversy it engendered, and the relation of
> these events to the Revolution.

725 Taylor, Robert J., ed. MASSACHUSETTS, COLONY TO COMMON-WEALTH: DOCUMENTS ON THE FORMATION OF ITS CONSTITUTION, 1775-1780. Chapel Hill: University of North Carolina Press, 1961. 177 p. Map.

> Includes materials by John Adams and others who were
> responsible for the formulation of one of the more stable
> and influential of the early state constitutions.

4. Prominent Individuals

GENERAL

726 Morris, Richard B. SEVEN WHO SHAPED OUR DESTINY: THE FOUND-ING FATHERS AS REVOLUTIONARIES. New York: Harper & Row, 1973. 334 p. Illus., ports.

> A collection of biographical sketches of significant
> figures in the Revolution and the founding of the new
> nation: Franklin, Washington, John Adams, Jefferson,

Jay, Madison, and Hamilton. Morris attempts to show
that each of these men underwent an identity crisis and
emerged a stable and balanced individual capable of
providing responsible leadership in the American cause.

JOHN ADAMS

727 Butterfield, Lyman H., et al., eds. ADAMS FAMILY CORRESPONDENCE.
2 vols. to date. Cambridge, Mass.: Harvard University Press, 1963- .
Illus., ports., maps, facsims., charts.

Projected at twenty volumes, the Adams family correspondence will run from 1761 to 1889. These present
volumes include the letters of John and Abigail Adams
to each other and to and from friends. Both make
incisive comments on the issues and personalities of
their day. Volume 1: DECEMBER 1761-MAY 1776;
volume 2: JUNE 1776-MARCH 1778.

728 _____. DIARY AND AUTOBIOGRAPHY OF JOHN ADAMS. 4 vols.
Cambridge, Mass.: Harvard University Press, 1961. Illus., ports.,
plates, facsims.

Part of the new edition of the Adams Papers. Adams's
diary is a revealing document in which he argues with
himself about his goals and accomplishments, and his
failings. It is a mine of information on the public and
private figures with whom he had dealings and on political and social affairs. The autobiography, which in
his papers is in chaotic state, is fragmentary but revealing of his personality and attitudes. Volume 1: DIARY,
1755-1770; volume 2: DIARY, 1771-1781; volume 3:
DIARY, 1782-1804; AUTOBIOGRAPHY, THROUGH
1776; volume 4: AUTOBIOGRAPHY, 1777-1780. Index.

729 _____. THE EARLIEST DIARY OF JOHN ADAMS. Cambridge, Mass.:
Harvard University Press, 1966. 142 p. Illus., ports., facsims.

Discovered after the main body of the Adams diaries
had been published, this earlier journal covers a period
of almost two years (June 1753-April 1754; September
1758-January 1759) and reveals the young man's thoughts
on many topics--natural law, reason, religion, justice--
as well as on his own reading in the classics and divi-
nity.

730 Cappon, Lester J., ed. THE ADAMS-JEFFERSON LETTERS: THE COM-
PLETE CORRESPONDENCE BETWEEN THOMAS JEFFERSON AND ABIGAIL
AND JOHN ADAMS. 2 vols. Chapel Hill: University of North Caro-
lina Press, 1959. Illus., fronts., ports.

A well-edited version of the letters John and Abigail
Adams and Thomas Jefferson exchanged over a fifty-year
period. The correspondence is particularly notable in
the years of their retirement from public office, when
Adams and Jefferson re-fought, in a much more philosophical vein, the old political battles and exchanged
thoughts on literature, history, philosophy, their contemporaries, and many other matters. Volume 1: 1777-
1804; volume 2: 1812-1826.

731 Chinard, Gilbert. HONEST JOHN ADAMS. Boston: Little, Brown,
1933. 371 p. Front., ports., plates.

A political biography, but one which necessarily relates
politics to Adams's personality and outlook on life.
Chinard conveys the disturbing thought that Adams was
often isolated and lonely because he was so open, blunt,
and honest. He bases his study primarily on original
sources.

732 Koch, Adrienne, and Peden, William, eds. THE SELECTED WRITINGS
OF JOHN AND JOHN QUINCY ADAMS. New York: Alfred A. Knopf,
1946. 483 p. Ports.

Excerpts from the letters, important publications, and
public papers of the two Adamses, father and son. The
editors provide biographical background on both. The
excerpts are relatively short, but informative.

733 Smith, Page. JOHN ADAMS. 2 vols. Garden City, N.Y.: Doubleday, 1962. Illus., ports.

The first biography to make full use of the recently
opened Adams Papers. Smith is particularly good at
sketching the relationship between Adams and his wife
Abigail; these volumes are studded with choice excerpts
from their letters. His stress on the everyday life of
the Adams family does not hinder him, however, from
giving a full account of Adams as intellectual, politician, and statesman.

734 Wroth, L. Kinvin, and Zobel, Hiller B. LEGAL PAPERS OF JOHN
ADAMS. 3 vols. Cambridge, Mass.: Harvard University Press, 1965.
Illus., ports., maps, plans, facsims.

Part of the extensive edition of the Adams Papers now
in progress. This is a selection from the many Adams
legal papers extant. From these papers emerge vivid
vignettes of revolutionary Massachusetts and character
sketches of such leading lights as James Otis. Volume
1: INTRODUCTION, CASES 1-30; volume 2: CASES

31-62; volume 3: CASES 63 AND 64--THE BOSTON
MASSACRE TRIALS. Chronology. Index.

SAMUEL ADAMS

735 Miller, John C. SAM ADAMS: PIONEER IN PROPAGANDA. 1936.
Reprint. Stanford, Calif.: Stanford University Press, 1960. 437 p. Illus.

An exposition of the means, fair and foul, that Adams
used to stir up revolutionary fervor. Miller guides the
readers through the ins and outs of Massachusetts politics.

ETHAN ALLEN

736 Holbrook, Stewart H. ETHAN ALLEN. 1940. Reprint. Portland, Oreg.:
Binfords & Mort, 1958. 283 p. Illus.

A biography that accents the profane, blasphemous,
riotous, bibulous aspects of the frontier hero's life.
Writing with a light touch, Holbrook gives a lively
account of Allen's achievements in the Revolution and
the efforts of his Green Mountain Boys to validate the
land grants made by New Hampshire, as opposed to
those made by New York, in what was to become Vermont. He also sets forth the ideas contained in Allen's
deistic writings.

737 Pell, John. ETHAN ALLEN. Boston: Houghton Mifflin, 1929. 344 p.
Front., ports., plates, map, plan, facsims.

An objective, scholarly biography of the "Green Mountain Boy" who made a name for himself in the Revolution and in the struggle to create the state of Vermont.
Pell also considers Allen's writings, including his deistic
work, REASON THE ONLY ORACLE OF MAN, q.v.,
no. 679.

BENEDICT ARNOLD

738 Wallace, Willard M. TRAITOROUS HERO: THE LIFE AND FORTUNES
OF BENEDICT ARNOLD. 1954. Reprint. Freeport, N.Y.: Books for
Libraries Press, 1970. 407 p. Illus., ports., maps, facsims.

This detailed biography covers Arnold's years as a businessman as well as a soldier. Wallace underlines the
impulsive and egocentric aspects of Arnold's personality
and indulges in a certain amount of psychologizing to
explain his motives for treason.

ISAAC BACKUS

739 McLoughlin, William G. ISAAC BACKUS AND THE AMERICAN PIETISTIC
     TRADITION. Boston: Little, Brown, 1967. 264 p.

> A leader of the Baptists, Backus made an important
> contribution to the struggle for the disestablishment of
> churches and the separation of church and state in the
> period before the Revolution. McLoughlin's study makes
> wide use of primary sources in setting forth the prickly
> personality of Backus and the religious view of the man
> and his times.

CADWALLADER COLDEN

740 Keys, Alice M. CADWALLADER COLDEN: A REPRESENTATIVE EIGH-
     TEENTH CENTURY OFFICIAL. New York: Columbia University Press,
     1906. 389 p.

> Colden, a leading figure in science in the eighteenth
> century Enlightenment, is given full treatment by the
> author, who concentrates on his public life as a royal
> official in the province of New York.

BENJAMIN FRANKLIN

741 Aldridge, Alfred O. BENJAMIN FRANKLIN, PHILOSOPHER AND MAN.
     Philadelphia: Lippincott, 1965. 450 p. Port.

> By a professor of literature, this biography stresses
> Franklin the human being rather than the scientist and
> statesman. Aldridge uses Franklin's writings fully, be-
> lieving that routine remarks and jests reveal more of
> a man than do the public positions he takes.

Cohen, I. Bernard. FRANKLIN AND NEWTON. See no. 589.

742 Crane, Verner W. BENJAMIN FRANKLIN AND A RISING PEOPLE.
     Boston: Little, Brown, 1954. 219 p.

> Deals with the manifold aspects of Franklin's career in
> a learned narrative. Crane, without bending to praise,
> makes it obvious why Franklin was so well appreciated
> by his fellow countrymen for his efforts on behalf of
> the Revolution.

743 Fleming, Thomas J. THE MAN WHO DARED THE LIGHTNING: A NEW
     LOOK AT BENJAMIN FRANKLIN. New York: William Morrow, 1971.
     542 p. Illus., ports.

> A very favorable picture of Franklin. Fleming concen-

trates on his mature years, especially those spent abroad
in service to the colonies.

744 _____, ed. BENJAMIN FRANKLIN: A BIOGRAPHY IN HIS OWN
WORDS. New York: Newsweek; distributed by Harper & Row, 1972.
416 p. Illus.

This skillful blend of the famous AUTOBIOGRAPHY with
other autobiographical elements in Franklin's writings
results in a very full presentation of his life. The editor's brief, informative comments connect the excerpts,
and the text is enhanced by many illustrations of Franklin and his various associates and surroundings.

745 Franklin, Benjamin. AUTOBIOGRAPHY. Edited by Leonard W. Labaree
et al. New Haven, Conn.: Yale University Press, 1964. 351 p. Port.

A revealing self-portrait of the prototype self-made
American. Franklin reveals the techniques he used to
achieve success as a printer, businessman, and politician, and his efforts on behalf of his adopted community
of Philadelphia. Unfortunately he never got to write
about the Revolution and his part in it; his account remains unfinished.

746 Hanna, William S. BENJAMIN FRANKLIN AND PENNSYLVANIA POLI-
TICS. Stanford, Calif.: Stanford University Press, 1964. 249 p.

Concentrates on the years immediately following Franklin's retirement as a printer, when he became active
in politics. A less-than-flattering portrait of the new
politician emerges. The study throws much new light
on Pennsylvania politics.

747 Labaree, Leonard W., and Willcox, William B., eds. THE PAPERS OF
BENJAMIN FRANKLIN. 18 vols. to date. New Haven, Conn.: Yale
University Press, 1959- . Illus., fronts., ports., plates, maps, plans,
facsims.

This masterfully edited series of volumes includes letters
to and from Franklin, his writings on electricity, the
famous POOR RICHARD ALMANACS, etc., and will
continue until all of the known pieces by Franklin have
been published. Each volume contains an introduction,
chronology, and explanatory notes on each item. Volume 1 begins with 6 January 1706; volume 18 ends with
31 December 1771.

748 Van Doren, Carl C. BENJAMIN FRANKLIN. 1938. Reprint. Westport, Conn.: Greenwood Press, 1973. 866 p. Ports.

This full biography depends heavily on Franklin's own

words, taken both from his AUTOBIOGRAPHY, q.v.,
no. 745, and from his extensive writings. Van Doren
skillfully reveals the wit and humanity of the man, as
well as his many accomplishments undertaken on behalf
of himself and humanity.

ALEXANDER GARDEN

749 Berkeley, Edmund, and Berkeley, Dorothy. DR. ALEXANDER GARDEN
OF CHARLES TOWN. Chapel Hill: University of North Carolina Press,
1969. 393 p. Illus.

As a young Scotsman in the eighteenth century, Garden
migrated to Charleston, South Carolina, where he set
up medical practice and began a career of biological
exploration which earned him international recognition.
During the Revolution he remained a quiet loyalist, but
he migrated to England when his property was confiscated
at the close of the war. The Berkeleys include many
illustrations of his botanical and zoological discoveries
in this informative biography.

ALEXANDER HAMILTON

750 Miller, John C. ALEXANDER HAMILTON: PORTRAIT IN PARADOX.
New York: Harper & Brothers, 1959. 659 p. Illus.

A sympathetic account but one which strives for objectivity. Miller is more concerned with Hamilton's service to the nation than with his personal life, stressing
his insistent efforts to create a strong union. The book
provides a good history of the period.

751 Mitchell, Broadus. ALEXANDER HAMILTON. 2 vols. New York: Macmillan, 1957-62.

A scholarly but very sympathetic presentation of Hamilton's life. Mitchell tends to concentrate on the public
Hamilton, although he does necessarily deal with such
personal matters as his affair with Mrs. Reynolds, of
which Hamilton himself published a statement. Volume
1: YOUTH TO MATURITY, 1755-1788; volume 2: THE
NATIONAL ADVENTURE, 1788-1804.

752 Rossiter, Clinton. ALEXANDER HAMILTON AND THE CONSTITUTION.
New York: Harcourt, Brace & World, 1964. 382 p.

Discusses Hamilton's theories of law and politics and
how they influenced his attitude and actions during
and after the Constitutional Convention.

753 Stouzh, Gerald. ALEXANDER HAMILTON AND THE IDEA OF REPUBLICAN
GOVERNMENT. Stanford, Calif.: Stanford University Press, 1970. 286 p.

An analysis of Hamilton's thinking on republican government as it has existed, and as it should exist, in the
United States. Stourzh traces Hamilton's intellectual
debt to British thinkers and outlines his views on government and foreign policy.

754 Syrett, Harold C., ed. THE PAPERS OF ALEXANDER HAMILTON. 21
vols. to date. New York: Columbia University Press, 1961- . Illus.,
fronts., ports., maps, plans, facsims.

The authoritative edition of Hamilton now in progress;
the series has reached July 1798 with volume 21. The
editor provides extensive notes on each item.

JOHN HANCOCK

755 Allan, Herbert S. JOHN HANCOCK: PATRIOT IN PURPLE. New York:
Macmillan, 1948. 422 p. Illus., ports.

A journalist's account of the flamboyant merchant (and
smuggler) who was a leader of the Revolutionary forces
in Massachusetts and across colonial lines. Much detail
of the times is included, and Allan's view of Hancock
combines his heroic and unheroic sides.

PATRICK HENRY

756 Meade, Robert D. PATRICK HENRY. 2 vols. Philadelphia: Lippincott,
1957-69. Illus., plates, facsims.

Draws on materials in archives in Britain as well as in
the United States. A sympathetic but balanced account.
Volume 1: PATRIOT IN THE MAKING; volume 2:
PRACTICAL REVOLUTIONARY.

757 Tyler, Moses Coit. PATRICK HENRY. 1898. Reprint. New York: AMS
Press, 1972. 464 p. Illus.

A literary scholar's evaluation of the famous firebrand.
Tyler describes Henry's self-education in law, which was
minimal, his career as a politician, and his struggle
against adoption of the Constitution and for a bill of
rights. First published in 1887.

THOMAS HUTCHINSON

758 Bailyn, Bernard. THE ORDEAL OF THOMAS HUTCHINSON. Cambridge,
Mass.: Harvard University Press, 1974. 443 p.

An account of the thought and actions of the Massachusetts royal official and historian. Bailyn analyzes the
rigidity in Hutchinson's personality, which he believes
kept him from adapting to changing conditions and led
to his departure as a loyalist to England during the Revolution.

JOHN JAY

759 Jay, William. THE LIFE OF JOHN JAY. 2 vols. 1833. Reprint.
Freeport, N.Y.: Books for Libraries Press, 1972.

Written by Jay's son, this biography has the virtue of
including extended excerpts from his letters and papers.
Jay's career as diplomat, politician, and jurist is fully
covered.   .

760 Johnston, Henry P., ed. CORRESPONDENCE AND PUBLIC PAPERS OF
JOHN JAY. 4 vols. in 1. 1890-93. Reprint. New York: DaCapo
Press, 1971.

Jay served in many capacities in the Revolutionary and
post-Revolutionary period. He was governor of New
York; on the national level, his name is connected
with the FEDERALIST, q.v., no. 707, a famous treaty,
and the Supreme Court, where he served as first Chief
Justice. His years of public service are well represented
in his public papers and in his correspondence with such
colleagues as Washington, Franklin, Jefferson, John
Adams, and Hamilton.

THOMAS JEFFERSON

761 Boyd, Julian P., ed. THE PAPERS OF THOMAS JEFFERSON. 19 vols.
to date. Princeton, N.J.: Princeton University Press, 1950- . Illus.,
fronts., ports., maps, plans, facsims.

When completed, this series will include all of the
known letters of Jefferson (about 18,000) and all of
the extant letters to him (about 25,000), as well as his
public papers and other writings. The volumes include
very full, informative notes and excellent illustrations.
Volume 1 begins with 14 January 1760; volume 19 ends
with 31 March 1791.

762 Fleming, Thomas J. THE MAN FROM MONTICELLO: AN INTIMATE
LIFE OF THOMAS JEFFERSON. New York: William Morrow, 1969.
409 p. Illus., ports.

This biography, directed at a popular audience and

stressing Jefferson's virtues is based on the Jefferson papers and scholarly works; it is gracefully written and well illustrated.

763 Koch, Adrienne. JEFFERSON AND MADISON: THE GREAT COLLABO-RATION. 1950. Reprint. New York: Oxford University Press, 1969. 320 p. Paperbound.

The thesis of the book is that Jefferson and Madison were close collaborators in many ventures and some of their most brilliant accomplishments. Koch illustrates this with a generous use of their correspondence.

764 _____. THE PHILOSOPHY OF THOMAS JEFFERSON. 1943. Reprint. Chicago: Quadrangle Books, 1964. 224 p. Paperbound.

Traces the development of various aspects of Jefferson's thought, showing his indebtedness to the ancients and to his contemporaries as well as his more original for-mulations. His views on philosophy, religion, ethics, and ideology are examined in turn. Helpful in creating an understanding of Jefferson and the American Enlighten-ment generally.

765 Koch, Adrienne, and Peden, William, eds. THE LIFE AND SELECTED WRITINGS OF THOMAS JEFFERSON. New York: Modern Library, 1944. 800 p. Front.

A carefully chosen selection from the large corpus of Jefferson papers. Includes his autobiography, the Anas, the NOTES ON THE STATE OF VIRGINIA, as well as his personal correspondence and political writings. Many of the selections are abridged. The editors provide an introduction and headnotes.

766 Lipscomb, Andrew A., and Bergh, Albert Ellery, eds. THE WRITINGS OF THOMAS JEFFERSON. 20 vols. Washington, D.C.: Thomas Jeffer-son Memorial Association, 1903. Illus., fronts., ports., facsims.

Contains the Autobiography, Anas, letters written by Jefferson, and such major writings as the NOTES ON THE STATE OF VIRGINIA. A useful set until the pro-jected sixty-volume edition of PAPERS, q.v., no. 761, is completed.

767 Malone, Dumas. JEFFERSON AND HIS TIME. 5 vols. to date. Boston: Little, Brown, 1948- . Illus., fronts., ports., maps.

The most extensive biography of Jefferson, including de-tailed analyses of his personal and private concerns, as well as his ideas and public life, written in graceful

prose. This is a definitive biography which will include
a sixth and final volume. Volume 1: JEFFERSON THE
VIRGINIAN; volume 2: JEFFERSON AND THE RIGHTS
OF MAN; volume 3: JEFFERSON AND THE ORDEAL
OF LIBERTY; volume 4: JEFFERSON THE PRESIDENT:
FIRST TERM, 1801-1805; volume 5: JEFFERSON THE
PRESIDENT: SECOND TERM, 1805-1809.

768   Peterson, Merrill D. THOMAS JEFFERSON AND THE NEW NATION:
A BIOGRAPHY. New York: Oxford University Press, 1970. 1,072 p.
Illus., front., ports., plans, facsims.

A comprehensive, one-volume portrait. Peterson, with
graceful clarity, deals fully with Jefferson's intellectual
development, his revolutionary involvements, and his
career as a political leader. He accents three dominant
themes in Jefferson's life: democracy, nationalism, and
Enlightenment.

JOHN PAUL JONES

769   Morison, Samuel Eliot. JOHN PAUL JONES: A SAILOR'S BIOGRAPHY.
Boston: Little, Brown, 1959. 475 p. Illus., ports., maps.

A biography that combines stirring narrative with
scholarly evaluation. Morison gives a vivid picture
of Jones's personality, habits, personal relationships,
as well as his exploits. He gives a good account of
the state of the American Navy along the way. Included also is an evaluation of previous biographies.

ROBERT R. LIVINGSTON

770   Dangerfield, George. CHANCELLOR ROBERT R. LIVINGSTON OF NEW
YORK. New York: Harcourt, Brace, 1960. 540 p. Port., geneal.
table.

A much-needed reexamination of the life of the New
York politician who played an important role in the
revolutionary and early national years. Dangerfield
examines Livingston's political, legal, and diplomatic
functions (he and James Monroe arranged the Louisiana
Purchase while Livingston was American minister in
France) and his various scientific interests.

JAMES MADISON

771   Brant, Irving. THE FOURTH PRESIDENT: A LIFE OF JAMES MADISON.
Indianapolis: Bobbs-Merrill, 1970. 681 p.

A condensation by the author of his massive six-volume work, q.v., no. 772. Although he follows the organization of the original, he has omitted the scholarly apparatus and, to a great extent, has rewritten the text.

772 _____. JAMES MADISON. 6 vols. Indianapolis: Bobbs-Merrill, 1941-61. Front., ports., plates, facsims.

The definitive biography of the "father" of the American Constitution, who served also as president. Brant often displays partisanship in his treatment and is particularly concerned with refuting such earlier historians as Henry Adams, who have tended to minimize Madison's contributions. Volume 1: THE VIRGINIA REVOLUTIONIST; volume 2: THE NATIONALIST, 1780-1787; volume 3: FATHER OF THE CONSTITUTION, 1787-1800; volume 4: SECRETARY OF STATE, 1800-1809; volume 5: THE PRESIDENT, 1809-1812; volume 6: COMMANDER-IN-CHIEF, 1812-1836.

773 Hutchinson, William T., et al., eds. THE PAPERS OF JAMES MADISON. 8 vols. to date. Chicago: University of Chicago Press, 1962- . Illus., fronts., ports., maps, facsims.

A work in progress. Letters to and from Madison, his private and public papers, and speeches. Each volume has an editorial introduction to, and chronology of, the time period covered, as well as explanatory notes to the items. Volume 1 begins with 16 March 1751; volume 8 ends with 28 March 1786.

774 Ketcham, Ralph. JAMES MADISON: A BIOGRAPHY. New York: Macmillan, 1971. 767 p. Port., plates, map.

A full account of Madison's life and thought by one of the editors of the Madison PAPERS, q.v., no. 773. Ketcham is discriminating in his choice of materials, stressing Madison's education in the law, his constitutional studies that stood him in good stead in the Constitutional Convention in 1787, and his political career as a friend of Jefferson, which led to his election as fourth president of the United States. He stresses Madison's conviction that democracy could promote social justice.

775 Padover, Saul, ed. THE COMPLETE MADISON: HIS BASIC WRITINGS. New York: Harper & Brothers, 1953. 370 p.

A selection of Madison's most important writings, which clearly demonstrates the main themes in his thinking.

GEORGE MASON

776 Rutland, Robert A. GEORGE MASON, RELUCTANT STATESMAN.
Williamsburg, Va.: Colonial Williamsburg; distributed, New York:
Holt, Rinehart and Winston, 1961. 123 p. Illus.

A brief but informative life by the editor of the PAPERS
OF GEORGE MASON, q.v., no. 777. Rutland deals
with Mason's many contributions to Virginia's public
life, his drafting of the Virginia Declaration of Rights
(the text of which is included), and his participation
in the federal Constitutional Convention.

777 _____, ed. THE PAPERS OF GEORGE MASON, 1725-1792. 3 vols.
Chapel Hill: University of North Carolina Press, 1970. Illus., ports.,
map.

Letters to and from others, as well as Mason's significant papers, such as the various drafts of the Virginia
Declaration of Rights and his objections to the U.S.
Constitution. Includes an editorial introduction to
George Mason, notes on the entries, and glossary
identifying persons and places mentioned. Volume 1:
1749-1778; volume 2: 1779-1786; volume 3: 1787-
1792.

GOUVERNEUR MORRIS

778 Mintz, Max M. GOUVERNEUR MORRIS AND THE AMERICAN REVOLU-
TION. Norman: University of Oklahoma Press, 1970. 297 p. Illus.,
ports.

Concentrates on Morris's public career, accenting particularly his activities in the Revolution and the writing
of the Constitution.

ROBERT MORRIS

779 Ferguson, E. James, et al., eds. PAPERS OF ROBERT MORRIS, 1781-
1784. 1 vol. to date. Pittsburgh: University of Pittsburgh Press, 1973-
Illus., ports., facsims.

Letters to and from Robert Morris. The editors have
interspersed entries from his diary with the correspondence
according to date. They provide an introduction and
notes on the entries. Volume 1: 7 FEBRUARY TO 31
JULY 1781.

780 Ver Steeg, Clarence L. ROBERT MORRIS, REVOLUTIONARY FINANCIER:
WITH AN ANALYSIS OF HIS EARLIER CAREER. 1954. Reprint. New

York: Octagon Books, 1972. 317 p.

Not a biography but a study of Morris as superintendent of finance in the Revolution, with background on what made him particularly suitable for that position.

THOMAS PAINE

781 Aldridge, Alfred O. MAN OF REASON: THE LIFE OF THOMAS PAINE. Philadelphia: Lippincott, 1959. 348 p. Illus.

A scholarly and balanced view of Paine, dealing in detail with his contribution to the American revolutionary cause and his promotion of other ideas which he believed were for the good of humanity, e.g., a league of nations, and social betterment under the sponsorship of government.

782 Foner, Philip S., ed. THE COMPLETE WRITINGS OF THOMAS PAINE. 2 vols. New York: Citadel Press, 1945. Front.

This scholarly edition of Paine's works includes many lesser known writings, as well as the works which made him famous: COMMON SENSE, THE AMERICAN CRISIS, THE RIGHTS OF MAN, and THE AGE OF REASON.

783 Hawke, David Freeman. PAINE. New York: Harper & Row, 1974. 500 p. Illus.

A biography of the English expatriate whose inflammatory writings did much to bring on the Revolution (COMMON SENSE) and to maintain flagging energies once it had begun (THE AMERICAN CRISIS). Hawkes gives a positive picture of Paine, but there is implied criticism of him in some of what he writes.

PAUL REVERE

784 Forbes, Esther. PAUL REVERE AND THE WORLD HE LIVED IN. Boston: Houghton Mifflin, 1942. 523 p. Illus., front., ports., plates, maps, facsims.

Revere, of the famous ride, was a silversmith, an etcher who put his talent to work in a print of the Boston Massacre, a bell caster, and much more. Novelist Esther Forbes presents a colorful life story based on much research.

DAVID RITTENHOUSE

785 Hindle, Brooke. DAVID RITTENHOUSE. Princeton, N.J.: Princeton

University Press, 1964. 403 p. Illus., port., maps.

A biography of the self-taught instrument maker and astronomer who was celebrated for his creation of an Orrery, a mechanical planetarium that represented the workings of the Newtonian universe, and for his scientific observations, especially the Transit of Venus in 1769. Hindle also deals with Rittenhouse's involvement in politics and his years of public service to Revolutionary Pennsylvania.

BENJAMIN RUSH

786 Binger, Carl. REVOLUTIONARY DOCTOR: BENJAMIN RUSH, 1746-1813. New York: W.W. Norton, 1966. 326 p. Port.

This book deals with all aspects of Rush's career but is particularly valuable for the insight it gives into eighteenth-century medical practice. Binger, a physician himself, writes authoritatively concerning Rush's contributions to medicine and psychiatry and of his actions in the yellow fever epidemic that swept Philadelphia.

787 Butterfield, Lyman H., ed. THE LETTERS OF BENJAMIN RUSH. 2 vols. Princeton, N.J.: Princeton University Press, 1951. Illus., ports., map.

The life of the contentious Philadelphia physician emerges vividly from his letters, which give much insight into his ideas on politics, society, reform, religion, and many other matters, and also on contemporary personalities and events. Volume 1: 1761-1792; volume 2: 1793-1813.

788 Corner, George, ed. THE AUTOBIOGRAPHY OF BENJAMIN RUSH: HIS "TRAVELS THROUGH LIFE" TOGETHER WITH HIS COMMONPLACE BOOK FOR 1789-1813. 1948. Reprint. Westport, Conn.: Greenwood Press, 1970. 399 p. Illus., ports., facsims.

A signer of the Declaration of Independence, Dr. Benjamin Rush was a well-known Philadelphia physician and advocate of reform causes. He was a friend of Adams and Jefferson and many other leading figures of his time. Written for the private use of his family, his autobiography and his commonplace book give much insight into his controversial personality and much information about his contemporaries.

789 Hawke, David Freeman. BENJAMIN RUSH: REVOLUTIONARY GADFLY. Indianapolis: Bobbs-Merrill, 1971. 490 p.

Deals with the earlier career of Rush, when he was most

active in politics in Philadelphia, a leading figure in
the events leading to the Revolution--he was a signer of
the Declaration of Independence--and the multitude of
reform activities, e.g. antislavery, temperance, universal education, with which he busied himself. Should
be supplemented, for Rush's medical career, by Carl
Binger, REVOLUTIONARY DOCTOR, q.v., no. 786.

GEORGE WASHINGTON

790 Cunliffe, Marcus. GEORGE WASHINGTON: MAN AND MONUMENT.
Boston: Little, Brown, 1958. 248 p. Front., maps.

Examines the man and the myth surrounding him. Cunliffe points up the difficulty of separating the two but
makes the attempt.

791 Fitzpatrick, John C., ed. THE WRITINGS OF GEORGE WASHINGTON
FROM THE ORIGINAL MANUSCRIPT SOURCES, 1745-1799. Prepared
under the direction of the George Washington Bicentennial Commission
and published by authority of Congress. 39 vols. Washington, D.C.:
Government Printing Office, 1931-44. Illus., fronts., ports., facsims.

Washington's letters, speeches, military dispatches,
memoranda, messages to Congress, etc. The final two
volumes contain a general index.

792 Flexner, James Thomas. GEORGE WASHINGTON. 4 vols. Boston:
Little, Brown, 1965-72. Illus., ports., maps, facsims.

An extensive, readable biography. Flexner's object is
to separate the historical Washington from the myth that
has accreted to his figure from his own time to the present. For a balanced view, the reader should supplement this with more scholarly investigations of the political developments during Washington's lifetime. Volume
1: THE FORGE OF EXPERIENCE, 1732-1775; volume
2: IN THE AMERICAN REVOLUTION, 1775-1783;
volume 3: THE NEW NATION, 1783-1793; volume 4:
ANGUISH AND FAREWELL, 1793-1799.

793 Freeman, Douglas Southall. GEORGE WASHINGTON: A BIOGRAPHY.
7 vols. New York: Charles Scribner's Sons, 1948-57. Ports., maps,
facsims.

This massive biography goes into great detail on all aspects of the private and public Washington and also
deals with the myth that has grown up around him. On
the death of Freeman, volume 7 was completed by his
research associates, John A. Carroll and Mary W. Ash-
worth. Volumes 1 and 2: YOUNG WASHINGTON;

volume 3: PLANTER AND PATRIOT; volume 4: LEAD-
ER OF THE REVOLUTION; volume 5: VICTORY WITH
THE HELP OF FRANCE; volume 6: PATRIOT AND
PRESIDENT; volume 7: FIRST IN PEACE, 1793-1799.

794   _____. GEORGE WASHINGTON: A BIOGRAPHY. Abridged by
Richard Harwell. New York: Charles Scribner's Sons, 1968. 796 p.
Ports., maps, facsims.

Makes available in much smaller compass the famous
Freeman biography, q.v., no. 793.

795 Weems, Mason Locke. THE LIFE OF WASHINGTON. Edited by Marcus
Cunliffe. Cambridge, Mass.: Harvard University Press, 1962. 288 p.
Illus., ports., facsims.

A classic of American myth-making, first published in
1800. Parson Weems tells not only what did happen in
the life of Washington but what should have happened.
Young George's cutting down of the cherry tree and
his admission of guilt is just one of Weems's famous
creations. The book should be read not for facts but
for what it tells us of the early American attitude toward Washington. This is the text of the ninth edition,
"greatly improved." Cunliffe provides an introduction
to Weems and the evolution of the book.

JAMES WILSON

796 McCloskey, Robert Green, ed. THE WORKS OF JAMES WILSON. 2
vols. Cambridge, Mass.: Harvard University Press, 1967.

Includes lectures on law (which deal with nature and
man as citizen and an analysis of the Constitution) and
his miscellaneous papers (orations, his famous publication denying the authority of Parliament over American
affairs, and his writing on the Bank of North America).
Since Wilson was a Signer, a member of the Constitutional Convention, and an associate justice of the first
Supreme Court, as well as prominent professor, attorney,
and speculator in land, his writings give a good insight
into the thoughts of leaders of the Revolutionary generation.

797 Smith, C. Page. JAMES WILSON, FOUNDING FATHER, 1742-1798.
Chapel Hill: University of North Carolina Press, 1956. 426 p.

A biography of the Scotsman who became a leading Revolutionary on his move to Pennsylvania. Wilson, who,
among other things, voted for independence in the Continental Congress and helped write the Constitution, is
given a balanced treatment.

Chapter 4

THE NEW NATION, 1789-1840

A. THE EARLY NATIONAL PERIOD

1. General

798   Adams, Henry. HISTORY OF THE UNITED STATES DURING THE AD-
MINISTRATIONS OF JEFFERSON AND MADISON. 9 vols. 1889-91.
Reprint. New York: Charles Scribner's Sons, 1921. Maps, plans.

> A classic of nineteenth-century historiography, display-
> ing learning and style. The reputations of Jefferson
> and Madison do not emerge unscathed at the hands of
> this descendant of John Adams. The first volume con-
> veys an excellent picture of the social history of the
> United States in 1800. Volumes 1 and 2: THE FIRST
> ADMINISTRATION OF THOMAS JEFFERSON, 1801-
> 1805; volumes 3 and 4: THE SECOND ADMINISTRA-
> TION OF THOMAS JEFFERSON, 1805-1809; volumes
> 5 and 6: THE FIRST ADMINISTRATION OF JAMES
> MADISON, 1809-1813; volumes 7, 8, and 9: THE
> SECOND ADMINISTRATION OF JAMES MADISON,
> 1813-1817.

799   _____. HISTORY OF THE UNITED STATES DURING THE ADMINIS-
TRATIONS OF JEFFERSON AND MADISON. Edited by Ernest Samuels.
Chicago: University of Chicago Press, 1967. 445 p. Port., maps.

> A one-volume abridgment of the original nine-volume
> HISTORY, q.v., no. 798.

Boorstin, Daniel. THE AMERICANS. Vol. 2. See
no. 213.

800   Cunliffe, Marcus. THE NATION TAKES SHAPE, 1789-1837. Chicago:
University of Chicago Press, 1959. 222 p. Illus.

This well-written interpretive history covers a broad
range of topics and does not go into detail. Cunliffe
covers all sections of the country, industry, trade, and
the more intangible aspects of the story: national feeling, conservatism, democracy, and the American character.

801   Dangerfield, George. THE AWAKENING OF AMERICAN NATIONALISM,
1815-1828. New York: Harper & Row, 1965. 344 p. Illus., ports.,
maps, facsims.

Covers the same ground as his earlier ERA OF GOOD
FEELING, q.v., no. 802, but takes into account scholarly works produced in the interim. Dangerfield, who
writes with the same flair as in the earlier work, is never
unwilling to see the humor in a situation.

802   _____. THE ERA OF GOOD FEELING. 1952. Reprint. New York:
Harcourt, Brace & World. 1963. 539 p. Paperbound.

An account of the administrations of James Monroe and
John Quincy Adams and the development of sentiment
for positive government action to promote internal improvements, a period characterized by much conflict
despite the name given it. Dangerfield writes with a
lively style and brilliantly characterizes the men of
the time.

803   Krout, John A., and Fox, Dixon Ryan. THE COMPLETION OF INDE-
PENDENCE, 1790-1830. 1944. Reprint. Chicago: Quadrangle Books,
1971. 510 p. Illus., ports., plates.

This social history treats every section of the early
republic in turn; the authors describe the moving frontier;
life on the farm and plantation, and in the towns; the
growth of American business and manufacturing; and the
digging of canals.

804   Smelser, Marshall. THE DEMOCRATIC REPUBLIC, 1801-1815. New York:
Harper & Row, 1968. 383 p. Illus., ports., maps, facsims.

A history of the years when Jefferson and Madison sat
in the White House. Smelser deals with political,
social, and cultural affairs. One of the few recent
treatments of the period.

805   Wiltse, Charles M. THE NEW NATION, 1800-1845. New York: Hill
and Wang, 1961. 252 p. Maps.

This concise account dwells less on detail than on interpretation of events. Wiltse believes the United States

achieved its own identity and unity in these years but then began to feel the disruption over slavery which was to lead to Civil War.

2. Topical

a. BUSINESS AND ECONOMICS

Davis, Joseph S. ESSAYS IN THE EARLIER HISTORY OF AMERICAN CORPORATIONS. See no. 536.

806 Morison, Samuel Eliot. THE MARITIME HISTORY OF MASSACHUSETTS, 1783-1860. 1921. Reprint. Boston: Houghton Mifflin, 1961. 420 p. Illus., ports., plates, facsims.

The emergence of the Bay State as a trading power in the days of sailing vessels. Morison, with graphic detail, describes the coast of Massachusetts and how the Commonwealth, from colonial days, developed the trade and fishing industry that was to take its ships to all parts of the earth.

807 Nettels, Curtis P. THE EMERGENCE OF A NATIONAL ECONOMY, 1775-1815. New York: Holt, Rinehart & Winston, 1962. 440 p. Illus., ports., maps, tables.

Nettels believes that the development of the American economy was intimately tied to political developments of the period: the Revolution, the establishment of a new government, and its modification with the adoption of the Constitution.

808 Rothbard, Murray N. THE PANIC OF 1819: REACTIONS AND POLICIES. New York: Columbia University Press, 1962. 267 p.

Rothbard describes the economic state of the nation in the years from 1815 to 1821 and the proposals set forth by diverse persons to meet the depression that began in 1819. The panaceas proposed included expansion of credit (although some advocated the reverse), plans for relief of those in debt, manipulation of the supply of money, and many more.

Ware, Caroline F. EARLY NEW ENGLAND COTTON MANUFACTURE. See no. 290.

b. CANALS

Goodrich, Carter. GOVERNMENT PROMOTION OF AMERICAN CANALS

AND RAILROADS. See no. 276.

809 Miller, Nathan. THE ENTERPRISE OF A FREE PEOPLE: ASPECTS OF
ECONOMIC DEVELOPMENT IN NEW YORK STATE DURING THE CANAL
PERIOD, 1792-1838. Ithaca, N.Y.: Cornell University Press, 1962.
308 p. Map.

> This narrative deals with the financing of the Erie and
> Champlain Canals and the policies of the commissioners
> in times of plenty and of economic panic.

810 Shaw, Ronald E. ERIE WATER WEST: A HISTORY OF THE ERIE CANAL,
1792-1854. Lexington: University Press of Kentucky, 1966. 461 p.
Illus., map.

> The political, economic, and technological history of
> the original canal and its enlargement. Shaw, in ad-
> dition, illustrates the impact of the canal on society.

811 Waggoner, Madeline S. THE LONG HAUL WEST: THE GREAT CANAL
ERA, 1817-1850. New York: G.P. Putnam's Sons, 1958. 320 p. Illus.

> How the canals were built, how they operated, and
> whom they served, in a scholarly and readable narrative.

c. DIPLOMACY

812 Bemis, Samuel Flagg. JAY'S TREATY: A STUDY IN COMMERCE AND
DIPLOMACY. 1924. Reprint. New Haven, Conn.: Yale University
Press, 1962. 546 p. Maps.

> A thorough analysis of the treaty, set in the context
> of Anglo-American relations and politics in the United
> States.

813 _____. PINCKNEY'S TREATY: A STUDY OF AMERICA'S ADVANTAGE
FROM EUROPE'S DISTRESS, 1783-1800. Rev. ed. New Haven, Conn.:
Yale University Press, 1960. 372 p. Illus.

> The Treaty of San Lorenzo by which Spain recognized
> U.S. southern and western boundaries (thirty-first paral-
> lel and the Mississippi River) and the right of navigation
> on the River, which Bemis sees as a great mistake on
> the part of Spain and as a great plus for the United
> States. Bemis sets the treaty in the context of European
> and American developments.

814 DeConde, Alexander. ENTANGLING ALLIANCE: POLITICS AND DI-
PLOMACY UNDER GEORGE WASHINGTON. Durham, N.C.: Duke

University Press, 1958. 550 p.

A history of the alliance of France and the United States
from 1778 through the presidency of George Washington.
Basing his study on archival material in Great Britain
and France, as well as the United States, DeConde
traces the deterioration of the relationship as the Revolution in France prompted the rise of anglophiles and
francophiles among the Americans and provided the setting
for the Genet affair. As Washington retired from the
presidency, war between the two nations was imminent.

815 _____. THE QUASI-WAR: THE POLITICS AND DIPLOMACY OF THE
UNDECLARED WAR WITH FRANCE, 1797-1801. New York: Charles
Scribner's Sons, 1966. 512 p. Illus., ports., map.

A sequel to the author's ENTANGLING ALLIANCE,
q.v., no. 814. DeConde sees Republican and Federalist rivalry as an important factor in the diplomacy of
the United States. He believes peace was maintained
because of the efforts of Adams and Talleyrand.

816 Gilbert, Felix. THE BEGINNINGS OF AMERICAN FOREIGN POLICY
TO THE FAREWELL ADDRESS. 1961. Reprint. New York: Harper &
Row, 1965. 192 p.

A study of the foreign policy of the new United States
under the Articles of Confederation and the administration of President Washington. The former colonies had
to meld their interests into one and decide whether to
seek foreign alliances when independence was declared
in 1776. Gilbert examines the views on diplomacy of
the Enlightenment in Europe and America and the practical aspects confronting the United States as well.

817 Perkins, Bradford. THE FIRST RAPPROCHEMENT: ENGLAND AND THE
UNITED STATES, 1795-1805. 1955. Reprint. Berkeley and Los Angeles:
University of California Press, 1967. 269 p. Ports., maps.

An examination of the relationship between the two
countries, which culminated in Jay's Treaty. Perkins
holds a positive view of the treaty because, despite its
shortcomings, it worked to the advantage of both parties
economically, and renewed traditional cultural bonds
severed by the Revolution.

818 Ritcheson, Charles R. AFTERMATH OF REVOLUTION: BRITISH POLICY
TOWARD THE UNITED STATES, 1783-1795. Dallas: Southern Methodist
University Press, 1969. 519 p. Tables.

An examination of official British attitudes and actions
toward the former colonies in the period immediately

following the Revolution. Ritcheson probes the reasons
for British coolness and refusal to settle differences with
the United States, and her unfavorable trade policies.
His extensive bibliography includes English materials.

819 Varg, Paul A. FOREIGN POLICIES OF THE FOUNDING FATHERS. East
Lansing: Michigan State University Press, 1964. 325 p.

A history of American diplomacy from the nonimportation
agreements of 1774 through the War of 1812. The author
includes the abortive effort to create a state of Franklin,
developments in the West, and events in Spanish Florida,
as well as the problems of shipping and the search for
new markets by the shipping centers.

820 Whitaker, Arthur P. THE MISSISSIPPI QUESTION, 1795-1803: A STUDY
IN TRADE, POLITICS, AND DIPLOMACY. 1934. Reprint. Gloucester,
Mass.: Peter Smith, 1962. 351 p. Map.

Problems of American navigation of the Mississippi before
it passed into U.S. hands with the Louisiana Purchase.
Whitaker gives a lucid account of a period of confusion
in diplomatic relations with Spain and France.

821 _____. THE UNITED STATES AND THE INDEPENDENCE OF LATIN
AMERICA, 1800-1830. 1941. Reprint. New York: Russell & Russell,
1962. 654 p.

Originally delivered as the Albert Shaw Lectures on
Diplomatic History in 1938 at the Walter Hines Page
School of International Relations. Whitaker seeks the
origins of American governmental attitudes toward Latin
America (he finds them in Jefferson, Monroe, Adams,
and Clay) and political and economic determinants.

d. EDUCATION

822 Cremin, Lawrence A. THE AMERICAN COMMON SCHOOL: AN HIS-
TORIC CONCEPTION. New York: Teachers College, Columbia University, 1951. 257 p.

Sets the rise of the common school in a political and
social context in the early national period. Cremin
quotes generously from the sources.

823 Rudolph, Frederick, ed. ESSAYS ON EDUCATION IN THE EARLY RE-
PUBLIC. Cambridge, Mass.: Harvard University Press, 1965. 414 p.

An enlightening collection of proposals for the expansion and improvement of education in the early national
period. Essays by Benjamin Rush, Noah Webster, Robert

Coram, Simeon Doggett, Samuel Harrison Smith, Amable-
Louis-Rose de Lafitte du Courteil, and Samuel Knox.

e. GOVERNMENT AND POLITICS

824   Abernethy, Thomas P. THE BURR CONSPIRACY. 1954. Reprint. Gloucester, Mass.: Peter Smith, 1968. 312 p. Ports., map.

Abernethy believes Burr was guilty of an attempt to
separate the western part of the United States and form
a new nation. He attempts to trace Burr's tortuous
movements to demonstrate the truth of his conclusions.

825   Aronson, Sidney H. STATUS AND KINSHIP IN THE HIGHER CIVIL SER-
VICE: STANDARDS OF SELECTION IN THE ADMINISTRATIONS OF
JOHN ADAMS, THOMAS JEFFERSON, AND ANDREW JACKSON. Cam-
bridge, Mass.: Harvard University Press, 1964. 287 p. Tables.

Compares the views of three presidents on the types of
persons (social class) who should be appointed to office.
Aronson then sets forth the result of his study of their
actual appointments to determine how well they implemented their beliefs.

826   Baldwin, Leland D. WHISKEY REBELS: THE STORY OF A FRONTIER
UPRISING. Pittsburgh: University of Pittsburgh Press, 1939. 332 p.

The first full account of the rebellion that broke out in
1794 when Washington's administration imposed an excise
tax on whiskey. The author details, in colorful prose,
federal policy and the psychology of the farmers in
their resistance, and describes the military force that
marched to western Pennsylvania to put down the rebels.

827   Balinky, Alexander. ALBERT GALLATIN: FISCAL THEORIES AND POLI-
CY. New Brunswick, N.J.: Rutgers University Press, 1958. 285 p.

Balinky analyzes Gallatin's career as secretary of the
treasury (following Hamilton) under the presidencies of
Jefferson and Madison; he discusses Gallatin's administration of the department and fiscal policy and does
not give him a high mark for his efforts.

828   Banner, James M., Jr. TO THE HARTFORD CONVENTION: THE FED-
ERALISTS AND THE ORIGINS OF PARTY POLITICS IN MASSACHUSETTS,
1789-1815. New York: Alfred A. Knopf, 1970. 430 p. Map, table.

A study of the Massachusetts wing of the Federalist
party in the context of political and social ideology.
Banner examines the make-up of the party and its internal workings and traces the events that led to the

Federalists' desire for a modification of the Constitution,
if not secession from the Union.

829 Beard, Charles A. ECONOMIC ORIGINS OF JEFFERSONIAN DEMO-
CRACY. 1915. Reprint. New York: Free Press, 1965. 474 p. Maps.

Beard carries into the early national period the approach
he used in AN ECONOMIC INTERPRETATION OF THE
CONSTITUTION, q.v., no. 693. He believes economic interest, or self-interest, was behind the struggles
of the period.

830 Bowers, Claude G. JEFFERSON AND HAMILTON: THE STRUGGLE FOR
DEMOCRACY IN AMERICA. 1925. Reprint. Boston: Houghton Mifflin,
1966. 545 p. Illus. Paperbound.

A colorful review of the ideological and political conflict between Jefferson and Hamilton, beginning with
the formation of the new government in which the former served as secretary of state and the latter as secretary of the treasury and ending with Jefferson in the
White House. Bowers is clearly on the side of Jefferson. Many interesting anecdotes.

831 _____. JEFFERSON IN POWER: THE DEATH STRUGGLE OF THE
FEDERALISTS. 1936. Reprint. Boston: Houghton Mifflin, 1967. 552
p. Illus. Paperbound.

A sequel to Bowers's JEFFERSON AND HAMILTON,
q.v., no. 830. Although a strong partisan of Jefferson, he attempts to maintain fairness to Hamilton. The
book is enlivened by colorful character sketches and a
full complement of stories and quotations.

832 Boyd, Julian. NUMBER 7: ALEXANDER HAMILTON'S SECRET ATTEMPTS
TO CONTROL AMERICAN FOREIGN POLICY, WITH SUPPORTING DOCU-
MENTS. Princeton, N.J.: Princeton University Press, 1964. 183 p.

The title of the book gives a good description of its
contents. Boyd, the editor of the Jefferson PAPERS,
q.v., no. 761, here publishes material from volume
17 of the PAPERS, seeking to demonstrate that Hamilton
was in touch with British agents, particularly Major
George Beckwith. "Number 7" was the code name for
Hamilton. Boyd adopts the tone and approach of a pro-
secutor in his presentation.

833 Buel, Richard. SECURING THE REVOLUTION: IDEOLOGY IN AMERI-
CAN POLITICS, 1789-1815. Ithaca, N.Y.: Cornell University Press,
1972. 391 p.

A history of the rise of the Federalist and Republican

parties in the new nation, concentrating on the national
level. The author explores the differences of opinion
on economic and foreign policies that led to the formation of these rival groups.

834 Chambers, William N. POLITICAL PARTIES IN A NEW NATION. New
     York: Oxford University Press, 1963. 231 p.

     The development of political parties from Washington to
     Jackson and the influence they had on the development
     of democracy. Chambers thinks newly born nations in
     our time can learn from the American experience.

835 Channing, Edward. THE JEFFERSONIAN SYSTEM. 1906. Reprint. New
     York: Cooper Square, 1968. 314 p. Front., maps.

     Stresses the departures Jefferson made from the practices
     of his Federalist predecessors in the presidency and car-
     ries the history into the administration of Madison to
     the War of 1812.

836 Charles, Joseph E. THE ORIGINS OF THE AMERICAN PARTY SYSTEM:
     THREE ESSAYS. 1956. Reprint. New York: Harper & Row, 1961.
     147 p.

     The essays deal with the following themes: the influence
     Hamilton had on Washington's thinking and policies; the
     role of Madison in the emergence of the Jeffersonian
     Republican party; and the importance of Jay's Treaty as
     an issue that stimulated the differentiation of two parties.

837 Cooke, Jacob E., ed. THE REPORTS OF ALEXANDER HAMILTON. New
     York: Harper & Row, 1964. 228 p.

     The recommendations of Hamilton on fiscal policy and
     manufacturing from the years 1790-91. Cooke, an as-
     sociate editor of the Hamilton PAPERS, q.v., no. 754,
     provides background information.

838 Corwin, Edward S. JOHN MARSHALL AND THE CONSTITUTION. New
     Haven, Conn.: Yale University Press, 1919. 251 p. Front., ports.,
     plates.

     A constitutional scholar's analysis of the legal thought
     of John Marshall and the significance for American
     history of the cases in which he participated. Corwin
     clearly sets forth the principles involved in each issue
     that came before the chief justice.

839 Cunningham, Noble E. THE JEFFERSONIAN REPUBLICANS: THE FOR-
     MATION OF PARTY ORGANIZATION, 1789-1801. Chapel Hill: Uni-

versity of North Carolina Press, 1957. 289 p.

Deals primarily with political organization and only by inference with wider aspects of Jeffersonianism. Cunningham sees the tie vote for the presidency between Jefferson and Burr and the way it was resolved as indicative of the growing sense of party identification and regularity.

840 _____. THE JEFFERSONIAN REPUBLICANS IN POWER: PARTY OPERATIONS, 1801-1809. Chapel Hill: University of North Carolina Press, 1963. 327 p.

A sequel to his earlier work, THE JEFFERSONIAN REPUBLICANS, q.v., no. 839. Cunningham sets forth the practical workings of party organization in what was still a formative period, dealing with leadership, campaign methods, patronage, etc. He devotes a large portion of the book to activities at the state level.

841 Dauer, Manning J. THE ADAMS FEDERALISTS. Baltimore: Johns Hopkins Press, 1953. 404 p. Maps, tables.

Identifies the Adams Federalists, as opposed to the Hamilton Federalists, by examining voting patterns in the Congress in light of Adams's views on various subjects. Dauer combines statistical analysis with political theory and biography.

842 Fischer, David Hackett. THE REVOLUTION OF AMERICAN CONSERVATISM: THE FEDERALIST PARTY IN THE ERA OF JEFFERSONIAN DEMOCRACY. New York: Harper & Row, 1965. 475 p.

Attempts to demonstrate that with the defeat of the Federalists by the Jeffersonians the younger Federalists became increasingly willing to use the rhetoric of the Jeffersonians in their striving for elective office.

843 Hazen, Charles D. CONTEMPORARY AMERICAN OPINION OF THE FRENCH REVOLUTION. 1897. Reprint. Gloucester, Mass.: Peter Smith, 1964. 325 p.

The work is divided into two parts: the first, an exposition of the opinions of Jefferson, Monroe, and Gouverneur Morris, who were abroad; the second, a review of public opinion and such groups as the Democratic Societies.

844 Kurtz, Stephen G. THE PRESIDENCY OF JOHN ADAMS: THE COLLAPSE OF FEDERALISM, 1795-1800. Philadelphia: University of Pennsylvania Press, 1957. 448 p. Illus.

Describes the policies of Adams and discusses the divisions between the several factions in the Federalist party. Adams's refusal to join those who held extreme anti-French views and his determination to settle differences with France without war exacerbated divisions in the party.

845   Levy, Leonard W. JEFFERSON AND CIVIL LIBERTIES: THE DARKER SIDE. Cambridge, Mass.: Harvard University Press, 1963. 240 p.

Concentrates on what the author considers Jefferson's betrayal of civil liberties in specific instances in his career. Levy believes that the civil libertarian side of Jefferson is well known but that this "darker side" is not; thus, he makes no attempt to put these failings in the context of Jefferson's positive achievements.

846   Livermore, Shaw, Jr. THE TWILIGHT OF FEDERALISM. 1962. Reprint. New York: Gordian Press, 1972. 301 p.

Attempts to show that Federalist principles lived on, even after the party's demise, at state and local levels.

847   Miller, John C. CRISIS IN FREEDOM: THE ALIEN AND SEDITION ACTS. Boston: Little, Brown, 1951. 253 p.

A colorful history of a tumultuous political crisis early in the nation's life. The Alien and Sedition Acts (1798), and the Kentucky and Virginia Resolutions that followed, had serious consequences then and later. Miller delves heavily into the newspaper and pamphlet literature as well as other primary sources.

848   _____. THE FEDERALIST ERA, 1789-1801. New York: Harper & Row, 1960. 304 p. Illus.

A history of the administrations of George Washington and John Adams and the emergence of the Federalist party as a result of political controversy. Miller is careful to differentiate the varieties of Federalism and gives a vivid picture of the excesses of which some were guilty.

849   Moore, Glover. THE MISSOURI CONTROVERSY, 1819-1821. Lexington: University of Kentucky Press, 1953. 391 p. Ports., map, facsim.

Develops the story of the political bargain of 1820 that led to the entrance of Missouri as a slave state and Maine as a free state, with 36°30' set as the line above which slavery would not be allowed. Moore treats sympathetically the personalities involved and gives a balanced view of the sectional interests at stake.

850 Risjord, Norman K. THE OLD REPUBLICANS: SOUTHERN CONSERVA-
TISM IN THE AGE OF JEFFERSON. New York: Columbia University
Press, 1965. 340 p.

> Shows that southern conservatism had its roots in Jeffer-
> sonianism. Risjord traces the development of the thought
> of the "Old Republican" group up to the age of Jackson.

851 Robinson, Donald L. SLAVERY IN THE STRUCTURE OF AMERICAN POLI-
TICS, 1765-1820. New York: Harcourt Brace Jovanovich, 1971. 576 p.

> Refutes the idea that the early leaders of the country
> ignored slavery as a problem because they were con-
> vinced that it would die a natural death. Robinson
> seeks to demonstrate that it was an intrinsic part of
> American life and that the national government had
> to deal with it long before the Missouri Compromise.

852 Sears, Louis M. JEFFERSON AND THE EMBARGO. 1927. Reprint.
New York: Octagon Books, 1966. 349 p.

> Sears begins with an exposition of Jefferson's attitude
> toward war and then goes on to examine the imposition
> of the embargo, foreign and American reactions, the
> crumbling of Republican support for the measure, and
> its final repeal.

853 Smith, James M. FREEDOM'S FETTERS: THE ALIEN AND SEDITION
LAWS AND AMERICAN CIVIL LIBERTIES. Ithaca, N.Y.: Cornell University Press, 1956. 480 p.

> A full discussion of the emergence of the legislation in
> John Adams's administration and how it was implemented.
> Smith goes into specific cases of prosecution in detail.

854 Starkey, Marion L. A LITTLE REBELLION. New York: Alfred A. Knopf,
1955. 258 p.

> A history of Shays's Rebellion in western Massachusetts,
> 1786-1787. The author explains the grievances that led
> to the outbreak and characterizes the participants, from
> humble radicals to prominent conservatives, on the basis
> of thorough research.

855 White, Leonard D. THE FEDERALISTS: A STUDY IN ADMINISTRATIVE
HISTORY. New York: Macmillan, 1948. 550 p.

> A history of public administration in the early years of
> the republic (1789-1801), based on primary sources.
> White gives Washington high marks as an administrator
> and gives an exposition of Hamilton's many contributions
> as a planner in the new government.

856 _____ . THE JEFFERSONIANS: A STUDY IN ADMINISTRATIVE HIS-
TORY, 1801-1829. New York: Macmillan, 1951. 586 p.

A history of public administration, covering the presidencies of Jefferson, Madison, Monroe, and John Quincy
Adams. White explores executive-legislative relations,
the executive departments and personnel policies, and
the problems that confronted successive administrations.

Wiltse, Charles M. JEFFERSONIAN TRADITION IN AMERICAN DE-
MOCRACY. See no. 356.

857 Young, James S. THE WASHINGTON COMMUNITY, 1800-1828. New
York: Columbia University Press, 1966. 323 p.

The evolution of a new society on the former mud flats
on the Potomac. Young explores the relationships of
the president to Congress and the government to the
citizens of the town. He attempts to show that there
was a correlation between voting patterns in Congress
and the boarding houses where congressmen lived.

f. INTELLECTUAL AND SOCIAL LIFE

858 Dwight, Timothy. TRAVELS IN NEW ENGLAND AND NEW YORK. Edited by Barbara M. Solomon and Patricia M. King. 4 vols. Cambridge,
Mass.: Harvard University Press, 1969. Maps, table.

This primary work gives keen insight into the mind of
the reverend president of Yale (Dwight served for twenty-
two years until his death in 1817). These journals,
first published in 1821-22, contain observations on the
manifold aspects of social and political life in Connecticut as well as much of New England and neighboring
New York.

859 Howard, Leon. THE CONNECTICUT WITS. Chicago: University of Chicago Press, 1943. 466 p.

An intellectual history of the group of writers who became known far beyond the borders of their native state.
Howard gives little biographical detail but concentrates
on their place in American thought in the last third of
the eighteenth century. Included are Joel Barlow,
Timothy Dwight, David Humphreys, John Trumbull.

860 Mudge, Eugene T. THE SOCIAL PHILOSOPHY OF JOHN TAYLOR OF
CAROLINE. New York: Columbia University Press, 1939. 239 p.

An exposition of the thought of the philosopher of
Jeffersonian democratic agrarianism. A clear, compre-

hensive analysis of the origins and development of Taylor's views on decentralization in government, fiscal policy, tariffs, religion, and many other matters.

861   Nye, Russel B. THE CULTURAL LIFE OF THE NEW NATION, 1776-1830. New York: Harper & Row, 1960. 336 p. Illus., ports.

Beginning with Enlightenment thought at its peak in the colonies at the start of the Revolution, Nye traces the transition to romanticism in the first third of the nineteenth century. He sees a definite connection between the American's faith in science and the kind of political structure he created. All aspects of American culture are discussed with encyclopedic detail.

Peterson, Merrill D. JEFFERSONIAN IMAGE IN THE AMERICAN MIND. See no. 391.

862   Wright, Frances. VIEWS OF SOCIETY AND MANNERS IN AMERICA. Edited by Paul R. Baker. Cambridge, Mass.: Harvard University Press, 1963. 316 p.

An account, in the form of letters, of her travels and experiences in America, published in 1821. Fanny Wright had not yet toured the country with General Lafayette on his triumphal visit (1824) or seen the failure of her Nashoba Community (1825-28), designed to train ex-slaves for freedom. So these are fresh impressions of America formed shortly after her arrival from Scotland. This edition has an introduction by the editor.

g. THE MONROE DOCTRINE

Logan, John A. NO TRANSFER: AN AMERICAN SECURITY PRINCIPLE. See no. 312.

863   Perkins, Dexter. A HISTORY OF THE MONROE DOCTRINE. Rev. ed. Boston: Little, Brown, 1963. 476 p.

Traces the origins of the doctrine and also shows that it has been reinterpreted to meet changing conditions and understandings of American interest.

864   Tatum, Edward H. THE UNITED STATES AND EUROPE, 1815-1823: A STUDY IN THE BACKGROUND OF THE MONROE DOCTRINE. 1936. Reprint. New York: Russell & Russell, 1967. 325 p.

Denies the traditional interpretation that the Monroe Doctrine originated in fear of possible designs of European nations and Russia on the New World. Tatum believes it was an expression of blossoming American nationalism.

h. THE SOUTH

865 Abernethy, Thomas P. THE SOUTH IN THE NEW NATION, 1789-1819. Baton Rouge: Louisiana State University Press, 1961. 543 p. Illus.

The fourth volume of ten, under the general title A HISTORY OF THE SOUTH, by a group of scholars. Abernethy deals with the region as a whole, but devotes much space to southern and western expansion.

j. THE WAR OF 1812

866 Brown, Roger H. THE REPUBLIC IN PERIL: 1812. New York: Columbia University Press, 1964. 245 p.

The thesis of the book is that the United States went to war to preserve the American republican "experiment" from the Federalists. Brown, therefore, believes internal political squabbling had more to do with the coming of war than British high-handedness.

867 Coles, Harry L. THE WAR OF 1812. Chicago: University of Chicago Press, 1965. 307 p. Illus., port., maps.

Deals with the war on sea and land. Coles views it from the standpoint of the main participants--Britain, Canada, and the United States--and places it in the context of the warfare between Britain and France.

868 Engleman, Fred L. THE PEACE OF CHRISTMAS EVE. New York: Harcourt, Brace & World, 1962. 333 p. Illus.

The negotiations that resulted in the Treaty of Ghent, ending the War of 1812; a detailed history based on much documentation, enlivened by a witty style.

869 Hitsman, J. Mackay. THE INCREDIBLE WAR OF 1812: A MILITARY HISTORY. Toronto: University of Toronto Press, 1965. 275 p. Illus., ports., maps, facsims.

Puts greater stress on Canadian aspects of the war and points out the resultant Canadian hostility to the United States, which prevailed for a number of years after it.

870 Horsman, Reginald. THE CAUSES OF THE WAR OF 1812. Philadelphia: University of Pennsylvania Press, 1962. 345 p.

A history setting forth in clear terms the complicated

diplomacy between the British and American governments, which was not successful in averting war. Horsman includes a consideration of British Indian policy in the West and Canada, but he concludes that the orders in council and impressment of American seamen were most directly responsible for the conflict.

871 _____. THE WAR OF 1812. New York: Alfred A. Knopf, 1969. 286 p. Illus., ports., maps.

The author gives a detailed history of the reasons for its outbreak and then methodically narrates each engagement.

872 Leach, Jack F. CONSCRIPTION IN THE UNITED STATES: HISTORICAL BACKGROUND. Rutland, Vt.: Charles E. Tuttle, 1952. 512 p.

A full discussion of the draft, from the War of 1812 through the Civil War. Leach deals with legislation, the administration of conscription laws, and public opinion.

873 Perkins, Bradford. PROLOGUE TO WAR: ENGLAND AND THE UNITED STATES, 1805-1812. Berkeley and Los Angeles: University of California Press, 1961. 467 p. Ports.

A sequel to THE FIRST RAPPROCHEMENT, q.v., no. 817 continuing the author's examination of British-American relations following independence. Perkins explores the causes of the War of 1812, concluding that the United States took up arms to maintain the principle of neutral rights on the sea against high-handed British actions.

874 Pratt, Julius W. EXPANSIONISTS OF 1812. 1925. Reprint. Glouces-ter, Mass.: Peter Smith, 1957. 309 p.

A consideration of the efforts of the expansionists and their part in bringing on the War of 1812. Pratt sets forth their attempts to gain Canada, the Floridas, and, possibly, Mexico, and looks at the views of President Madison and Secretary of State Monroe.

875 White, Patrick C.T. A NATION ON TRIAL: AMERICA AND THE WAR OF 1812. New York: Wiley, 1965. 177 p. Illus., maps.

Dwells to a large extent on diplomacy in the pre-war and war periods. White believes that the United States was to a large extent caught up in European quarrels and had to fight to establish the American nationality.

k. WESTERN EXPLORATION AND SETTLEMENT

876 Bakeless, John E. LEWIS AND CLARK, PARTNERS IN DISCOVERY. New
York: William Morrow, 1947. 510 p. Illus., ports., maps.

This joint biography of Meriwether Lewis and William
Clark inevitably devotes much attention to their great
feat of exploration. Detailed and well-developed.

877 Billington, Ray A. WESTWARD EXPANSION: A HISTORY OF THE AMERI-
CAN FRONTIER. 3d ed. New York: Macmillan, 1967. 950 p. Maps.

This comprehensive history treats successive frontiers in
the development of the United States: the Colonial, the
trans-Appalachian, and the trans-Mississippi. Billington
then summarizes the meaning of the frontier in American
experience, dealing with economic, political, and social consequences.

878 Clark, Thomas D. FRONTIER AMERICA: THE STORY OF THE WESTWARD
MOVEMENT. 2d ed. New York: Charles Scribner's Sons, 1969. 848
p. Illus., maps, tables.

Primarily a political and social history, but Clark also
includes the impact of the arts and sciences on the frontier.

879 De Voto, Bernard. ACROSS THE WIDE MISSOURI. Boston: Houghton
Mifflin, 1947. 510 p. Plates, maps.

A noted literary critic and novelist deals with the mountain men who, in the 1830s, preceded the migrations of
pioneers into the West. DeVoto deals with their day-
to-day lives and with their economic and other relations
with the Indians. A social history richly illustrated
with the works of Alfred Jacob Miller, Charles Bodmer,
and George Catlin, artists who captured the spirit of
the West.

880 Foreman, Grant. INDIAN REMOVAL: THE EMIGRATION OF THE FIVE
CIVILIZED TRIBES. 1932. Reprint. Norman: University of Oklahoma
Press, 1953. 415 p. Illus., ports., maps.

This scholarly work draws on the archives of national
and state governments to show the origin of the Indian
removals and traces the actual movements of the Choc-
taws, Creeks, Chickasaws, Cherokees, and Seminoles
from the Southeast to the trans-Mississippi West.

881 Horsman, Reginald. EXPANSION AND AMERICAN INDIAN POLICY,
1783-1812. East Lansing: Michigan State University Press, 1967. 209 p.

A study of the American government's policies toward
the Indian. Horsman believes that a policy of fairness
was intended but not at the expense of expansion.

882   Johnson, Charles A. THE FRONTIER CAMP MEETING: RELIGION'S
HARVEST TIME. Dallas: Southern Methodist University Press, 1955. 334
p. Illus., ports., plans, facsim.

A scholarly and colorful history of the phenomenon that
swept the trans-Allegheny West in the early decades of
the nineteenth century. Developed by the Presbyterians,
the camp meeting was successfully used by the Methodists to swell their ranks. Johnson examines the aber-
rations associated with it as well as its successes.

883   Kincaid, Robert L. THE WILDERNESS ROAD. Indianapolis: Bobbs-
Merrill, 1949. 392 p. Illus., front., ports., plates, maps, facsims.

The Wilderness Road, running from the eastern piedmont
of Virginia via Tennessee to Kentucky, the first route
across the Appalachian barrier, carried immigrants west.
It is best known for its association with Daniel Boone
and later was an important road for the movement of
troops in the Civil War.

884   Lewis, Meriwether, and Clark, William. THE JOURNALS OF LEWIS AND
CLARK. Edited by Bernard De Voto. Boston: Houghton Mifflin, 1953.
557 p. Maps.

A condensation of the famous journals, also available in
complete form in eight volumes, q.v., no. 885.

885   _____. ORIGINAL JOURNALS OF THE LEWIS AND CLARK EXPEDI-
TION, 1804-1806. Edited by Reuben Gold Thwaites. 8 vols. 1904-5.
Reprint. New York: Arno Press, 1969. Illus., maps, tables.

The most complete edition describing the significant exploration of the Northwest carried out at the instigation
of President Jefferson by his secretary Meriwether Lewis
and others. Thwaites included informative notes in his
edition, and this reprint includes an introduction by
Bernard De Voto taken from his abridged edition, q.v.,
no. 884.

886   Philbrick, Francis S. THE RISE OF THE WEST, 1754-1830. New York:
Harper & Row, 1965. 415 p. Illus., ports., maps.

This scholarly analysis attempts to dispel the romanticism
that has grown up about the settlement of the West.
Philbrick is particularly critical of Frederick Jackson
Turner. He covers the highlights of western settlement.

887   Prucha, Francis P. AMERICAN INDIAN POLICY IN THE FORMATIVE
      YEARS: THE INDIAN TRADE AND INTERCOURSE ACTS, 1790-1834.
      Cambridge, Mass.: Harvard University Press, 1962. 311 p.

      > The actions of white men toward the Indians. The Ameri-
      > can government proceeded by trial and error in dealing
      > with such matters as trade and Indian lands. The legi-
      > slative acts of the 1830s finally brought a semblance
      > of consistent policy.

888   Ridge, Martin, and Billington, Ray A., eds. AMERICA'S FRONTIER
      STORY: A DOCUMENTARY HISTORY OF WESTWARD EXPANSION. New
      York: Holt, Rinehart and Winston, 1969. 680 p. Illus.

      > The frontier story from the beginning, in primary docu-
      > ments. The editors go back to Columbus, deal with the
      > frontiers of the various settlements in the colonial period,
      > and conclude with material from 1939 on social problems
      > of the new West. The editors supply a headnote to each
      > selection.

889   Riegel, Robert E., and Athearn, Robert G. AMERICA MOVES WEST.
      5th ed. New York: Holt, Rinehart and Winston, 1971. 612 p. Illus.,
      ports., maps.

      > The various stages of westward movement are plotted.
      > The authors stress the economic and social elements that
      > motivated the pioneers.

890   Van Every, Dale. MEN OF THE WESTERN WATERS: A SECOND LOOK
      AT THE FIRST AMERICANS. Boston: Houghton Mifflin, 1956. 244 p.
      Illus.

      > A popular presentation by a novelist and historian,
      > tracing movement along the Wilderness Road into the
      > Ohio Valley from 1781 to the Battle of Fallen Timbers
      > in 1794. Van Every dramatically portrays the trials con-
      > fronted by these pioneers.

891   Wade, Richard C. THE URBAN FRONTIER: PIONEER LIFE IN EARLY
      PITTSBURGH, CINCINNATI, LEXINGTON, LOUISVILLE, AND ST. LOUIS.
      1959. Reprint. Chicago: University of Chicago Press, 1967. 360 p.
      Paperbound.

      > The subtitle in the original edition: The Rise of Western
      > Cities, 1790-1830. Wade believes that the West had
      > two types of societies--urban and rural. He makes heavy
      > use of the newspapers of these frontier communities to
      > trace their colorful rise.

Weinberg, Albert K. MANIFEST DESTINY. See no. 245.

892 Whitaker, Arthur P. THE SPANISH-AMERICAN FRONTIER, 1783-1795:
THE WESTWARD MOVEMENT AND THE SPANISH RETREAT IN THE MIS-
SISSIPPI VALLEY. 1927. Reprint. Lincoln: University of Nebraska
Press, 1969. 263 p. Maps.

> A history of Spanish and American conflict in the Missis-
> sippi Valley, from the conclusion of the Revolution with
> the Treaty of Paris in 1783. Whitaker, using primary
> material from Spanish archives, explores Spanish fears
> of a growing American population in the Valley and
> the resultant possible loss of the river as a waterway.
> The Americans skillfully delayed negotiations, looking
> forward to their dominance of the area.

893 Wright, Louis B. CULTURE ON THE MOVING FRONTIER. 1955. Reprint. New York: Harper & Row, 1961. 276 p. Paperbound.

> Originally a set of lectures delivered at Indiana Univer-
> sity, 1953. Succinctly, and with a light touch, Wright
> tells of the effort to perpetuate culture and repel bar-
> barism on the frontier.

3. Prominent Individuals

See also the section on Prominent Individuals, 3,C,4.

CHARLES FRANCIS ADAMS

894 Donald, Aida Di Pace, and Donald, David, eds. DIARY OF CHARLES
FRANCIS ADAMS. 6 vols. to date. Cambridge, Mass.: Harvard University Press, 1964- . Illus., ports., plates, facsims., cartoons.

> Part of the ongoing Adams Papers project. C.F. Adams,
> lawyer, politician, and diplomat, was the son of John
> Quincy Adams. The DIARY, projected at eighteen vol-
> umes, according to the editors, is "a cool, precise, and
> informed record of most of the important men and events
> in mid-nineteenth-century American history, from the
> presidency of James Monroe to the election of James
> Garfield." Volume 1 begins with 1820; volume 6 ends
> with 1836.

JOHN QUINCY ADAMS

895 Adams, Charles Francis, ed. MEMOIRS OF JOHN QUINCY ADAMS,
COMPRISING PORTIONS OF HIS DIARY FROM 1795 TO 1848. 12
vols. 1874-77. Reprint. Freeport, N.Y.: Books for Libraries Press,
1969. Fronts., ports.

> Provides insight into the character and thinking of J.Q.

Adams and the events of a long life of public service.

896 Bemis, Samuel Flagg. JOHN QUINCY ADAMS AND THE FOUNDATIONS OF AMERICAN FOREIGN POLICY. New York: Alfred A. Knopf, 1949. 622 p.

Along with JOHN QUINCY ADAMS AND THE UNION, q.v., no. 1084, this makes up a work that concentrates less on the person than on his career. Here, Bemis deals with the years when Adams's contribution was to the formation of foreign policy both as secretary of state under Monroe and as president.

897 Ford, Worthington Chauncey, ed. WRITINGS OF JOHN QUINCY ADAMS. 7 vols. 1913-17. Reprint. New York: Greenwood Press, 1968. Front.

A selection of papers and letters, dating from 1779 to 1823, the year before Adams became president. The table of contents in each volume gives summaries of the contents of each item.

Koch, Adrienne, and Peden, William, eds. SELECTED WRITINGS OF JOHN AND JOHN QUINCY ADAMS. See no. 732.

898 Nevins, Allan, ed. DIARY OF JOHN QUINCY ADAMS, 1794-1845: AMERICAN POLITICAL, SOCIAL AND INTELLECTUAL LIFE FROM WASH-INGTON TO POLK. 1928. Reprint. New York: Charles Scribner's Sons, 1951. 621 p.

An abridgment of Adams's multivolume MEMOIRS, q.v., no. 895.

For the later career of John Quincy Adams see the section on Prominent Individuals, 5,B,3.

JOHN JACOB ASTOR

899 Porter, Kenneth W. JOHN JACOB ASTOR, BUSINESS MAN. 2 vols. 1931. Reprint. New York: Russell & Russell, 1966. Fronts., ports., plates, facsim.

This biography is primarily concerned with Astor's role in the development of business. Based to a large extent on business records.

AARON BURR

900 Schachner, Nathan. AARON BURR: A BIOGRAPHY. New York: Frederick A. Stokes, 1937. 575 p. Front., ports., plates, facsims.

This sympathetic treatment of Burr relieves him of the
onus of treason and gives a very positive account of
his activities. The book is based on much research but
is very argumentative in tone.

JOHN SINGLETON COPLEY

901   Prown, Jules D. JOHN SINGLETON COPLEY. 2 vols. Cambridge,
Mass.: Harvard University Press, 1966. Illus., ports., geneal. tables.

The career of the famous painter in the context of the
art of his day, with a consideration of contemporary
political and social life. Volume 1: IN AMERICA,
1738-1774; volume 2: IN ENGLAND, 1774-1815.

ALBERT GALLATIN

902   Adams, Henry, ed. THE WRITINGS OF ALBERT GALLATIN. 3 vols.
1879. Reprint. New York: Antiquarian Press, 1960.

A selection of significant papers of the politician, diplomat, and secretary of the treasury in the administrations
of Jefferson and Madison. Volumes 1 and 2 are made
up of his letters, plus some letters of distinguished persons to him. Volume 3 includes Gallatin's essays and
other significant papers, a list of his writings, a list
of letters to and from him, a list of miscellaneous letters and papers, the Gallatin genealogy, and a general
index.

WILLIAM MACLAY

903   Maclay, William. THE JOURNAL OF WILLIAM MACLAY: UNITED
STATES SENATOR FROM PENNSYLVANIA. New York: Albert and
Charles Boni, 1927. 450 p. Front.

Maclay was a democratic, "leveling" politician who
served in the Senate in its first years. His shrewd,
humorous, outspoken account (1789-91) gives much insight into the personalities and actions of his political
contemporaries. It has been drawn on many times by
historians of the period. This edition includes an introduction by Charles A. Beard.

JOHN MARSHALL

904   Beveridge, Albert J. THE LIFE OF JOHN MARSHALL. 4 vols. in 2.
1916-19. Reprint. Boston: Houghton Mifflin, 1945. Fronts.

A lengthy biography by a Progressive Era Republican
senator. Beveridge brings his own experience in politics
to bear in his interpretation of Marshall's career. He
sees him as largely responsible for the triumph of nationalism over sectionalism.

JAMES MONROE

905 Hamilton, Stanislaus Murray, ed. THE WRITINGS OF JAMES MONROE:
     INCLUDING A COLLECTION OF HIS PUBLIC AND PRIVATE PAPERS AND
     CORRESPONDENCE NOW FOR THE FIRST TIME PRINTED. 7 vols. 1898-
     1903. Reprint. New York: AMS Press, 1969. Front.

     Monroe's letters, as well as his papers. The table of
     contents briefly summarizes the nature of each item.
     Volume 1 begins with 1778; volume 7 concludes with
     1831.

906 Ammon, Harry. JAMES MONROE: THE QUEST FOR NATIONAL IDEN-
     TITY. New York: McGraw-Hill Book Co., 1971. 717 p.

     A scholarly analysis, concentrating on Monroe as diplo-
     matist. Ammon has delved into sources not used before
     in arriving at his interpretation of Monroe's contribution.

JOHN RANDOLPH

907 Kirk, Russell A. RANDOLPH OF ROANOKE: A STUDY IN CONSER-
     VATIVE THOUGHT. Chicago: University of Chicago Press, 1951. 193
     p. Port.

     Treats only briefly the details of John Randolph's life
     in order to concentrate on his political thought. From
     1799 to 1829 Randolph served in Congress, entering as
     a Jeffersonian and standing up for the old principles
     when his contemporaries put their minds to other things.

ELI WHITNEY

908 Green, Constance M. ELI WHITNEY AND THE BIRTH OF AMERICAN
     TECHNOLOGY. Boston: Little, Brown, 1956. 215 p.

     A biography stressing Whitney's greatest contribution to
     technology, i.e., the invention of interchangeable parts.
     The author inevitably deals with Whitney's other accom-
     plishments, most notably the invention of the cotton
     gin.

B. THE AGE OF JACKSON

1. General

909 Bowers, Claude G. THE PARTY BATTLES OF THE JACKSON PERIOD.
Boston: Houghton Mifflin, 1922. 535 p. Front., ports.

> Written with gusto. The political turbulence of the
> eight years covered loses nothing in the telling. Al-
> though Jacksonian in his sympathies, Bowers tries to be
> fair to the president's opponents.

910 Meyers, Marvin. THE JACKSONIAN PERSUASION: POLITICS AND
BELIEF. 1957. Reprint. Stanford, Calif.: Stanford University Press,
1960. 316 p. Paperbound.

> This study sees Jacksonian democracy not as a consistent
> doctrine but as a "persuasion": "a broad judgment of
> public affairs informed by common sentiments and beliefs
> about the good life in America." Meyers examines the
> various interpretations and interpreters in a stimulating
> amalgam of political and intellectual history and social
> psychology.

911 Pessen, Edward. JACKSONIAN AMERICA: SOCIETY, PERSONALITY,
AND POLITICS. Homewood, Ill.: Dorsey Press, 1969. 419 p.

> An examination of intellectual, social, and economic
> developments and their interplay with politics in the
> Jacksonian era. Pessen bases his work on primary
> sources as well as the large amount of scholarship de-
> voted to the subject in recent years.

912 _____, ed. NEW PERSPECTIVES ON JACKSONIAN PARTIES AND
POLITICS. Boston: Allyn and Bacon, 1969. 291 p. Tables.

> A collection of recent articles by leading historians on
> various phases of Jacksonian politics.

913 Schlesinger, Arthur M., Jr. THE AGE OF JACKSON. Boston: Little,
Brown, 1945. 592 p.

> A detailed treatment of the United States from the first
> election of Jackson--with flashbacks to the early repub-
> lic--to the eve of the Civil War. Schlesinger looks at
> Jacksonianism not only in the political realm, but also
> in various cultural and economic manifestations. His
> view, that Eastern labor added a radical element to
> the movement and that a major concern of Jacksonians
> was to curb business activity, has been disputed by
> other historians.

914   Van Deusen, Glyndon G.   THE JACKSONIAN ERA, 1828-1848.   New
York: Harper & Row, 1959.   Illus., ports., maps.

> Surveys the American scene from the election of Jackson
> to that of Taylor.   Van Deusen considers the findings of
> recent scholarship in dealing with such matters as the
> national bank, tariffs, and slavery.

2. Topical

a. THE BANK WAR AND ECONOMICS

915   Catterall, Ralph C.H.   THE SECOND BANK OF THE UNITED STATES.
1903.   Reprint.   Chicago: University of Chicago Press, 1960.   538 p.
Illus.

> A classic study of the bank and its policies, with much
> detail on how its practices affected the political climate
> as well as the nation's economy.

916   McGrane, Reginald C.   THE PANIC OF 1837:   SOME FINANCIAL PROB-
LEMS OF THE JACKSONIAN ERA.   Chicago: University of Chicago Press,
1924.   267 p.

> How leaders coped with the panic that came on after
> a period of rapid growth in all parts of the country with
> attendant financial speculation and abuses.

917   Smith, Walter B.   THE ECONOMIC ASPECTS OF THE SECOND BANK
OF THE UNITED STATES.   1953.   Reprint.   New York: Greenwood
Press, 1969.   326 p.   Illus.

> An economist's examination of the policies of Nicholas
> Biddle and the Second Bank of the United States.   Smith
> looks at the internal organization of the bank, how it
> managed its money, and the impact its policies had on
> the economic life of the nation.

918   Temin, Peter.   THE JACKSONIAN ECONOMY.   New York: W.W. Norton, 1969.   208 p.

> Removes from Jackson's shoulders the responsibility for
> the boom and bust of the 1830s.   Temin attempts to
> show that the president's rejection of the Second Bank
> of the United States did not cause the economic fluc-
> tuation.   It was the result of factors beyond his control,
> including the international economic situation.

919   Wilburn, Jean A.   BIDDLE'S BANK: THE CRUCIAL YEARS.   New York:
Columbia University Press, 1967.   149 p.   Maps.

Asks what kind of support the Second Bank of the United States had on the eve of Jackson's veto of the bill to recharter it. Wilburn finds that, judging from memorials to Congress advocating renewal of the charter, support was given by many banks at the state level.

b. GOVERNMENT AND POLITICS

920 Benson, Lee. THE CONCEPT OF JACKSONIAN DEMOCRACY: NEW YORK AS A TEST CASE. 1961. Reprint. Princeton, N.J.: Princeton University Press, 1970. 368 p. Paperbound.

Covers the years 1816-44, examining actions of groups on the state and local levels in order to determine whether the concept of Jacksonian democracy was viable. Benson believes it was not and would substitute "the Age of Egalitarianism" for "the Age of Jackson." A very argumentative book.

921 Carroll, E. Malcolm. ORIGINS OF THE WHIG PARTY. 1925. Reprint. New York: DaCapo Press, 1970. 274 p. Maps.

The emergence of a new party in 1834 as the disintegration of the Jeffersonian Republican party became more pronounced. Carroll deals with John Quincy Adams and the National Republican party, the campaign of 1832, the Crisis of 1833, and party strategy and new leadership.

922 Gunderson, Robert G. THE LOG-CABIN CAMPAIGN. Lexington: University of Kentucky Press, 1957. 292 p. Illus.

Interprets the strategies used in the election of 1840 as the beginning of a politics based on appeal to the masses.

923 Hugins, Walter E. JACKSONIAN DEMOCRACY AND THE WORKING CLASS: A STUDY OF THE NEW YORK WORKINGMEN'S MOVEMENT, 1829-1837. Stanford, Calif.: Stanford University Press, 1960. 292 p. Tables.

The author has tracked down biographical and occupational data on a sizable number of members of the Workingmen's Movement. He analyzes the make-up of the movement and its relationship to Jacksonian democracy.

924 McCormick, Richard P. THE SECOND AMERICAN PARTY SYSTEM: PARTY FORMATION IN THE JACKSONIAN ERA. Chapel Hill: University of North Carolina Press, 1966. 399 p.

A study of the emergence of political parties in the various states in the presidential campaigns from 1824 to 1840. McCormick has collected data to show how they organized and promoted candidates and makes comparisons among them.

925 Miller, Douglas T. JACKSONIAN ARISTOCRACY: CLASS AND DEMOCRACY IN NEW YORK, 1830-1860. New York: Oxford University Press, 1967. 241 p.

Miller uses New York City and State as a test case to determine whether democratic tendencies became more widespread in the Jacksonian era. He concludes that, although measured by the franchise, political democracy advanced, social and economic divisions became more pronounced.

926 Remini, Robert V. THE ELECTION OF ANDREW JACKSON. Philadelphia: Lippincott, 1963. 224 p. Paperbound.

Interprets the election of 1828 as "political revolution" which, though it did not represent the triumph of the common man, revived the two-party system. J.Q. Adams had a better program, but Jackson had better managers and party machinery.

927 White, Leonard D. THE JACKSONIANS: A STUDY IN ADMINISTRATIVE HISTORY, 1829-1861. New York: Macmillan, 1954. 605 p.

Concentrates on how the government actually operated, rather than on political philosophy or rhetoric, covering all aspects, from how postmasters were chosen to the establishment of the naval academy.

c. INTELLECTUAL AND SOCIAL LIFE

928 Brooks, Van Wyck. THE WORLD OF WASHINGTON IRVING. 1944. Reprint. New York: E.P. Dutton, 1950. 514 p.

Irving is just one of a number of well-known authors with whom Brooks deals in this cultural and literary history of the years from 1800 to mid-century. He analyzes the contributions of such men as James Fenimore Cooper, William Cullen Bryant, and William Gilmore Simms.

929 Cooper, James Fenimore. THE AMERICAN DEMOCRAT. Edited by H.L. Mencken. New York: Alfred A. Knopf, 1931. 204 p.

A biting satire on the leveling spirit of the new democracy, whose vulgarity the noted author rejected in this book, first published in 1838. The noted latter-day critic of American democracy provides an editorial introduction to this edition.

930 Grund, Francis J. ARISTOCRACY IN AMERICA: FROM THE SKETCH-BOOK OF A GERMAN NOBLEMAN. 1839. Reprint. Gloucester, Mass.: Peter Smith, 1968. 319 p.

Grund was not happy with the social pretensions of the American upper class. He was a staunch Jacksonian democrat.

931 Martineau, Harriet. SOCIETY IN AMERICA. 3 vols. 1837. Reprint. New York: AMS Press, 1966.

The result of two years of travel in the United States, begun in 1834. Miss Martineau traveled as far west as Chicago and as far south as New Orleans before returning to England. She was hospitably received until her outspoken antislavery views became known. This book tells of her experiences, is sympathetic to American society, and was well received.

932 Pierson, George Wilson. TOCQUEVILLE IN AMERICA. Abridged by Dudley C. Lunt. 1959. Reprint. Gloucester, Mass.: Peter Smith, 1969. 520 p.

Pierson used Alexis de Tocqueville's writings and manuscript diaries and letters to reconstruct his travels with his associate Gustave de Beaumont. It was this journey, ostensibly an inspection of American prisons, which provided Tocqueville with the information that was to be incorporated into his classic DEMOCRACY IN AMERICA, q.v., no. 933. Pierson's account gives much interesting detail on the Americans who entertained the young Frenchmen. The unabridged version, TOCQUEVILLE AND BEAUMONT IN AMERICA, was published in 1938.

933 Tocqueville, Alexis de. DEMOCRACY IN AMERICA. Edited by J.P. Mayer. Garden City, N.Y.: Doubleday, 1969. 792 p.

Tocqueville's perceptive analysis of the political and sociological composition of the United States in the 1830s has become a classic and has had vast influence on scholarship since. This edition contains a new translation by George Lawrence.

934 Trollope, Frances. DOMESTIC MANNERS OF THE AMERICANS. Edited by Donald Smalley. New York: Alfred A. Knopf, 1960. 562 p. Illus. Paperbound.

Trollope spent several years in America, 1827-30,
managing a department store in Cincinnati and traveling
about. Her outspoken account, which is critical of the
leveling tendencies of American democracy and the un-
couth habits of the frontier, has upset Americans ever
since it was published in 1832. Smalley's introduction
is very full and excellent in its analysis.

935 Ward, John William. ANDREW JACKSON: SYMBOL FOR AN AGE.
1955. Reprint. New York: Oxford University Press, 1962. 286 p.
Ports., plates, facsim. Paperbound.

Ward has drawn on all the elements of popular culture--
ballads, campaign songs, cartoons, etc.--as well as such
efforts as Fourth of July orations and funeral sermons.
The result tells us much about the American people who
made Jackson their folk hero.

d. THE NULLIFICATION CONTROVERSY

936 Freehling, William W. PRELUDE TO CIVIL WAR: THE NULLIFICATION
CONTROVERSY IN SOUTH CAROLINA, 1816-1836. New York: Harper
& Row, 1966. 408 p. Maps.

Freehling sees the attitudes of South Carolinians fostered
in the Nullification Controversy as a direct cause of
the Civil War. He treats social and intellectual as
well as political themes and brings out the humanity
of the leaders of the opposing camps, Jackson and
Calhoun.

937 _____, ed. THE NULLIFICATION ERA: A DOCUMENTARY RECORD.
New York: Harper & Row, 1967. 224 p. Paperbound.

A collection of primary materials on the Nullification
Controversy stirred up by South Carolina in 1832.
Freehling gives excerpts from speeches and writings of
John Calhoun, Thomas Cooper, Robert Y. Hayne,
Andrew Jackson, Daniel Webster, James Madison, and
others. He provides a brief introduction and headnotes
to the selections.

3. Prominent Individuals

THOMAS HART BENTON

938 Benton, Thomas Hart. THIRTY YEARS' VIEW: OR, A HISTORY OF THE
WORKING OF THE AMERICAN GOVERNMENT FOR THIRTY YEARS,

FROM 1820 TO 1850. 2 vols. 1854-56. Reprint. New York: Green-wood Press, 1968. Fronts.

> A leading western Jacksonian expresses his democratic sentiments in an outspoken manner. He was involved in most of the great issues over the years covered.

939 Chambers, William N. OLD BULLION BENTON, SENATOR FROM THE NEW WEST. Boston: Little, Brown, 1956. 517 p. Illus.

> Thomas Hart Benton was one of the first two senators elected from Missouri and represented his state through countless battles to the eve of the Civil War. His loud, driving personality and his career as lawyer, soldier, author, and politician are colorfully recreated in this biography.

NICHOLAS BIDDLE

940 Govan, Thomas P. NICHOLAS BIDDLE: NATIONALIST AND PUBLIC BANKER, 1786-1844. Chicago: University of Chicago Press, 1959. 440 p. Ports., plates.

> A highly partisan defense of Biddle. Govan reckons him right on practically every question. The biographical elements are mingled with questions of financial policy and banking practices. Based on much research.

For works on John C. Calhoun, see the section on Prominent Individuals, 5,B, 3.

WILLIAM HENRY HARRISON

941 Green, James A. WILLIAM HENRY HARRISON: HIS LIFE AND TIMES. Richmond, Va.: Garrett and Massie, 1941. 548 p. Front., ports., plates, map, facsims.

> This detailed picture of the military man and ninth president magnifies the role of the West and somewhat minimizes the importance of the East. Harrison emerges as a hero. Green quotes extensively from contemporary sources.

WASHINGTON IRVING

942 Hedges, William L. WASHINGTON IRVING: AN AMERICAN STUDY, 1802-1832. Baltimore: Johns Hopkins Press, 1965. 288 p.

> Devoted to Irving's contribution to the romantic literary movement in America. His work is placed in the con-

text of what others, such as Poe, Cooper, Emerson,
Hawthorne, and Melville, were doing at the same time.

943 Williams, Stanley T. THE LIFE OF WASHINGTON IRVING. 2 vols.
1935. Reprint. New York: Octagon Books, 1971. Illus.

A full discussion of Irving's careers as literary man,
diplomat, and, in his closing years, biographer of Washington. Williams bases his study on extensive research
in the Irving manuscripts.

ANDREW JACKSON

944 Bassett, John Spencer. THE LIFE OF ANDREW JACKSON. 2 vols. in
1. 1931. Reprint. Hamden, Conn.: Shoe String Press, 1967. Front.,
ports., plates, maps.

A standard biography, first published in 1911. Bassett
was the first scholar to benefit from the opening of the
Jackson letters. He concentrates on Jackson and somewhat neglects what was happening in the country except
where it directly bears on his subject.

945 James, Marquis. THE LIFE OF ANDREW JACKSON. 2 vols. in 1. 1933-
37. Reprint. Indianapolis: Bobbs-Merrill, 1938. Front., ports., plates,
maps, facsims.

Based on much primary material; a colorful, vivid biography. Part 1: THE BORDER CAPTAIN; part 2: POR-
TRAIT OF A PRESIDENT.

946 Remini, Robert V. ANDREW JACKSON. New York: Twayne, 1966.
212 p. Maps.

A biography stressing Jackson as politician and president.
Remini tries to show that Jackson was eager for a political role and that he was a deft politician, as demonstrated by his handling of Calhoun and the bank war.

MARTIN VAN BUREN

947 Curtis, James C. THE FOX AT BAY: MARTIN VAN BUREN AND THE
PRESIDENCY, 1837-1841. Lexington: University Press of Kentucky, 1970.
233 p.

This examination of Van Buren's years in the White House
contrasts him with his predecessor, Jackson, and examines
his role in domestic and international affairs. Over all,
Curtis evaluates him positively.

948   Remini, Robert V. MARTIN VAN BUREN AND THE MAKING OF THE
       DEMOCRATIC PARTY. 1959. Reprint. New York: W.W. Norton,
       1970. 280 p.

       Remini refurbishes the reputation of Van Buren; he pictures
       him as an important shaper of the Democratic party and
       its principles.

949   Van Buren, Martin. THE AUTOBIOGRAPHY OF MARTIN VAN BUREN.
       Edited by John C. Fitzpatrick. 2 vols. 1920. Reprint. New York:
       DaCapo Press, 1973.

       This chatty autobiography gives Van Buren's views frankly
       on the ins and outs of politics and political machina-
       tions. Van Buren was in his seventies when he wrote it
       and carried it only to 1832, four years short of his
       election to the presidency. This edition is a reprinting
       of the autobiography as it appeared in the ANNUAL
       REPORT OF THE AMERICAN HISTORICAL ASSOCIA-
       TION FOR THE YEAR 1918 (Washington, D.C., 1920)
       in one volume.

Chapter 5

THE ANTE-BELLUM YEARS, 1840-60

A. REFORM AND RENAISSANCE

1. Reform Movements

a. GENERAL

950 Griffin, C.S. THEIR BROTHERS' KEEPERS: MORAL STEWARDSHIP IN THE UNITED STATES, 1800-1865. New Brunswick, N.J.: Rutgers University Press, 1960. 332 p.

> The activities of societies formed to encourage post-Puritan Americans to walk the straight and narrow path. Griffin is quite critical of the trustees of these groups for forcing their moral zeal on others. He includes the American Education Society, Home Missionary Society, Bible Society, Tract Society, Sunday School Union, Peace Society, Society for the Promotion of Temperance, and the Antislavery Society.

951 Hugins, Walter E., ed. THE REFORM IMPULSE, 1825-1850. Columbia: University of South Carolina Press, 1972. 270 p.

> A collection of primary materials with an introduction and a headnote to each selection by the editor. Sections deal with the roots of reform and such specific topics as labor, women, education, blacks, temperance, utopian societies, government, and criticisms of reform.

b. TOPICAL

i. The Abolition Movement

952 Barnes, Gilbert H. THE ANTI-SLAVERY IMPULSE, 1830-1844. New York: Appleton-Century, 1933. 307 p.

> Traces the growth of the antislavery movement from small

beginnings. Barnes attempts to minimize the importance
of William Lloyd Garrison and to magnify the role of
Theodore Dwight Weld. The book draws heavily on the
Weld papers.

953 Duberman, Martin, ed. THE ANTISLAVERY VANGUARD: NEW ESSAYS
ON THE ABOLITIONISTS. 1965. Reprint. Princeton, N.J.: Princeton
University Press, 1970. 518 p. Paperbound.

A series of learned articles which, generally speaking,
refurbishes the reputations of the abolitionists. Among
the contributors are Fawn M. Brodie, David Brion Davis,
Larry Gara, Leon F. Litwack, Benjamin Quarles, Willie
Lee Rose, John L. Thomas, and Robin W. Winks.

954 Dumond, Dwight L. ANTISLAVERY: THE CRUSADE FOR FREEDOM IN
AMERICA. Ann Arbor: University of Michigan Press, 1961. 432 p. Illus., ports., maps, facsims.

The result of a great deal of research in the original
sources. Dumond tells the story from the pre-Revolutionary
period to the eve of the Civil War in passionate terms.
He believes not only that slavery was wrong but that
southern whites should have done something about it
without the necessity of a war. Profusely illustrated.

955 Filler, Louis. THE CRUSADE AGAINST SLAVERY, 1830-1860. New
York: Harper & Row, 1960. 318 p. Illus., ports.

A history of abolitionism, but much more. Filler shows
the relationships of various reform movements to the
antislavery campaign. His pages are crowded with facts
and personalities.

956 Fladeland, Betty L. MEN AND BROTHERS: ANGLO-AMERICAN ANTI-
SLAVERY COOPERATION. Urbana: University of Illinois Press, 1972.
492 p.

Traces the relations of American and British antislavery
leaders and their influence on each other from the settlement of the American colonies to the U.S. Civil War.
The author weaves into the history the diplomatic con-
tacts bearing on the slave question. A study based on
British and American sources.

957 Kraditor, Aileen S. MEANS AND ENDS IN AMERICAN ABOLITIONISM:
GARRISON AND HIS CRITICS ON STRATEGY AND TACTICS, 1834-1850.
New York: Pantheon Books, 1969. 312 p.

Using Garrison as a focal point, the author examines the
arguments among the antislavery forces that led to divi-

sion into radical and conservative camps. This is primarily a history of ideas, with little attention given to
personalities. Excellent on the relationship of abolitionism to other reform causes.

958 Quarles, Benjamin. BLACK ABOLITIONISTS. New York: Oxford University Press, 1969. 320 p.

Establishes the importance of blacks in the struggle to
abolish slavery. Quarles has studied the role of black
preachers and orators, the black press, and abolition
societies; he has found a large measure of cooperation
between them and white abolitionists.

959 Staudenraus, P.J. THE AFRICAN COLONIZATION MOVEMENT, 1816-
1865. New York: Columbia University Press, 1961. 332 p.

Traces the rise of sentiment for colonization of slaves
and black free men in Africa and the attempts to implement the plan. Unlike some historians who have charged
that backers of colonization were hypocrites, Staudenraus believes they hoped to atone for the slave trade
and to restore the blacks to their own continent.

960 Stowe, Harriet Beecher. THE KEY TO UNCLE TOM'S CABIN. New
York: Arno Press, 1969. 516 p.

Written by Stowe in 1853 to demonstrate the verisimili-
tude of her novel UNCLE TOM'S CABIN, q.v., no.
961, in refutation of her detractors. She devotes a
chapter to each of her leading characters, attempting
to show that they were drawn from real life, and then
deals with many issues concerning slavery--its morality,
legality, etc.--and the role of the clergy in its perpetuation. A powerful indictment of slavery and hypocrisy.

961 _____. UNCLE TOM'S CABIN. New York: E.P. Dutton, 1970. 456
p.

Stowe's famous novel about a black slave, who died a
martyr's death rather than renounce Christian love, appeared in installments in a well-known periodical of
the day and was published as a book in 1852. Although
she did not view the evil of slavery as a sectional
matter for which the South was to be condemned, her
book soon became the object of pro-slavery denuncia-
tion and a national issue. This edition has an introduction by Van Wyck Brooks.

962 Thomas, John L., ed. SLAVERY ATTACKED: THE ABOLITIONIST CRU-
SADE. Englewood Cliffs, N.J.: Prentice-Hall, 1965. 190 p. Paperbound.

A collection of excerpts from the writings of the abolitionists, with introductory comments to each piece by
the editor. The selections cover the attack on slavery,
the organization of antislavery efforts, differences among
the reformers, and pieces on the eve and aftermath of
the Civil War.

963   Weld, Timothy Dwight. AMERICAN SLAVERY AS IT IS: TESTIMONY OF
A THOUSAND WITNESSES. New York: Arno Press, 1968. 228 p.

Written and compiled by the abolitionist preacher, and
published in 1839, to convict slaveholders with words
out of their own mouths. The book contains hundreds
of advertisements from newspapers in the slave states
calling for the return of runaway slaves, ads that make
it clear that the slaves have been branded, maimed,
and generally abused. To these Weld has added the
personal testimonies of observers. A searing indictment
of the system.

ii. Education

Curti, Merle. SOCIAL IDEAS OF AMERICAN EDUCATORS. See no. 320.

Elson, Ruth M. GUARDIANS OF TRADITION. See no. 322.

iii. Religion

964   Hutchison, William R. THE TRANSCENDENTALIST MINISTERS: CHURCH
REFORM IN THE NEW ENGLAND RENAISSANCE. New Haven, Conn.:
Yale University Press, 1959. 254 p. Illus.

Transcendentalism was a religious sentiment which in its
literary expression became famous. Hutchison concentrates on the impact it had on the life of the church
in theology and social action.

965   Smith, Timothy L. REVIVALISM AND SOCIAL REFORM: AMERICAN
PROTESTANTISM ON THE EVE OF THE CIVIL WAR. 1957. Reprint.
New York: Harper & Row, 1965. 254 p. Paperbound.

Attempts to demonstrate that the Social Gospel had its
origins in the work of revivalists, a group usually inter-
preted as unconcerned with social matters.

iv. The Underground Railroad

966   Breyfogle, William A. MAKE FREE: THE STORY OF THE UNDERGROUND

RAILROAD. Philadelphia: Lippincott, 1958. 287 p.

> A popularization of the history of the "railroad," set
> in the context of the over-all antislavery movement.
> Breyfogle uses his historical imagination to supply
> sketches of typical "passengers" and "station masters"
> on the line.

967 Gara, Larry. THE LIBERTY LINE: THE LEGEND OF THE UNDERGROUND
RAILROAD. Lexington: University of Kentucky Press, 1961. 210 p.

> A critical evaluation of the legends that grew up around
> the Underground Railroad and the histories that have been
> based on them. Gara raises serious questions as to wheth-
> er the Railroad's accomplishments have been inflated
> out of all due proportion.

v. Utopian Communities

968 Bestor, Arthur E., Jr. BACKWOODS UTOPIAS: THE SECTARIAN AND
OWENITE PHASES OF COMMUNITARIAN SOCIALISM IN AMERICA,
1663-1829. Philadelphia: University of Pennsylvania Press, 1950. 299
p.

> A scholarly, well-documented study of a series of com-
> munistic experiments, the most striking of which were
> tried in the nineteenth century. Bestor carefully analy-
> zes the motivations and implementations of a number of
> these groups, including Robert Owen's New Harmony,
> the Shakers, the Rappites, and the Separatists of Zoar.

969 Nordhoff, Charles. THE COMMUNISTIC SOCIETIES OF THE UNITED
STATES: FROM PERSONAL VISIT AND OBSERVATION. 1875. Reprint.
New York: Hillary House, 1960. 440 p. Illus., front.

> A book based on both the writings of the communitarian
> societies and on keen personal observation by the author.
> He covers the Amana Society, the Harmonists at Econ-
> omy, the Separatists of Zoar, the Shakers, the Oneida
> and Wallingford Perfectionists, Aurora, Bethel, the
> Icarians, Bishop Hill, Cedar Vale, the Social Freedom
> Commune, and several others, and makes a comparison
> of their lives and characters. Nordhoff was an editor
> of HARPER'S and the NEW YORK EVENING POST.

970 Richard, Jerry, ed. THE GOOD LIFE. New York: New American Library, 1973. 316 p. Paperbound.

> Brings together contemporary materials and commentaries
> on the successes and failures of nineteenth and twentieth
> century utopian communities and communes. Richard

provides a general introduction and a headnote to each selection.

971   Sams, Henry W., ed. AUTOBIOGRAPHY OF BROOK FARM. Englewood Cliffs, N.J.: Prentice-Hall, 1958. 282 p. Maps. Paperbound.

Excerpts from the writings of the participants in the utopian experiment and of some who observed it. Included are George and Sophia Ripley, Margaret Fuller, Nathaniel Hawthorne, Ralph Waldo Emerson, and many more.

Tyler, Alice Felt. FREEDOM'S FERMENT. See no. 394.

972   Wilson, William E. THE ANGEL AND THE SERPENT: THE STORY OF NEW HARMONY. Bloomington: Indiana University Press, 1964. 256 p. Illus.

A history of the utopian community in Indiana, both in its Rappite phase, under the German pietist George Rapp, and the Owenite phase, when Robert Owen bought him out. Wilson spices his narrative with many anecdotes.

2. Cultural Renaissance

a. GENERAL

973   Bartlett, Irving H. THE AMERICAN MIND IN THE MID-NINETEENTH CENTURY. New York: Crowell, 1967. 140 p.

A brief, perceptive interpretation of American thinking at mid-century.

974   Ekirch, Arthur A., Jr. THE IDEA OF PROGRESS IN AMERICA, 1815-1860. New York: Columbia University Press, 1944. 305 p.

This intellectual history illustrates the development of the idea of progress, using the writings and statements of many figures of the period. Ekirch sets the history into the context of social developments.

Gabriel, Ralph H. COURSE OF AMERICAN DEMOCRATIC THOUGHT. See no. 383.

b. TOPICAL

i. Literature

975   Brooks, Van Wyck. THE FLOWERING OF NEW ENGLAND, 1815-1865.

1936. Reprint. New York: E.P. Dutton, 1952. 556 p.

Brooks's impressionistic prose is evocative of the mood of Emerson and Thoreau, and their forerunners and followers, who were responsible for the "New England Renaissance."

976 _____. THE TIMES OF MELVILLE AND WHITMAN. 1947. Reprint. New York: E.P. Dutton, 1953. 507 p.

Literary developments from the late 1840s to the 1880s, concentrating primarily on Melville, Whitman, and Mark Twain, whose works are discussed against a background of contemporary social and cultural developments.

977 Lewis, Richard W.B. THE AMERICAN ADAM: INNOCENCE, TRAGEDY, AND TRADITION IN THE NINETEENTH CENTURY. Chicago: University of Chicago Press, 1955. 208 p.

An examination of the myth of the American as a "figure of heroic innocence and vast potentialities" in U.S. literature between 1820 and 1860. Lewis deals with such thinkers as Cooper, Hawthorne, Holmes, Melville, Parker, and Whitman.

978 Marx, Leo. THE MACHINE IN THE GARDEN: TECHNOLOGY AND THE PASTORAL IDEAL IN AMERICA. New York: Oxford University Press, 1964. 392 p. Illus.

A literary and social historical study of the emerging dominance of the machine and the longing for a past, simpler age. Marx explores this theme in the writings of Thoreau, Hawthorne, Melville, Mark Twain, Henry James, Henry Adams, and F. Scott Fitzgerald, among others, and harks back even to Virgil and Shakespeare.

979 Matthiessen, F.O. AMERICAN RENAISSANCE: ART AND EXPRESSION IN THE AGE OF EMERSON AND WHITMAN. 1941. Reprint. New York: Oxford University Press, 1968. 704 p. Illus., front., ports. Paperbound.

Literary criticism on historical principles of the writings of Emerson, Thoreau, Hawthorne, Melville, and Whitman, which were published in a five-year period, 1850-55. Using the form and content of this remarkable group of books, Matthiessen sets forth the authors' thoughts on literature and its function.

980 Miller, Perry, ed. THE AMERICAN TRANSCENDENTALISTS: THEIR PROSE AND POETRY. Garden City, N.Y.: Doubleday, 1957. 399 p. Paperbound.

An offshoot of Miller's more comprehensive volume,
THE TRANSCENDENTALISTS, q.v., no. 981. He provides headnotes to the selections.

981   _____, ed. THE TRANSCENDENTALISTS: AN ANTHOLOGY. Cambridge, Mass.: Harvard University Press, 1960. 538 p.

An admirable collection which has culled materials from
periodicals as well as books of the period to illustrate
the emergence of the movement. Emerson and Thoreau
are included, as are many others who have been eclipsed
by these greater contemporaries.

982   Mumford, Lewis. THE GOLDEN DAY: A STUDY IN AMERICAN LITERA-
TURE AND CULTURE. 1926. Reprint. Boston: Beacon Press, 1957.
174 p. Paperbound.

One of the first works to give literature and art their
due in the study of American history. An analysis of
the American mind from the romantics to the pragmatism
of John Dewey.

Parrington, Vernon L. MAIN CURRENTS IN AMERICAN THOUGHT.
Vol. 2. See no. 389.

ii. Popular Culture

983   Bode, Carl. THE AMERICAN LYCEUM: TOWN MEETING OF THE
MIND. New York: Oxford University Press, 1956. 287 p. Illus.

The first full study of the institution which brought cultural programs to hundreds of American towns in the
nineteenth century and provided platforms to many of
the leading reformers. Bode's work is based on wide-
ranging research.

984   _____. THE ANATOMY OF POPULAR CULTURE, 1840-1861. Berkeley
and Los Angeles: University of California Press, 1959. 313 p.

Deals with the mass culture of the period, ignoring the
major figures to concentrate on the lesser, ephemeral
ones who were most influential with the people. Bode
touches on such themes as patriotism, piety, materialism,
and sentimentality.

3. Prominent Individuals

BRONSON ALCOTT

985   Shepard, Odell. PEDLAR'S PROGRESS: THE LIFE OF BRONSON AL-

COTT. Boston: Little, Brown, 1937. 562 p. Front., plates, facsims.

A colorful portrait of the transcendentalist which recounts
his early days as a pedlar, his career as schoolmaster
and lecturer, and deals fully with his relationship with
Emerson and the other members of the school.

JAMES GILLESPIE BIRNEY

986 Dumond, Dwight L., ed. LETTERS OF JAMES GILLESPIE BIRNEY, 1831-
1857. 2 vols. New York: Appleton-Century, 1938. Fronts., facsims.

The correspondence with associates of the Kentucky-born
attorney and slaveholder who became one of the more
prominent antislavery leaders. The letters give a revealing picture of the movement and are supplemented
by excellent editorial notes.

987 Fladeland, Betty L. JAMES GILLESPIE BIRNEY: SLAVEHOLDER TO
ABOLITIONIST. 1955. Reprint. New York: Greenwood Press, 1969.
332 p. Port.

This scholarly biography traces Birney's rise to fame as
an abolitionist and his subsequent lapse into obscurity.
The author has made extensive use of the Birney papers.

WILLIAM ELLERY CHANNING

988 Brown, Arthur W. ALWAYS YOUNG FOR LIBERTY: A BIOGRAPHY OF
WILLIAM ELLERY CHANNING. Syracuse, N.Y.: Syracuse University
Press, 1956. 280 p.

The leading liberal minister in Boston who helped formu-
late the Unitarian position within the Congregational
churches, Channing was internationally known for his
literary criticism as well. Brown, a professor of literature, analyzes the various aspects of his career.

DOROTHEA DIX

989 Marshall, Helen E. DOROTHEA DIX: FORGOTTEN SAMARITAN. Chapel Hill: University of North Carolina Press, 1937. 309 p. Front.,
ports., plates.

A life of the nineteenth-century reformer, who devoted
her life to the improvement of the care of the mentally
ill. The author portrays her work among the unfortunate
and her constant lobbying among political and other
leaders for the establishment of asylums.

FREDERICK DOUGLAS

990 Foner, Philip S. FREDERICK DOUGLASS: A BIOGRAPHY. 1950-55. Reprint. New York: Citadel Press, 1964. 444 p. Illus.

> The biographical sections from Foner's LIFE AND WRIT-INGS OF FREDERICK DOUGLASS, q.v., no. 991, have been separated out and published in this one-volume work.

991 _____, ed. THE LIFE AND WRITINGS OF FREDERICK DOUGLASS. 4 vols. New York: International Publishers, 1950-55. Ports.

> Foner combines a biography of the great ex-slave and abolitionist with writings from each period of his career. Volume 1: EARLY YEARS, 1817-1849; volume 2: PRE-CIVIL WAR DECADE, 1850-1860; volume 3: THE CIVIL WAR, 1861-1865; volume 4: RECONSTRUCTION AND AFTER.

RALPH WALDO EMERSON

992 Rusk, Ralph L. THE LIFE OF RALPH WALDO EMERSON. New York: Charles Scribner's Sons, 1949. 601 p. Front.

> The most complete modern biography, by a well-known scholar of American literature. Rusk gives full play to Emerson's personal trials and shows how they were reflected in his writings.

MARGARET FULLER

993 Miller, Perry, ed. MARGARET FULLER, AMERICAN ROMANTIC: A SELECTION FROM HER WRITINGS AND CORRESPONDENCE. Garden City, N.Y.: Doubleday, 1963. 352 p. Paperbound.

> Miller guides the reader through the course of Margaret Fuller's life, giving generous excerpts from her formal pieces and her private correspondence, including her famous feminist work, WOMAN IN THE NINETEENTH CENTURY.

WILLIAM LLOYD GARRISON

994 Merrill, Walter M. AGAINST WIND AND TIDE: A BIOGRAPHY OF WILLIAM LLOYD GARRISON. Cambridge, Mass.: Harvard University Press, 1963. 406 p. Illus., ports.

> This biography traces Garrison's career from his early days as an editor in Vermont to his establishment of THE

LIBERATOR and his rise to fame as a leading abolitionist. Merrill does a good job of showing how Garrison's multifarious reform interests related to his abolitionism.

995 Merrill, Walter M., and Rucharmes, Louis, eds. THE LETTERS OF WILLIAM LLOYD GARRISON. 3 vols. to date. Cambridge, Mass.: Harvard University Press, 1971- . Illus., fronts., ports.

The correspondence of the noted abolitionist, a series which is in progress. Volume 1: I WILL BE HEARD, 1822-1835; volume 2: A HOUSE DIVIDING AGAINST ITSELF, 1836-1840; volume 3: NO UNION WITH SLAVEHOLDERS, 1841-1849.

996 Nye, Russel B. WILLIAM LLOYD GARRISON AND THE HUMANITARIAN REFORMERS. Boston: Little, Brown, 1955. 215 p.

This brief biography concentrates on the multitudinous reform causes that engaged Garrison's attention, particularly abolition. Nye stresses Garrison's simple religious faith and belief that moral opposition to slavery, rather than political action, would win the day.

997 Thomas, John L. THE LIBERATOR: WILLIAM LLOYD GARRISON: A BIOGRAPHY. Boston: Little, Brown, 1963. 502 p. Illus.

Places Garrison in the center of many reform causes, such as women's rights and pacifism, as well as abolitionism, and treats the leaders of these movements as well. A detailed, well-written narrative which makes vivid Garrison's difficult personality.

HORACE GREELEY

998 Van Deusen, Glyndon G. HORACE GREELEY, NINETEENTH-CENTURY CRUSADER. 1953. Reprint. New York: Hill and Wang, 1964. 444 p. Illus., ports.

A scholarly biography with touches of humor. Van Deusen deals with Greeley's many reform interests (some solid, some eccentric), his political ambitions, and his editing of the NEW YORK TRIBUNE.

ANGELINA AND SARAH GRIMKE

999 Lerner, Gerda. THE GRIMKE SISTERS FROM SOUTH CAROLINA: REBELS AGAINST SLAVERY. Boston: Houghton Mifflin, 1967. 493 p. Illus., ports., facsim.

A joint biography of the South Carolinians who were in the forefront of abolitionist activity and became pioneers

in the women's rights movement. The author gives a
full picture of their times and of such associates as
Theodore Weld, who was married to Angelina. Speeches
of Angelina are appended.

NATHANIEL HAWTHORNE

1000 Van Doren, Mark. NATHANIEL HAWTHORNE. 1949. Reprint. Westport, Conn.: Greenwood Press, 1972. 298 p. Port.

A work of critical scholarship which discusses Hawthorne
as man and literary artist. Van Doren is warmly sympathetic to the man but balances this sympathy with criticism of his weaknesses.

THOMAS WENTWORTH HIGGINSON

1001 Edelstein, Tilden. STRANGE ENTHUSIASM: A LIFE OF THOMAS WENT-
WORTH HIGGINSON. New Haven, Conn.: Yale University Press, 1968.
425 p.

Higginson (1823-1911), a Unitarian minister in the New
England tradition, lived a long and fruitful life which
included involvement in many reform movements and
service as head of the Black Regiment in the Civil War.
He was a close friend and encourager of the poet Emily
Dickinson and was involved with many prominent figures
of his time. Edelstein traces Higginson's career in
detail and applies psychological analysis to explain his
motivations and actions.

ELIJAH P. LOVEJOY

1002 Dillon, Merton L. ELIJAH P. LOVEJOY, ABOLITIONIST EDITOR. Urbana: University of Illinois Press, 1961. 202 p.

A biography of the abolitionist editor, who was murdered
by a mob while protecting his press in Alton, Illinois.
The author believes a study of Lovejoy's life helps reveal why men were attracted to the abolitionist cause.

HORACE MANN

1003 Messerli, Jonathan. HORACE MANN: A BIOGRAPHY. New York: Alfred A. Knopf, 1972. 659 p. Illus., ports.

The only recent, scholarly account of the life of the
attorney, politician, reformer, and educator, that deals
fully with his thought and varied career.

HERMAN MELVILLE

1004 Arvin, Newton. HERMAN MELVILLE. New York: William Sloane, 1950. 329 p.

> This biographical and literary study leans heavily on psychoanalytic theory; Arvin devotes a full measure of space to MOBY DICK.

THEODORE PARKER

1005 Commager, Henry Steele. THEODORE PARKER. Boston: Beacon Press, 1947. 352 p. Illus., ports.

> A somewhat impressionistic biography of the Boston Unitarian minister best known for his reform activities in religion and in the abolitionist crusade.

WENDELL PHILLIPS

1006 Filler, Louis, ed. WENDELL PHILLIPS ON CIVIL RIGHTS AND FREEDOM. New York: Hill and Wang, 1965. 246 p.

> The editor includes fourteen lectures and speeches drawn from collections published in 1864 and 1891. Phillips's great oratorical ability is obvious, even on the printed page, in such selections as "In Defense of Lovejoy," "John Brown and Harper's Ferry," and "Abraham Lincoln Assassinated." Filler also provides an introduction and choice excerpts entitled "Some Thoughts and Deeds of Wendell Phillips."

1007 Bartlett, Irving H. WENDELL PHILLIPS: BRAHMIN RADICAL. Boston: Beacon Press, 1961. 446 p.

> Traces in detail the varied group of reform causes Phillips advocated over a long life, but is particularly informative on his relationship with Garrison.

EDGAR ALLAN POE

1008 Wagenknecht, Edward C. EDGAR ALLAN POE: THE MAN BEHIND THE LEGEND. New York: Oxford University Press, 1963. 276 p. Port.

> The author attempts to make Poe understandable as a human being and does not deal to any great extent with his writings. He succeeds in his object.

JOSEPH SMITH

1009 Brodie, Fawn M. NO MAN KNOWS MY HISTORY: THE LIFE OF JO-
SEPH SMITH, THE MORMON PROPHET. 2d ed., rev. and enl. New
York: Alfred A. Knopf, 1971. 532 p. Illus., ports., map.

> The founder of the Mormon movement, in an impartial,
> scholarly biography based on diaries, manuscripts, and
> other documentation.

SOJOURNER TRUTH

1010 Bernard, Jacqueline. JOURNEY TOWARD FREEDOM: THE STORY OF
SOJOURNER TRUTH. New York: W.W. Norton, 1967. 279 p. Illus.,
ports.

> A biography of the ex-slave Isabelle Hardenbergh, who
> chose a pseudonym when she began her career as itiner-
> ant speaker on behalf of abolition. Designed for the
> younger set, the book is nonetheless useful to older
> readers.

LEWIS TAPPAN

1011 Wyatt-Brown, Bertram. LEWIS TAPPAN AND THE EVANGELICAL WAR
AGAINST SLAVERY. Cleveland: Press of Case Western Reserve University, 1969. 397 p.

> A biography of the Yankee who, with his brother Arthur,
> combined successful business practice in Boston and New
> York with zeal for a number of reform causes, most
> notably abolitionism.

HENRY DAVID THOREAU

1012 Canby, Henry Seidel. THOREAU. 1939. Reprint. Gloucester, Mass.:
Peter Smith, 1965. 528 p.

> A biography which explains Thoreau's transcendentalism
> and individualism as outgrowths of his own experience,
> fed by his extensive reading.

HARRIET TUBMAN

1013 Conrad, Earl. HARRIET TUBMAN. Washington, D.C.: Associated Publishers, 1943. 262 p.

> A sympathetic biography of the ex-slave and antislavery
> orator who served as a "conductor" on the Underground
> Railroad.

THEODORE DWIGHT WELD

1014 Barnes, Gilbert H., and Dumond, Dwight L., eds. LETTERS OF THEO-
DORE DWIGHT WELD, ANGELINA GRIMKE WELD, AND SARAH GRIM-
KE, 1822-1844. 2 vols. 1934. Reprint. Gloucester, Mass.: Peter
Smith, 1965.

> The letters of Weld, his wife, and his sister-in-law,
> between themselves and fellow abolitionists, give much
> information and great insight into the organization and
> mood of the antislavery forces. The letters are placed
> in context by the editors in an introduction. Volume 1:
> 1822-1837; volume 2: 1838-1844.

1015 Thomas, Benjamin P. THEODORE WELD, CRUSADER FOR FREEDOM.
New Brunswick, N.J.: Rutgers University Press, 1950. 319 p. Port.

> The first biographical study of the abolitionist preacher,
> based on much original research. Weld and his wife,
> Angelina Grimke, are credited with making a substantial
> contribution to the cause.

WALT WHITMAN

1016 Allen, Gay Wilson. THE SOLITARY SINGER: A CRITICAL BIOGRAPHY
OF WALT WHITMAN. New York: Macmillan, 1955. 628 p. Illus.,
ports., maps.

> A scholarly treatment of the man and his work by a
> specialist on Whitman. The analyses of the poems are
> informed by Allen's great knowledge of their background.

JOHN GREENLEAF WHITTIER

1017 Bennett, Whitman. WHITTIER: BARD OF FREEDOM. 1941. Reprint.
Port Washington, N.Y.: Kennikat Press, 1971. 374 p. Front., ports.,
plates, facsims.

> A study of the Quaker newspaper editor and poet which
> stresses his activities in behalf of abolition and other
> reform causes.

B. THE CRISIS OF THE UNION

1. General

1018 Craven, Avery O. THE COMING OF THE CIVIL WAR. 2d ed. Chicago: University of Chicago Press, 1957. 491 p.

An exposition of events from 1820 to 1840. Craven
points out many blunders on the part of political leaders
which resulted in what he does not believe was an inevitable war.

1019 Nichols, Roy F. THE DISRUPTION OF AMERICAN DEMOCRACY. 1948.
Reprint. New York: Free Press, 1967. 605 p. Illus., ports. Paperbound.

Deals with the interplay of forces in the years 1856 to
1861 and the persons whose disagreements disrupted the
Democratic party and the nation. A well-documented,
vivid history.

1020 Simms, Henry H. A DECADE OF SECTIONAL CONTROVERSY, 1851-
1861. Chapel Hill: University of North Carolina Press, 1942. 295 p.

The turbulent debate in the crucial decade that preceded
the outbreak of the Civil War.

2. Topical

a. THE "KNOW-NOTHING" PARTY

1021 Beals, Carlton. BRASS-KNUCKLE CRUSADE: THE GREAT KNOW-
NOTHING CONSPIRACY, 1820-1860. New York: Hastings House, 1960.
312 p. Illus.

A history of nativism and bigotry replete with indignation
from the author. The seamy history of the movement is
told with detail as well as verve.

1022 Overdyke, William D. THE KNOW-NOTHING PARTY IN THE SOUTH.
1950. Reprint. Gloucester, Mass.: Peter Smith, 1968. 328 p. Facsims.

The American, or Know-Nothing, party achieved a large
measure of popularity in the South, the author believes,
because it took people's minds off the sectional controversy. He looks at the structure of the party and its
relations with the northern wing.

b. "MANIFEST DESTINY" AND THE WAR WITH MEXICO

1023 Bill, Alfred H. REHEARSAL FOR CONFLICT: THE WAR WITH MEXICO,
1846-1848. 1947. Reprint. New York: Cooper Square, 1969. 363 p.
Illus., ports.

The military developments of the Mexican War are put
in context of the political developments. Bill attempts
to exculpate President Polk from responsibility for the
war. He interprets the conflict as a forerunner of the
Civil War.

1024 Binkley, William C. THE TEXAS REVOLUTION. Baton Rouge: Louisiana State University Press, 1952. 139 p.

> The early years of the Republic of Texas in a brief account originally delivered as the Walter Lynwood Fleming Lectures in Southern History, 1950, Louisiana State University.

1025 Graebner, Norman A. EMPIRE ON THE PACIFIC: A STUDY IN AMERICAN CONTINENTAL EXPANSION. New York: Ronald Press, 1955. 287 p. Maps.

> A study of the pressures for expansion of the nation. Graebner is less concerned with pioneers and more with diplomacy in the 1840s.

1026 Henry, Robert S. THE STORY OF THE MEXICAN WAR. Indianapolis: Bobbs-Merrill, 1950. 424 p. Illus., maps, table.

> A lively account filled with colorful stories and based on much primary as well as secondary material. Henry investigates the causes of the war and traces its course.

1027 Lavender, David S. WESTWARD VISION: THE STORY OF THE OREGON TRAIL. New York: McGraw-Hill Book Co., 1963. 424 p. Illus., maps.

> A popular history written in a colorful narrative style. Lavender devotes a great deal of the book to a background of the trail and deals with its actual use in the remaining chapters; he traversed part of the trail in preparation for this work.

1028 Merk, Frederick. THE MONROE DOCTRINE AND AMERICAN EXPANSIONISM, 1843-1849. New York: Alfred A. Knopf, 1966. 312 p. Illus., map.

> A study of the expansionist period, which included the Mexican War. Merk takes a dim view of President Polk, believing that his achievements were based on dishonest policy. He examines in psychological terms the fears, desires, and suspicions of those involved.

1029 _____. THE OREGON QUESTION: ESSAYS IN ANGLO-AMERICAN DIPLOMACY AND POLITICS. Cambridge, Mass.: Harvard University Press, 1967. 441 p. Map.

> A collection of essays, some of which were originally published in scholarly journals, tracing the series of negotiations over the Oregon border dispute between the years 1818 and 1846. A perceptive analysis by the leading expert on the subject.

1030 Parkman, Francis. THE OREGON TRAIL. Edited by E.N. Feltskog. Madison: University of Wisconsin Press, 1969. 778 p. Illus., maps.

> The authoritative edition of a classic work which is available in several reprintings. This is a facsimile of the 1892 edition (the book was first published in 1849), the last before Parkman's death the following year. Illustrations by Frederick Remington enhance the graceful text. Feltskog provides an extended introduction with comment on Parkman's life and the writing of the book.

1031 Pletcher, David M. THE DIPLOMACY OF ANNEXATION: TEXAS, OREGON, AND THE MEXICAN WAR. Columbia: University of Missouri Press, 1973. 669 p. Maps.

> A comprehensive history of American expansion to the West. Pletcher gives a thorough account based on material in the archives of five nations, private papers of the leaders involved, and printed materials.

1032 Siegel, Stanley. A POLITICAL HISTORY OF THE TEXAS REPUBLIC, 1836-1845. Austin: University of Texas Press, 1956. 295 p. Illus., ports., map, facsims.

> Siegel interprets these early years of Texas as a time when, in economic and social developments, it became identified with the South in sentiment and fact.

1033 Singletary, Otis A. THE MEXICAN WAR. Chicago: University of Chicago Press, 1960. 181 p. Illus.

> The political, diplomatic, and military aspects of what the author considers the first offensive war in the history of the United States; includes colorful accounts of what happened in the field.

1034 Smith, Justin H. THE WAR WITH MEXICO. 2 vols. New York: Macmillan, 1919.

> A full, well-documented discussion of the war. Smith traces the history of Mexico under Spain and as an independent nation, discusses its relations with the United States, and gives detailed descriptions of the battles. His interpretation, on the whole, favors the United States.

Weinberg, Albert K. MANIFEST DESTINY. See no. 245.

c. NATIONAL TURMOIL OVER SLAVERY

See also the section on the Abolition Movement, 5,A,1,b,i.

1035 Angle, Paul M., ed. CREATED EQUAL? THE COMPLETE LINCOLN-DOUGLAS DEBATES OF 1858. Chicago: University of Chicago Press, 1958. 454 p.

> The debates during the senatorial election in Illinois. The editor, a well-known Lincoln scholar, supplies an illuminating introduction.

1036 Berwanger, Eugene H. FRONTIER AGAINST SLAVERY: WESTERN ANTI-NEGRO PREJUDICE AND THE SLAVERY EXTENSION CONTROVERSY. Urbana: University of Illinois Press, 1967. 184 p.

> That Americans found it possible to be both opposed to slavery and prejudiced against blacks is the theme of this book. Berwanger used election results, census reports, and other data to determine the attitudes of regional, religious, and ethnic groups toward blacks. He believes the attempt to limit slavery to the South was at least partly motivated by anti-black sentiment.

1037 Campbell, Stanley W. THE SLAVE CATCHERS: ENFORCEMENT OF THE FUGITIVE SLAVE LAW, 1850-1860. Chapel Hill: University of North Carolina Press, 1970. 244 p.

> An examination of the political compromise of 1850, which led to adoption of the Fugitive Slave Law and the features of that measure. Campbell maintains that, despite southern claims to the contrary, the federal government adequately enforced the law in the North. He goes into specific cases.

1038 Floan, Howard R. THE SOUTH IN NORTHERN EYES, 1831 TO 1861. Austin: University of Texas Press, 1958. 209 p.

> The attitudes of major northern writers toward the South. Floan finds the greatest criticism among New Englanders, while New Yorkers were more sympathetic. Among those discussed are Emerson, Bryant, Garrison, Hawthorne, Holmes, Longfellow, Lowell, Melville, Phillips, Thoreau, Whitman, and Whittier.

1039 Foner, Eric. FREE SOIL, FREE LABOR, FREE MEN: THE IDEOLOGY OF THE REPUBLICAN PARTY BEFORE THE CIVIL WAR. New York: Oxford University Press, 1970. 353 p.

> A penetrating study of the minds of the men who formed the new Republican party in the decade before the outbreak of war. Foner contrasts their view of the North as a free society with opportunity for upward economic and social mobility with their opinion of the South as a stagnant society dragged down by slavery. He stresses the importance of ideology as a motivating factor in their willingness to go to war.

1040 Hamilton, Holman. PROLOGUE TO CONFLICT: THE CRISIS AND COM-
PROMISE OF 1850. Lexington: University of Kentucky Press, 1964. 244
p. Maps, tables.

> Rehearses the great debate on the future of the territories
> and slavery, attempting to look at the problem through
> the eyes of contemporaries and yet bring to bear more
> recent understanding of the forces at work in the struggle.
> An incisive analysis. Includes House and Senate roll
> calls and excerpts from the text of the compromise.

1041 Hopkins, Vincent C. DRED SCOTT'S CASE. 1951. Reprint. New York:
Russell & Russell, 1967. 213 p.

> The landmark case reviewed in all of its legal detail.
> Hopkins sets forth the reasons for the slave's claim to
> freedom, the counter-arguments that were accepted by
> the Supreme Court, and the Court's decision to make a
> sweeping statement concerning congressional authority
> over the territories.

1042 Howard, Warren S. AMERICAN SLAVERS AND THE FEDERAL LAW, 1837-1862.
Berkeley and Los Angeles: University of California Press, 1963. 348 p. Illus.

> The African slave trade flourished, with the help of
> American ships and sailors, even though it was forbidden
> by law. Howard shows how the Americans transported
> slaves to Cuba and Brazil and smuggled them into the
> United States, and how the federal government was in-
> capable of dealing with the situation both at sea and in
> the courtroom.

1043 Jaffa, Harry V. CRISIS OF THE HOUSE DIVIDED: AN INTERPRETATION
OF THE ISSUES IN THE LINCOLN-DOUGLAS DEBATES. 1959. Reprint.
Seattle: University of Washington Press, 1973. 451 p.

> A comprehensive discussion of the philosophical and
> political issues involved in the Lincoln-Douglas debates
> of 1858. Jaffa sheds light on many of the issues, but
> his attitude toward historians who differ with his inter-
> pretation is quite acerbic.

1044 Litwack, Leon F. NORTH OF SLAVERY: THE NEGRO IN THE FREE
STATES, 1790-1860. Chicago: University of Chicago Press, 1961. 318 p.

> A discussion of the treatment accorded the free black
> in the North from the beginnings of the nation to the
> eve of the Civil War. Litwack demonstrates that the
> Negro had to contend with both social and legal dis-
> crimination and that his economic status in the North
> was little better than that of the free black in the
> South, since only the most menial of jobs were avail-
> able to him.

1045 Malin, James C. THE NEBRASKA QUESTION, 1852-1854. 1953. Reprint. Gloucester, Mass.: Peter Smith, 1968. 455 p.

> This account of Nebraska's time of troubles deals with state political development in the context of the controversy between North and South on the national level.

1046 Nichols, Alice. BLEEDING KANSAS. New York: Oxford University Press, 1954. 307 p.

> The bloody contest between pro and antislavery forces for control of the new state, 1854-57. A colorful account in which the author attempts to balance the claims of North and South.

1047 O'Connor, Thomas H. LORDS OF THE LOOM: THE COTTON WHIGS AND THE COMING OF THE CIVIL WAR. New York: Charles Scribner's Sons, 1968. 223 p. Illus., ports., facsims.

> In this case study of the Whig party in Massachusetts, O'Connor examines the split between the "cotton" and the "conscience" Whigs; he seeks to demonstrate that there was no monolithic industrial community and that the war was not a result of the clash of two divergent economic systems.

1048 Richards, Leonard L. "GENTLEMEN OF PROPERTY AND STANDING": ANTI-ABOLITION MOBS IN JACKSONIAN AMERICA. New York: Oxford University Press, 1970. 205 p. Illus.

> By an analysis of the make-up of mobs in several American cities (Utica, Alton, Cincinnati, New York) the author attempts to demonstrate that they were led by prominent individuals and that there was a direct connection between the increase of abolitionist propaganda and such outbreaks of violence. The upper classes, trying to preserve the status quo, were joined by lower-class workers afraid that freedom for the Negro slave would lead to miscegenation and amalgamation of the races. Richards holds that the riots were carefully planned and executed by lawyers, judges, congressmen, and other officials; he makes convincing use of statistics.

1049 Zilversmit, Arthur. THE FIRST EMANCIPATION: THE ABOLITION OF SLAVERY IN THE NORTH. Chicago: University of Chicago Press, 1967. 272 p.

> Why abolition succeeded in the North but not in the South. Using primary sources, Zilversmit reveals the attitudes of northerners on the subject and also the economics of slavery: the skills of black workers, prices

slaves brought on the market, the profitability of the
institution, etc.

d. SLAVERY

1050 Aptheker, Herbert. AMERICAN NEGRO SLAVE REVOLTS. Reprint. 1943.
New York: International Publishers, 1963. 409 p.

A pioneer work in its field. Aptheker demonstrates that
the southern fear of slave revolts was justified, for there
were, indeed, many of them. He has isolated 250 cases.

1051 Bontemps, Arna W., ed. GREAT SLAVE NARRATIVES. Boston: Beacon
Press, 1969. 350 p.

An essay by Bontemps on the genre of the slave narrative,
with prime examples by Gustavus Vassa, Rev. James W.
C. Pennington, and William and Ellen Craft.

1052 Davis, David Brion. THE PROBLEM OF SLAVERY IN WESTERN CULTURE.
Ithaca, N.Y.: Cornell University Press, 1966. 520 p.

A study, in great depth, of slavery in the western world,
with attention paid to developments in the United States.
Davis examines the sources of slavery in antiquity and
how the major thinkers of western civilization reacted
to it.

1053 Elkins, Stanley M. SLAVERY: A PROBLEM IN AMERICAN INSTITUTION-
AL AND INTELLECTUAL LIFE. 2d ed. Chicago: University of Chicago
Press, 1968. 271 p.

A controversial book which attempts to explain the psychological make-up and the outward behavior of American slaves by analogy to the characteristics developed
by the Jews in Nazi concentration camps. Elkins contends that both slavery and the concentration camps
reduced their human victims to a dependent status.

1054 Genovese, Eugene D. IN RED AND BLACK: MARXIAN EXPLORATIONS
IN SOUTHERN AND AFRO-AMERICAN HISTORY. New York: Random
House, 1971. 435 p.

A collection of essays applying the Marxian concept of
economic and class struggle to themes in the history of
the South and slavery and to the black power movement
of the twentieth century. For the advanced student;
these pieces should be read in conjunction with Genovese's POLITICAL ECONOMY OF SLAVERY, q.v., no.
1055, and THE WORLD THE SLAVEHOLDERS MADE,
q.v., no. 1056.

1055 _____. THE POLITICAL ECONOMY OF SLAVERY: STUDIES IN THE ECONOMY AND SOCIETY OF THE SLAVE SOUTH. New York: Pantheon Books, 1964. 318 p.

> A series of essays on important aspects of the peculiar institution. The author views the system as patriarchal, the enslaved being subject to the paternalism of the master and his family. Slavery was inefficient, Genovese claims, because the masters fed slaves poorly, were reluctant to train them, and had no interest in adopting improved tools and methods of agriculture. The planters' money was tied up in land, slaves, and comfortable living. Such conditions did not allow for investment of capital and the development of industry.

1056 _____. THE WORLD THE SLAVEHOLDERS MADE: TWO ESSAYS IN INTERPRETATION. New York: Pantheon Books, 1969. 286 p.

> The first of the essays deals with the slaveholders of the Caribbean and Latin America, the second with those of the American South, especially the nineteenth-century apologist, George Fitzhugh of Virginia, an attorney and newspaper writer who stressed the paternalistic features of slavery and insisted the system was preferable to northern industrialism.

Mannix, Daniel P., and Cowley, Malcolm. BLACK CARGOES. See no. 263.

Mullin, Gerald W. FLIGHT AND REBELLION. See no. 508.

1057 Phillips, Ulrich B. AMERICAN NEGRO SLAVERY: A SURVEY OF THE SUPPLY, EMPLOYMENT AND CONTROL OF NEGRO LABOR AS DETERMINED BY THE PLANTATION REGIME. 1918. Reprint. New York: Appleton-Century, 1940. 540 p.

> A history based on journals and records of several large plantations. Phillips devoted a life-time to scholarship on the old South. He was a Georgian, born in 1877, and shared southern racial attitudes toward the black which are reflected in his approach. Nonetheless, his research produced a better understanding of the ante-bellum South.

Robinson, Donald L. SLAVERY IN THE STRUCTURE OF AMERICAN POLITICS, 1765-1820. See no. 851.

1058 Stampp, Kenneth M. THE PECULIAR INSTITUTION: SLAVERY IN THE ANTE-BELLUM SOUTH. 1956. Reprint. New York: Vintage Books, 1964. 459 p.

> A discussion of all aspects of slavery in the South.

Stampp deals with the introduction of slavery and its utilization on various types of plantations, describing the daily routine and the lot of the black man. Stampp believes that the slaves pretended to be docile and naive in order to pacify their masters; he deals with abuse of slaves and other evils of the system.

1059 Tannenbaum, Frank. SLAVE AND CITIZEN: THE NEGRO IN THE AMERI-CAS. New York: Alfred A. Knopf, 1946. 149 p. Table.

A comparative study of white attitudes toward the black in Latin and English-speaking America. Tannenbaum discusses the introduction of slavery among the Portuguese in 1442. From Cicero, Seneca, and St. Paul, they derived the message that a slave was a man with rights and privileges. This attitude, codified earlier in Spain in the thirteenth century, was brought to the New World by the Latins and contrasted sharply with the attitudes of the British colonies, where the slave was treated as a domestic animal. Tannenbaum discusses at length the consequences for the slave of these divergent views.

1060 Wade, Richard C. SLAVERY IN THE CITIES: THE SOUTH, 1820-1860. New York: Oxford University Press, 1964. 350 p.

Discusses conditions of life for slaves in an urban environment. Wade has studied the records of a substantial number of larger towns and cities in the South and reveals the slaves' housing conditions, hiring practices, legal controls on them, punishments imposed, and the incidence of escape.

1061 Weinstein, Allen, and Gatell, Frank Otto, eds. AMERICAN NEGRO SLAVERY: A MODERN READER. 2d ed. New York: Oxford University Press, 1973. 439 p.

This collection of articles and extracts from books gives a good picture of the state of scholarship on the subject. The editors have reached back to the works of Ulrich B. Phillips for an excerpt; otherwise the selection is from the work of contemporaries setting forth their own views and commenting on those of others. Among those represented: David Brion Davis, Stanley Elkins, John Hope Franklin, Eugene Genovese, Winthrop Jordan, Arnold Sio, Kenneth M. Stampp.

1062 Wish, Harvey, ed. SLAVERY IN THE SOUTH: FIRST-HAND ACCOUNTS OF THE ANTE-BELLUM AMERICAN SOUTHLAND FROM NORTHERN & SOUTHERN WHITES, NEGROES, & FOREIGN OBSERVERS. New York: Farrar, Straus, 1964. 313 p. Facsim.

An anthology which includes materials from three groups: blacks who had known slavery, southern whites, and northerners and British visitors. Wish provides a perceptive introduction and a headnote on each selection.

e. THE SOUTH

1063 Carpenter, Jesse T. THE SOUTH AS A CONSCIOUS MINORITY, 1789-1861: A STUDY IN POLITICAL THOUGHT. 1930. Reprint. Gloucester, Mass.: Peter Smith, 1963. 315 p.

The phases southern thought went through in the effort to maintain sectional identity, from the beginnings of the nation to the Civil War. Carpenter bases his conclusions on debates in constitutional conventions, the Congress, state legislatures, and pamphlet and periodical literature.

1064 Cash, Wilbur J. THE MIND OF THE SOUTH. 1941. Reprint. New York: Alfred A. Knopf, 1960. 455 p.

A southern newspaperman's classic historical and sociological analysis of the southern outlook on life. Cash delves into the colonial and Confederate past in order to illumine the relationship of social classes to each other and to provide an understanding of the South in the twentieth century.

1065 Craven, Avery O. CIVIL WAR IN THE MAKING, 1815-1860. Baton Rouge: Louisiana State University Press, 1959. 115 p.

An investigation of the sources of the war, originally the Walter Lynwood Fleming Lectures in Southern History at Louisiana State University. Craven sees a transition in the 1840s from a recognition of "realities" of the situation to an acceptance of "abstractions" as the source of growing hostility. He likens pre-Civil War days to the contemporary "Cold War."

1066 _____. THE GROWTH OF SOUTHERN NATIONALISM, 1848-1861. Baton Rouge: Louisiana State University Press, 1953. 444 p. Illus., port.

The development of sectional antagonism in the South, placed in the context of national developments. Craven thinks southern constitutional claims were strong until the eve of the Civil War, when passion overcame reason. This is volume 6 in the cooperative venture, A HISTORY OF THE SOUTH.

1067 Eaton, Clement. THE FREEDOM-OF-THOUGHT STRUGGLE IN THE OLD

SOUTH. 1940. Reprint. New York: Harper & Row, 1964. 431 p. Illus., ports.

> The transformation of the South from a liberal, if aristocratic, agrarian civilization to a militant, authoritarian, closed society. The section was transformed, of course, over the issue of slavery and abolitionism.

1068 _____. THE GROWTH OF SOUTHERN CIVILIZATION, 1790-1860. New York: Harper & Row, 1961. 370 p. Illus., ports.

> This work stresses the variety of southern life, from the Creoles of New Orleans to the hill folk, based to a large extent on the writings of the period covered. A rich, thoughtful interpretation.

1069 _____. A HISTORY OF THE OLD SOUTH. 1949. Reprint. New York: Macmillan, 1966. 596 p. Illus., ports., maps.

> A liberal's survey of the southern way of life, from colonial settlement to the eve of the Civil War. Eaton deals with economic factors (including the effect on agriculture of dependence on one crop), political practices, slavery, education, religion, literature.

1070 _____. THE MIND OF THE OLD SOUTH. Rev. ed. Baton Rouge: Louisiana State University Press, 1967. 359 p. Ports.

> Explains the evolution of southern thought from a variety of points of view to a unity on the race question by the time of the Civil War.

1071 Fitzhugh, George. CANNIBALS ALL! OR SLAVES WITHOUT MASTERS. Edited by C. Vann Woodward. Cambridge, Mass.: Harvard University Press, 1960. 264 p.

> Fitzhugh, a Virginia attorney and small plantation owner, became one of the most original advocates of slavery. In periodicals and books he attempted to show that the southern slaves received benevolent treatment when compared to the industrial workers in the North and in England. He held that, ideally, there should be two levels in society, masters and slaves (white slaves as well as black). In this work, first published in 1857, Fitzhugh uses statistics to indicate that slavery is superior to a free-labor system. This edition contains a full introductory essay by a leading historian of the South.

1072 Franklin, John Hope. THE MILITANT SOUTH, 1800-1861. Cambridge, Mass.: Harvard University Press, 1956. 317 p.

> Attempts to explain the growth of the martial spirit in

the South. Franklin isolates many causes for such a
development: continued danger from the Indians, fear
of slaves and possible uprisings, a rural environment,
etc. He details how martial attitudes were fostered
by such things as military academies, militia musters,
and even verse.

1073 Hentz, Caroline Lee. THE PLANTER'S NORTHERN BRIDE. Chapel Hill:
University of North Carolina Press, 1970. 602 p. Paperbound.

One of several "answers" in novel form to Harriet
Beecher Stowe's UNCLE TOM'S CABIN, q.v., no. 961.
Hentz, a New Englander residing in the South, devises
a plot which brings a southern planter to the North,
where he falls in love with the chastely beautiful daugh-
ter of a leading abolitionist. The pair wed and live
happily ever after in the idyllic setting of a southern
plantation, surrounded by happy, devoted slaves. An
extremely popular novel when published in 1854. This
edition contains an introduction by Rhoda Coleman El-
lison.

1074 Jenkins, William S. PRO-SLAVERY THOUGHT IN THE OLD SOUTH.
Chapel Hill: University of North Carolina Press, 1935. 392 p.

Makes it clear that much of the intellectual energy of
the ante-bellum South went into the justification of
slavery. Jenkins summarizes the legal, religious, and
ethical arguments given. Although he traces the story
from the beginning, he concentrates on the later years.
Heavily documented.

1075 McKitrick, Eric L., ed. SLAVERY DEFENDED: THE VIEWS OF THE OLD
SOUTH. Englewood Cliffs, N.J.: Prentice-Hall, 1963. 188 p. Paperbound.

A well-chosen selection of excerpts from writings of
those who advocated slavery. The editor provides headnotes to the pieces, which are derived from politicians,
publicists, and academics.

1076 Olmsted, Frederick Law. THE COTTON KINGDOM: A TRAVELLER'S
OBSERVATIONS ON COTTON AND SLAVERY IN THE AMERICAN SLAVE
STATES. Edited by Arthur M. Schlesinger. New York: Alfred A. Knopf,
1953. 705 p. Facsim.

As a reporter for the NEW YORK TIMES in the 1850s,
Olmsted traveled through various parts of the South observing life there and interviewing many whites and
slaves. Although he had kind remarks for some aspects
of southern society, his evaluation of slavery was almost

wholly negative. A reliable, first-hand account.

1077 Osterweiss, Rollin G. ROMANTICISM AND NATIONALISM IN THE OLD
SOUTH. 1949. Reprint. Baton Rouge: Louisiana State University Press,
1967. 285 p.

Osterweiss examines the romantic outlook as expressed in
four sections of the South: the Upper South, with its
center at Richmond; the Coastal South, with its center
at Charleston; the Gulf area and New Orleans; and the
southwest frontier. He depends heavily on famous magazines of the day for his picture.

1078 Owsley, Frank L. PLAIN FOLK OF THE OLD SOUTH. Baton Rouge:
Louisiana State University Press, 1949. 256 p. Maps, tables.

Originally the Walter Lynwood Fleming Lectures in
Southern History for 1948 at the Louisiana State University. Owsley has used such sources as tax lists and the
census reports of 1850 and 1860 to derive a picture of
the southern middle class.

1079 Phillips, Ulrich B. LIFE AND LABOR IN THE OLD SOUTH. 1929. Reprint. Boston: Little, Brown, 1963. 394 p. Illus., maps, diagrs. Paperbound.

A history of the development of the southern way of
life. Phillips deals with all aspects of the plantation:
masters, overseers, slaves, climate, soil, and varieties
of cotton. Since his work is permeated by the southern
view of race, he tends to minimize or ignore the more
unpleasant aspects of plantation life.

1080 Robert, Joseph Clarke. THE ROAD FROM MONTICELLO: A STUDY OF
THE VIRGINIA SLAVERY DEBATE OF 1832. 1941. Reprint. New York:
AMS Press, 1970. 136 p. Maps.

The Nat Turner rebellion occurred in the summer of
1831. In January 1832 the Virginia Assembly debated
proposals to abolish slavery. Robert has provided background to the debate and the main thrust of the argument presented. The decision to retain slavery, made
by a narrow margin, had grave consequences for the
future. Increasingly the institution was defended as a
positive good.

Scott, Anne Fior. THE SOUTHERN LADY. See no. 331.

1081 Simkins, Francis B., and Roland, Charles Pierce. A HISTORY OF THE
SOUTH. 4th ed. New York: Alfred A. Knopf, 1972. 739 p.

Originally published by Simkins in 1947 as THE SOUTH,
OLD AND NEW. Believing that the South became a
conscious political entity with the Missouri Compromise
of 1820, the authors begin the history with that event.
The greater part of the book is devoted to the period
since the Civil War.

1082 Sydnor, Charles S. THE DEVELOPMENT OF SOUTHERN SECTIONALISM,
1819-1848. Baton Rouge: Louisiana State University Press, 1948. 415
p. Illus., ports., maps.

A sympathetic but nonpartisan account of the strains
that developed between the South and the rest of the
country over the slavery issue. This is a volume in
the series, A HISTORY OF THE SOUTH, by a number
of authorities on the section.

1083 Taylor, William R. CAVALIER AND YANKEE: THE OLD SOUTH AND
AMERICAN NATIONAL CHARACTER. New York: George Braziller,
1961. 384 p.

The growth of the myth in the ante-bellum South, which
pictured southern civilization essentially different from
that of the North. Taylor explains the political and
sociological conditions that supplied the motive for this
development.

3. Prominent Individuals

JOHN QUINCY ADAMS

1084 Bemis, Samuel Flagg. JOHN QUINCY ADAMS AND THE UNION. New
York: Alfred A. Knopf, 1956. 580 p. Illus., ports.

In JOHN QUINCY ADAMS AND THE FOUNDATIONS
OF AMERICAN FOREIGN POLICY, q.v., no. 896,
Bemis dealt with Adams's "first career." Here he deals
with him as a member of the House of Representatives,
where "Old Man Eloquent" served for many years upon his
retirement from the presidency and fought, among many
other battles, his great campaign against the "gag rule."

For the earlier career of John Quincy Adams, see the section on Prominent Individuals, 5,A,3.

JOHN BROWN

1085 Oates, Stephen B. TO PURGE THIS LAND WITH BLOOD: A BIOGRAPHY
OF JOHN BROWN. New York: Harper & Row, 1970. 434 p. Illus.

A biography based to a great extent on original sources.
Brown emerges in this portrait as a failure in his worldly
pursuits, but as a person so honest and firm in his convictions that he was capable of inspiring men to follow
him in his various antislavery ventures. Oates judges
him to have been sane, although Brown became convinced that he had been chosen by God to strike against
slavery.

JAMES BUCHANAN

1086 Klein, Philip S. PRESIDENT JAMES BUCHANAN: A BIOGRAPHY. University Park: Pennsylvania State University Press, 1962. 524 p. Illus.,
ports.

A sympathetic portrait. Klein pictures Buchanan as a
man dedicated to peace and orderly procedure and rejects the usual charge that he was a doughface.

1087 Moore, John Bassett, ed. THE WORKS OF JAMES BUCHANAN: COM-
PRISING HIS SPEECHES, STATE PAPERS, AND PRIVATE CORRESPON-
DENCE. 12 vols. 1908-11. Reprint. New York: Antiquarian Press,
1960. Fronts., ports.

The first eleven volumes contain material arranged
chronologically. Volume 12 is made up of an autobiographical sketch and biographical sketches by others.

JOHN C. CALHOUN

1088 Coit, Margaret L. JOHN C. CALHOUN: AMERICAN PORTRAIT. Boston: Houghton Mifflin, 1950. 608 p.

This full biography sympathetically treats Calhoun's view
that the United States was a federal union of states
rather than a centralized nation.

1089 Meriwether, Robert L., ed. THE PAPERS OF JOHN C. CALHOUN. 7
vols. to date. Columbia: University of South Carolina Press, 1959- .
Illus., fronts., ports.

Projected at fifteen volumes. The editor provides full
explanatory notes on the materials included. Volume 1
begins with 1801; volume 7 runs through March 1823.

1090 Wiltse, Charles M. JOHN C. CALHOUN. 3 vols. Indianapolis: Bobbs-
Merrill, 1944-51. Illus., ports., maps.

A biography in which Wiltse attempts to reveal the humanity of his subject and to give a sympathetic hearing

to the principles for which he stood. Volume 1: NA-
TIONALIST, 1782-1828; volume 2: NULLIFIER, 1829-
1839; volume 3: SECTIONALIST, 1840-1850.

HENRY CLAY

1091 Eaton, Clement. HENRY CLAY AND THE ART OF AMERICAN POLITICS.
Boston: Little, Brown, 1957. 209 p.

A sympathetic biography which includes a perceptive
analysis of Clay's political program for the United States.

1092 Hopkins, James F., and Hargreaves, Mary W.M., eds. THE PAPERS OF
HENRY CLAY. 5 vols. to date. Lexington: University of Kentucky Press,
1959-   . Illus., fronts., ports.

This collection is annotated, with full index and cross
references. The series so far extends to 1826, when
Clay served as secretary of state under President John
Quincy Adams.

1093 Mayo, Bernard. HENRY CLAY: SPOKESMAN OF THE NEW WEST. Boston: Houghton Mifflin, 1937. 583 p. Front., ports., plates, facsim.

The early career of Clay as one of the "War Hawks."
Mayo presents in detail the social as well as the political events of the time and gives a vivid representation
of Clay's response to them.

1094 Van Deusen, Glyndon G. THE LIFE OF HENRY CLAY. Boston: Little,
Brown, 1937. 453 p. Front., ports., plates, facsims.

A balanced, scholarly political biography which is also
readable.

STEPHEN A. DOUGLAS

1095 Capers, Gerald M. STEPHEN A. DOUGLAS: DEFENDER OF THE UNION.
Boston: Little, Brown, 1959. 249 p.

A biography of the leading Democratic figure and antag-
onist of Lincoln set in the context of the political battles of the pre-Civil War years.

1096 Johannsen, Robert W. STEPHEN A. DOUGLAS. New York: Oxford University Press, 1973. 1,005 p. Illus.

A central political figure of his day, Senator Douglas of
Illinois is intimately associated with the question of slavery in the territories. His proposal that Kansans and

Nebraskans decide for themselves whether to allow slavery ("popular sovereignty") and subsequent bloodshed was a prelude to Civil War. The author of this biography is the leading Douglas scholar. The definitive study.

1097 ____, ed. THE LETTERS OF STEPHEN A. DOUGLAS. Urbana: University of Illinois Press, 1961. 590 p. Illus., ports.

All of the extant, significant letters of Douglas are included. The editor provides explanatory notes and an introduction on the significance of Douglas in the American life and politics of his day.

MILLARD FILLMORE

1098 Rayback, Robert J. MILLARD FILLMORE: BIOGRAPHY OF A PRESIDENT. Buffalo, N.Y.: H. Stewart, 1959. 484 p. Ports., plates.

The first substantial biography, much of it based on documents in central and western New York State. Fillmore emerges from these pages as a man of dignity and principle.

FRANKLIN PIERCE

1099 Nichols, Roy F. FRANKLIN PIERCE, YOUNG HICKORY OF THE GRANITE HILLS. Rev. ed. Philadelphia: University of Pennsylvania Press, 1958. 642 p. Front., ports., maps, facsims.

A full biography of President Pierce as an individual and as a type of those who labored to save the Union.

JAMES K. POLK

1100 Nevins, Allan, ed. POLK: THE DIARY OF A PRESIDENT, 1845-1849, COVERING THE MEXICAN WAR, THE ACQUISITION OF OREGON, AND THE CONQUEST OF CALIFORNIA AND THE SOUTHWEST. 1952. Reprint. New York: Capricorn Books, 1968. 446 p. Paperbound.

The diary, kept by Polk while he was in the White House, gives a good indication of his personality and attitudes on policy. Nevins has condensed it from the four-volume original.

1101 Sellers, Charles Grier. JAMES K. POLK. 2 vols. to date. Princeton, N.J.: Princeton University Press, 1957- .

Projected at three volumes. A well-written, at times humorous, account of a major figure in a turbulent pe-

riod. Sellers deals with Polk's driving political career
in Tennessee and in Washington in the large framework
of what was happening around him. Volume 1: JACK-
SONIAN, 1795-1843; volume 2: CONTINENTALIST,
1843-1846.

1102 Weaver, Herbert, ed. CORRESPONDENCE OF JAMES K. POLK. 1 vol.
to date. Nashville, Tenn.: Vanderbilt University Press, 1969- . Front.,
map, facsims.

The first volume in a projected series. Letters from and
to Polk, with notes by the editor. Dates covered: 1817-
1832.

WILLIAM GILMORE SIMMS

1103 Wakelyn, Jon. THE POLITICS OF A LITERARY MAN: WILLIAM GIL-
MORE SIMMS. Westport, Conn.: Greenwood Press, 1973. 320 p.

Places Simms in the context of South Carolinian and
southern politics, in which he was particularly involved
as an editor before he gained recognition for his fic-
tional writing. Wakelyn skillfully demonstrates the interplay of Simms's political and writing careers.

ZACHARY TAYLOR

1104 Hamilton, Holman. ZACHARY TAYLOR. 2 vols. 1941-57. Reprint.
Hamden, Conn.: Archon Books, 1966. Illus., ports., maps, facsim.

A well-documented, thorough study of Taylor, stressing
his participation in the War of 1812 and the Mexican
War and his time as president. Volume 1: SOLDIER
OF THE REPUBLIC; volume 2: SOLDIER IN THE WHITE
HOUSE.

JOHN TYLER

1105 Seager, Robert II. AND TYLER TOO: A BIOGRAPHY OF JOHN AND
JULIA GARDINER TYLER. New York: McGraw-Hill Book Co., 1963.
698 p.

Combines the romance and marriage of the principals
with the involved political machinations of the time.
Seager traces the evolution of Tyler's states rights position to one of secession.

DANIEL WEBSTER

1106 Brown, Norman D. DANIEL WEBSTER AND THE POLITICS OF AVAIL-

ABILITY. Athens: University of Georgia Press, 1969. 191 p.

A detailed study of particularly significant years in Webster's development as a politician (1830-36), a period which saw emergence of the Whigs, the controversy over President Andrew Jackson's bank policies, and the Nullification Controversy.

1107 Current, Richard N. DANIEL WEBSTER AND THE RISE OF NATIONAL CONSERVATISM. Boston: Little, Brown, 1955. 215 p.

The book centers on Webster's exposition of conservative politics as his ideas matured between 1820 and 1850.

1108 Fuess, Claude M. DANIEL WEBSTER. 2 vols. Boston: Little, Brown, 1930. Fronts., ports., plates, facsims.

A full, informative biography, stressing Webster's political career and the many controversies in which he took part.

Chapter 6

DISRUPTION AND RECONSTRUCTION
OF THE UNION, 1860-77

A. CIVIL WAR

1. General

1109 Basler, Roy P. A SHORT HISTORY OF THE AMERICAN CIVIL WAR. New
York: Basic Books, 1967. 159 p. Illus., ports., facsims.

A compact history, useful for gaining a quick overview
of events. Excellent illustrations.

1110 Catton, Bruce. CENTENNIAL HISTORY OF THE CIVIL WAR. 3 vols.
Garden City, N.Y. Doubleday, 1961-65.

The culmination of many years of research and publishing on the Civil War. Catton's narrative is dramatic
and colorful. Volume 1: THE COMING FURY; volume
2: TERRIBLE SWIFT SWORD; volume 3: NEVER CALL
RETREAT.

1111 Cole, Arthur C. THE IRREPRESSIBLE CONFLICT, 1850-1865. 1934. Reprint. St. Clair Shores, Mich.: Scholarly Press, 1971. 483 p. Illus.

Stresses the differences between the ways of life of North
and South and the schism which grew and deepened until the only alternative seen was war.

1112 Commager, Henry Steele, ed. THE BLUE AND THE GRAY: THE STORY
OF THE CIVIL WAR AS TOLD BY PARTICIPANTS. 2 vols. Indianapolis:
Bobbs-Merrill, 1950. Illus., maps.

Commager ransacked the contemporary literature of the
war and put together an intriguing anthology. He provides a general introduction and pithy headnotes to the
selections.

1113 Donald, David. LINCOLN RECONSIDERED: ESSAYS ON THE CIVIL
WAR ERA. 2d ed., enl. New York: Alfred A. Knopf, 1961. 275 p.
Paperbound.

This series of essays on various aspects of Lincoln and
the Civil War is more concerned with interpretation and
less concerned with restating what the author believes
are now well-established facts. Donald includes such
matters as Lincoln as a politician and as a Whig, his
relations with the Radicals, and his place in folklore.

1114 _____, ed. WHY THE NORTH WON THE CIVIL WAR. Baton Rouge:
Louisiana State University Press, 1960. 128 p.

A collection of lectures by leading authorities, delivered
at Gettysburg College. Included are the editor, on the
structure of the Confederacy; Richard N. Current, on
the war-making abilities of the two sections; David M.
Potter, on political parties in the North; T. Harry Williams,
on military developments; and Norman A. Graebner, on
foreign affairs of the North and South.

1115 Long, E.B. THE CIVIL WAR DAY BY DAY: AN ALMANAC, 1861-1865.
Garden City, N.Y.: Doubleday, 1971. 1,149 p. Maps.

The author, who was in charge of research for Bruce
Catton's CENTENNIAL HISTORY OF THE CIVIL WAR,
q.v., no. 1110, has here gathered together in almanac
form developments in the conflict from November 1860
to May 1865. He precedes his account of each month
with an overview of political and military events for the
period and includes a section on statistical information
and an exhaustive bibliography. Each item in the index
is dated.

1116 Nevins, Allan. ORDEAL OF THE UNION. 8 vols. New York: Charles
Scribner's Sons, 1947-71. Illus., ports., maps.

A comprehensive history covering the years 1857-65.
The three segments of the history stand independent of
one another, Nevins having decided to continue the
story after the publication of the first two volumes. His
stance is generally conservative, e.g., in regard to such
abolitionists as Congressman Horace Mann, whom he
thought mischievous. Volumes 1 and 2: THE ORDEAL
OF THE UNION; volumes 3 and 4: THE EMERGENCE
OF LINCOLN; volumes 5 to 8: THE WAR FOR THE
UNION.

1117 Nichols, Roy F. THE STAKES OF POWER, 1845-1877. New York: Hill
and Wang, 1961. 246 p. Maps.

An analysis of the ante-bellum period which stresses the strains in the relationship between North and South and the constant angling for position and superiority in national councils and in economic matters.

1118 Randall, James, and Donald, David. THE CIVIL WAR AND RECONSTRUCTION. 2d rev. ed. Boston: D.C. Heath, 1969. 866 p. Illus., maps.

A standard text in a revised edition. Randall's original volume appeared in 1937. Donald, in 1961, accomplished the first revision to take cognizance of later scholarship. This edition is substantially the same but includes additional bibliographical material.

1119 Stampp, Kenneth M., ed. THE CAUSES OF THE CIVIL WAR. Rev. ed. Englewood Cliffs, N.J.: Prentice-Hall, 1965. 192 p. Paperbound.

A mixture of contemporary materials and recent articles by scholars in the field. The selections, which are quite brief, are grouped under such headings as State Rights and Nationalism, The Right and Wrong of Slavery, and Majority Rule and Minority Rights.

1120 U.S. Naval War Records Office. OFFICIAL RECORDS OF THE UNION AND CONFEDERATE NAVIES IN THE WAR OF THE REBELLION. 30 vols. Washington, D.C.: Government Printing Office, 1894-1922. Illus., ports., maps.

Complements the army records in THE WAR OF THE REBELLION, q.v., no. 1121.

1121 U.S. War Department. THE WAR OF THE REBELLION: A COMPILATION OF THE OFFICIAL RECORDS OF THE UNION AND CONFEDERATE ARMIES. 128 vols. 1881-1900. Reprint. Gettysburg, Pa.: National Historical Society, 1972-   .

A storehouse of material containing not only official records of the armies on both sides of the conflict but documents of the Union and Confederate governments and materials from private sources as well. The material is arranged in the volumes by topic; the general index volume is an excellent key to the contents.

2. Sectional

a. THE CONFEDERACY

1122 Coulter, E. Merton. THE CONFEDERATE STATES OF AMERICA, 1861-1865. Baton Rouge: Louisiana State University Press, 1950. 658 p. Illus.

Focuses on the South at war. In this volume in the joint
venture, A HISTORY OF THE SOUTH, Coulter deals with
all aspects of the wartime experience--military, political,
economic, and social. He believes the South lost because the people did not have the will to carry on.

1123 Dowdey, Clifford. THE LAND THEY FOUGHT FOR: THE STORY OF THE
SOUTH AS THE CONFEDERACY, 1832-1865. Garden City, N.Y.: Doubleday, 1955. 446 p. Map.

Dowdey harks back to the Nullification Controversy of
1832 in order to explain the development of the South's
sectional feeling and its alienation from the rest of the
nation. He brings to the narrative his skill as a novelist. A book filled with partisan, i.e., Confederate,
feeling.

1124 Eaton, Clement. A HISTORY OF THE SOUTHERN CONFEDERACY. New
York: Macmillan, 1954. 351 p.

A well-rounded account, making much use of primary
material. Eaton uses a topical arrangement and deals
with aspects of both civilian and military life.

1125 Owsley, Frank L. KING COTTON DIPLOMACY: FOREIGN RELATIONS
OF THE CONFEDERATE STATES OF AMERICA. 2d ed., rev. Chicago:
University of Chicago Press, 1959. 638 p. Tables.

A full history of the diplomacy of the Confederate states.
Owsley makes it clear that cotton was the major consideration in southern foreign affairs. This revision is
by Harriet Chappell Owsley.

1126 Patrick, Rembert W. JEFFERSON DAVIS AND HIS CABINET. 1944. Reprint. Baton Rouge: Louisiana State University Press, 1961. 411 p.

The operations of the Confederate cabinet during the
war. Patrick evaluates the contributions of the various
members and also considers them as personalities in the
social life of the capitals.

1127 Roland, Charles P. THE CONFEDERACY. Chicago: University of Chicago Press, 1960. 218 p. Illus.

Covers, in brief compass, all aspects of the struggle of
the Confederacy for independence. A balanced view
that fails, however, to cover fully the South's share of
the responsibility for what happened at Sumter.

1128 Wiley, Bell I., and Milhollen, Hirst D. EMBATTLED CONFEDERATES:
AN ILLUSTRATED HISTORY OF SOUTHERNERS AT WAR. New York: Har-

per & Row, 1964. 300 p. Illus., ports., map, facsims., tables.

Text by Wiley, pictures compiled by Milhollen. The collection gives examples of the varied life on the home front. Appendices give lists of members of the Congress, the cabinet, governors, generals, and even vital statistics of a "typical" infantry company.

1129 Yearns, Wilfred B. THE CONFEDERATE CONGRESS. Athens: University of Georgia Press, 1960. 293 p.

A detailed study of the workings of the Confederate Congress. Yearns reviews its organization and operation, its leading personalities, and the important question of how it got on with President Jefferson Davis.

b. THE UNION

1130 Fite, Emerson D. SOCIAL AND INDUSTRIAL CONDITIONS IN THE NORTH DURING THE CIVIL WAR. 1910. Reprint. New York: Frederick Ungar, 1963. 325 p.

An economic study based primarily on original sources. Concentrates on the development of industry and the social consequences of the war.

1131 Freidel, Frank, ed. UNION PAMPHLETS OF THE CIVIL WAR, 1861-1865. 2 vols. Cambridge, Mass.: Harvard University Press, 1967. Illus., facsims.

Pamphlets that created a stir at the time are included, with editorial introductions placing them in context.

1132 Gray, Wood. THE HIDDEN CIVIL WAR: THE STORY OF THE COPPER-HEADS. New York: Viking Press, 1942. 314 p. Illus., ports., plates, maps, facsims.

A study of those in the North who advocated a settlement of the war on southern terms and those who attempted to sabotage the Union effort. Gray makes good use of contemporary newspapers.

1133 Hesseltine, William B. LINCOLN AND THE WAR GOVERNORS. New York: Alfred A. Knopf, 1948. 437 p.

The relations of Lincoln and the northern governors, a story of many disagreements. Hesseltine shows that Lincoln was able to unite them and thus the Union into an effective force.

1134 _____. LINCOLN'S PLAN OF RECONSTRUCTION. 1960. Reprint.

Chicago: Quadrangle Books, 1967. 154 p.

Examines the widely held belief that had Lincoln lived
he would have successfully guided the nation through
Reconstruction. The author concludes that the president
had not developed a plan at the time of his death.

1135 Klement, Frank L. THE COPPERHEADS IN THE MIDDLE WEST. Chicago:
University of Chicago Press, 1960. 354 p. Ports., facsims.

A revisionist history. Klement attempts to overturn the
view that the Copperheads were pro-South and disloyal
to the Union. He, indeed, believes Republican politicians achieved their goal of getting the Copperheads to
support the war effort.

1136 Leech, Margaret. REVEILLE IN WASHINGTON, 1860-1865. New York:
Harper & Brothers, 1941. 493 p. Illus., maps, facsim.

A social, political study of the capital in wartime. All
aspects of life are dealt with--serious and frivolous--and
many notable persons are sketched. A well-documented
work, written in vivid prose.

1137 Trefousse, Hans L. THE RADICAL REPUBLICANS: LINCOLN'S VANGUARD
FOR RACIAL JUSTICE. New York: Alfred A. Knopf, 1969. 524 p.
Illus., ports.

A study of the leading Radicals and their part in forming
the Republican party and in the struggle for equal rights
for blacks. Trefousse pays particular attention to Sumner, Stevens, Wade, and Chandler.

1138 Williams, T. Harry. LINCOLN AND THE RADICALS. Madison: University of Wisconsin Press, 1941. 419 p. Illus., ports.

The struggle between Lincoln, who first and foremost
sought to preserve the Union, and the Radicals in the
Republican party and the Congress who sought to promote
social revolution in the South. A lively account, somewhat slanted against the Radicals.

3. Topical

a. AGRICULTURE

1139 Gates, Paul W. AGRICULTURE AND THE CIVIL WAR. New York: Alfred A. Knopf, 1965. 406 p. Illus., ports., maps, facsims.

The relative accomplishments of agriculture in the North
and South during the war and changes brought about as

a result of it. The book is based on contemporary records.

b. BLACK AMERICANS

1140 Cornish, Dudley T. THE SABLE ARM: NEGRO TROOPS IN THE UNION ARMY, 1861-1865. 1956. Reprint. New York: W.W. Norton, 1966. 337 p.

The debate over whether to recruit black troops and, when the question was decided affirmatively, how they performed in the Union armies. Cornish has amassed a great deal of documentary evidence.

1141 Du Bois, W.E.B. BLACK RECONSTRUCTION IN AMERICA: AN ESSAY TOWARD A HISTORY OF THE PART WHICH BLACK FOLK PLAYED IN THE ATTEMPT TO RECONSTRUCT DEMOCRACY IN AMERICA, 1860-1880. 1935. Reprint. New York: Russell & Russell, 1966. 746 p.

An analysis of the role of the freedman in the Civil War and Reconstruction. Du Bois sets forth the successes due to Negro efforts in both periods and attempts to revise the negative opinions of white historians of this period toward Reconstruction governments. He is critical of whites for holding the view that the black man is inferior and of blacks for accepting that evaluation. Had the federal government provided land and other economic help for the freedman, he believes the outcome of Reconstruction would have been quite different.

1142 Gerteis, Louis S. FROM CONTRABAND TO FREEDMAN: FEDERAL POLICY TOWARD SOUTHERN BLACKS, 1861-1865. Westport, Conn.: Greenwood Press, 1973. 255 p.

An analysis of the changing status of the black from slave to freedman in the South during the Civil War. Gerteis dwells on the relationship of the slave with the northern armies and officials.

1143 Higginson, Thomas Wentworth. ARMY LIFE IN A BLACK REGIMENT. Edited by John Hope Franklin. Boston: Beacon Press, 1962. 302 p. Paperbound.

An intriguing primary source of the Civil War, originally published in 1869. Higginson, a Unitarian minister and reformer, led the first black army unit to be formed by the Union in its operation along the southern Atlantic coast; here he details their day-to-day problems and accomplishments. The editor provides a biographical introduction of Higginson.

1144 McPherson, James M. THE STRUGGLE FOR EQUALITY: ABOLITIONISTS AND THE NEGRO IN THE CIVIL WAR AND RECONSTRUCTION. Princeton, N.J.: Princeton University Press, 1964. 485 p. Illus.

The role the abolitionists played in the Civil War and Reconstruction. McPherson shows that, contrary to popular belief, they did not neglect the black man on emancipation but teamed up with black groups to promote the attainment of civil rights.

1145 _____, ed. THE NEGRO'S CIVIL WAR: HOW AMERICAN NEGROES FELT AND ACTED DURING THE WAR FOR THE UNION. New York: Pantheon Books, 1965. 370 p. Illus., ports.

Material drawn from many types of persons--soldiers, editors, schoolteachers, nurses, workers, etc.--bridged by an informative narrative by the editor.

1146 Quarles, Benjamin. LINCOLN AND THE NEGRO. New York: Oxford University Press, 1962. 275 p. Illus.

The attitudes of Lincoln toward blacks and vice versa. Lincoln, Quarles asserts, put the survival of the Union before the abolition of slavery, thus disappointing the blacks; but when he emancipated the slaves in the District of Columbia and issued the Emancipation Proclamation he became a hero. Quarles provides details on Lincoln's thoughts on colonization, use of blacks in the military forces, etc.

1147 Wiley, Bell I. SOUTHERN NEGROES, 1861-1865. 1938. Reprint. New Haven, Conn.: Yale University Press, 1965. 376 p.

The lives of blacks in the Confederate states and in the areas controlled by the Union forces. Wiley considers laboring conditions, the behavior of the slaves, their education and religious life, and their service in the armies.

c. CONSTITUTIONAL DEVELOPMENTS

1148 Hyman, Harold M. A MORE PERFECT UNION: THE IMPACT OF THE CIVIL WAR AND RECONSTRUCTION OF THE CONSTITUTION. New York: Alfred A. Knopf, 1973. 562 p.

Hyman takes the position that the Civil War and Reconstruction had a serious impact on succeeding interpretations of the Constitution. He traces the successful attempt of the Republicans to mold that instrument to meet the needs of the political situation in a time of crisis.

1149 Randall, James G. CONSTITUTIONAL PROBLEMS UNDER LINCOLN.
Rev. ed. 1951. Reprint. Gloucester, Mass.: Peter Smith, 1963. 603
p.

> A thorough analysis, based on documentary sources, of
> how the Constitution was stretched to meet wartime con-
> ditions, by a scholar of Lincoln and the Civil War.
> Randall deals with treason, habeas corpus, military rule,
> martial law, confiscation, emancipation, the partition
> of Virginia, and many other issues. This edition con-
> tains a foreword by the author on new sources and com-
> ments made on the original edition of 1926.

d. ECONOMICS

1150 Andreano, Ralph, ed. THE ECONOMIC IMPACT OF THE AMERICAN
CIVIL WAR. Rev. ed. Cambridge, Mass.: Schenkman, 1967. 244 p.
Tables. Paperbound.

> The editor includes recent articles by scholars making
> use of quantitative methods. In addition, he includes
> statistical tables for consideration by the reader. Topics
> covered: internal economic adjustments during the war;
> monetary and physical costs of the war; national econo-
> mic policy, business interests, and political power; the
> tariff issue; the war and national economic growth.

1151 Gilchrist, David T., and Lewis, David W., eds. ECONOMIC CHANGE
IN THE CIVIL WAR ERA. Greenville, Del.: Eleutherian Mills-Hagley
Foundation, 1965. 190 p. Map, tables.

> The proceedings of a conference on American economic
> institutional change, 1850-1873, and the impact of the
> Civil War, held in 1964. The papers and commentaries
> by leading scholars deal with the national economy,
> commercial banking, foreign investment in the United
> States, the international market for agricultural commod-
> ities, government-business relations, science and tech-
> nology, and manufacturing and transportation.

1152 Sharkey, Robert P. MONEY, CLASS AND PARTY: AN ECONOMIC
STUDY OF CIVIL WAR AND RECONSTRUCTION. Baltimore: Johns Hopkins Press, 1959. 346 p.

> A revisionist study which sets out to destroy the thesis
> of Charles A. Beard that eastern capitalists advocated
> contraction of the currency while Democratic western
> farmers favored inflation. Sharkey's figures indicate that
> what is called for is a general overhaul of the conven-
> tional wisdom.

e. THE EMANCIPATION PROCLAMATION

1153 Donovan, Frank R. MR. LINCOLN'S PROCLAMATION: THE STORY OF
THE EMANCIPATION PROCLAMATION. New York: Dodd, Mead, 1964.
150 p. Illus., ports.

> Donovan deals with Lincoln's motivations in issuing the
> Proclamation, claiming that his first concern was mili-
> tary. The political and moral effects it might have in
> the states of the Union and abroad were secondary con-
> siderations.

1154 Franklin, John Hope. THE EMANCIPATION PROCLAMATION. Garden
City, N.Y.: Doubleday, 1963. 181 p. Illus.

> The circumstances leading up to Lincoln's proclamation.
> Franklin assesses the political and military situation and
> analyzes Lincoln's motivations.

f. FOREIGN REACTIONS

1155 Adams, Ephraim D. GREAT BRITAIN AND THE AMERICAN CIVIL WAR.
2 vols. New York: Longmans, Green, 1925. Front., ports., plates.

> Based on archival material and the contemporary press
> accounts. Adams maintains that the British government
> was properly neutral in the war, while important social
> leaders, such as Bright and Cobden, were outspokenly
> in favor of the cause of the North.

1156 Jordan, Donaldson, and Pratt, Edwin J. EUROPE AND THE AMERICAN
CIVIL WAR. 1931. Reprint. New York: Octagon Books, 1969. 311
p. Illus.

> European reactions are mirrored in one-third of the book,
> those of the English in about two-thirds. The authors
> have delved deeply into the sources.

g. INTELLECTUAL AND SOCIAL LIFE

1157 Chesnut, Mary B. A DIARY FROM DIXIE. Edited by Ben Ames Williams.
Boston: Houghton Mifflin, 1949. 584 p.

> Chesnut of South Carolina, wife of a brigadier general
> in the Confederate army, filled her pages with gossip,
> laughter, and risque stories, as well as the serious busi-
> ness of a nation at war. Her diary provides a remark-
> able picture of the time.

1158 Fredrickson, George M. THE INNER CIVIL WAR: NORTHERN INTEL-

LECTUALS AND THE CRISIS OF THE UNION. New York: Harper & Row, 1965. 285 p.

A discussion of how Americans viewed the Civil War as it progressed, with particular accent on such northern intellectuals as Thoreau, Whitman, and Holmes.

1159 Wilson, Edmund. PATRIOTIC GORE: STUDIES IN THE LITERATURE OF THE AMERICAN CIVIL WAR. New York: Oxford University Press, 1962. 849 p.

A literary critic examines the writings of significant figures, North and South, with insight and sensitivity. Wilson evaluates the work of such writers as Harriet Beecher Stowe, Ambrose Bierce, Thomas Nelson Page, and Sidney Lanier, and also delves into the thought of political and military figures such as Lincoln, Lee, Sherman, and Grant.

h. THE SECESSION CRISIS

1160 Current, Richard N. LINCOLN AND THE FIRST SHOT. Philadelphia: Lippincott, 1963. 223 p. Map.

The events of March and April 1861, leading up to the firing on Fort Sumter. Current explains Lincoln's thoughts and actions in this period. He thinks the president believed war was inevitable and that it was vital that, if it came, the South should have responsibility for starting it.

1161 Dumond, Dwight L. THE SECESSION MOVEMENT, 1860-1861. 1931. Reprint. New York: Octagon Books, 1963. 300 p.

Traces the contention between North and South over interpretation of the Constitution and the process by which secession took place. A compact narrative based on archival materials.

1162 _____, ed. SOUTHERN EDITORIALS ON SECESSION. 1931. Reprint. Gloucester, Mass.: Peter Smith, 1964. 561 p.

Dumond examined approximately 2,000 editorials in more than seventy papers in order to derive a representative sample. The 183 published here show differences of opinion as well as agreement on the momentous issue.

1163 Potter, David M. LINCOLN AND HIS PARTY IN THE SECESSION CRISIS. 1942. Reprint. New Haven, Conn.: Yale University Press, 1962. 440 p.

The critical period between the election of Lincoln and

the bombardment of Fort Sumter. Potter gives an un-
flattering appraisal of the actions both of Lincoln and
certain intemperate southern politicians.

1164 Stampp, Kenneth M. AND THE WAR CAME: THE NORTH AND THE
SECESSION CRISIS, 1860-1861. 1950. Reprint. Baton Rouge: Louisiana
State University Press, 1970. 348 p. Port. Paperbound.

A study of the conflicting sentiments in the days immediately prior to the outbreak of war. Stampp analyzes
the positions taken for and against maintaining the Union
and the personalities involved in the debate.

1165 Wooster, Ralph A. THE SECESSION CONVENTIONS OF THE SOUTH.
Princeton, N.J.: Princeton University Press, 1962. 302 p. Maps.

A statistical study of the conventions in each state in
1860-61. By comparing places of birth, ages, occupations, and such matters as slaveholding, gained from
census reports and sources, Wooster derives what he considers typical characteristics of the members of the conventions.

j. WARFARE

1166 Bruce, Robert V. LINCOLN AND THE TOOLS OF WAR. Indianapolis:
Bobbs-Merrill, 1956. 379 p. Illus., ports.

The development of improved weaponry and Lincoln's
part in it. Bruce has delved deeply into the records
and has produced a detailed work that is also rich in
anecdotal material and humor.

1167 Catton, Bruce. GLORY ROAD: THE BLOODY ROUTE FROM FREDERICKS-
BURG TO GETTYSBURG. Garden City, N.Y.: Doubleday, 1952. 416
p. Maps.

The second in Catton's series on the Army of the Potomac. (See also MR. LINCOLN'S ARMY, no. 1168,
and A STILLNESS AT APPOMATTOX, no. 1169.)
This volume concentrates on the bloody battles of
Fredericksburg, Chancellorsville, and Gettysburg in
1862-63. Catton uses official reports, regimental histories, private letters and diaries, newspaper accounts,
etc., and distills them into a moving narrative.

1168 _____. MR. LINCOLN'S ARMY. Garden City, N.Y.: Doubleday,
1951. 372 p. Maps.

The Army of the Potomac under General George B.
McClellan. The first of Catton's trilogy (see also GLORY

ROAD, no 1167, and A STILLNESS AT APPOMAT-
TOX, no. 1169), it starts with the Second Battle
of Bull Run and is crammed with colorful details of
army life.

1169 _____. A STILLNESS AT APPOMATTOX. Garden City, N.Y.: Doubleday, 1953. 448 p.

The final year of the Civil War, ending with Grant and
Lee meeting at Appomattox Court House. Catton describes such engagements as the Battle of the Wilderness
and the siege of Petersburg in graphic detail. This is
the third in his trilogy on the Army of the Potomac,
with MR. LINCOLN'S ARMY, q.v., no. 1168, and
GLORY ROAD, q.v., no. 1167.

1170 _____. THIS HALLOWED GROUND: THE STORY OF THE UNION SIDE
OF THE CIVIL WAR. Garden City, N.Y.: Doubleday, 1956. 446 p.
Maps.

Reviews the entire military history of the war with verve,
color, and keen analysis. Brilliant sketches of the personalities, political as well as military, are included.

1171 Freeman, Douglas Southall. LEE'S LIEUTENANTS: A STUDY IN COM-
MAND. 3 vols. New York: Charles Scribner's Sons, 1942-44. Illus.,
ports., maps.

Supplementing his earlier work, R.E. LEE, q.v., no.
1183, Freeman examines the personalities and accomplishments of Lee's chief cohorts in the Army of Northern Virginia, with particular attention to their relationships to their chief.

Leach, Jack F. CONSCRIPTION IN THE UNITED STATES. See no. 872.

1172 Shannon, Fred A. ORGANIZATION AND ADMINISTRATION OF THE
UNION ARMY, 1861-1865. 2 vols. 1928. Reprint. Gloucester, Mass.:
Peter Smith, 1965. Illus., port.

A comprehensive picture of what was going on behind
the lines. Shannon has made extensive use of original
sources. His view of what went on is somber, but his
presentation is vivid.

1173 Vandiver, Frank E. REBEL BRASS: THE CONFEDERATE COMMAND SYS-
TEM. 1956. Reprint. New York: Greenwood Press, 1969. 159 p. Illus., ports., map.

The direction of the Confederate war effort. Vandiver
looks at the problem of fighting a total war, for which

231

the South was not prepared, the relation of the civil
administration to the military command, and the problems
of logistics.

1174 Wiley, Bell I. THE LIFE OF BILLY YANK: THE COMMON SOLDIER OF
THE UNION. 1952. Reprint. Garden City, N.Y.: Doubleday, 1971.
454 p. Front.

> The author does for the Union soldier what he did for
> the Confederate in his earlier work, THE LIFE OF JOHNNY
> REB, q.v., no. 1175.

1175 _____. THE LIFE OF JOHNNY REB: THE COMMON SOLDIER OF THE
CONFEDERACY. 1943. Reprint. Garden City, N.Y.: Doubleday,
1971. 444 p. Front.

> Looks at the lot of the common soldier in the southern
> forces in the Civil War: his training, food, the strains
> of combat, and problems of morale. Wiley bases his
> work on letters and diaries of participants, supplemented
> by interviews with veterans. He treats the Union sol-
> diers in THE LIFE OF BILLY YANK, q.v., no. 1174.

1176 Williams, Kenneth P. LINCOLN FINDS A GENERAL: A MILITARY STUDY
OF THE CIVIL WAR. 5 vols. New York: Macmillan, 1949-59. Ports.,
maps.

> The trials and tribulations experienced by Lincoln in his
> search for a competent military leader. Williams exa-
> mines the personalities of the Union officers and eval-
> uates their strategy and tactics.

1177 Williams, T. Harry. LINCOLN AND HIS GENERALS. New York: Alfred
A. Knopf, 1952. 375 p. Ports., map.

> Evaluates Lincoln in his role as commander-in-chief.
> Using the standards of modern warfare, Williams gives
> Lincoln a high grade.

4. Prominent Individuals

CHARLES FRANCIS ADAMS

For C.F. Adams' DIARY (his early years), see no. 894.

1178 Duberman, Martin. CHARLES FRANCIS ADAMS, 1807-1886. Boston:
Houghton Mifflin, 1961. 525 p. Illus., ports.

> A solid biography which deals less with the private man
> than with his public career. Duberman traces in detail

Adams's involvement in Massachusetts politics, his service in the House of Representatives, and his crucial role as the Union's minister to Great Britain.

JAY COOKE

1179 Oberholtzer, Ellis P. JAY COOKE, FINANCIER OF THE CIVIL WAR. 2 vols. 1907. Reprint. New York: Burt Franklin, 1969. Illus., front., ports., plates, map, facsims.

A very favorable view of the financier in a lengthy biography, much of it based on family papers.

JEFFERSON DAVIS

1180 Rowland, Dunbar, ed. JEFFERSON DAVIS, CONSTITUTIONALIST: HIS LETTERS, PAPERS, AND SPEECHES. 10 vols. Jackson: Mississippi Department of Archives and History, 1923. Fronts., ports.

The materials are arranged chronologically; editorial notes are not extensive.

1181 Strode, Hudson. JEFFERSON DAVIS. 3 vols. New York: Harcourt, Brace, 1955-64. Ports.

A sympathetic biography which, however, does not completely gloss over Davis's weak points. His rigidity shines through. Volume 1: AMERICAN PATRIOT, 1808-1861; volume 2: CONFEDERATE PRESIDENT; volume 3: TRAGIC HERO: THE LAST TWENTY-FIVE YEARS, 1864-1889.

THOMAS JONATHAN JACKSON

1182 Vandiver, Frank E. MIGHTY STONEWALL. New York: McGraw-Hill Book Co., 1957. 558 p. Illus., ports., maps.

A biography of the famous Confederate general, Thomas Jonathan Jackson. Vandiver covers his complete career but inevitably dwells to a greater extent on his role in the Civil War.

ROBERT E. LEE

1183 Freeman, Douglas Southall. R.E. LEE. 4 vols. 1934-35. Reprint. New York: Charles Scribner's Sons, 1949. Fronts., ports., plates, maps, facsims.

A massive biography of the South's leading general and

citizen. Freeman pays particular attention to Lee's strategy in the Civil War.

ABRAHAM LINCOLN

1184 Basler, Roy P., ed. THE COLLECTED WORKS OF ABRAHAM LINCOLN. 9 vols. New Brunswick, N.J.: Rutgers University Press, 1953-55. Illus., ports., facsims.

The speeches, state papers, and extant personal letters of Lincoln, in a well-edited collection. No tables of contents are included, but volume 9 is a general index.

1185 _____. THE COLLECTED WORKS OF ABRAHAM LINCOLN: SUPPLE-MENT, 1832-1865. Westport, Conn.: Greenwood Press, 1974. 320 p.

Brings together previously unpublished materials and therefore fills gaps in the original collection, q.v., no. 1184. More routine matters in Lincoln's career are dealt with here.

1186 Current, Richard N. THE LINCOLN NOBODY KNOWS. 1958. Reprint. New York: Hill and Wang, 1964. 320 p.

A discussion of aspects of Lincoln's life under dispute by historians. Among the topics dealt with are Lincoln as a family man, a politician, leader in war, peacemaker. Many of Current's conclusions are tentative.

1187 Fehrenbacher, Don E. PRELUDE TO GREATNESS: LINCOLN IN THE 1850's. Stanford, Calif.: Stanford University Press, 1962. 205 p.

A collection of the author's essays, some of which appeared earlier. Fehrenbacher deals with such matters as Lincoln as a politician and his role in the development of the Republican party, and with historiographical matters.

1188 Randall, James G. LINCOLN, THE PRESIDENT. 4 vols. New York: Dodd, Mead, 1945-55. Illus., ports., maps, facsims.

Removes Lincoln from his pedestal and deals with him as a fallible human being seeking the right solutions to very confusing problems. A dispassionate evaluation. On the death of Randall, volume 4 was completed by Richard N. Current. Volumes 1 and 2: SPRINGFIELD TO GETTYSBURG; volume 3: MIDSTREAM; volume 4: LAST FULL MEASURE.

1189 Sandburg, Carl. ABRAHAM LINCOLN. 6 vols. New York: Harcourt,

Brace, 1926-39. Illus., fronts., ports., plates, maps, facsims.

This poetic treatment of Lincoln's life and times is a
mine of information, a mammoth work which tells not
only what Lincoln thought, said, and did but what
others thought, said, and did about him. Volumes 1
and 2: THE PRAIRIE YEARS; volumes 3-6: THE WAR
YEARS.

1190 Thomas, Benjamin P. ABRAHAM LINCOLN: A BIOGRAPHY. 1952.
Reprint. New York: Modern Library, 1968. 560 p.

Rated by many scholars as the best single-volume biography of Lincoln. Thomas displays deep and intimate
knowledge of the sources and writes in a pleasurable
style.

EDMUND RUFFIN

1191 Craven, Avery O. EDMUND RUFFIN, SOUTHERNER. 1932. Reprint.
Baton Rouge: Louisiana State University Press, 1966. 302 p. Illus.,
ports.

A study of the Virginia agriculturist and radical who
fired the first shot at Fort Sumter. Craven sees Ruffin
as a type in the Old South that was responsible for the
violent emotionalism that fed the fires of secession.

WILLIAM HENRY SEWARD

1192 Van Deusen, Glyndon G. WILLIAM HENRY SEWARD. New York: Oxford University Press, 1967. 677 p. Illus., ports.

A detailed biography of the New York governor who
served as secretary of state in the Lincoln and Johnson
administrations. Van Deusen concentrates on Seward's
public life.

EDWIN STANTON

1193 Thomas, Benjamin P., and Hyman, Harold M. STANTON: THE LIFE AND
TIMES OF LINCOLN'S SECRETARY OF WAR. New York: Alfred A. Knopf,
1962. 659 p. Illus., ports., facsim.

Begun by Thomas but, on his death, completed by Hyman. An impartial, judicious study. Edwin Stanton's
personality, which was "explosive," comes through the
mass of scholarly detail.

CHARLES SUMNER

1194 Donald, David H. CHARLES SUMNER. 2 vols. New York: Alfred A. Knopf, 1960-70. Illus., ports.

> Donald traces Sumner's career in Massachusetts and then his establishment as a force in Washington. Donald's analysis of Sumner's lingering illness after his beating on the Senate floor has become famous. Volume 1: THE COMING OF THE CIVIL WAR; volume 2: THE RIGHTS OF MAN.

B. RECONSTRUCTION

1. General

1195 Belz, Herman. RECONSTRUCTING THE UNION: THEORY AND POLICY DURING THE CIVIL WAR. Ithaca, N.Y.: Cornell University Press, 1969. 345 p.

> The shifting policies of the president and Congress toward Reconstruction, 1861-64. Provides a good background for what actually did happen at war's close.

1196 Bowers, Claude G. THE TRAGIC ERA: THE REVOLUTION AFTER LINCOLN. Cambridge, Mass.: Houghton Mifflin, 1929. 589 p. Illus., front., ports., plates, facsim.

> This popularization supports President Andrew Johnson's plan for a lenient reconstruction of the South and sees him as maligned by his opponents. Bowers's bias becomes obvious when he defends the formation and activities of the Ku Klux Klan, which originated, he claims, among fun-loving folk out on a spree but was then transformed into a vehicle of oppression when poor whites enlisted in the ranks. As in all of his writings, Bowers includes here many entertaining stories.

1197 Buck, Paul H. THE ROAD TO REUNION, 1865-1900. 1937. Reprint. Boston: Little, Brown, 1947. 331 p.

> A study of the forces--economic, social and cultural-- that led to a healing of the wounds of the Civil War. Despite the waving of the "bloody shirt" and other divisive appeals of the political parties that perpetuated hard feelings, and despite the intransigence of the South on the subject of Negro rights, Buck states that the passage of time softened sectional animosities until at the turn of the twentieth century they had subsided.

1198 Craven, Avery O. RECONSTRUCTION: THE ENDING OF THE CIVIL WAR. New York: Holt, Rinehart and Winston, 1969. 336 p.

Traces the conflicting presidential and congressional plans for reconstruction through the presidency of U.S. Grant. Craven claims that among the failings of leaders of the period was an unwillingness to confront such problems as the place of the freedmen in American life. The results of such inaction are being visited on the present generation.

1199 Dunning, William A. RECONSTRUCTION, POLITICAL AND ECONOMIC, 1865-1877. 1907. Reprint. New York: Harper & Row, 1968. 394 p. Front., maps. Paperbound.

An influential book by the leader of a school of historians that took a critical view of northern attempts at reconstruction and fostered the doctrine of white supremacy. Dunning condemned the radical governments as evil and hypocritical. The blacks are denigrated, as are the carpetbaggers, scalawags, and the Republican party. An important book in the history of American historiography.

1200 Franklin, John Hope. RECONSTRUCTION: AFTER THE CIVIL WAR. Chicago: University of Chicago Press, 1962. 258 p. Illus.

Gives special attention to the role of blacks in the Reconstruction governments of the South, judging them, over-all, to have done a good job. They lacked vindictiveness toward their former masters, a feeling not reciprocated. Franklin details the rise of the Ku Klux Klan and the efforts of the Redeemers to thwart the will of the North. He believes that only with a greater concentration of federal troops in the South could Reconstruction as envisaged by the Radicals have been a success.

1201 Patrick, Rembert W. THE RECONSTRUCTION OF THE NATION. New York: Oxford University Press, 1967. 335 p. Illus., ports., maps.

An attempt to balance the views of past historians with those of present-day revisionists. Patrick deals with social and economic factors but concentrates on political developments. He believes that President Johnson had a definite plan for reconstruction and that the southern states were on their way to achieving stability when emergence of the Black Codes caused a vigorous reaction in the North.

Randall, James G., and Donald, D. CIVIL WAR AND RECONSTRUCTION. See no. 1118.

1202 Stampp, Kenneth M. THE ERA OF RECONSTRUCTION, 1865-1877. New
York: Alfred A. Knopf, 1965. 237 p.

> Refutes the older view that the South was reincorporated
> in the Union by harsh methods. Stampp believes that,
> although shabbiness and corruption marred the process,
> never in history had a conquered people been treated
> so gently. The campaign of the Radical Republicans
> was responsible for the acceptance in the Constitution's
> Fourteenth and Fifteenth Amendments of the humanity of
> four million black people. Stampp includes evaluations
> of the personal and political characters of Presidents
> Lincoln and Johnson.

1203 Stampp, Kenneth M., and Litwack, Leon, eds. RECONSTRUCTION: AN
ANTHOLOGY OF REVISIONIST WRITINGS. Baton Rouge: Louisiana
State University Press, 1969. 543 p.

> A collection of pieces from the pens of leading revision-
> ist historians, examining the views and policies of Lin-
> coln, Johnson, and the Radical Republicans, the origin
> of the Fourteenth Amendment, and accomplishments of
> the freedmen. Among the contributors: Stanley Cohen,
> John and La Wanda Cox, Richard Current, H.J. Gra-
> ham, Eric McKitrick, Jack B. Scraggs, V.L. Wharton,
> C. Vann Woodward.

2. Topical

a. BLACK AMERICANS

1204 Bentley, George R. A HISTORY OF THE FREEDMEN'S BUREAU. 1955.
Reprint. New York: Octagon Books, 1970. 298 p.

> The successes and failures of the bureau on the national
> and state levels are carefully detailed, from its organi-
> zation to its dissolution in 1872.

1205 Cruden, Robert. THE NEGRO IN RECONSTRUCTION. Englewood Cliffs,
N.J.: Prentice-Hall, 1969. 191 p.

> The positive accomplishments of blacks under the mil-
> itary phase of Reconstruction and the great setback
> that occurred when the troops were withdrawn.

Du Bois, W.E.B. BLACK RECONSTRUCTION. See no. 1141.

McPherson, James M. STRUGGLE FOR EQUALITY. See no. 1144.

1206 Rose, Willie Lee. REHEARSAL FOR RECONSTRUCTION: THE PORT ROY-

AL EXPERIMENT. Indianapolis: Bobbs-Merrill, 1964. 460 p. Illus., ports., maps.

An examination of the attempt in 1861 to prepare former slaves for life in a free society on the islands off the South Carolina coast. The departure of the plantation owners left the blacks, in effect, free. Rose recounts the attempts of northern abolitionists ("Gideonites") to educate them for freedom. She details the obstacles in the way of success: civilian-military disagreements, the failure of the government to take decisive action in distributing land to the freedmen, the land hunger of the northern whites, etc. These were among the problems that would recur during Reconstruction.

1207 Wharton, Vernon Lane. THE NEGRO IN MISSISSIPPI, 1865-1890. 1947. Reprint. New York: Harper & Row, 1965. 298 p. Paperbound.

Describes the accomplishments of blacks during Reconstruction, when they enjoyed legal rights. With the reassertion of Democratic control, they were restricted by codes designed to maintain white supremacy.

1208 Williamson, Joel. AFTER SLAVERY: THE NEGRO IN SOUTH CAROLINA DURING RECONSTRUCTION, 1861-1877. Chapel Hill: University of North Carolina Press, 1965. 451 p.

This revisionist work seeks to demonstrate that the ex-slave accomplished much in politics in the state immediately after the war, only to be set back by the return of control to the former Confederates.

b. CONSTITUTIONAL DEVELOPMENTS

Hyman, H.M. A MORE PERFECT UNION. See no. 1148.

1209 Kutler, Stanley I. JUDICIAL POWER AND RECONSTRUCTION POLITICS. Chicago: University of Chicago Press, 1968. 178 p. Port.

The growth of the power of the Supreme Court as a result of the constitutional issues posed in the aftermath of the war.

c. GOVERNMENT AND POLITICS

1210 Brock, W.R. AN AMERICAN CRISIS: CONGRESS AND RECONSTRUCTION, 1865-1867. New York: St. Martin's Press, 1963. 324 p.

A British historian's analysis of the workings of Congress in the critical years following the Civil War. Brock

scrutinizes the policies and actions of the parties and
concludes that seldom has a congressional majority been
as united in purpose as were the Republican Radicals in
their attempt to unseat Johnson. Their failure to convict and remove Johnson was followed by a growing disillusionment with the theory of equality. On the other
hand, Brock maintains the Negro has worked within the
system to achieve his rights because these rights were
inscribed in the law of land, however neglected they
may have been in practice.

1211 Cox, La Wanda, and Cox, John H. POLITICS, PRINCIPLE, AND PRE-
JUDICE, 1865-1866: DILEMMA OF RECONSTRUCTION AMERICA. New
York: Free Press of Glencoe, 1963. 294 p.

Examines the contest between the Radicals and President
Johnson for control of Reconstruction. The Coxes believe that, with all his political experience, Johnson
handled matters badly. They trace the complex of political machinations and debate over the civil rights of
the freedmen.

1212 Donald, David H. THE POLITICS OF RECONSTRUCTION, 1863-1867.
Baton Rouge: Louisiana State University Press, 1965. 123 p. Illus.

A study of congressional voting records in an attempt to
identify the Radical Republicans on the basis of their
actions rather than their rhetoric. Using this method,
Donald is able to name a core group. Originally delivered as a series of lectures at Louisiana State University.

1213 Gillette, William. THE RIGHT TO VOTE: POLITICS AND THE PASSAGE
OF THE FIFTEENTH AMENDMENT. Baltimore: Johns Hopkins Press, 1965.
206 p. Front., tables.

The struggle to secure suffrage for the former slaves.
Gillette traces the history from the closing days of the
Civil War to adoption of suffrage and explains why the
federal government failed to enforce the black's right
to vote in the South.

1214 Hyman, Harold M., ed. THE RADICAL REPUBLICANS AND RECONSTRUC-
TION, 1861-1870. Indianapolis: Bobbs-Merrill, 1967. 624 p.

An authority on the subject has collected prime writings
of the period. Hyman provides an introduction to the
times and the material.

1215 James, Joseph B. THE FRAMING OF THE FOURTEENTH AMENDMENT.
Urbana: University of Illinois Press, 1956. 229 p.

The motivations of the framers and the political action

that resulted in the amendment. James reviews the history of its various sections, basing his findings on official documents, newspaper accounts, diaries, letters, and biographies.

1216 Sefton, James E. THE UNITED STATES ARMY AND RECONSTRUCTION, 1865-1877. Baton Rouge: Louisiana State University Press, 1967. 304 p. Illus.

A study which attributes an important role to the army in the Reconstruction South. Sefton deals with political, constitutional, and social questions and the relation of the occupation force to them.

d. JOHNSON AND IMPEACHMENT

1217 Beale, Howard K. THE CRITICAL YEAR: A STUDY OF ANDREW JOHNSON AND RECONSTRUCTION. New York: Harcourt, 1930. 463 p. Illus., front., plates.

A study of Johnson's relations with the Radicals in the Republican party and suggestions as to what might have been if Johnson had acted differently. Beale, influenced by Charles Beard's interpretation of the role of economics in history, insists that the Radicals were more interested in the domination of American politics by big business than in the fate of the Negro. The Fourteenth Amendment was viewed by some, even then, as a means to protect business interests. The election year of 1866 was crucial. Beale believes Johnson should have rid his cabinet of members who worked surreptitiously against him and brought the issues to the people via a third party.

1218 Lomask, Milton. ANDREW JOHNSON: PRESIDENT ON TRIAL. New York: Farrar, Straus, & Cudahy, 1960. 376 p.

A colorful retelling of the story of the impeachment of President Johnson. Lomask covers the period from the assassination of Lincoln to the casting of the crucial vote in the Senate. His view of Johnson is sympathetic, but he does not overlook his faults. Lomask believes the move against Johnson was an attempt to alter the government to a parliamentary system.

1219 McKitrick, Eric L. ANDREW JOHNSON AND RECONSTRUCTION. Chicago: University of Chicago Press, 1960. 542 p.

A study of the relations of President Andrew Johnson with the Congress from the time of his assumption of office to his impeachment. McKitrick believes that since he was from outside the Republican party, Johnson should have sought the advice of party leaders but did not. His policy toward the South was ill-advised, since he expected that section voluntarily to show some sign of remorse, which it did not. This failure aggravated the situation in the North. McKitrick is critical of Johnson as a man and as a politician, and this study should be read as corrective to those that have portrayed him as "misunderstood statesman."

e. THE SOUTH

1220 Alexander, Thomas B. POLITICAL RECONSTRUCTION IN TENNESSEE. Nashville, Tenn.: Vanderbilt University Press, 1950. 292 p.

Attempts to cut through the tangle of events in the political sphere. Tennessee saw the reestablishment of civil government by local Unionists. The Radicals who dominated for a time were, the author says, "home-grown."

1221 Carter, Hodding. THE ANGRY SCAR: THE STORY OF RECONSTRUCTION. New York: Doubleday, 1959. 425 p.

A southern writer's attempt at an objective account of the emotional period of Reconstruction. Carpetbaggers and scalawags fill these pages as do the struggles for the establishment of the rights of the black man. Carter does not take account of more recent interpretations of the period.

1222 Chalmers, David M. HOODED AMERICANISM: THE FIRST CENTURY OF THE KU KLUX KLAN, 1865-1965. Garden City, N.Y.: Doubleday, 1965. 432 p. Illus., maps, facsims.

Traces the development of the Klan in various parts of the country. Chalmers analyzes not only the political and social reasons for its existence, but also ventures a psychological interpretation.

1223 Clark, Thomas D., and Kirwan, Albert D. THE SOUTH SINCE APPOMATTOX: A CENTURY OF REGIONAL CHANGE. New York: Oxford University Press, 1967. 445 p. Illus., ports., maps.

Examines various aspects of southern history since the Civil War, including Reconstruction, industrialization, education, race relations, and civil rights. The authors, southerners themselves, write fondly of the section but seek to destroy some of the more popular legends.

1224 Coulter, E. Merton. THE SOUTH DURING RECONSTRUCTION, 1865-1877. Baton Rouge: Louisiana State University Press, 1947. 441 p. Illus.

Presents Reconstruction as southerners saw it, with much documentation from southern sources. A volume in the series A HISTORY OF THE SOUTH, by several authors.

1225 Perman, Michael. REUNION WITHOUT COMPROMISE: THE SOUTH AND RECONSTRUCTION, 1865-1868. New York: Cambridge University Press, 1973. 376 p. Tables.

A study of the attitudes and actions of a cross section of the leaders of the rebellious South. Perman concludes that they were not willing to compromise and suggests that a more successful reconstruction would have been an enforced one. This study is based to a large extent on southern archives.

1226 Simkins, Francis B., and Woody, Robert H. SOUTH CAROLINA DURING RECONSTRUCTION. 1932. Reprint. Gloucester, Mass.: Peter Smith, 1966. 604 p. Illus., ports., map.

The successes and failures of Reconstruction in South Carolina in politics, economics, social life, religion, and education. The authors point to the intransigence of the whites on the subject of rights of the blacks and their open destruction of those rights, but they claim that freedmen fell far short of what northerners had expected of them. Limited successes included the establishment of black churches and schools.

1227 Wish, Harvey, ed. RECONSTRUCTION IN THE SOUTH, 1865-1877: FIRST-HAND ACCOUNTS OF THE AMERICAN SOUTHLAND AFTER THE CIVIL WAR BY NORTHERNERS AND SOUTHERNERS. New York: Farrar, Straus and Giroux, 1965. 360 p.

A collection of primary accounts by southerners and by travelers through the South, including persons on official business. A limited selection, but one revealing contemporary attitudes and conditions.

1228 Woodward, C. Vann. THE ORIGINS OF THE NEW SOUTH, 1877-1913. Baton Rouge: Louisiana State University Press, 1951. 557 p. Illus.

The years between the end of Reconstruction and the eve of World War I, examined by a leading scholar of the section. Woodward gives a lucid exposition of the development of industry, the continuing problems of the farmer, resentment against the North, and, of course, white supremacy and the black man. A volume in the cooperative venture, A HISTORY OF THE SOUTH.

1229 _____. REUNION AND REACTION: THE COMPROMISE OF 1877 AND

THE END OF RECONSTRUCTION. 1951. Reprint. Boston: Little, Brown, 1966. 275 p.

An examination of the disputed Hayes-Tilden election of 1877 and the rejection of idealism and humanitarianism in favor of economic considerations. The deal that made Rutherford B. Hayes president included the withdrawal of Union troops from the South and the promise to support a southern route for a transcontinental railroad to the West. Woodward casts much light on the contending political and economic forces at work.

1230 _____. THE STRANGE CAREER OF JIM CROW. 3d rev. ed. New York: Oxford University Press, 1974. 250 p.

Demonstrates that Jim Crow laws and practices were instituted in the period after Reconstruction. Thus segregation was a product of the late nineteenth century.

3. Prominent Individuals

See also the section on Prominent Individuals, 6,A,4.

1231 Nevins, Allan. HAMILTON FISH: THE INNER HISTORY OF THE GRANT ADMINISTRATION. 2 vols. 1936. Reprint. New York: Frederick Ungar, 1957. Illus., fronts., ports., plates, facsim.

This biography makes heavy use of Fish's diary. He served as secretary of state under Grant and Hayes.

1232 Simon, John Y., ed. THE PAPERS OF ULYSSES S. GRANT. 5 vols. to date. Carbondale: Southern Illinois University Press, 1967- . Illus., fronts., ports.

A series in progress; each volume contains a chronology, a calendar of material, and an index, and the editor provides extensive notes on items. Volume 1 starts with 1837; volume 5 concludes with 31 August 1862.

1233 Grant, Ulysses S. PERSONAL MEMOIRS. New York: AMS Press, 1972. 666 p. Illus.

Reveals Grant as a simple, straightforward man. The work appeared originally in two volumes in 1885. Grant arranged that the proceeds be used to support his family after his death.

1234 Catton, Bruce. U.S. GRANT AND THE AMERICAN MILITARY TRADITION. Boston: Little, Brown, 1954. 211 p.

Reviews Grant's early years but dwells on his career as

a soldier and as president--the first, ultimately a success, the second, a terrible failure. A readable, penetrating study.

1235 Hesseltine, William B. ULYSSES S. GRANT, POLITICIAN. 1935. Reprint. New York: Frederick Ungar, 1957. 480 p. Illus., ports.

The transition of Grant from soldier to party politician. Hesseltine believes that Grant at first wanted to be president of all the people, but that he gradually made the transition to the point where he represented "the more reactionary economic interests . . . ."

1236 Graf, Leroy P., and Haskins, Ralph W., eds. THE PAPERS OF ANDREW JOHNSON. 2 vols. to date. Knoxville: University of Tennessee Press, 1967- . Illus., fronts., ports., facsims.

A work in progress. Includes letters to and from Johnson, speeches, bills introduced in the Tennessee legislature and U.S. House of Representatives, and materials relating to his governorship. Each volume contains an editorial introduction and chronology of the years covered, and each item is annotated.

1237 Brodie, Fawn M. THADDEUS STEVENS, SCOURGE OF THE SOUTH. 1959. Reprint. New York: W.W. Norton, 1966. 448 p. Illus., ports. Paperbound.

A biography of one of the chief architects of Reconstruction and sponsor of the Fourteenth Amendment. The author seeks to explain Stevens's motives as well as his career.

Chapter 7

THE GILDED AGE, 1877-1900

A. THE TRANS-MISSISSIPPI WEST AND THE INDIANS

1. The Western Movement

a. GENERAL

1238 Billington, Ray A. AMERICA'S FRONTIER HERITAGE. New York: Holt, Rinehart & Winston, 1966. 316 p.

Using the literature of the social and behavioral sciences, Billington examines the various points raised by Frederick Jackson Turner's work on the frontier in American history. He believes they can be demonstrated to be correct.

1239 _____. THE FAR WESTERN FRONTIER, 1830-1860. New York: Harper & Row, 1956. 343 p.

The movement of settlers into Texas, California, Utah, New Mexico, and Oregon, from 1830 to 1860. A work of scholarship, vividly presented.

_____. WESTWARD EXPANSION. See no. 877.

Clark, Thomas D. FRONTIER AMERICA. See no. 878.

1240 De Voto, Bernard. THE YEAR OF DECISION, 1846. Boston: Little, Brown, 1943. 553 p. Maps.

A dramatic portrayal of one of the most significant years in American history, a year that included the beginning of the War with Mexico, the emigration to Oregon and California, the taking of New Mexico, the Donner Party, and more. An outstanding narrative history.

1241 Hawgood, John A. AMERICA'S WESTERN FRONTIERS: THE EXPLORA-
TION AND SETTLEMENT OF THE TRANS-MISSISSIPPI WEST. New York:
Alfred A. Knopf, 1967. 473 p. Illus., ports., maps, facsims.

> A detailed history of the moving frontier by a British
> historian. Hawgood uses a blend of objective fact and
> anecdotal material to produce a colorful account.

Ridge, Martin, and Billington, Ray A., eds. AMERICA'S FRONTIER
STORY. See no. 888.

Riegel, Robert E., and Athearn, Robert G. AMERICA MOVES WEST.
See no. 889

1242 Turner, Frederick Jackson. THE FRONTIER IN AMERICAN HISTORY.
1920. Reprint. New York: Holt, Rinehart and Winston, 1962. 395 p.

> This volume contains thirteen essays, including "The
> Significance of the Frontier in American History" (1893),
> a famous work in American historiography. Turner was
> convinced that the frontier was responsible for the devel-
> opment of democracy as the population moved West and be-
> came more detached from its European roots. It was on the
> frontier that America developed its distinctive character.
> These points, and several others included here, stimulated
> the growth of a school of western historiography. This edi-
> tion has a foreword by Ray Allen Billington.

1243 Webb, Walter Prescott. THE GREAT FRONTIER. 1952. Reprint. Austin:
University of Texas Press, 1964. 452 p. Illus., maps.

> A work rich in interpretation on the role of the West
> in American history. Webb believes it loomed large in
> the minds of Americans and Europeans. The availability
> of vast expanses of land, for instance, had an important
> impact for several centuries.

1244 _____. THE GREAT PLAINS. 1931. Reprint. New York: Grosset &
Dunlap, 1957. 533 p. Maps. Paperbound.

> This pioneer work has come to be rated as a classic.
> Webb's is a comprehensive history, based on primary
> sources, and presented in readable style. He deals with
> the physical setting, the Plains Indians, and the coming
> of the Spanish and English-speaking peoples.

b. TOPICAL

i. Agriculture

1245 Fite, Gilbert C. THE FARMERS' FRONTIER, 1865-1900. New York:

Holt, Rinehart and Winston, 1966. 286 p. Illus., ports., maps.

> The author uses a mass of statistics to indicate the importance of the role of the farmer in the settlement and the civilizing of the frontier territories of the West.

1246 Shannon, Fred A. THE FARMER'S LAST FRONTIER: AGRICULTURE, 1860-1897. New York: Farrar & Rinehart, 1945. 446 p. Front., plates, maps.

> A fully documented account, dealing with all aspects of agriculture; particularly useful for a picture of the spread of agriculture into the western territories and new states.

ii. Cattlemen

1247 Abbott, Edward C. ("Teddy Blue"), and Smith, Helena H. WE POINTED THEM NORTH: RECOLLECTIONS OF A COWPUNCHER. 1939. Reprint. Norman: University of Oklahoma Press, 1971. 247 p. Illus.

> "Teddy Blue" drove cattle in Montana and Wyoming in the 1870s and 1880s. He gave his impressions of the cowboy's life, the landscape, the Plains Indians, and much more to Helena Smith, who transcribed them.

1248 Atherton, Lewis E. THE CATTLE KINGS. Bloomington: Indiana University Press, 1961. 308 p. Illus., front., ports., map.

> A study of cattle ranchers, not of cowboys. The rancher, the author believes, was far more important in shaping the culture and environment of the West. Based on documentary materials.

1249 Frantz, Joe B., and Choate, Julian E., Jr. THE AMERICAN COWBOY: THE MYTH AND THE REALITY. Norman: University of Oklahoma Press, 1955. 232 p. Illus.

> A scholarly study. The authors trace the rise of the cowboy, using many contemporary sources, and then discuss the place he had held in the imaginations of Americans.

1250 Osgood, Ernest S. THE DAY OF THE CATTLEMAN: A STUDY OF THE NORTHERN RANGE, 1845-1890. 1929. Reprint. Chicago: University of Chicago Press, 1957. 295 p. Front., maps, plan, facsims., diagrs. Paperbound.

> Does not romanticize the cowboy but deals with the economics of the cattle business. The result of thorough research.

iii. Intellectual and Social Life

1251 Dick, Everett. THE SOD-HOUSE FRONTIER, 1854-1890: A SOCIAL HIS-
TORY OF THE NORTHERN PLAINS FROM THE CREATION OF KANSAS
AND NEBRASKA TO THE ADMISSION OF THE DAKOTAS. New York:
Appleton, 1937. 568 p. Front., port., plates, maps.

A history of the area represented in contemporary gossip
as a Great American Desert, posing insurmountable dif-
ficulties to the pioneer. Dick deals with the everyday
life of the settler: farming, political development, relations with the Indians, etc.

1252 Smith, Henry Nash. VIRGIN LAND: THE AMERICAN WEST AS SYMBOL
AND MYTH. 1950. Reprint. Cambridge, Mass.: Harvard University Press,
1971. 323 p. Illus.

Smith examines nineteenth-century novels, poetry, periodicals, and other literature, to determine the place the
West and its pioneers held in American thought. A stim-
ulating analysis.

1253 Stegner, Wallace. BEYOND THE HUNDREDTH MERIDIAN: JOHN WESLEY
POWELL AND THE SECOND OPENING OF THE WEST. Boston: Houghton
Mifflin, 1954. 461 p. Illus., ports., plate, maps.

The public life of a man whose scientific work had much
influence in spreading knowledge of, and interest in,
the West. Powell, who was engaged in geology and
ethnology of the Indians, influenced public land policy.
Stegner's is a well-written, scholarly presentation.

1254 _____. THE GATHERING OF ZION: THE STORY OF THE MORMON
TRAIL. New York: McGraw-Hill Book Co., 1964. 331 p. Illus.,
maps.

A history of the Mormon trek west after the group was
driven from Nauvoo, Illinois, in 1845. Stegner, with
his great interest in the environment, presents a colorful
and convincing description of the climate and terrain
and deals with the migration itself in objective terms.

1255 Taft, Robert. ARTISTS AND ILLUSTRATORS OF THE OLD WEST, 1850-
1900. New York: Charles Scribner's Sons, 1953. 417 p. Illus., plates,
maps.

Deals with use of illustrations in the study of history.
Using their personal papers, Taft provides information
on the artists and the relevance of their pictures.

Wright, Louis B. CULTURE ON THE MOVING FRONTIER. See no. 893.

iv. Mining

1256 Greever, William S. THE BONANZA WEST: THE STORY OF THE WEST-
ERN MINING RUSHES, 1848-1900. Norman: University of Oklahoma
Press, 1963. 430 p. Illus.

> Traces the movement of miners West and illustrates how
> they were followed by permanent settlers. Greever
> deals with mining booms in Montana, Colorado, Califor-
> nia, South Dakota, Idaho, Nevada, and Alaska and
> traces the economic and social developments that led
> to the cultural enrichment of such places as Central
> City, Colorado, and Butte, Montana. He includes
> colorful anecdotes.

1257 Paul, Rodman W. MINING FRONTIERS OF THE FAR WEST, 1848-1880.
New York: Holt, Rinehart and Winston, 1963. 236 p. Illus.

> A scholarly examination, heavily dependent on primary
> sources. Paul attempts to separate fact from the color-
> ful tall tales which have romanticized this story. He
> examines the economics of mining, traces the develop-
> ment of machinery, and deals with the many other as-
> pects of mining as an industry.

v. Mountain Men

1258 Cleland, Robert G. THIS RECKLESS BREED OF MEN: THE TRAPPERS
AND FUR TRADERS OF THE SOUTHWEST. 1950. Reprint. New York:
Alfred A. Knopf, 1963. 396 p. Illus., maps.

> A study of the mountain men who explored the Southwest
> from the 1820s to 1840s. Using much primary material,
> Cleland creates a picture of their daily lives and the
> hazards they confronted, concentrating on such colorful
> figures as Jedediah S. Smith and Joseph Reddeford Walker.

De Voto, Bernard. ACROSS THE WIDE MISSOURI. See no. 879.

vi. Transportation

1259 Riegel, Robert E. THE STORY OF THE WESTERN RAILROADS: FROM
1852 THROUGH THE REIGN OF THE GIANTS. New York: Macmillan,
1926. 360 p.

> An early history of the railroad and its role in bringing
> civilization to the West. Although written before the
> airplane and truck had encroached on the railroad em-
> pire, and though it includes elements of boosterism, this
> is still valuable for the information Riegel presents on

the bearing of the roads on the lives of the Indian, the
pioneer farmer, and the development of urban centers.
He also covers laws passed to control the roads, financial details, and the technological improvements in the
rolling stock.

1260 Winther, Oscar O. THE TRANSPORTATION FRONTIER: TRANS-MISSISSIPPI
WEST, 1865-1890. New York: Holt, Rinehart and Winston, 1964. 238
p. Illus., maps, facsims.

A thorough survey of all modes of transportation used in
the West--stagecoach, railroad, wagon, riverboat, net-
works of roads for the automobile and even bicycles--and
their relationship to the taming of the area. A work of
scholarship based on many primary sources.

2. The Indians

a. GENERAL

See also relevant sections of works listed under Indians, 2,B,13.

1261 Brown, Dee. BURY MY HEART AT WOUNDED KNEE: AN INDIAN HIS-
TORY OF THE AMERICAN WEST. New York: Holt, Rinehart and Winston, 1971. 504 p. Illus., ports., music.

An Indian view of dealings with the white man from
1860 to 1890, as the frontier relentlessly moved into
Indian territories. Brown provides detailed treatment
of what he considers the duplicity of the whites, and
provides a multitude of examples of gore and massacre.
The book also provides much information on the Indians
of the Plains and the Rocky Mountains.

b. TOPICAL

i. Attitudes of the White Man

For white attitudes in the earlier period see Foreman, Grant. INDIAN REMOVAL,
no. 880, and Horsman, Reginald. EXPANSION AND AMERICAN INDIAN POLI-
CY, no. 881.

1262 Finerty, John F. WAR-PATH AND BIVOUAC; OR, THE CONQUEST OF
THE SIOUX: A NARRATIVE OF STIRRING PERSONAL EXPERIENCES AND
ADVENTURES IN THE BIG HORN AND YELLOWSTONE EXPEDITION OF
1876, AND IN THE CAMPAIGN ON THE BRITISH BORDER IN 1879. Norman: University of Oklahoma Press, 1961. 358 p. Illus.

The personal experiences of a member of the editorial

staff of THE CHICAGO TIMES, who accompanied the
troops. Originally published in 1890. This edition
contains an introduction by Oliver Knight.

1263 Fritz, Henry E. THE MOVEMENT FOR INDIAN ASSIMILATION, 1860-
1890. Philadelphia: University of Pennsylvania Press, 1963. 244 p.
Illus., maps.

A study of attempts to assimilate the Indian into white
American society, beginning with President Grant's
"peace policy" after the Civil War. Fritz examines
the attitudes of Protestants, Catholics, and other groups,
and concludes that the efforts were a failure because a
political democracy has always served the interests of
powerful groups and ignored minorities.

1264 Jackson, Helen Hunt. A CENTURY OF DISHONOR: THE EARLY CRU-
SADE FOR INDIAN REFORM. Edited by Andrew F. Rolle. New York:
Harper & Row, 1965. 364 p.

A famous indictment of American governmental policy
toward the Indians and a plea for relief of their desper-
ate plight, published first in 1881. The editor provides
an introduction.

1265 Prucha, Francis P., ed. AMERICANIZING THE AMERICAN INDIANS:
WRITINGS BY THE "FRIENDS OF THE INDIAN," 1880-1900. Cambridge,
Mass.: Harvard University Press, 1973. 358 p.

A collection of writings by those who sought to reform
U.S. government Indian policies in the late nineteenth
century. They sought, among other things, citizenship
for the Indian distribution of land to individual Indians,
and establishment of an educational system.

ii. The Indian Wars

1266 Andrist, Ralph K. THE LONG DEATH: THE LAST DAYS OF THE PLAINS
INDIAN. New York: Macmillan, 1964. 380 p. Illus., ports., maps.

A vivid history which is also an indictment of white
Americans. Andrist tells the story of the conquest of
the Plains, which culminated in the Battle of Wounded
Knee in South Dakota in 1890.

1267 Brown, Mark H. THE FLIGHT OF THE NEZ PERCE. New York: G.P.
Putnam's Sons, 1967. 480 p. Maps.

Based to a large extent on eyewitness accounts. Brown,
a military man, traces the progress of the war between
federal troops and the Indians in realistic detail. The

whites do not come out very well in this account.

1268 Dunn, J.P. MASSACRES OF THE MOUNTAINS: A HISTORY OF THE INDIAN WARS OF THE FAR WEST, 1815-1875. 1886. Reprint. New York: G.P. Putnam's Sons, 1969. 658 p. Illus. Paperbound.

This contemporary account gives insight into attitudes of the participants as well as details of the campaigns.

1269 Josephy, Alvin M., Jr. THE NEZ PERCE INDIANS AND THE OPENING OF THE NORTHWEST. New Haven, Conn.: Yale University Press, 1965. 725 p. Illus., ports., maps.

The Nez Perce had been a peaceful tribe from the time they helped Lewis and Clark until, goaded by broken treaties and attempts to take their land, they struck back at the whites in 1877. Josephy deals with these events and the settlement of Oregon, Washington, Idaho, and Montana.

1270 Leckie, William H. THE MILITARY CONQUEST OF THE SOUTHERN PLAINS. Norman: University of Oklahoma Press, 1963. 281 p. Illus.

A history of the sporadic warfare in the 1860s and 1870s between the white man and the Indian in the extensive area that includes present-day Texas, Oklahoma, and New Mexico.

1271 Utley, Robert M. LAST DAYS OF THE SIOUX NATION. New Haven, Conn.: Yale University Press, 1963. 314 p. Illus., maps.

The events leading to the Battle of Wounded Knee Creek (1890). Utley discusses the influence of the Ghost Dance Religion in feeding Indian dissatisfaction with the reservation life imposed on them by the American government.

B. INDUSTRIALIZATION AND URBANIZATION

1. General

1272 Bryce, James. THE AMERICAN COMMONWEALTH. 3 vols. 1888. Reprint. New York: AMS Press, 1973.

A classic study of the United States in the last quarter of the nineteenth century, by an English liberal statesman. Lord Bryce's acute but sympathetic eye noted many aspects of American life, from governmental operations to hymn-singing. Volume 1: THE NATIONAL GOVERNMENT, THE STATE GOVERNMENTS; volume 2: THE PARTY SYSTEM; volume 3: PUBLIC OPINION, IL-

LUSTRATIONS AND REFLECTIONS, SOCIAL INSTITU-
TIONS.

1273 Cochran, Thomas C., and Miller, William. THE AGE OF ENTERPRISE:
A SOCIAL HISTORY OF INDUSTRIAL AMERICA. Rev. ed. New York:
Harper & Row, 1961. 412 p.

> The rise of industry and its effect on American society,
> from 1800 on. The authors deal with commerce, labor,
> agriculture, the development of canals, railroads, and
> aviation as well.

1274 Diamond, Sigmund, ed. THE NATION TRANSFORMED: THE CREATION
OF AN INDUSTRIAL SOCIETY. New York: George Braziller, 1963.
542 p.

> An anthology which covers the years 1876 to 1904.
> Diamond has culled from contemporary materials a color-
> ful and enlightening assortment. Both the unknown im-
> migrant and the famous are represented.

1275 Faulkner, Harold U. POLITICS, REFORM, AND EXPANSION, 1890-1900.
New York: Harper & Brothers, 1959. 312 p. Illus.

> A survey of the politics, economics, attempts at reform,
> and war in the ten-year period. Faulkner sees this time
> as a watershed in U.S. history, since Americans then
> plunged into industrialization and imperialism.

1276 Garraty, John A. THE NEW COMMONWEALTH, 1877-1890. New York:
Harper & Row, 1968. 379 p. Illus., ports.

> A survey which interprets the period as a time of trans-
> formation from the individualism of laissez-faire to the
> collective approach in confronting problems. A politi-
> cal, economic, and social history.

1277 Ginger, Ray. THE AGE OF EXCESS: THE UNITED STATES FROM 1877
TO 1914. New York: Macmillan, 1965. 396 p.

> An attempt to make sense out of what the author con-
> siders a confusing period in U.S. history. He deals
> with political, social, and intellectual consequences of
> the great change from a rural, agrarian society to an
> urban, industrial one. Many persons and anecdotes
> crowd his pages.

1278 Hays, Samuel P. THE RESPONSE TO INDUSTRIALISM, 1885-1914. Chicago: University of Chicago Press, 1957. 210 p.

> A general survey of the acceleration of industrial growth

and the consequences for American life.

1279 Holbrook, Stewart H. THE AGE OF THE MOGULS. Garden City, N.Y.: Doubleday, 1953. 383 p. Ports.

An entertaining survey, rich in anecdotes, of the careers of the leading capitalists and entrepreneurs of the years between the Civil War and the Great Depression. Among those covered are the Vanderbilts, Carnegie, Rockefeller, the Guggenheims, the DuPonts, Ford, Hearst.

1280 Morgan, H. Wayne, ed. THE GILDED AGE. Rev. and enl. ed. Syracuse, N.Y.: Syracuse University Press, 1970. 336 p. Illus., ports., facsim.

Articles written for this collection by leading scholars on the period, dealing with such topics as big business, civil service reform, public morality, Populism, and foreign affairs.

1281 Nevins, Allan. THE EMERGENCE OF MODERN AMERICA, 1865-1878. 1927. Reprint. Chicago: Quadrangle Books, 1971. 465 p. Paperbound.

Nevins's theme is that a new America emerged as a result of the Civil War. He traces political developments and gives a great deal of attention to social matters, particularly the life of the common man in the period.

1282 Randel, William Peirce. CENTENNIAL: AMERICAN LIFE IN 1876. Philadelphia: Chilton, 1969. 485 p.

Using the Centennial Exhibition in Philadelphia as a springboard, the author sets forth a comprehensive picture of life in America in the centennial year of 1876; he deals with politics, social life, economics, religion, thought.

2. Topical

a. BUSINESS AND ECONOMICS

1283 Carnegie, Andrew. THE GOSPEL OF WEALTH, AND OTHER TIMELY ESSAYS. Edited by Edward C. Kirkland. Cambridge, Mass.: Harvard University Press, 1962. 259 p.

The famous financier and philanthropist sets forth his credo in this modern printing, edited by a historian of American business. Kirkland provides an introduction which sets the essays in context.

1284 Corey, Lewis. THE HOUSE OF MORGAN: A SOCIAL BIOGRAPHY OF THE MASTERS OF MONEY. New York: G.H. Watt, 1930. 479 p. Front., ports., plates, maps, diagrs.

The rise of J.P. and the Morgan family in financial circles, with glimpses of the workings of Wall Street.

1285 Hacker, Louis M. THE WORLD OF ANDREW CARNEGIE, 1865-1901. Philadelphia: Lippincott, 1968. 510 p.

An account that is basically sympathetic to Carnegie and his industrialist contemporaries. Hacker, unlike most, even takes a positive view of Henry Clay Frick's actions in the Homestead Strike. The entrepreneurs, he believes, were to a large extent responsible for the transformation of the United States into the strongest industrial nation in the world.

1286 Harvey, William H. COIN'S FINANCIAL SCHOOL. Edited by Richard Hofstadter. Cambridge, Mass.: Harvard University Press, 1963. 260 p. Illus., tables, diagrs.

A best seller of 1896. Coin, a young financier, gives the answers to society's ills in his advocacy of free sil- ver. A perceptive introduction by the editor.

1287 Josephson, Matthew. THE ROBBER BARONS: THE GREAT AMERICAN CAPITALISTS, 1861-1901. 1934. Reprint. New York: Harcourt, Brace & World, 1962. 474 p.

The emergence of the great capitalists during and follow- ing the Civil War. A lively account of financial trans- actions and the other doings of Gould, Morgan, the Vanderbilts, Carnegie, Rockefeller, Hill, Harriman, Huntingdon, Frick, et al.

1288 Kirkland, Edward C. DREAM AND THOUGHT IN THE BUSINESS COM- MUNITY, 1860-1900. 1956. Reprint. Chicago: Quadrangle Books, 1964. 176 p.

American business ideas, as expressed by business leaders in the press, in testimony before Congress, in personal and business correspondence, etc. Kirkland conveys their thinking on many social and economic matters, such as higher education, civil service reform, and government commissions.

1289 _____. INDUSTRY COMES OF AGE: BUSINESS, LABOR, AND PUBLIC POLICY, 1860-1897. 1961. Reprint. Chicago: Quadrangle Books, 1967. 456 p. Paperbound.

This economic history of the period attempts to look at

the problems as they were seen by contemporaries. Kirkland, in addition to treating areas listed in the subtitle,
devotes extensive space to the railroads and also touches
on the development of urban areas.

1290 Lloyd, Henry Demarest. WEALTH AGAINST COMMONWEALTH. Edited
by Thomas C. Cochran. Englewood Cliffs, N.J.: Prentice-Hall, 1963.
184 p. Paperbound.

A well-documented attack on industrial trusts, particularly the Standard Oil Company, published in 1894 by
one of the inaugurators of muckraking journalism. An
introduction by the editor is included.

1291 Nugent, Walter T.K. MONEY AND AMERICAN SOCIETY, 1865-1880.
New York: Free Press, 1968. 315 p.

Nugent uses the money question as a vehicle for a consideration of the points of view of various interest groups
in the United States. In addition, he places the monetary question in a context that includes Europe. He
believes Americans were so preoccupied with the subject
that they missed the opportunity to explore alternative
solutions to the problems posed by the upsurge of industrialization.

1292 Sobel, Robert. THE BIG BOARD: A HISTORY OF THE NEW YORK STOCK
MARKET. New York: Free Press, 1965. 408 p. Tables.

The stock market and the figures who have attempted to
dominate it--Gould, Fisk, Vanderbilt, and others--are
treated in a colorful manner. Sobel attempts to show
how political and social matters bear on what happens
to the market.

1293 Tarbell, Ida M. THE NATIONALIZING OF BUSINESS, 1878-1898. 1936.
Reprint. Chicago: Quadrangle Books, 1971. 330 p. Illus., front.,
ports., plates.

The consolidation of industry into large corporate units
and trusts in the late nineteenth century. Tarbell, a
leading muckraker, had the background needed to write
such a history.

1294 Unger, Irwin. THE GREENBACK ERA: A SOCIAL AND POLITICAL HIS-
TORY OF AMERICAN FINANCE, 1865-1879. Princeton, N.J.: Princeton
University Press, 1964. 467 p.

The debates between the advocates of "hard" and "soft"
money, especially in the political parties. Unger disputes the view of Charles Beard and others that power

shifted from rural agrarian to urban, industrial interests
as a result of the Civil War.

1295 Veblen, Thorstein. THE THEORY OF THE LEISURE CLASS: AN ECO-
NOMIC STUDY OF INSTITUTIONS. 1899. Reprint. New York:
Augustus M. Kelley, 1965. 400 p. Facsim.

A classic analysis of the commercial values of America's
moneyed class. "Conspicuous consumption," and other
concepts in the book, became famous. This edition
contains a review by William Dean Howells.

1296 Williamson, Harold F., and Daum, Arnold R. THE AMERICAN PETROLE-
UM INDUSTRY. 2 vols. Evanston, Ill.: Northwestern University Press,
1959-63. Illus., ports., maps, facsims., tables, diagrs.

The phases through which the petroleum industry has
passed, in a detailed, scholarly study. Volume 1: THE
AGE OF ILLUMINATION, 1859-1899; volume 2: THE
AGE OF ENERGY, 1899-1959.

b. GOVERNMENT AND POLITICS

1297 Clancy, Herbert J. THE PRESIDENTIAL ELECTION OF 1880. Chicago:
Loyola University Press, 1958. 306 p.

A detailed study of the election in which James A.
Garfield defeated Winfield Scott Hancock for the presidency. The author traces the electoral process from
the nominating conventions through the election and
concludes with the assassination of President Garfield.

1298 De Santis, Vincent P. REPUBLICANS FACE THE SOUTHERN QUESTION:
THE NEW DEPARTURE YEARS, 1877-1897. 1959. Reprint. Westport,
Conn.: Negro Universities Press, 1969. 275 p. Maps.

Republican party attempts to win support in the South in
the period of the reestablishment of home rule following
Reconstruction. DeSantis shows that Presidents Hayes,
Garfield, Arthur, and Harrison, and party officials,
engaged in the effort with no success.

1299 Durden, Robert F. THE CLIMAX OF POPULISM: THE ELECTION OF
1896. Lexington: University of Kentucky Press, 1965. 202 p.

A favorable view of the People's party, which lost the
election of 1896 not because of its own weakness, says
the author, but because of circumstances it could not
control. Durden makes heavy use of the papers of
Marion Butler, a Populist senator from North Carolina.

1300 Glad, Paul W. MCKINLEY, BRYAN AND THE PEOPLE. Philadelphia: Lippincott, 1964. 222 p.

The issues in the election of 1896 and the personalities of the candidates are described in a competent narrative.

1301 Hirshon, Stanley P. FAREWELL TO THE BLOODY SHIRT: NORTHERN REPUBLICANS AND THE SOUTHERN NEGRO, 1877-1893. 1962. Reprint. Gloucester, Mass.: Peter Smith, 1968. 334 p.

The abandonment of the black man in the South by Republican politicians of the North with the end of Reconstruction. Hirshon investigates the contending pressures, political and economic, within the party.

1302 Hollingsworth, J. Rogers. THE WHIRLIGIG OF POLITICS: THE DEMOCRACY OF CLEVELAND AND BRYAN. Chicago: University of Chicago Press, 1963. 275 p. Illus., ports.

The divisions and tensions within the Democratic party and how they affected the country, from the second term of Cleveland through the election of 1904. A thoughtful analysis.

1303 Hoogenboom, Ari. OUTLAWING THE SPOILS: A HISTORY OF THE CIVIL SERVICE REFORM MOVEMENT, 1865-1883. Urbana: University of Illinois Press, 1961. 306 p.

Hoogenboom looks at the motivations of the reformers (he considers them an "out" group) as well as at what they tried to accomplish.

1304 Jones, Stanley L. THE PRESIDENTIAL ELECTION OF 1896. Madison: University of Wisconsin Press, 1964. 446 p. Illus., ports., facsims.

A study of the contest between Bryan and McKinley. Jones explores in detail the issue of free coinage of silver and the workings of the two party structures.

1305 Josephson, Matthew. THE POLITICOS, 1865-1896. New York: Harcourt, Brace, 1938. 769 p.

A sequel to THE ROBBER BARONS, q.v., no. 1287, Josephson recounts the slavish toadying of certain politicians to the dominant financiers of the period.

1306 Knoles, George H. THE PRESIDENTIAL CAMPAIGN AND ELECTION OF 1892. 1942. Reprint. New York: AMS Press, 1971. 268 p. Map.

Traces the campaign from the nominating conventions to the election. Knoles places populism in the context of political and social developments.

1307 Leech, Margaret. IN THE DAYS OF MCKINLEY. New York: Harper & Brothers, 1959. 694 p. Illus., ports., facsims.

> Deals fully with the man and the lively times in which he lived. This colorful presentation gives a much more positive evaluation of McKinley than has been customary.

1308 Letwin, William. LAW AND ECONOMIC POLICY IN AMERICA: THE EVOLUTION OF THE SHERMAN ANTI-TRUST ACT. New York: Random House, 1965. 313 p.

> Provides precedents from English and American history for the Sherman Act and shows what the U.S. population generally thought about monopolies. Letwin then explains the political process by which the Sherman Act was adopted and the major cases which arose in its early years.

1309 Merrill, Horace Samuel. BOURBON DEMOCRACY OF THE MIDDLE WEST, 1865-1896. 1953. Reprint. Seattle: University of Washington Press, 1967. 314 p. Illus., ports.

> A study of the conservative elements in the Democratic party, which sought to protect big business in the years following the Civil War. Merrill deals with Ohio, Indiana, Illinois, Nebraska, Iowa, Minnesota, and Wisconsin.

1310 Morgan, H. Wayne. FROM HAYES TO MCKINLEY: NATIONAL PARTY POLITICS, 1877-1896. Syracuse, N.Y.: Syracuse University Press, 1969. 628 p. Illus., ports.

> From the end of Reconstruction to the rise of Progressivism. A political history of "the Gilded Age," written with color and artistry.

1311 Quint, Howard H. THE FORGING OF AMERICAN SOCIALISM: ORIGINS OF THE MODERN MOVEMENT. Columbia: University of South Carolina Press, 1953. 418 p.

> The years from 1886 to 1901 when the movement was emerging from various beginnings. Quint shows the effect it had on intellectuals and the society as a whole.

1312 Rothman, David J. POLITICS AND POWER: THE UNITED STATES SENATE, 1869-1901. Cambridge, Mass.: Harvard University Press, 1966. 358 p. Illus., ports.

> Attempts to demonstrate that a transformation occurred in the Senate, in the years studied, that was to have decided consequences for American political life.

1313 Thorelli, Hans B. THE FEDERAL ANTITRUST POLICY: ORIGINATION OF AN AMERICAN TRADITION. Baltimore: Johns Hopkins Press, 1954. 674 p. Illus.

> A thorough discussion of the origins of antitrust sentiment and the adoption of the Sherman Act, followed by an analysis of what happened in the early years of its implementation.

1314 White, Leonard D. THE REPUBLICAN ERA, 1869-1901: A STUDY IN ADMINISTRATIVE HISTORY. New York: Macmillan, 1958. 406 p.

> The government's administrative practices in a long period dominated by Republicans. White views the country from the perspective of the executive office but lightens his pages with sparkling personalities like Theodore Roosevelt and Carl Schurz and campaigns such as that for reform of the civil service.

c. IMMIGRATION

1315 DeConde, Alexander. HALF-BITTER, HALF-SWEET: AN EXCURSION INTO ITALIAN-AMERICAN HISTORY. New York: Charles Scribner's Sons, 1972. 466 p.

> Deals with Italian immigrants in the United States. De Conde, a historian of diplomacy, traces the relationship between Italy and the United States, but stresses the mingling of Old and New World influences in the lives of this major ethnic group, concentrating on the twentieth century. Combats common stereotypes of the Italian-American.

1316 Erickson, Charlotte. AMERICAN INDUSTRY AND THE EUROPEAN IMMIGRANT, 1860-1885. 1957. Reprint. New York: Russell & Russell, 1967. 279 p.

> A study of the attempt of the labor unions to exclude contract labor from the United States. Erickson contends that American industry did not make use of much labor of this type but that the craft unions feared importation of skilled laborers from Europe who might act as strike breakers. Organized efforts resulted in the Foran Act of 1885, which excluded contract labor of all types.

1317 Handlin, Oscar. BOSTON'S IMMIGRANTS, 1790-1880: A STUDY IN ACCULTURATION. Rev. ed. Cambridge, Mass.: Harvard University Press, 1959. 382 p. Illus., maps, plans, tables, diagrs.

> The history of a culturally homogeneous city transformed by the influx of thousands of immigrants into a metropo-

lis torn by intergroup conflict. Handlin bases his work on federal and state statistics as well as public documents and the immigrant press. He deals with the arrival of the immigrants and their adjustment to their new physical surroundings, their economic problems, their development of a group consciousness, and their relations with the older settlers.

_____. RACE AND NATIONALITY IN AMERICAN LIFE. See no. 359.

1318 _____. THE UPROOTED. 2d ed. Boston: Little, Brown, 1973.

Rather than a factual history, this is an impressionistic, poetic evocation of what immigrants experienced in leaving the Old World and adapting to the environment of the New. First edition published in 1951.

1319 Park, Robert E., and Miller, Herbert A. OLD WORLD TRAITS TRANS-PLANTED. New York: Harper & Brothers, 1921. 314 p. Front., maps, plan, diagr.

Approaches the problems of the immigrant's adaptation to America from an anthropological point of view. The authors believed assimilation was inevitable. Rich in detail.

1320 Potter, George W. TO THE GOLDEN DOOR: THE STORY OF THE IRISH IN IRELAND AND AMERICA. Boston: Little, Brown, 1960. 631 p. Illus.

The Irish in their homeland, the years of the potato famine, and their migration and adaptation to America. The book is based on serious research but is filled with humorous anecdotes.

Taylor, Phillip A.M. DISTANT MAGNET. See no. 364.

1321 Wittke, Carl F. THE IRISH IN AMERICA. 1956. Reprint. New York: Russell & Russell, 1970. 330 p.

An authority on immigrant history traces the experience of the Irish in America from the period of their great migration in the 1830s and 1840s. Wittke deals with problems confronting them, using a topical approach.

d. INTELLECTUAL AND SOCIAL LIFE

Higham, John. STRANGERS IN THE LAND. See no. 362.

1322 Meier, August. NEGRO THOUGHT IN AMERICA, 1880-1915: RACIAL IDEOLOGIES IN THE AGE OF BOOKER T. WASHINGTON. Ann Arbor: University of Michigan Press, 1963. 346 p.

An exposition of the black man's thought concerning his place in American life in a period dominated by the personality of Booker T. Washington.

1323 Miller, Perry, ed. AMERICAN THOUGHT: CIVIL WAR TO WORLD WAR I. New York: Holt, Rinehart and Winston, 1954. 408 p. Paperbound.

An anthology which accents the role of American men of thought. Miller presents selections from Josiah Royce, Chauncey Wright, Henry George, William Graham Sumner, Lester Ward, Charles Sanders Peirce, William James, Oliver Wendell Holmes, John Dewey, Brooks Adams, Henry Adams, Thorstein Veblen, and Louis D. Brandeis, with a thoughtful general introduction analyzing their thought.

1324 Mumford, Lewis. THE BROWN DECADES: A STUDY OF THE ARTS IN AMERICA, 1865-1895. 2d rev. ed. 1955. Reprint. New York: Dover, 1959. 266 p. Illus.

A well-known, impressionistic study of the arts in a period which, Mumford believes, was still overshadowed by the Civil War. He evaluates architecture, city planning, landscape architecture, painting, and literature.

1325 Riis, Jacob. HOW THE OTHER HALF LIVES: STUDIES AMONG THE TENEMENTS OF NEW YORK. Edited by Sam Bass Warner, Jr. Cambridge, Mass.: Harvard University Press, 1970. 265 p. Illus., plans.

Riis, who moved to New York from Denmark in 1870, established himself as a journalist and reformer. This book, published first in 1890, is an expose of life in the slums and of the practices of the slum lords.

1326 Solomon, Barbara M. ANCESTORS AND IMMIGRANTS: A CHANGING NEW ENGLAND TRADITION. Cambridge, Mass.: Harvard University Press, 1956. 285 p.

Views the self-image of the old families of New England, using their attitudes toward immigrants as a vehicle. Their attempts to restrict immigration were given ideological respectability by the writings of Henry Adams, Herbert Baxter, Barrett Wendell, and others who insisted on the superiority of the Anglo-Saxon heritage. Solomon has examined much primary material--public documents, personal interviews, autobiographies, memoirs, correspondence--as well as periodicals, newspapers, literary and sociological works.

Weiss, Richard. AMERICAN MYTH OF SUCCESS. See no. 246.

1327 White, Morton G. SOCIAL THOUGHT IN AMERICA: THE REVOLT AGAINST FORMALISM. 1949. Reprint. Boston: Beacon Press, 1957. 315 p. Paperbound.

> An examination of the thought of Oliver Wendell Holmes, Thorstein Veblen, Charles Beard, and James Harvey Robinson, figures the author believes were most influential in the formulation of twentieth-century liberal thought.

i. Social Darwinism

1328 Fine, Sidney. LAISSEZ-FAIRE AND THE GENERAL WELFARE STATE: A STUDY IN CONFLICT IN AMERICAN THOUGHT, 1865-1901. Ann Arbor: University of Michigan Press, 1956. 478 p.

> Looks at both sides of the argument between the Social Darwinists and their opponents, delving fully into the contending ideas on society and economy.

1329 Hofstadter, Richard. SOCIAL DARWINISM IN AMERICAN THOUGHT. Rev. ed. Boston: Beacon Press, 1955. 254 p. Paperbound.

> When Darwinian ideas were applied to the social realm they were used to justify laissez-faire and the economic survival of the fittest. Hofstadter explores the formulations of such thinkers as William Graham Sumner and the opposition of such as Lester Ward.

1330 McCloskey, Robert G. AMERICAN CONSERVATISM IN THE AGE OF ENTERPRISE: A STUDY OF WILLIAM GRAHAM SUMNER, STEPHEN J. FIELD, AND ANDREW CARNEGIE. Cambridge, Mass.: Harvard University Press, 1951. 204 p.

> The leading exponents of laissez-faire: Sumner the scholar, Field the jurist, Carnegie the businessman. McCloskey makes a critical examination of their ideas in the years between the close of the Civil War and World War I.

1331 Wilson, R. Jackson, ed. DARWINISM AND THE AMERICAN INTELLECTUAL: A BOOK OF READINGS. Homewood, Ill.: Dorsey Press, 1967. 215 p. Paperbound.

> Materials drawn from the period of debate over Darwinian evolution. Wilson covers Darwinism as scientific theory and as a way of thinking and its bearing on religion and social ethics; he introduces each section and includes readings from the famous persons in the debate.

ii. The Social Gospel

1332 Hopkins, Charles H. THE RISE OF THE SOCIAL GOSPEL IN AMERICAN
PROTESTANTISM, 1865-1915. New Haven, Conn.: Yale University Press,
1940. 364 p.

> A history of the process by which the American churches,
> reacting to an industrial society, began to look beyond
> salvation for the individual to the salvation of society.
> Hopkins provides much detail and deals with both fa-
> mous and less well-known leaders.

1333 May, Henry F. PROTESTANT CHURCHES AND INDUSTRIAL AMERICA.
1949. Reprint. New York: Octagon Books, 1963. 307 p.

> The Social Gospel as it emerged among the major Ameri-
> can Protestant denominations. May examines the atti-
> tudes of the Baptists, Congregationalists, Episcopalians,
> Methodists, and Presbyterians, in the context of the
> industrial and social developments of the period.

1334 Strong, Josiah. OUR COUNTRY. Edited by Jurgen Herbst. Cambridge,
Mass.: Harvard University Press, 1963. 291 p. Illus., map, facsim.

> A famous product of the Social Gospel published in
> 1885. Strong, a Congregational minister, advocated the
> Christianization of capitalism and the dominance of what
> he considered superior Anglo-Saxon ways throughout the
> world.

e. LABOR

1335 Brody, David. STEELWORKERS IN AMERICA: THE NONUNION ERA.
Cambridge, Mass.: Harvard University Press, 1960. 401 p.

> On the basis of examination of management and union
> records and public statements, Brody sets forth steel-
> workers attitudes as well as their actions from about
> the 1880s to the 1920s. This aspect of labor history is
> not usually dealt with in such detail.

1336 Bruce, Robert V. 1877: YEAR OF VIOLENCE. Indianapolis: Bobbs-
Merrill, 1959. 384 p.

> An account of the strike against the Baltimore and Ohio
> Railroad that broke out in Martinsburg, West Virginia,
> and spread to Pittsburgh and into the West. Bruce paints
> an unflattering picture of the United States in the period,
> stressing political corruption and crime. Federal troops
> were used to put down the strikers, with two dozen per-
> sons being killed and rioting which resulted in millions
> of dollars in property damage.

1337 David, Henry. HISTORY OF THE HAYMARKET AFFAIR: A STUDY IN THE AMERICAN SOCIAL-REVOLUTIONARY AND LABOR MOVEMENTS. Rev. ed. New York: Collier, 1963. 479 p.

> David traces the events leading to and following the 1886 bomb explosion that killed several policemen and workmen in Haymarket Square, Chicago, after police broke up an anarchist meeting. The strike at the Mc-Cormick Harvesting Machine Company, which occasioned the meeting, the trials and execution of the accused, and the wave of anti-radical activities that followed, are examined in detail.

1338 Dubofsky, Melvyn. WE SHALL BE ALL: A HISTORY OF THE INDUSTRI-AL WORKERS OF THE WORLD. Chicago: Quadrangle Books, 1969. 575 p. Illus.

> A comprehensive history of an early attempt at unioniza-tion. Dubofsky believes the IWW was more significant in determining the shape of labor's future than scholars have recognized heretofore. He includes the legacy of the "Wobblies" in American music and literature.

1339 Grob, Gerald N. WORKERS AND UTOPIA: A STUDY OF IDEOLOGI-CAL CONFLICT IN THE AMERICAN LABOR MOVEMENT, 1865-1900. Evanston, Ill.: Northwestern University Press, 1961. 232 p.

> Seeks to place the ideology of American labor in the context of the society and culture. Grob specifically examines the National Labor Movement, the Knights of Labor, and the American Federation of Labor.

1340 Lindsey, Almont. THE PULLMAN STRIKE: THE STORY OF A UNIQUE EXPERIMENT AND OF A GREAT LABOR UPHEAVAL. 1942. Reprint. Chicago: University of Chicago Press, 1964. 396 p. Illus., ports. Paperbound.

> In this objective account of the great strike of 1894, which had national consequences, Lindsey explores the motivations and actions of such principals in the dispute as Attorney General Richard Olney and Eugene Debs, as well as George Pullman.

1341 Wolff, Leon. LOCKOUT: THE STORY OF THE HOMESTEAD STRIKE OF 1892: A STUDY OF VIOLENCE, UNIONISM AND THE CARNEGIE STEEL EMPIRE. New York: Harper & Row, 1965. 308 p. Illus., ports., maps.

> A great strike that failed. Henry Clay Frick managed to break the union at the Homestead mill in Pennsyl-vania. Wolff's impartial study gives both sides of the story, using contemporary materials as his source.

f. LITERATURE

1342 Brooks, Van Wyck. THE CONFIDENT YEARS, 1885-1915. New York: E.P. Dutton, 1952. 635 p.

> A literary history. Brooks combines an impressive grasp of the social and political milieu in which his subjects wrote with rare literary grace. He touches on many, including Theodore Dreiser, H.L. Mencken, Gertrude Stein, Edith Wharton, Paul Elmer More.

1343 _____. HOWELLS: HIS LIFE AND WORLD. New York: E.P. Dutton, 1959. 296 p. Illus.

> The arbiter of literary taste is pictured, in Brooks's usual lush style, as a friendly, helpful, dignified person. More important, he shows the growth of Howells's literary abilities and weighs his accomplishments.

1344 _____. NEW ENGLAND: INDIAN SUMMER, 1865-1915. 1940. Reprint. New York: E.P. Dutton, 1950. 569 p.

> A sequel to his FLOWERING OF NEW ENGLAND, q.v., no. 975, Brooks deals with many of the literary men of the period, with particular attention to Henry Adams, Henry James, Francis Parkman, and William Dean Howells. Rich and colorful text.

1345 Carter, Everett. HOWELLS AND THE AGE OF REALISM. 1954. Reprint. Hamden, Conn.: Archon Books, 1966. 307 p.

> A biography which places the famous author in the context of his time. Carter believes Howells to have been the dominant literary figure of the period.

1346 Cox, James M. MARK TWAIN: THE FATE OF HUMOR. Princeton, N.J.: Princeton University Press, 1966. 329 p.

> A critical analysis of the man and his writings. Cox makes distinctions among types of humor, considers the place Mrs. Clemens held as censor, and looks at many other aspects of Twain's career.

1347 Ziff, Larzer. THE AMERICAN 1890s: LIFE AND TIMES OF A LOST GENERATION. New York: Viking Press, 1966. 384 p.

> A discussion of literary trends, with attention given magazines and newspapers as well as leading literary figures. Among others, Ziff analyzes the writings of Howells, Twain, James, Garland, Bierce, Crane, Henry Adams, Norris, Robinson, and Dreiser.

g. POPULISM

1348 Buck, Solon J. THE AGRARIAN CRUSADE: A CHRONICLE OF THE
FARMER IN POLITICS. New Haven, Conn.: Yale University Press, 1920.
224 p. Front., ports.

> A general treatment of the rise of political conscious-
> ness on the part of the farmer as it expressed itself in
> the Granger movement, the Farmers' Alliance, and the
> Populist party.

1349 _____. THE GRANGER MOVEMENT: A STUDY OF AGRICULTURAL
ORGANIZATION AND ITS POLITICAL, ECONOMIC, AND SOCIAL
MANIFESTATIONS, 1870-1880. 1913. Reprint. Lincoln: University
of Nebraska Press, 1963. 384 p. Illus.

> A scholarly examination of various farmer organizations,
> with particular concern for the rise of the Grangers.
> Buck goes deeply into the economic factors.

1350 Hackney, Sheldon, ed. POPULISM: THE CRITICAL ISSUES. Boston:
Little, Brown, 1971. 190 p.

> A collection of articles on the concerns of the Populists
> by leading scholars. They include Robert Durden,
> Richard Hofstadter, Walter T.K. Nugent, C. Vann
> Woodward, the editor, and others.

1351 Hicks, John D. THE POPULIST REVOLT: A HISTORY OF THE FARMERS'
ALLIANCE AND THE PEOPLE'S PARTY. 1931. Reprint. Lincoln: University of Nebraska Press, 1961. 473 p. Illus.

> A description, by an expert in the field, of the coali-
> tion and the personalities that made up the Populist
> party. Hicks analyzes the financial situation of the
> farmer in the 1880s and 1890s and gives a clear formu-
> lation of Populist ideas.

1352 Hofstadter, Richard. THE AGE OF REFORM: FROM BRYAN TO F.D.R.
1955. Reprint. New York: Alfred A. Knopf, n.d. 351 p. Paperbound.

> A broad, interpretive study. Hofstadter deals with Bryan,
> Populism, and Progressivism, to the First World War, and
> then draws parallels between this earlier period and the
> later New Deal.

1353 Nugent, Walter T.K. THE TOLERANT POPULISTS: KANSAS POPULISM
AND NATIVISM. Chicago: University of Chicago Press, 1963. 256 p.

> Covers the dozen years of 1888 to 1900. The author at-

tempts to show that the People's party was neither nativ-
ist nor anti-Semitic and included in its ranks many
foreign-born Kansans.

1354 Pollack, Norman. THE POPULIST RESPONSE TO INDUSTRIAL AMERICA:
MIDWESTERN POPULIST THOUGHT. Cambridge, Mass.: Harvard University Press, 1962. 166 p.

Deals with Minnesota, Nebraska, Wisconsin, and Kansas. Pollack attempts to show that the movement was
forward-looking, rather than retrogressive, as is often
thought. He thinks Populism accepted the industrial
age but sought to ameliorate its harsh features. Because
of this it gained adherents among industrial workers and
intellectuals.

1355 Tindall, George B., ed. A POPULIST READER: SELECTIONS FROM THE
WORKS OF AMERICAN POPULIST LEADERS. New York: Harper & Row,
1966. 251 p. Paperbound.

A collection of contemporary source materials. Includes
party platforms, speeches of candidates, policy statements, etc.

h. RAILROADS

1356 Campbell, E.G. THE REORGANIZATION OF THE AMERICAN RAILROAD
SYSTEM, 1893-1900: A STUDY OF THE EFFECTS OF THE PANIC OF
1893, THE ENSUING DEPRESSION, AND THE FIRST YEARS OF RECOV-
ERY ON RAILROAD ORGANIZATION AND FINANCING. New York:
Columbia University Press. 1938. 366 p.

Campbell identifies incompetence and financial mismanagement as the main reasons for the problems confronting the roads.

1357 Cochran, Thomas C. RAILROAD LEADERS, 1845-1890: THE BUSINESS
MIND IN ACTION. 1953. Reprint. New York: Russell & Russell,
1966. 583 p. Maps.

Concentrates on the attitudes, not the accomplishments,
of sixty railroad entrepreneurs. Cochran deals with their
ideas on government, labor, the public, customers, competition, etc., supplementing his analysis with extensive
extracts from their letters.

1358 Fogel, Robert W. THE UNION PACIFIC RAILROAD: A CASE IN PRE-
MATURE ENTERPRISE. Baltimore: Johns Hopkins Press, 1960. 129 p.

On the basis of microeconomic theory and analysis,
Fogel concludes that the basis for financing the railroad

was all wrong. He suggests what may have worked better.

Goodrich, Carter. GOVERNMENT PROMOTION OF AMERICAN CANALS AND RAILROADS. See no. 276.

1359 Griswold, Wesley S. A WORK OF GIANTS: BUILDING THE FIRST TRANSCONTINENTAL RAILROAD. New York: McGraw-Hill Book Co., 1962. 367 p. Illus.

The linking of East and West with the building of Central Pacific and Union Pacific Railroads, 1863-69. Griswold touches lightly on the political and economic questions involved and concentrates on producing a dramatic account of the obstacles overcome by the builders and the managers.

1360 Grodinsky, Julius. TRANSCONTINENTAL RAILWAY STRATEGY, 1869-1893: A STUDY OF BUSINESSMEN. Philadelphia: University of Pennsylvania Press, 1962. 468 p. Maps, tables.

The ups and downs of investors in the railroads. Grodinsky deals with the expansion of the roads, competition among them, and their relation to the national economy.

1361 Holbrook, Stewart H. THE STORY OF AMERICAN RAILROADS. New York: Crown, 1947. 478 p. Illus., ports., maps.

A popularization written in Holbrook's usual winning style. He deals with the planners, the builders, and those who ran the roads.

1362 Kolko, Gabriel. RAILROADS AND REGULATION, 1877-1916. 1965. Reprint. New York: W.W. Norton, 1970. 273 p.

Takes the position that the railroad managers themselves were in favor of federal regulation and arranged it in order to cut down on competition. Kolko claims that they had easy access to the White House.

Riegel, Robert E. STORY OF THE WESTERN RAILROADS. See no. 1259.

1363 Stover, John F. AMERICAN RAILROADS. Chicago: University of Chicago Press, 1961. 316 p. Illus., ports., plates, maps, chart.

A general history of the railroads: their development, the linking of East and West, the competition among them, and the problems confronting them. The author includes a chronology.

1364 Taylor, George Rogers, and Neu, Irene D. THE AMERICAN RAILROAD NETWORK, 1861-1890. Cambridge, Mass.: Harvard University Press, 1956. 126 p. Maps.

> The authors point out that the country did not have a connected railroad system in 1861, since various problems such as "gauge differentials" kept the roads apart. They give a history of the development of the roads and the move toward integration.

j. URBAN LIFE

1365 Callow, Alexander B., Jr. THE TWEED RING. New York: Oxford University Press, 1966. 362 p. Illus.

> A study of the Tweed political organization in New York City, 1866-71. Callow examines the personalities of the members and shows how they manipulated Tammany Hall and the state legislature and used patronage, the police, the courts, and the immigrants for their purposes.

1366 Green, Constance M. AMERICAN CITIES IN THE GROWTH OF THE NATION. New York: J. DeGraff, 1957. 258 p. Illus.

> In original form, lectures delivered at London University in 1951. The author deals with clusters of cities, showing their common characteristics and problems: Boston, New York, Philadelphia, Baltimore, and Charleston as seaboard cities; Cincinnati, St. Louis, and New Orleans, as river cities; etc.

1367 McKelvey, Blake. THE URBANIZATION OF AMERICA, 1860-1915. New Brunswick, N.J.: Rutgers University Press, 1963. 370 p. Illus.

> Urban expansion from its beginnings to the point where half of the population was living in urban areas. McKelvey sets forth the causes for growth and the impact of the city on the society generally. Excellent illustrations.

1368 Mandelbaum, Seymour J. BOSS TWEED'S NEW YORK. New York: Wiley, 1965. 205 p. Illus., map.

> Mandelbaum makes an imaginative use of sources to discover the dynamics at work in New York City in the late 1860s and early 1870s. He shows how William Marcy Tweed used the political payoff to accomplish his ends and how Horace Greeley, Samuel J. Tilden, et al., and the TIMES succeeded in their demands for reform.

1369 Mann, Arthur. YANKEE REFORMERS IN THE URBAN AGE: SOCIAL RE-
FORM IN BOSTON, 1880-1900. 1954. Reprint. New York: Harper &
Row, 1966. 326 p. Paperbound.

> Deals primarily with humanitarian concerns in the Boston
> area, and such figures as Edward Everett Hale, in an
> age of industrialization and urbanization.

1370 Patton, Clifford W. THE BATTLE FOR MUNICIPAL REFORM: MOBILIZA-
TION AND ATTACK, 1875-1900. 1940. Reprint. College Park, Md.:
McGrath Publishing Co., 1969. 91 p.

> Machine politics and the battles of reformers to clean
> up municipal corruption.

1371 Schlesinger, Arthur M. THE RISE OF THE CITY, 1878-1898. 1933. Reprint. Chicago: Quadrangle Books, 1971. 508 p. Paperbound.

> The transition from a rural to an urban and industrial
> nation in the 1880s and 1890s. Schlesinger gives much
> detail on social and intellectual developments.

1372 Ward, David. CITIES AND IMMIGRANTS: A GEOGRAPHY OF CHANGE
IN NINETEENTH-CENTURY AMERICA. New York: Oxford University
Press, 1971. 180 p. Illus., maps, tables.

> A study of the changing nature of the city as it was
> affected by the influx of immigrants. An excellent
> selection of drawings, photographs, and maps comple-
> ments the text.

3. Prominent Individuals

HENRY ADAMS

1373 Adams, Henry. THE EDUCATION OF HENRY ADAMS. Edited by Ernest
Samuels. Boston: Houghton Mifflin, 1974. 735 p.

> Originally written for Adams's friends, but published in
> 1918. An intimate picture of the life-long education
> of a Boston Brahmin that tells much about the times.

LOUIS AGASSIZ

1374 Lurie, Edward. LOUIS AGASSIZ: A LIFE IN SCIENCE. Chicago: University of Chicago Press, 1960. 463 p. Illus., ports.

> The Swiss-born naturalist who, at Harvard, became an
> important opponent of Darwin's evolutionary theory and
> of its advocate, his colleague Asa Gray. Lurie gives

a critical evaluation of Agassiz's contributions.

HENRY WARD BEECHER

1375 Hibben, Paxton. HENRY WARD BEECHER: AN AMERICAN PORTRAIT.
New York: Doran, 1927. 390 p. Front., ports., plates.

A biography, somewhat sarcastic in tone, that deflates
the reputation of the famous preacher of the Plymouth
Church in Brooklyn and leading proponent of the application of Darwinism to religion. Hibben supplies psychological explanations for Beecher's actions.

ALEXANDER GRAHAM BELL

1376 Bruce, Robert V. BELL: ALEXANDER GRAHAM BELL AND THE CON-
QUEST OF SOLITUDE. Boston: Little, Brown, 1973. 575 p. Illus.

A full biography, with accent on the intellectual process by which Bell worked through the obstacles to the
invention of the telephone.

EDWARD BELLAMY

1377 Bowman, Sylvia E. THE YEAR 2000: A CRITICAL BIOGRAPHY OF ED-
WARD BELLAMY. New York: Bookman, 1958. 404 p. Illus.

Bellamy's LOOKING BACKWARD, published in 1888,
became one of the best-known of utopian novels. Bowman, an authority on such writings, traces the sources
of Bellamy's discontent and recounts what he did about
them.

JAMES G. BLAINE

1378 Muzzey, David S. JAMES G. BLAINE: A POLITICAL IDOL OF OTHER
DAYS. New York: Dodd, Mead, 1934. 525 p. Front., ports., plates,
facsims.

Blaine of Maine, the "Plumed Knight," who was a force
in the Republican party and candidate for president in 1884,
in a biography written with detachment by a leading
American historian earlier in this century.

WILLIAM JENNINGS BRYAN

1379 Coletta, Paolo E. WILLIAM JENNINGS BRYAN. 3 vols. Lincoln: University of Nebraska Press, 1964-69. Illus., ports., maps.

This detailed biography is quite sympathetic to Bryan.
Volume 1: POLITICAL EVANGELIST, 1860-1908; volume 2: PROGRESSIVE POLITICIAN AND MORAL STATESMAN, 1909-1915; volume 3: POLITICAL PURITAN, 1915-1925.

1380 Glad, Paul W. THE TRUMPET SOUNDETH: WILLIAM JENNINGS BRYAN AND HIS DEMOCRACY, 1896-1912. Lincoln: University of Nebraska Press, 1960. 254 p. Illus., ports.

Analyzes the ideas of Bryan in these important years in his career as a party leader and shows how they stemmed from his background. Glad demonstrates that Bryan was a significant figure in his time.

ANDREW CARNEGIE

1381 Wall, Joseph F. ANDREW CARNEGIE. New York: Oxford University Press, 1970. 1,149 p. Illus., ports.

A lengthy biography which is sympathetic but balanced. Wall deals with Carnegie's many business involvements in great detail and points up the importance of the technological innovations which he fostered.

GROVER CLEVELAND

1382 Merrill, Horace Samuel. BOURBON LEADER: GROVER CLEVELAND AND THE DEMOCRATIC PARTY. Boston: Little, Brown, 1957. 224 p.

A study of the conservative president and his two administrations. Merrill deals with Cleveland's accomplishments and failures fairly.

1383 Nevins, Allan. GROVER CLEVELAND: A STUDY IN COURAGE. 1932. Reprint. New York: Dodd, Mead, 1948. 845 p. Front., ports., plates.

Portrays Cleveland as a man of character and integrity but not of great intellect. A balanced picture of the man emerges, along with a skillfull representation of his times.

ANTHONY COMSTOCK

1384 Broun, Heywood C., and Leech, Margaret. ANTHONY COMSTOCK, ROUNDSMAN OF THE LORD. New York: Albert & Charles Boni, 1927. 285 p. Ports., plates, facsims.

A highly critical study of Comstock's various campaigns for moral purity at the expense of freedom of press and

expression. The authors, to a certain extent, deal with
his psychological motivations.

EMILY DICKINSON

1385 Johnson, Thomas H. EMILY DICKINSON: AN INTERPRETIVE BIOGRAPHY.
Cambridge, Mass.: Harvard University Press, 1955. 286 p. Illus., ports.

> A scholarly biography by an editor of her poems. John-
> son analyzes the famous recluse in her family setting,
> with her friends, and as she reveals herself in her writing.

MARY BAKER EDDY

1386 Peel, Robert. MARY BAKER EDDY. 2 vols. New York: Holt, Rinehart and Winston, 1966-71. Ports.

> A biography of the founder of Christian Science by a
> member of the group who had access to church records.
> Peel sets Eddy in the social and intellectual context of
> her time. Volume 1: THE YEARS OF DISCOVERY;
> volume 2: THE YEARS OF TRIAL.

THOMAS ALVA EDISON

1387 Josephson, Matthew. EDISON: A BIOGRAPHY. New York: McGraw-
Hill Book Co., 1959. 511 p. Illus.

> Edison's inventive genius is placed in the framework of
> American life; not only is his life given in full, but the
> impact of his work on society is measured. A warm por-
> trait of a colorful figure.

CHARLES W. ELIOT

1388 Hawkins, Hugh. BETWEEN HARVARD AND AMERICA: THE EDUCATION-
AL LEADERSHIP OF CHARLES W. ELIOT. New York: Oxford University
Press, 1972. 415 p. Port.

> Covers the years 1849-1909: Eliot as student and then
> as president of Harvard University for forty years. It
> was under Eliot that Harvard was transformed into a
> great secular university. Hawkins is concerned to show
> Eliot and his school in the context of American social
> and intellectual life.

JAMES ABRAM GARFIELD

1389 Hinsdale, Burke A., ed. THE WORKS OF JAMES ABRAM GARFIELD.
2 vols. 1882. Reprint. Freeport, N.Y.: Books for Libraries Press,

1970. Fronts., ports.

Speeches and addresses arranged chronologically from 1864 to 1880, years during which Garfield served in the House of Representatives. The collection concludes with his inaugural address as president in 1881. No correspondence is included. Volume 2 contains an index.

1390 Smith, Theodore Clarke. LIFE AND LETTERS OF JAMES ABRAM GAR-FIELD. 2 vols. 1925. Reprint. Hamden, Conn.: Archon Books, 1968. Ports.

Using family papers, Smith wrote an account of the president's life that is objective but at the same time sympathetic.

HENRY GEORGE

1391 Barker, Charles A. HENRY GEORGE. New York: Oxford University Press, 1955. 713 p. Port.

The reformer and advocate of the "single tax" is pictured with both his virtues and his faults in a scholarly biography. Barker subjects George's social and economic views to a rigorous analysis.

SAMUEL GOMPERS

1392 Gompers, Samuel. SEVENTY YEARS OF LIFE AND LABOR: AN AUTO-BIOGRAPHY. 2 vols. 1953. Reprint. New York: Augustus M. Kelley, 1967.

In his old age, Gompers set down his reminiscences of his years in labor as head of the American Federation of Labor. His self-portrait is quite conservative.

1393 Mandel, Bernard. SAMUEL GOMPERS: A BIOGRAPHY. Yellow Springs, Ohio: Antioch Press, 1963. 588 p. Illus., ports.

Labor developments from 1875 to 1925 are treated in the life of the most important labor leader of the time. Gompers's formation of the American Federation of Labor and his campaigns for child labor laws, the eight-hour day, and other reforms, are reported in detail. The book includes an introduction by Louis Filler: "Samuel Gompers: Labor Statesman or Labor Faker?"

ASA GRAY

1394 Dupree, A. Hunter. ASA GRAY, 1810-1888. Cambridge, Mass.: Harvard University Press, 1959. 515 p. Illus., ports.

A solidly documented study of the Harvard botanist who
related the flora of North America to those of North-
east Asia (thus supporting Darwin's theories) and became
an advocate of Darwinism in the great debate on evolution.

MARCUS ALONZO HANNA

1395 Croly, Herbert. MARCUS ALONZO HANNA: HIS LIFE AND WORK.
1912. Reprint. Hamden, Conn.: Archon Books, 1965. 508 p. Ports.,
plates, facsims.

A frank portrait of Hanna as successful businessman and
politico, with a revealing account of Republican politics over a thirty-year period. Since documents were
scarce, Croly turned to acquaintances of Hanna for information and reminiscences.

BENJAMIN HARRISON

1396 Harrison, Benjamin. PUBLIC PAPERS AND ADDRESSES OF BENJAMIN
HARRISON, TWENTY-THIRD PRESIDENT OF THE UNITED STATES. 1893.
Reprint. New York: Kraus Reprint Co., 1969. 302 p.

Includes materials dated from 4 March 1889 to 4 March
1893. Originally published by Government Printing
Office.

1397 Sievers, Harry J. BENJAMIN HARRISON. 3 vols. Chicago: Henry
Regnery, 1952-68. Illus., ports., maps.

Portrays a warm-hearted Harrison within the cold exterior
seen by his contemporaries. Sievers had use of the extensive Harrison papers. Volume 1: HOOSIER WAR-
RIOR, 1833-1865; volume 2: HOOSIER STATESMAN:
FROM THE CIVIL WAR TO THE WHITE HOUSE, 1865-
1888; volume 3: HOOSIER PRESIDENT: THE WHITE
HOUSE AND AFTER.

JOHN HAY

1398 Dennett, Tyler. JOHN HAY: FROM POETRY TO POLITICS. 1933. Reprint. Port Washington, N.Y.: Kennikat Press, 1963. 476 p. Illus.,
ports., facsim.

Hay's career included time as secretary to Lincoln, the
writing of poetry, novels, and, with Nicolay, a history
of Lincoln's times, and holding the position of sec-

retary of state under McKinley and Theodore Roosevelt.
Dennett's account is based on Hay's papers.

RUTHERFORD B. HAYES

1399 Barnard, Harry. RUTHERFORD B. HAYES AND HIS AMERICA. 1954.
Reprint. New York: Russell & Russell, 1967. 606 p. Illus., ports.,
facsim.

> This biography of the president is both a study of his
> psychological makeup and of his career. Barnard pic-
> tures Hayes as an effective executive.

1400 Williams, Charles Richard, ed. DIARY AND LETTERS OF RUTHERFORD
BIRCHARD HAYES. 5 vols. Columbus: Ohio State Archaeological and
Historical Society, 1922-26. Illus., fronts., ports., plates, maps, plans.

> Items are dated from 1834 to 1892 and concern personal
> and public matters. The DIARY is made up mostly of
> brief entries.

WILLIAM RANDOLPH HEARST

1401 Swanberg, W.A. CITIZEN HEARST: A BIOGRAPHY OF WILLIAM RAN-
DOLPH HEARST. New York: Charles Scribner's Sons, 1961. 555 p.
Illus., ports.

> The builder and maintainer of the great newspaper chain
> is shown with his strengths and weaknesses. Swanberg
> describes Hearst's many-sided life with verve and color.

HENRY JAMES

1402 Edel, Leon. HENRY JAMES. 5 vols. Philadelphia: Lippincott, 1953-
72. Illus., ports.

> This exhaustive biography of the expatriate American
> novelist deals skillfully with the relationship of his per-
> sonality to the themes explored in his works. Volume
> 1: THE UNTRIED YEARS, 1843-1870; volume 2: THE
> CONQUEST OF LONDON, 1870-1881; volume 3: THE
> MIDDLE YEARS, 1882-1895; volume 4: THE TREACH-
> EROUS YEARS, 1895-1901; volume 5: THE MASTER,
> 1901-1916.

WILLIAM JAMES

1403 Perry, Ralph Barton. THE THOUGHT AND CHARACTER OF WILLIAM
JAMES. 1948. Reprint. Cambridge, Mass.: Harvard University Press,

1967. 412 p. Port.

A briefer version of Perry's two-volume work of 1935.
Perry, who had studied with the philosopher, skillfully
sketches his personality and thought and includes many
excerpts from his correspondence.

WILLIAM McKINLEY

1404 Morgan, H. Wayne. WILLIAM McKINLEY AND HIS AMERICA. Syracuse,
N.Y.: Syracuse University Press, 1963. 606 p. Illus., ports.

A favorable evaluation of the political career and contributions of the twenty-fifth president. Morgan believes
that McKinley could not have avoided the war with
Spain and that he was internationalistic, rather than
imperialistic, in his outlook.

J.P. MORGAN

1405 Allen, Frederick Lewis. THE GREAT PIERPONT MORGAN. New York:
Harper & Brothers, 1949. 316 p. Port.

Deals with J.P. Morgan as a financier, intentionally
neglecting his private life. Allen weighs the ethical
implications of his various dealings. On the whole, a
sympathetic account.

TERENCE POWDERLY

1406 Powderly, Terence. THIRTY YEARS OF LABOR, 1859 TO 1889. 1890.
Reprint. New York: Augustus M. Kelley, 1962. 372 p. Front.

The experiences of a well-known labor leader who
served as Grand Master Workman of the Knights of
Labor (1879-93) and advocated abolition of the wage
system in favor of cooperatives. First published in
1889.

JOHN D. ROCKEFELLER

1407 Nevins, Allan. STUDY IN POWER: JOHN D. ROCKEFELLER, INDUS-
TRIALIST AND PHILANTHROPIST. 2 vols. New York: Charles Scribner's
Sons, 1953. Illus., ports., maps.

Nevins's second version of Rockefeller's career, the first
having been published in 1940. This is much expanded,
making use of new documentary material. A sympathetic book which attempts to rehabilitate Rockefeller, long
considered one of the "robber barons."

CARL SCHURZ

1408 Fuess, Claude M. CARL SCHURZ, REFORMER (1829-1906). New York: Dodd, Mead, 1932. 436 p. Front., ports., plates.

A balanced picture of the German immigrant who became a leading force for reform in American political life. Schurz's contribution to liberal Republicanism, humane Indian policy, and reform of the civil service, are dealt with in detail.

LOUIS SULLIVAN

1409 Paul, Sherman. LOUIS SULLIVAN, AN ARCHITECT IN AMERICAN THOUGHT. Englewood Cliffs, N.J.: Prentice-Hall, 1962. 176 p. Illus. Paperbound.

The philosophical views of the great architect as contained in his writings. Paul traces Sullivan's intellectual indebtedness to such seminal thinkers as Whitman, Veblen, William James, and Dewey.

CORNELIUS VANDERBILT

1410 Lane, Wheaton J. COMMODORE VANDERBILT: AN EPIC OF THE STEAM AGE. New York: Alfred A. Knopf, 1942. 383 p. Front., ports., plates, maps, facsims.

Concentrates on Vanderbilt as a businessman, with little attention to personal matters. A scholarly, unsensational picture of an adventurous, rugged character.

THORSTEIN VEBLEN

1411 Riesman, David. THORSTEIN VEBLEN: A CRITICAL INTERPRETATION. 1953. Reprint. New York: Charles Scribner's Sons, 1960. 221 p. Paperbound.

A penetrating study of the provocative pioneer American sociologist and his scathing analyses of America's moneyed classes.

LESTER F. WARD

1412 Chugerman, Samuel. LESTER F. WARD, THE AMERICAN ARISTOTLE: A SUMMARY AND INTERPRETATION OF HIS SOCIOLOGY. 1939. Reprint. New York: Octagon Books, 1965. 604 p. Illus., ports.

An intellectual portrait of the influential sociologist who sought to establish the principle of cooperation against the Social Darwinism of William Graham Sumner, Herbert Spencer et al.

BOOKER T. WASHINGTON

1413 Harlan, Louis R. BOOKER T. WASHINGTON. 1 vol. to date. New York: Oxford University Press, 1972- . Illus., ports.

The first volume of a new, two-volume biography in process, by the editor of the Washington PAPERS, q.v., no. 1414. Harlan points up the complexity of Washington's actions in various aspects of his career, such as the image he projected of the compliant black accepting white supremacy at the same time that, behind the scenes, he was supporting legal action against segregation. Volume 1: THE MAKING OF A BLACK LEADER, 1856-1901.

1414 _____, ed. THE BOOKER T. WASHINGTON PAPERS. 3 vols. to date. Urbana: University of Illinois Press, 1972- . Illus., ports.

This collection enhances our understanding of Washington and the problems of American blacks in accommodating to the white power structure in the United States following the Civil War. The first volume includes his famous UP FROM SLAVERY and other autobiographical writings. Volume 1: AUTOBIOGRAPHICAL WRITINGS; volume 2: 1860-1889; volume 3: 1889-1895.

1415 Spencer, Samuel R. BOOKER T. WASHINGTON AND THE NEGRO'S PLACE IN AMERICAN LIFE. Boston: Little, Brown, 1955. 212 p.

A positive picture of the black leader which concentrates on an analysis of his view of how the black man could best fit into American life after emancipation.

1416 Washington, Booker T. UP FROM SLAVERY: AN AUTOBIOGRAPHY. New York: Dodd, Mead, 1965. 212 p. Illus., ports.

The autobiography of the black educator. Washington tells of his birth in slavery and his ascent to head of the Tuskegee Institute and fame as a leader of his people. This edition includes an introduction by Langston Hughes.

C. IMPERIALIST EXPANSION

1. General

1417 Dulles, Foster Rhea. THE IMPERIAL YEARS. New York: Crowell, 1956.

340 p. Illus.

Covers the period 1885 to 1909. Dulles traces the origin of imperialistic sentiment in an understanding manner and shows how the Americans went about the task of building an empire.

1418 LaFeber, Walter. THE NEW EMPIRE: AN INTERPRETATION OF AMERICAN EXPANSION, 1860-1898. Ithaca, N.Y.: Cornell University Press, 1963. 457 p.

Traces the connection between the growth of business and the development of foreign markets and America's growing interest in achieving the status of a world power. LaFeber believes that big business came to dominate U.S. foreign policy in the last two generations of the nineteenth century. In the case of Cuba, for instance, an interest in the protection of American investments led to war with Spain.

1419 Mahan, Alfred T. THE INFLUENCE OF SEA POWER UPON HISTORY, 1660-1783. New York: Sagamore Press, 1957. 495 p. Illus.

The work, first published in 1890 had great influence on the development of the American navy and imperialistic thought in the United States. This edition has an introduction by Louis M. Hacker.

1420 May, Ernest R. IMPERIAL DEMOCRACY: THE EMERGENCE OF AMERICA AS A GREAT POWER. New York: Harcourt, Brace & World, 1961. 318 p.

Deals with the years 1893-98, during which the United States took a place among the powerful nations of the earth. May has used foreign as well as American archives; he assesses the roles of U.S. diplomacy and public opinion in America's imperialist beginning.

1421 Pratt, Julius W. AMERICA'S COLONIAL EXPERIMENT: HOW THE UNITED STATES GAINED, GOVERNED, AND IN PART GAVE AWAY A COLONIAL EMPIRE. 1950. Reprint. Gloucester, Mass.: Peter Smith, 1964. 417 p. Maps.

The account by a historian of diplomacy of the acquisition of territories in America's imperial period and their later disposal. Pratt traces in detail the dealings of the United States with each of its possessions, and the impact the American presence had on the colony.

1422 _____. EXPANSIONISTS OF 1898. 1936. Reprint. Chicago: Quadrangle Books, 1964. 402 p. Paperbound.

The 1936 Albert Shaw Lectures on Diplomatic History at the Walter Hines Page School of International Relations, Johns Hopkins University. Pratt sees the beginning of U.S. imperialism in the administration of Benjamin Harrison and traces its development.

Weinberg, Alfred K. MANIFEST DESTINY. See no. 245.

2. Topical

a. CUBA AND THE CARIBBEAN

1423 Callcott, Wilfrid H. THE CARIBBEAN POLICY OF THE UNITED STATES, 1890-1920. Baltimore: Johns Hopkins Press, 1942. 538 p.

The Albert Shaw Lectures on Diplomatic History for 1942 at the Walter Hines Page School of International Relations. Deals with Mexico as well as the Caribbean. Callcott has made use of the papers of House, Knox, Lansing, Root, and Wilson in assessing American intentions.

1424 Ealy, Lawrence O. YANQUI POLITICS AND THE ISTHMIAN CANAL. University Park: Pennsylvania State University Press, 1971. 192 p.

Discusses the relationship between the United States and what became of the country of Panama. Ealy begins his account with the discovery of the Pacific by Balboa in 1513. A thorough, scholarly treatment of the development of the area and the particular interest the United States was to maintain in it as it expanded westward and looked increasingly to a water route from east to west.

1425 Healy, David F. THE UNITED STATES IN CUBA, 1898-1902: GENERALS, POLITICIANS, AND THE SEARCH FOR POLICY. Madison: University of Wisconsin Press, 1963. 260 p. Illus.

A clear analysis of the muddle out of which emerged U.S. policy toward Cuba, which was taken over in the Spanish-American War. The author compares it with the United States approach to the Philippines.

1426 Munro, Dana G. INTERVENTION AND DOLLAR DIPLOMACY IN THE CARIBBEAN, 1900-1921. Princeton, N.J.: Princeton University Press, 1964. 562 p. Map.

The motives of American intervention in various crises in Cuba and Central America are examined by a scholar who served earlier in the Latin American section of the State Department. Munro believes American actions were due to political rather than economic concerns.

1427 Roosevelt, Theodore. THE ROUGH RIDERS. 1899. Reprint. Williams-
town, Mass.: Corner House, 1971. 330 p.

A day-by-day account of the volunteer cavalry recruited
to fight in Cuba. This book reveals Roosevelt's attitudes
toward war and the place of the United States in world
affairs. He preached intervention and enjoyed every
battle once the U.S. forces had landed on the island.

b. DIPLOMACY

1428 Campbell, Charles S., Jr. ANGLO-AMERICAN UNDERSTANDING, 1898-
1903. Baltimore: Johns Hopkins Press, 1957. 392 p. Map.

The trouble between Britain and the United States gener-
ated by differences of opinion on the Isthmian canal and
the location of the Alaska boundary.

1429 Grenville, John A.S., and Young, George B. POLITICS, STRATEGY,
AND AMERICAN DIPLOMACY: STUDIES IN FOREIGN POLICY, 1873-
1917. New Haven, Conn.: Yale University Press, 1966. 370 p.

An Anglo-American team of scholars reexamines foreign
policy in a series of essays. Many themes are dealt
with; particularly important are those dealing with U.S.
imperialistic ambitions.

1430 Pletcher, David M. THE AWKWARD YEARS: AMERICAN FOREIGN RE-
LATIONS UNDER GARFIELD AND ARTHUR. Columbia: University of
Missouri Press, 1962. 381 p.

An analysis of political machinations within the executive
department in two administrations and the resultant inept
attempts to implement expansionist policies.

1431 Zabriskie, Edward H. AMERICAN-RUSSIAN RIVALRY IN THE FAR EAST:
A STUDY IN DIPLOMACY AND POWER POLITICS, 1895-1914. Philadelphia: University of Pennsylvania Press, 1946. 234 p. Map.

A diplomatic history which does not take into account
economic rivalry between the two nations. Zabriskie
begins his history with the signing of the peace agreement at the end of the Chinese-Japanese War. Well
documented.

c. ECONOMIC IMPERIALISM

1432 Campbell, Charles S., Jr. SPECIAL BUSINESS INTERESTS AND THE OPEN

DOOR POLICY. 1951. Reprint. Hamden, Conn.: Shoe String Press, 1968. 88 p.

A very brief account of the pressures exerted by business on government in behalf of the Open Door Policy in China. Businessmen were anxious to find a large market for their surplus products.

1433 Gardner, Lloyd C., ed. A DIFFERENT FRONTIER: SELECTED READINGS IN THE FOUNDATIONS OF AMERICAN ECONOMIC EXPANSION. Chicago: Quadrangle Books, 1966. 190 p.

The editor has collected documents to illustrate the economic pressures that worked for imperialistic expansion once the western frontier was closed.

1434 McCormick, Thomas J. CHINA MARKET: AMERICA'S QUEST FOR INFORMAL EMPIRE, 1893-1901. Chicago: Quadrangle Books, 1967. 241 p.

An economic interpretation of U.S. expansionism. The author believes that Presidents Cleveland and McKinley promoted American business interests in China as a part of government policy because of assumed economic need.

d. HAWAII AND THE PHILIPPINES

1435 Russ, William A., Jr. THE HAWAIIAN REPUBLIC, 1894-98, AND ITS STRUGGLE TO WIN ANNEXATION. Selinsgrove, Pa.: Susquehanna University Press, 1961. 406 p.

A sequel to the author's HAWAIIAN REVOLUTION, q.v., no. 1436. He deals here with the establishment of, and various threats to, the republic and the annexation to the United States during the wave of imperialist sentiment.

1436 _____. THE HAWAIIAN REVOLUTION, 1893-94. Selinsgrove, Pa.: Susquehanna University Press, 1959. 372 p.

A history of the fall of the Hawaiian monarchy, growing sentiment on the islands for annexation to the United States, and an exploration of American governmental and public attitudes.

1437 Stevens, Sylvester K. AMERICAN EXPANSION IN HAWAII, 1842-1898. 1945. Reprint. New York: Russell & Russell, 1968. 320 p. Map.

The development of American interest in the Hawaiian Islands from its beginnings to the annexation in 1898.

Stevens' study is a thorough one, based on primary
materials.

1438 Wolff, Leon. LITTLE BROWN BROTHER: AMERICA'S FORGOTTEN BID
FOR EMPIRE WHICH COST 250,000 LIVES. 1961. Reprint. New York:
Kraus Reprint Co., 1970. 383 p. Illus., ports., maps.

A heavily ironic account of America's imperialist adventure. Wolff makes it clear that he considers U.S.
policy at the time reprehensible.

e. THE SPANISH-AMERICAN WAR

1439 Braisted, W.R. THE UNITED STATES NAVY IN THE PACIFIC, 1897-1909.
Austin: University of Texas Press, 1958. 294 p. Map.

A history of the navy in a period of expansion. Braisted evaluates its impact on American foreign policy.
Among the topics dealt with are the Spanish-American
War and the navy's role in the absorption of Hawaii
and the Philippines. Its role in the Boxer Rebellion,
the Open Door Policy, and the Russo-Japanese War
is also considered.

1440 Freidel, Frank. THE SPLENDID LITTLE WAR. Boston: Little, Brown,
1958. 314 p. Illus.

A pictorial history of the Spanish-American War. The
title is derived from John Hay in a letter to Theodore
Roosevelt. Freidel makes it clear, in his selection of
striking photographs and illustrations, that the war was
anything but splendid.

1441 Millis, Walter. THE MARTIAL SPIRIT. 1931. Reprint. New York:
Viking Press, 1965. 442 p. Illus. Paperbound.

Traces the growth of militancy in the United States in
the last half of the nineteenth century, which resulted
in the war with Spain. Millis examines the political
situation, the economic factors, and the sensational
journalistic efforts of William Randolph Hearst and Joseph
Pulitzer. He also deals with the individuals and groups
that advocated and opposed the war.

1442 Morgan, H. Wayne. AMERICA'S ROAD TO EMPIRE: THE WAR WITH
SPAIN AND OVERSEAS EXPANSION. New York: Wiley, 1965. 137
p. Maps.

In this brief presentation dealing with diplomacy leading
to the Spanish-American War, Morgan attempts to show
that the United States was provoked to go to war by

Spanish policy and not by hysteria over the sinking of
the MAINE or the agitation of the yellow press. The
action was a conscious attempt to extend American power.

3. Prominent Individuals

1443 Beisner, Robert L. TWELVE AGAINST EMPIRE: THE ANTI-IMPERIALISTS,
1898-1900. New York: McGraw-Hill Book Co., 1968. 326 p. Ports.

The opposition by a group of prominent persons to the
Spanish-American War and the trend toward imperialism,
set forth in well-drawn biographical sketches. The fig-
ures are William James, Andrew Carnegie, Carl Schurz,
E.L. Godkin, Charles Eliot Norton, Edward Atkinson,
Charles Francis Adams, Senator George F. Hoar, George
Boutwell, Thomas Reed, John Sherman, ex-President
Benjamin Harrison.

1444 West, Richard S. ADMIRALS OF THE AMERICAN EMPIRE: THE COM-
BINED STORY OF GEORGE DEWEY, ALFRED THAYER MAHAN, WIN-
FIELD SCOTT SCHLEY, AND WILLIAM THOMAS SAMPSON. 1948. Re-
print. Westport, Conn.: Greenwood Press, 1971. 354 p. Illus., maps.

A joint biography of influential figures in the development of the U.S. Navy over a thirty-year period. West
deals with such conflicts as the battles of Manila Bay
and Santiago.

Chapter 8

EARLY TWENTIETH CENTURY, 1900-1945

A. THE PROGRESSIVE ERA

1. General

1445 Chamberlain, John. FAREWELL TO REFORM: THE RISE, LIFE AND DE-
CAY OF THE PROGRESSIVE MIND IN AMERICA. 1932. Reprint. Chicago: Quadrangle Books, 1965. 344 p.

> From Populism to Wilson and World War I. Chamberlain
> is quite critical of what he considers ill-conceived mea-
> sures of the reformers; he believes the future belongs to
> revolution. Filled with personalities and detail.

1446 Faulkner, Harold U. THE QUEST FOR SOCIAL JUSTICE, 1898-1914.
1931. Reprint. Chicago: Quadrangle Books, 1971. 390 p. Illus.,
ports., plates.

> An objective, general overview of the period which
> sees a transition from concern for laissez-faire to reform
> of various types: education, child welfare, women's
> rights, labor, conservation, etc.

1447 Goldman, Eric F. RENDEZVOUS WITH DESTINY: A HISTORY OF MODERN
AMERICAN REFORM. Rev. ed. 1952. Reprint. New York: Alfred A.
Knopf, 1956. 414 p. Paperbound.

> The sweep of American reform from the years after the
> Civil War to mid-twentieth century, touching particu-
> larly on such movements as progressivism and the New
> Deal. Colorful, lively presentation.

1448 Kolko, Gabriel. THE TRIUMPH OF CONSERVATISM: A RE-INTERPRETA-
TION OF AMERICAN HISTORY, 1900-1916. New York: Free Press of
Glencoe, 1963. 344 p.

> A revisionist view of the Progressive era. Kolko claims

that large industry and banking interests sought regulation by the federal government in order to restrict competition and that politicians were responding to their
desires in writing "reform" legislation.

1449 Link, Arthur S. WOODROW WILSON AND THE PROGRESSIVE ERA,
1900-1917. 1954. Reprint. New York: Harper & Row, 1963. 347 p.
Illus., ports., maps, cartoons. Paperbound.

Essentially a history of Wilson's first term, by the editor
of the Wilson PAPERS, q.v., no. 1523, and the author
of an extensive biography, WILSON, q.v., no. 1522.
A result of deep scholarship.

1450 Mowry, George E. THE ERA OF THEODORE ROOSEVELT AND THE BIRTH
OF MODERN AMERICA, 1900-1912. New York: Harper & Brothers,
1958. 330 p. Illus.

A scholarly and readable history dealing with social and
intellectual themes as well as political and economic
ones. The author sets forth the principles of progressivism, deals with the campaigns against monopoly and for
municipal reform, among many others, and chronicles
the presidencies of Roosevelt and Taft.

1451 _____. THEODORE ROOSEVELT AND THE PROGRESSIVE MOVEMENT.
Madison: University of Wisconsin Press, 1946. 415 p. Illus., front.,
ports.

The influences of TR and the progressive movement on
each other. Mowry makes use of the extensive Roosevelt
manuscript collection.

1452 Resek, Carl, ed. THE PROGRESSIVES. Indianapolis: Bobbs-Merrill,
1967. 435 p.

This collection includes selections from such contemporary
figures as Jane Addams, W.E.B. Du Bois, Vernon L. Parrington, Margaret Sanger, and Ida Tarbell. Topics include the universities, poverty, big business, democracy,
and war.

2. Topical

a. BUSINESS AND ECONOMICS

1453 Brandeis, Louis D. OTHER PEOPLE'S MONEY AND HOW THE BANKERS
USE IT. New York: Harper & Row, 1967. 196 p.

Originally published as articles in HARPER'S WEEKLY,

1913-14, and as a book in 1914. Brandeis attempts to show that borrowing and lending tends to concentrate wealth and that the lenders enrich themselves with no service to society. He deals with such matters as interlocking directorates, problems of bigness, etc.

1454 Faulkner, Harold U. THE DECLINE OF LAISSEZ FAIRE, 1899-1917. New York: Rinehart, 1951. 447 p. Illus., ports.

An interpretive history of the rise of big business. Faulkner explains why demands were made for regulation by government.

1455 Haber, Samuel. EFFICIENCY AND UPLIFT: SCIENTIFIC MANAGEMENT IN THE PROGRESSIVE ERA, 1890-1920. Chicago: University of Chicago Press, 1964. 194 p.

Concern with "efficiency" was a child of the Progressive era. "Scientific" management invaded all areas of life, including the churches, became identified with what was "good," and swept all before it. Haber tells how it happened.

1456 Tarbell, Ida M. THE HISTORY OF THE STANDARD OIL COMPANY. Edited by David M. Chalmers. New York: Harper and Row, 1966. 252 p. Paperbound.

This is an abridged version of the famous expose by a leading muckraker, drawn from her articles in McCLURE'S magazine, published in two volumes in 1904. Tarbell includes much detail on the ruthless business practices of the day.

1457 Weinstein, James. THE CORPORATE IDEAL IN THE LIBERAL STATE, 1900-1918. Boston: Beacon Press, 1968. 280 p.

The author sets out to show that the large corporations and financial organizations promoted reforms when they found it in their interest to do so. Weinstein discusses such innovations as introduction of city managers, the Federal Trade Commission, workmen's compensation, and agencies created by the government in the First World War.

1458 Wiebe, Robert H. BUSINESSMEN AND REFORM: A STUDY OF THE PROGRESSIVE MOVEMENT. Cambridge, Mass.: Harvard University Press, 1962. 283 p.

Attempts to refurbish the image of the business community by showing that part of it, at least, enlisted in the campaign for reform.

b. CONSERVATION

1459 Hays, Samuel P. CONSERVATION AND THE GOSPEL OF EFFICIENCY: THE PROGRESSIVE CONSERVATION MOVEMENT, 1890-1920. 1959. Reprint. New York: Atheneum, 1969. 297 p.

> A discussion of conflicting policies advocated for the use and protection of the nation's waterways, forests, range lands, etc. The contest, according to Hays, was between those who advocated control by scientists and technicians and those who advocated control on the local level through elected representatives.

c. DIPLOMACY

1460 Bailey, Thomas A. THEODORE ROOSEVELT AND THE JAPANESE-AMERICAN CRISIS: AN ACCOUNT OF THE INTERNATIONAL COMPLICATIONS ARISING FROM THE RACE PROBLEM ON THE PACIFIC COAST. Stanford, Calif.: Stanford University Press, 1934. 362 p.

> Deals with California's effort to turn off further immigration from Japan and the resultant international complications faced by TR, 1906-9. Bailey concentrates on the diplomatic aspects of the problem.

1461 Beale, Howard K. THEODORE ROOSEVELT AND THE RISE OF AMERICA TO WORLD POWER. Baltimore: Johns Hopkins Press, 1956. 600 p.

> Beale's thorough probing of TR's involvement in foreign affairs sets forth his attitudes toward various nations and tells how he dealt with them. Beale attributes great influence on world developments to the president.

1462 Esthus, Raymond. THEODORE ROOSEVELT AND JAPAN. Seattle: University of Washington Press, 1967. 329 p.

> The author reviews the beginnings of the American-Japanese relationship, which has been both friendly and antagonistic, in the years Roosevelt served in the presidency (1901-9). Esthus examines Roosevelt's mediating role in the peace conference that concluded the Russo-Japanese War and in the Open Door Policy in China. He also looks at the significance of Japan's designs on Korea and Manchuria and the anti-Japanese campaign on the West Coast of the United States.

d. EDUCATION

Cremin, Lawrence A. TRANSFORMATION OF THE SCHOOL. See no. 318.

Curti, Merle. SOCIAL IDEAS OF AMERICAN EDUCATORS. See no. 320.

1463 Dewey, John. DEMOCRACY AND EDUCATION: AN INTRODUCTION TO THE PHILOSOPHY OF EDUCATION. 1916. Reprint. New York: Free Press, 1966. 378 p. Paperbound.

The philosopher of progressive education expounds his ideas on why a democratic society must incorporate democracy in its educational practices.

1464 _____. THE SCHOOL AND SOCIETY. Rev. ed. Chicago: University of Chicago Press, 1915. 179 p.

The leading exponent of progressive education looks at the schools and education practices of his day in a series of lectures: The School and Social Progress, The School and the Life of the Child, Waste in Education, The Psychology of Elementary Education, Froebel's Educational Principles, The Psychology of Occupations, The Development of Attention, The Aim of History in Elementary Education.

e. FEMINISM AND WOMEN'S SUFFRAGE

1465 Grimes, Alan P. THE PURITAN ETHIC AND WOMAN SUFFRAGE. New York: Oxford University Press, 1967. 172 p.

The author's thesis is that the woman's suffrage movement in the West was successful because it formed an alliance with those supporting Prohibition and restrictive immigration policies, who thought women would uphold their causes in the voting booth. Grimes does not, however, deal with the "Puritan ethic."

1466 Kraditor, Aileen S. THE IDEAS OF THE WOMAN SUFFRAGE MOVEMENT 1890-1920. New York: Columbia University Press, 1965. 325 p.

The author analyzes the movement and the ideas and personalities of its leaders. She demonstrates that the movement drew its support from the bourgeois elements and that a high percentage of the leadership was college-educated.

f. GOVERNMENT AND POLITICS

1467 Bell, H.C.F. WOODROW WILSON AND THE PEOPLE. Garden City, N.Y.: Doubleday, Doran, 1945. 396 p.

This biographical study concentrates on the years of Wilson's presidency. The author attempts to demonstrate Wilson's efforts to remain in contact with the people.

He explores Wilson's personality and character to show
his strengths and weaknesses and the reasons for his
successes and failures.

1468 Blum, John M. THE REPUBLICAN ROOSEVELT. Cambridge, Mass.: Harvard University Press, 1954. 170 p.

An interpretation of Theodore Roosevelt as a politician.
Blum, who assisted in the editing of the TR LETTERS,
q.v., no. 1512, makes a balanced evaluation of his
strengths and weaknesses.

1469 Croly, Herbert. THE PROMISE OF AMERICAN LIFE. Edited by Arthur
M. Schlesinger, Jr. Cambridge, Mass.: Harvard University Press, 1965.
495 p.

A call for reform by an influential figure among the
Progressives, originally published in 1909. Includes an
introduction by the editor.

1470 Kipnis, Ira. THE AMERICAN SOCIALIST MOVEMENT, 1897-1912. 1952.
Reprint. New York: Greenwood Press, 1968. 496 p.

A history of the Socialist party in its early years. Kipnis has made a detailed study of the literature and re-
suscitates many of the intraparty arguments to illumine
the spirit of the movement.

1471 Mackay, Kenneth Campbell. THE PROGRESSIVE MOVEMENT OF 1924.
1947. Reprint. New York: Octagon Books, 1966. 298 p. Maps.

An analysis of the Progressive party's fortunes in the
campaign of 1924 and a discussion of the problems that
confront third parties in the American political system.

1472 Maxwell, Robert S. LA FOLLETTE AND THE RISE OF THE PROGRESSIVES
IN WISCONSIN. Madison: State Historical Society of Wisconsin, 1956.
279 p. Illus., ports.

La Follette on the state scene. Maxwell evaluates the
quality of his leadership and tells of his success in
building a powerful political organization. Not a completely favorable picture of the man emerges.

1473 Nye, Russel B. MIDWESTERN PROGRESSIVE POLITICS: A HISTORICAL
STUDY OF ITS ORIGINS AND DEVELOPMENT, 1870-1950. East Lansing:
Michigan State College Press, 1951. 422 p. Illus., ports.

The Midwest contributed many leaders and ideas to the
upsurge of progressivism. Nye looks at it as an entity
in itself and relates it to the larger movement.

1474 Shannon, David A. THE SOCIALIST PARTY OF AMERICA: A HISTORY. 1955. Reprint. Chicago: Quadrangle Books, 1967. 320 p. Paperbound.

> An objective account of the rise and fall of the Socialist party, from Eugene Debs to Norman Thomas. Shannon provides reasons why the party did not succeed.

1475 Steffens, Lincoln. THE SHAME OF THE CITIES. New York: Sagamore Press, 1957. 214 p.

> A famous muckraking attack on municipal corruption and its relationship to business interests, first published in 1904.

1476 Warner, Hoyt L. PROGRESSIVISM IN OHIO, 1897-1917. Columbus: Ohio State University Press, 1964. 569 p.

> The successes and failures of the Progressive movement in Ohio, told in detail and with clarity.

1477 Weyl, Walter. THE NEW DEMOCRACY: AN ESSAY ON CERTAIN PO- LITICAL AND ECONOMIC TENDENCIES IN THE UNITED STATES. 1920. Reprint. New York: Harper & Row, 1964. 390 p. Paperbound.

> Published first in 1912. Weyl saw plutocracy and a new democracy locked in battle to control the future of the country. He deals with such matters as the trust, monopoly, government regulation, the labor union, con- servation, immigration, initiative, and recall. This edi- tion has an introduction by Charles B. Forcey.

1478 Wilson, Woodrow. THE NEW FREEDOM: A CALL FOR THE EMANCI- PATION OF THE GENEROUS ENERGIES OF A PEOPLE. Englewood Cliffs, N.J.: Prentice-Hall, 1961. 173 p. Paperbound.

> Wilson's famous formulation of his domestic policies, first published in 1913. This edition has an introduc- tion and notes by William E. Leuchtenburg.

g. INTELLECTUAL AND SOCIAL LIFE

1479 Addams, Jane. TWENTY YEARS AT HULL HOUSE, WITH AUTOBIOGRAPHI- CAL NOTES. New York: New American Library, 1961. 320 p. Illus. Paperbound.

> The reformer tells of the work of the social settlement house in Chicago, which made her famous. Originally published in 1910. This edition includes drawings by Norah Hamilton and a foreword by Henry Steele Com- mager.

1480 Bremner, Robert H. FROM THE DEPTHS: THE DISCOVERY OF POVERTY IN THE UNITED STATES. New York: New York University Press, 1956. 377 p. Illus.

> A history of the growing awareness of poverty as a social problem and attempts of social workers to meet it. Bremner traces developments from mid-nineteenth century and concentrates on developments in the twentieth.

1481 Davis, Allen F. SPEARHEADS OF REFORM: THE SOCIAL SETTLEMENTS AND THE PROGRESSIVE MOVEMENT, 1890-1914. New York: Oxford University Press, 1967. 340 p.

> The leading personalities in the settlement houses in Boston, New York, and Chicago, and the work they did in education, labor, housing, the protection of child labor, and for immigrants and blacks.

1482 Du Bois, W.E.B. THE SOULS OF BLACK FOLK. 1903. Reprint. Millwood, N.Y.: Kraus-Thomson, 1973. 325 p. Illus.

> What it meant to be black at the beginning of the twentieth century. Du Bois examines the past of blacks as slaves, the accommodations made by such men as Booker T. Washington, and hopes for the future, in a collection of articles published earlier in periodicals. This edition has an introduction by Herbert Aptheker.

1483 Forcey, Charles. THE CROSSROADS OF LIBERALISM: CROLY, WEYL, LIPPMANN, AND THE PROGRESSIVE ERA, 1900-1925. New York: Oxford University Press, 1961. 358 p.

> An interpretation of the thought of three Progressive editors; their new vehicle, THE NEW REPUBLIC, founded in 1914; and their campaign for a "democratic nationalism."

1484 Lippmann, Walter. DRIFT AND MASTERY: AN ATTEMPT TO DIAGNOSE THE CURRENT UNREST. Englewood Cliffs, N.J.: Prentice-Hall, 1961. 177 p. Paperbound.

> An analysis of the social ills of the nation, first published in 1914. Lippmann seeks democratic solutions to problems in politics, industry, the family, religion, etc. This edition has an introduction and notes by William E. Leuchtenburg.

1485 May, Henry F. THE END OF AMERICAN INNOCENCE: A STUDY OF THE FIRST YEARS OF OUR OWN TIME, 1912-1917. 1959. Reprint. Chicago: Quadrangle Books, 1964. 429 p. Paperbound.

> An intellectual history of the passing of Victorian ideas

and the transition to the twentieth century, a process
May believes was well underway before the outbreak of
World War I. Among the many figures evaluated are
Thorstein Veblen, Irving Babbitt, Walter Lippmann,
Mabel Dodge, Van Wyck Brooks, and John Dewey.

1486 Newby, Idus A. JIM CROW'S DEFENSE: ANTI-NEGRO THOUGHT IN
AMERICA, 1900-1930. Baton Rouge: Louisiana State University Press,
1965. 245 p.

An examination of racist thinking, of both North and
South, in the early years of the century. Newby analyzes the writings of those who were influential in prop-
agating an antiblack bias.

1487 Noble, David W. THE PARADOX OF PROGRESSIVE THOUGHT. Minneapolis: University of Minnesota Press, 1958. 280 p.

A group of individuals is studied in order to derive the
principles of Progressive thought. They are H. Croly,
editor and philosopher; J.M. Baldwin, social psycholo-
gist; H.D. Lloyd, publicist; C.H. Cooley, sociologist;
W. Rauschenbusch, preacher; R.T. Ely, S. Patten, and
T. Veblen, economists.

1488 Woods, Robert A., ed. THE CITY WILDERNESS: A SETTLEMENT STUDY
BY RESIDENTS AND ASSOCIATES OF THE SOUTH END HOUSE. 1898.
Reprint. New York: Garrett Press, 1970. 342 p. Illus., maps, plans.

A sociological discussion by members of a notable settlement house in Boston, edited by the director. Topics
covered: history, population, public health, work and
wages, politics, crime, amusements, churches, education, and "social recovery." This edition has a present-
day introduction by David N. Alloway.

h. THE MUCKRAKERS

1489 Chalmers, David M. THE SOCIAL AND POLITICAL IDEAS OF THE MUCK-
RAKERS. New York: Citadel Press, 1964. 127 p.

The muckrakers analyzed are: Lincoln Steffens, Ida M.
Tarbell, Ray Stannard Baker, David Graham Phillips,
Upton Sinclair, Will Irwin, Burton I. Hendrick, George
Kibbe Turner, Christopher P. Connolly, Alfred Henry
Lewis, Samuel Hopkins Adams, Thomas Lawson, and
Charles Edward Russell.

1490 Filler, Louis. CRUSADERS FOR AMERICAN LIBERALISM. New ed. Yellow Springs, Ohio: Antioch Press, 1964. 450 p. Illus.

A full, penetrating analysis of the muckrakers. Filler's serious approach does not exclude the more humorous aspects of the story.

1491 Regier, Cornelius C. THE ERA OF THE MUCKRAKERS. Chapel Hill: University of North Carolina Press, 1932. 267 p. Front., ports.

Examines the conditions that brought forth the muck-raking movement, with particular attention to the contributions of its leading lights: Lincoln Steffens, Ida Tarbell, Ray S. Baker, Gustavus Myers, et al.

1492 Weinberg, Arthur, and Weinberg, Lila, eds. THE MUCKRAKERS: THE ERA IN JOURNALISM THAT MOVED AMERICA TO REFORM: THE MOST SIGNIFICANT MAGAZINE ARTICLES OF 1902-1912. New York: Simon and Schuster, 1961. 449 p.

Articles by Lincoln Steffens, Ida Tarbell, Upton Sinclair, Samuel Hopkins Adams, Edwin Markham, Mark Sullivan, Will Irwin, Charles Edward Russell, Thomas W. Lawson, Ray Stannard Baker, et al, derived from McCLURE'S and other muckraking journals.

3. Prominent Individuals

GENERAL

1493 Aaron, Daniel. MEN OF GOOD HOPE: A STORY OF AMERICAN PRO-GRESSIVES. 1951. Reprint. New York: Oxford University Press, 1967. 343 p.

A series of biographical sketches, with an attempt to place the subjects in the historical context of their time and to evaluate their significance in American thought. Among those discussed are Emerson, Parker, George, Bellamy, Lloyd, Howells, Veblen, as genuine progressives, and Theodore Roosevelt and Brooks Adams as "pseudo-progressives."

ALBERT BEVERIDGE

1494 Bowers, Claude G. BEVERIDGE AND THE PROGRESSIVE ERA. Boston: Houghton Mifflin, 1932. 634 p. Front., ports., plates, facsim.

A leading senator of the era in a biography by a leading journalist, historian, and diplomat. A balanced view, based to a great extent on Beveridge manuscripts.

LOUIS BRANDEIS

1495 Bickel, Alexander M., ed. THE UNPUBLISHED OPINIONS OF MR. JUS-

TICE BRANDEIS: THE SUPREME COURT AT WORK. Cambridge, Mass.: Harvard University Press, 1957. 299 p. Ports., facsims.

> The editor, who once served as clerk to Justice Brandeis, has isolated ten unpublished opinions from the voluminous Brandeis papers at Harvard and adds comments on their significance. The book reveals how the Supreme Court goes about its task.

1496 Mason, Alpheus T. BRANDEIS: LAWYER AND JUDGE IN THE MODERN STATE. Princeton, N.J.: Princeton University Press, 1933. 209 p.

> Not a complete biography, but a rigorous analysis of Justice Brandeis's legal, economic, political, and social views.

EUGENE VICTOR DEBS

1497 Ginger, Ray. THE BENDING CROSS: A BIOGRAPHY OF EUGENE VICTOR DEBS. 1949. Reprint. New York: Russell & Russell, 1969. 526 p. Port.

> A biography of the noted socialist leader and presidential candidate, with an evaluation of the role he played in organizing labor in the United States. Debs's experience in federal prison, for exercising free speech in opposition to the First World War, is treated sympathetically.

JOHN DEWEY

1498 Hook, Sidney. JOHN DEWEY: AN INTELLECTUAL PORTRAIT. 1939. Reprint. Westport, Conn.: Greenwood Press, 1971. 251 p.

> A philosopher's summary of the views of the famous philosopher. Hook deals briefly with biographical matters and then proceeds to an analysis of the Dewey system.

W.E.B. DU BOIS

1499 Du Bois, W.E.B. THE AUTOBIOGRAPHY OF W.E.B. Du BOIS: A SOLILOQUY ON VIEWING MY LIFE FROM THE LAST DECADE OF ITS FIRST CENTURY. Edited by Herbert Aptheker. New York: International Publishers, 1968. 448 p.

> The famous black leader was over ninety when he finished this version of his life in 1960. (Other versions had been published earlier.) He gives a reflective, quite objective view of his years of struggle on behalf of his people.

1500 Rudwick, Elliott M. W.E.B. Du BOIS: A STUDY IN MINORITY GROUP
LEADERSHIP. Philadelphia: University of Pennsylvania Press, 1960. 382
p.

> A biography of Du Bois concentrating on the part he
> played in ameliorating the condition of the black man.
> Rudwick describes his role as a propagandist and his
> leadership in such organizations as the National Asso-
> ciation for the Advancement of Colored People.

OLIVER WENDELL HOLMES

1501 Bowen, Catherine Drinker. YANKEE FROM OLYMPUS: JUSTICE HOLMES
AND HIS FAMILY. Boston: Little, Brown, 1944. 492 p. Illus., front.,
ports., facsim., geneal. tables.

> A history of the distinguished family, beginning with
> the grandfather, minister Abiel; and then on to the two
> Olivers, father, the doctor and literary man; and son,
> the famous jurist. A colorful, anecdotal account.

1502 Frankfurter, Felix. MR. JUSTICE HOLMES AND THE SUPREME COURT.
2d ed. Cambridge, Mass.: Harvard University Press, 1961. 112 p.

> A combining of lectures delivered by Frankfurter when
> he was a professor at Harvard with the biographical
> article on Holmes he wrote for the DICTIONARY OF
> AMERICAN BIOGRAPHY. A keen analysis of the man
> and his legal and social views.

1503 Howe, Mark DeWolfe. JUSTICE OLIVER WENDELL HOLMES. 2 vols.
Cambridge, Mass.: Harvard University Press, 1957-63. Illus., ports.

> An intellectual biography of the famous member of the
> Supreme Court. Howe, a legal scholar who served as
> a youth as a secretary to Holmes, pictures him in the
> context of the intellectual currents of his time. Volume
> 1: THE SHAPING YEARS, 1841-1870; volume 2: THE
> PROVING YEARS, 1870-1882.

1504 Lerner, Max, ed. THE MIND AND FAITH OF JUSTICE HOLMES: HIS
SPEECHES, ESSAYS, LETTERS AND JUDICIAL OPINIONS. Boston: Little,
Brown, 1943. 524 p. Front.

> The editor attempts a "rounded portrait" of the man in
> the selections included. He concentrates on Holmes as
> a humanitarian thinker rather than as a legal figure.

ROBERT LA FOLLETTE

1505 La Follette, Robert M. AUTOBIOGRAPHY: A PERSONAL NARRATIVE OF

POLITICAL EXPERIENCES. Madison: University of Wisconsin Press, 1960. 349 p. Illus.

In these pages the Progressive senator from Wisconsin fights again the old battles for reform as well as those he was still engaged in when the book was first published in 1913. This edition has a foreword by Allan Nevins.

HENRY CABOT LODGE

1506 Garraty, John A. HENRY CABOT LODGE: A BIOGRAPHY. New York: Alfred A. Knopf, 1953. 462 p. Ports.

A biography which maintains scholarly detachment even in the section dealing with the bitter confrontation between Senator Lodge and President Wilson over American membership in the League of Nations. Well documented.

GEORGE W. NORRIS

1507 Lowitt, Richard. GEORGE W. NORRIS. 2 vols. to date. Vol. 1. Syracuse, N.Y.: Syracuse University Press, 1963. Vol. 2. Urbana: University of Illinois Press, 1971. Illus., ports.

A biography, projected at three volumes, of the Progressive senator from Nebraska. A balanced, scholarly work which makes full use of the Norris papers. Volume 1: THE MAKING OF A PROGRESSIVE, 1861-1912; volume 2: THE PERSISTENCE OF A PROGRESSIVE, 1913-1933.

MITCHELL PALMER

1508 Coben, Stanley. A. MITCHELL PALMER, POLITICIAN. New York: Columbia University Press, 1963. 351 p. Illus.

A biography of the politician best known for his raids on supposed radicals in the Red Scare, 1919-20, in Wilson's administration. Coben speculates on Palmer's motives but provides solid information on the concerns of the time: unemployment, strikes, Communist activities, inflation, etc.

GIFFORD PINCHOT

1509 Fausold, Martin L. GIFFORD PINCHOT, BULL MOOSE PROGRESSIVE. Syracuse, N.Y.: Syracuse University Press, 1961. 278 p. Illus., ports., cartoons.

This biography of a leading conservationist also provides an insight into the radicalism of the Progressive years, 1910-17. Fausold has delved deeply into manuscript sources, especially the Pinchot papers.

1510 Pinkett, Harold T. GIFFORD PINCHOT, PRIVATE AND PUBLIC FORES-TER. Urbana: University of Illinois Press, 1970. 167 p. Illus., ports.

This biographical study of an outstanding leader of the conservation movement deals with his career in forestry in North Carolina and New York and as an adviser to Theodore Roosevelt. A sympathetic but balanced view.

THEODORE ROOSEVELT

1511 Harbaugh, William H. LIFE AND TIMES OF THEODORE ROOSEVELT. Rev. ed. New York: Collier, 1963. 540 p.

A large, colorful biography that is sympathetic to Roosevelt and interprets his role in politics as a responsible one. The original edition of 1961 was entitled POWER AND RESPONSIBILITY.

1512 Morison, Elting E., ed. THE LETTERS OF THEODORE ROOSEVELT. 8 vols. Cambridge, Mass.: Harvard University Press, 1951-54. Illus., ports., geneal. tables, cartoons.

Roosevelt's letters to others, with notes by the editor on individual items. Each volume contains a chronological table. Volumes 1 and 2: THE YEARS OF PREPARATION, 1868-1900; volumes 3 and 4: THE SQUARE DEAL, 1900-1905; volumes 5 and 6: THE BIG STICK, 1905-1909; volumes 7 and 8: THE DAYS OF ARMAGEDDON, 1909-1919.

1513 Pringle, Henry F. THEODORE ROOSEVELT: A BIOGRAPHY. Rev. ed. New York: Harcourt, Brace, 1956. 445 p.

A not-very-flattering biography. Pringle represents TR as somewhat immature in his attitudes and basically a conservative who used liberal rhetoric.

1514 Roosevelt, Theodore. PRESIDENTIAL ADDRESSES AND STATE PAPERS OF THEODORE ROOSEVELT. 4 vols. in 2. N.d. Reprint. New York: Kraus Reprint Co., 1970. Fronts.

Also contains some of his papers from his time as governor of New York. The introduction is by Albert Shaw.

ELIHU ROOT

1515 Leopold, Richard W. ELIHU ROOT AND THE CONSERVATIVE TRADITION.
Boston: Little, Brown, 1954. 222 p.

> Leopold concentrates on the thought and public career
> of the man rather than on his personal life. He briefly
> describes Root's years as a businessman in a conservative
> milieu and then deals at greater length with his service
> as secretary of war, secretary of state, and as a senator.

LINCOLN STEFFENS

1516 Kaplan, Justin. LINCOLN STEFFENS: A BIOGRAPHY. New York:
Simon and Schuster, 1974. 380 p. Illus.

> A life of the foremost of the muckrakers, in a readable
> style. Complements Steffens's famous AUTOBIOGRAPHY,
> q.v., no. 1517.

1517 Steffens, Lincoln. AUTOBIOGRAPHY. 2 vols. New York: Harcourt,
Brace & World, 1968. Illus., facsim. Paperbound.

> The leading muckraking journalist's famous account of
> his own career, written with humorous skepticism. First
> published in 1931.

WILLIAM HOWARD TAFT

1518 Pringle, Henry F. THE LIFE AND TIMES OF WILLIAM HOWARD TAFT.
2 vols. 1939. Reprint. Hamden, Conn.: Shoe String Press, 1965.
Fronts., ports., plates, facsims.

> A biography that draws heavily on the Taft papers.
> Pringle presents Taft as a down-to-earth man who sought
> to do what he considered best for the country.

HARVEY WILEY

1519 Anderson, Oscar E. THE HEALTH OF A NATION: HARVEY WILEY AND
THE FIGHT FOR PURE FOOD. Chicago: University of Chicago Press,
1958. 332 p.

> A biography of the physician and scientist who cam-
> paigned for pure food laws. Anderson briefly deals with
> the time Wiley spent as a physician in Indiana, concen-
> trating the greater part of the book on his years in
> Washington as chief chemist of the Department of Agri-
> culture, his advocacy of reform, and his problems of
> enforcement once the Pure Food and Drug Act was
> passed in 1906.

WOODROW WILSON

1520 Blum, John M. WOODROW WILSON AND THE POLITICS OF MORAL-
ITY. Boston: Little, Brown, 1956. 215 p.

> Blum analyzes Wilson's moral dedication and relates it
> to the crises he confronted in his years of political
> leadership. A thoughtful interpretation.

1521 Garraty, John A. WOODROW WILSON: A GREAT LIFE IN BRIEF. New
York: Alfred A. Knopf, 1956. 206 p.

> A biography that looks both at Wilson's personal and
> public lives. A thoughtful, readable account which
> strives for objectivity.

1522 Link, Arthur S. WILSON. 5 vols. to date. Princeton, N.J.: Princeton University Press, 1947- . Illus., ports., plates.

> A biography in progress, based on years of research, by
> the editor of the Wilson PAPERS, q.v., no.1523. Link
> maintains objectivity, refusing to become an apologist
> for his subject but attempting to give him his due.
> Volume 1: THE ROAD TO THE WHITE HOUSE; volume
> 2: THE NEW FREEDOM; volume 3: THE STRUGGLE
> FOR NEUTRALITY, 1914-1915; volume 4: CONFU-
> SIONS AND CRISES, 1915-1916; volume 5: CAM-
> PAIGNS FOR PROGRESSIVISM AND PEACE, 1916-1917.

1523 _____, ed. THE PAPERS OF WOODROW WILSON. 17 vols. to date.
Princeton, N.J.: Princeton University Press, 1966- . Illus., ports.,
facsims.

> An exhaustive, scholarly edition in progress. The editor
> supplies explanatory notes on the items included. Thus
> far the PAPERS consist of letters to and from Wilson
> and his lectures on various themes. Volume 1 begins
> with the year 1856; volume 17 reaches 1908.

1524 Smith, Gene. WHEN THE CHEERING STOPPED: THE LAST YEARS OF
WOODROW WILSON. New York: William Morrow, 1964. 318 p. Illus., ports.

> A newspaperman's dramatic portrait of an incapacitated
> president and the wife who carried on the affairs of
> government in his stead. Strong on human emotions,
> weak on evidence for many of the contentions made.
> Introduction by Allan Nevins.

1525 Walworth, Arthur C. WOODROW WILSON. 2d ed., rev. Boston:
Houghton Mifflin, 1965. 889 p. Port.

Originally published in two volumes in 1958. Walworth concentrates on Wilson's life and thought and slights the political developments of the time. He interprets Wilson as a prophetic figure.

WRIGHT BROTHERS

1526 Kelly, Fred C. WRIGHT BROTHERS: A BIOGRAPHY AUTHORIZED BY ORVILLE WRIGHT. New York: Harcourt, Brace, 1943. 347 p. Ports., plates, facsims., diagrs.

A nontechnical account of the work of the pioneers in aviation, written by a friend. Kelly clearly sets forth an account of their experiments and significance of them.

B. WORLD WAR I

1. General

1527 Paxson, Frederic L. AMERICAN DEMOCRACY AND THE WORLD WAR. 3 vols. 1936-48. Reprint. New York: Cooper Square, 1966.

The comprehensive and scholarly survey starts with the years immediately preceding American entry into the First World War and ends with the twenties. Aside from the manifold political questions of the day, Paxson deals with such topics as the campaign for women's rights, problems of immigration, the income tax amendment, and developing class consciousness in American society. Volume 1: PRE-WAR YEARS, 1913-1917; volume 2: AMERICA AT WAR, 1917-1918; volume 3: POSTWAR YEARS: NORMALCY, 1918-1923.

1528 Slosson, Preston W. THE GREAT CRUSADE AND AFTER, 1914-1928. 1930. Reprint. Chicago: Quadrangle Books, 1971. 504 p. Front., plates, facsims. Paperbound.

In this social history, Slosson deals with various aspects of American life through the period of the war and into the years of "normalcy." He covers much territory. Written with verve.

1529 Smith, Daniel M. THE GREAT DEPARTURE: THE UNITED STATES AND WORLD WAR I, 1914-1920. New York: Wiley, 1965. 229 p.

This history of the Great War accents the diplomatic aspects of the struggle. Smith also deals with military, economic, and social matters in the context of the objectives of President Wilson and his advisors. The "Great

Departure" from America's supposed tradition of neutrality, he thinks, was due to Wilson's desire to pursue an
idealistic but practical foreign policy.

2. Topical

a. DIPLOMACY AND THE LEAGUE OF NATIONS

1530 Bailey, Thomas A. WILSON AND THE PEACEMAKERS: COMBINING
WOODROW WILSON AND THE LOST PEACE AND WOODROW WILSON
AND THE GREAT BETRAYAL. 2 vols. in 1. New York: Macmillan,
1947. Illus., maps.

The first volume contains an analysis of the peace conference and sketches of the participants; it is sympathetic to what Wilson tried to accomplish but makes clear
his inadequacies. The second volume deals with Wilson's unsuccessful efforts to achieve American membership in the League of Nations and is as critical of him
for his unwillingness to compromise as it is of those who
refused to support the international organization.

1531 Curry, Roy W. WOODROW WILSON AND FAR EASTERN POLICY, 1913-
1921. 1957. Reprint. New York: Octagon Books, 1968. 411 p.

The author attempts to demonstrate that European preoc-
cupation with its own conflict in World War I left Japan greater latitude in the Far East. She encroached
on the American "Open Door" in China, and so were
planted the seeds of later antagonism between the United States and Japan.

1532 Fleming, D.F. THE UNITED STATES AND THE LEAGUE OF NATIONS,
1918-1920. 1932. Reprint. New York: Russell & Russell, 1968. 568
p. Front., ports., plates.

A thorough review of President Wilson's efforts to bring
the United States into the League of Nations and of the
arguments and actions of those who opposed him. Flem-
i::g takes Wilson's side of the argument.

1533 Kennan, George F. SOVIET-AMERICAN RELATIONS, 1917-1920. 2 vols.
Princeton, N.J.: Princeton University Press, 1956-58. Illus., ports.,
maps.

A specialist on Russia, formerly in the American diplomatic service, provides an illuminating work on the relations of the U.S. and Soviet governments in World
War I and in western intervention in the Russian Revolution. Volume 1: RUSSIA LEAVES THE WAR; volume 2:
THE DECISION TO INTERVENE.

1534 Levin, N. Gordon, Jr. WOODROW WILSON AND WORLD POLITICS: AMERICA'S RESPONSE TO WAR AND REVOLUTION. New York: Oxford University Press, 1968. 352 p.

Takes the view that Wilson's "liberal-capitalist internationalism" has been determinative of American policy ever since. The United States has attempted to construct a world order incorporating these elements.

1535 Link, Arthur S. WILSON THE DIPLOMATIST: A LOOK AT HIS MAJOR FOREIGN POLICIES. Baltimore: Johns Hopkins Press, 1951. 165 p.

Originally delivered as the Albert Shaw Lectures on Diplomatic History for 1956 at Johns Hopkins University. Link looks at Wilson's foreign policy in detail and points up the conflict between his idealism and rigidity and the narrow nationalistic views of his opponents.

1536 May, Ernest R. THE WORLD WAR AND AMERICAN ISOLATION, 1914-1917. Cambridge, Mass.: Harvard University Press, 1959. 490 p.

A history based on the archives of the United States and the European powers. May presents the internal politics of the nations involved and relates them to their diplomacy. He believes Wilson was an idealist who sought to avoid war but had to bend to the practical political situation when American interests were threatened by Germany.

1537 Mayer, Arno J. POLITICS AND DIPLOMACY OF PEACEMAKING: CONTAINMENT AND COUNTERREVOLUTION AT VERSAILLES, 1918-1919. New York: Alfred A. Knopf, 1967. 946 p. Map.

A sequel to the author's POLITICAL ORIGINS OF THE NEW DIPLOMACY, q.v., no. 1538. Mayer examines the currents running through the peace conference, the pressures applied by events in eastern Europe, etc. He believes Wilson failed because he became captive of the anti-Bolshevik point of view of reactionary groups.

1538 _____. POLITICAL ORIGINS OF THE NEW DIPLOMACY, 1917-1918. 1959. Reprint. New York: Howard Fertig, 1969. 449 p.

Mayer examines the emergence among the Allies and the continental powers of their war and diplomatic aims, and the influence that Wilson's idealistic approach had on them in the period immediately preceding U.S. entry into the war.

1539 Notter, Harley. THE ORIGINS OF THE FOREIGN POLICY OF WOODROW WILSON. 1937. Reprint. New York: Russell & Russell, 1965. 701 p.

Notter attempts to find the germs of Wilson's foreign
policy in his years as professor and college president
and then discusses his efforts to arrive at a workable
policy of neutrality before he reluctantly decided the
country must enter the war.

1540 Seymour, Charles. AMERICAN DIPLOMACY DURING THE WORLD WAR.
1934. Reprint. Hamden, Conn.: Archon Books, 1964. 445 p.

The Albert Shaw Lectures on Diplomatic History for 1933
at Johns Hopkins University. Seymour traces the steps
by which Wilson and the nation went from neutrality
to participation in the war, stressing German submarine
warfare as the crucial factor.

b. GOVERNMENT AND POLITICS

1541 Creel, George. HOW WE ADVERTISED AMERICA: THE FIRST TELLING
OF THE AMAZING STORY OF THE COMMITTEE ON PUBLIC INFORMA-
TION THAT CARRIED THE GOSPEL OF AMERICANISM TO EVERY COR-
NER OF THE GLOBE. New York: Harper & Brothers, 1920. 483 p.
Front., ports., plates.

By the man who headed the internal propaganda effort
during World War I. Based on his earlier official version, Creel deals with organization of the committee,
its objectives, and those persons who were employed in
carrying out its functions. Creel believes President
Wilson was wise in forming the committee, and he takes
a quite optimistic view of its role and accomplishments.

1542 Gelfand, Lawrence E. THE INQUIRY: AMERICAN PREPARATIONS FOR
PEACE, 1917-1919. New Haven, Conn.: Yale University Press, 1963.
401 p.

An account of the study group Wilson set up to prepare
a government program for peace. Headed by Colonel
Edward M. House, it included Sidney E. Mezes, Charles
Seymour, Isaiah Bowman, David Hunter Miller, Walter
Lippmann, and James T. Shotwell. Gelfand describes
the workings of the group; he is somewhat critical of its
accomplishments, and laces his account with humor.

1543 Livermore, Seward W. POLITICS IS ADJOURNED: WOODROW WILSON
AND THE WAR CONGRESS, 1916-1918. Middletown, Conn.: Wesleyan
University Press, 1966. 324 p.

Political bickering continued unabated in this time of
national crisis. Livermore examines the issues and the
personalities, with an accent on the role of the Congress.

1544 Millis, Walter. THE ROAD TO WAR: AMERICA, 1914-1917. 1935.
Reprint. New York: Howard Fertig, 1969. 475 p. Front., ports.,
plates, facsims.

> A severe stricture of American governmental actions
> which led to involvement in World War I. Millis claims
> involvement was due not to policy decisions but to so-
> cial and economic pressures. A "somnolent State De-
> partment" did not realize the extent of the crisis until
> it was too late for Americans to avoid becoming em-
> broiled.

1545 Mock, James R., and Larson, Cedric. WORDS THAT WON THE WAR:
THE STORY OF THE COMMITTEE ON PUBLIC INFORMATION, 1917-
1919. Princeton, N.J.: Princeton University Press, 1939. 388 p. Illus., front., ports., plates, maps, facsims.

> Based on the records of the committee, discovered twenty
> years after it went out of existence. The authors are
> positive in their evaluation of George Creel's chairman-
> ship of this propaganda effort on the homefront.

1546 Peterson, Horace C. PROPAGANDA FOR WAR: THE CAMPAIGN AGAINST
AMERICAN NEUTRALITY, 1914-1917. 1939. Reprint. Port Washington,
N.Y.: Kennikat Press, 1968. 371 p. Ports., plates, facsims.

> A useful and colorful study of the means used to draw
> the United States into the First World War, stressing the
> propaganda efforts of the British government. American
> leaders, Peterson believes, gave way to their own emo-
> tions and to the forces of public opinion rather than
> being governed by a dispassionate view of American in-
> terests. He has set forth in detail the techniques used
> by the British in controlling American access to views
> of what was transpiring in Europe and how American
> politicians, journalists, teachers, and preachers perpetu-
> ated the British line.

1547 Seymour, Charles. AMERICAN NEUTRALITY, 1914-1917: ESSAYS ON
THE CAUSES OF AMERICAN INTERVENTION IN THE WORLD WAR. 1935.
Reprint. Hamden, Conn.: Archon Books, 1967. 194 p.

> Asserts that the threat to American shipping by German
> submarine warfare was the prime cause for the abandon-
> ment of U.S. neutrality. Although Seymour recognizes
> the influence of other factors, such as British propagan-
> da and the presence of munitions makers, he attempts to
> refute the reports of the Nye Committee, denying that
> these elements were determinative.

1548 Tansill, Charles C. AMERICA GOES TO WAR. 1938. Reprint. Gloucester, Mass.: Peter Smith, 1963. 741 p.

> The result of extensive research in German and American manuscripts from the years 1914 to 1917. Tansill is unsympathetic to the actions of the Allies and critical of U.S. entry into the war. He traces American involvement step by step.

1549 Willoughby, William F. GOVERNMENT ORGANIZATION IN WARTIME AND AFTER: A SURVEY OF THE FEDERAL CIVIL AGENCIES CREATED FOR THE PROSECUTION OF THE WAR. New York: Appleton, 1919. 389 p.

> Sets forth the legislation adopted by Congress to mobilize the country for war and describes how the agencies it established went about their tasks.

c. LABOR

1550 Brody, David. LABOR IN CRISIS: THE STEEL STRIKE OF 1919. Philadelphia: Lippincott, 1965. 208 p.

> A case study used by the author to show why labor was unsuccessful in achieving its goals until later under the New Deal. He looks at the words and actions of management, labor and government, and also at public opinion.

d. PACIFISM

1551 Chatfield, Charles. FOR PEACE AND JUSTICE: PACIFISM IN AMERICA, 1914-1941. Knoxville: University of Tennessee Press, 1971. 455 p. Illus., ports.

> A thorough discussion of pacifist ideas in America, from World War I to U.S. involvement in World War II, by a leading interpreter of the movement. Chatfield analyzes belle-lettres and expressions of the popular media and makes use of interviews with leaders of the movement, as well as manuscript sources.

1552 Peterson, Horace C., and Fite, Gilbert C. OPPONENTS OF WAR, 1917-1918. Madison: University of Wisconsin Press, 1957. 412 p. Illus., ports.

> A detailed history of the vigorous suppression of dissent in the United States during World War I. The authors deal with attempts to silence professors, teachers, and clergymen, and to control expression on stage and screen, as well as attempts to suppress freedom of the press where it was critical of American actions.

e. THE RED SCARE AND CIVIL LIBERTIES

1553 Johnson, Donald O. THE CHALLENGE TO AMERICAN FREEDOMS:
WORLD WAR I AND THE RISE OF THE AMERICAN CIVIL LIBERTIES
UNION. Lexington: University of Kentucky Press, 1963. 243 p.

It was in the days following World War I, with the Red
Scare and accompanying attacks on freedom of thought,
speech, and association, that the ACLU was formed.
Johnson discusses the issues and the leaders who guided
the organization in the early years.

1554 Murray, Robert K. THE RED SCARE: A STUDY IN NATIONAL HYSTERIA,
1919-1920. Minneapolis: University of Minnesota Press, 1955. 337 p.
Illus.

An account of the "rank intolerance and mob violence"
that broke out in the United States during the "Red
Scare" following World War I. The author looks at the
activities of the radicals, the Boston police strike, other
labor matters, etc., in seeking explanations for the reactions of government and public.

1555 Preston, William. ALIENS AND DISSENTERS: FEDERAL SUPPRESSION
OF RADICALS, 1903-1933. Cambridge, Mass.: Harvard University Press,
1963. 352 p.

A study of the treatment of dissent among the immigrants
to the United States. Often coming from a rural setting
in Europe to an urban setting in America, the alien was
confronted with massive problems of adaptation. Solutions
were offered by radicals, socialists, and communists.
Preston concludes that suppression of these elements was
most often carried out by administrative action rather
than by the courts. The ultimate weapon of deportation
was used vigorously, especially in wartime.

1556 Scheiber, Harry N. THE WILSON ADMINISTRATION AND CIVIL LIBER-
TIES, 1917-1921. Ithaca, N.Y.: Cornell University Press, 1960. 78 p.

A grim picture of encroachments on civil liberties during
and following World War I. Scheiber analyzes federal
legislation passed to promote security and how it was
implemented by federal officials.

f. WARFARE

AMERICAN HERITAGE HISTORY OF FLIGHT. See no. 448.

1557 THE AMERICAN HERITAGE HISTORY OF WORLD WAR I. Edited by Alvin M. Josephy, Jr. New York: American Heritage Publishing Co.; distributed by Simon & Schuster, 1964. 384 p. Illus., ports., maps.

> An account illustrated with contemporary photographs, well-prepared maps, and sketches. The narrative is by S.L.A. Marshall.

1558 Baldwin, Hanson W. WORLD WAR I: AN OUTLINE HISTORY. New York: Harper & Row, 1962. 181 p. Illus.

> A military affairs editor puts in chronological order the battles, political events, and other occurrences of the war and gives brief sketches of the leading participants.

1559 Coffman, Edward M. THE WAR TO END ALL WARS: THE AMERICAN MILITARY EXPERIENCE IN WORLD WAR I. New York: Oxford University Press, 1968. 428 p. Illus., ports., plans.

> An account of how the Americans prepared for war and how they waged it. Coffman stresses what the war meant to the individuals involved.

1560 DeWeerd, Harvey A. PRESIDENT WILSON FIGHTS HIS WAR: WORLD WAR I AND THE AMERICAN INTERVENTION. New York: Macmillan, 1968. 478 p. Illus., maps.

> Actually deals little with Wilson but concerns itself with American preparation for, and waging of, the war. De Weerd places American battle strategy in the context of what was happening to the other armies on the continent.

1561 Freidel, Frank. OVER THERE: THE STORY OF AMERICA'S FIRST GREAT OVERSEAS CRUSADE. Boston: Little, Brown, 1964. 396 p. Illus., ports., maps.

> Friedel deals with the years 1917-18 in a popular account, quoting wherever possible, the words of those who participated in battle; he provides a generous selection of photographs.

1562 Stallings, Laurence. THE DOUGHBOYS: THE STORY OF THE AEF, 1917-18. New York: Harper & Row, 1963. 404 p. Illus., maps, plans.

> A chronicle that dramatically conveys the color and the horror of the war. Stallings starts his account with the arrival in France of General John D. Pershing and the American Expeditionary Force, and concludes it with the armistice. He skillfully weaves sketches of personalities and battles into his narrative.

1563 Tuchman, Barbara. THE GUNS OF AUGUST. New York: Macmillan, 1962. 511 p. Illus., maps.

A dramatically written account of the early battles of
the war, with excellent word sketches of the participants. The author touches on the question of America's
rights as a neutral nation.

3. Prominent Individuals

For prominent individuals of this period, see 8,A,3.

C. THE TWENTIES

1. General

1564 Abels, Jules. IN THE TIME OF SILENT CAL. New York: G.P. Putnam's Sons, 1969. 320 p. Illus.

Using the presidency of Calvin Coolidge as a framework,
Abels presents a colorful picture of the 1920s, dwelling
primarily on social history—introduction of the automobile to a mass market, development of radio and sound
motion pictures, along with events more disturbing to
the peace, i.e., the Ku Klux Klan, Prohibition, and serious strikes. Entertaining, popular approach.

1565 Allen, Frederick Lewis. ONLY YESTERDAY: AN INFORMAL HISTORY
OF THE NINETEEN-TWENTIES. 1931. Reprint. New York: Harper &
Brothers, 1957. 370 p.

This lively, popular social history by a journalist deals
with the transformations in society caused by the coming
of the motor car, the Red Scare, the agitation for women's suffrage, Prohibition, etc., from the armistice of
1918 to the stock market crash of 1929.

1566 Braeman, John, et al., eds. CHANGE AND CONTINUITY IN AMERI-
CA: THE 1920's. Columbus: Ohio State University Press, 1968. 465 p.

A collection of essays by a dozen historians dealing
with various aspects of life in the twenties. Among the
topics dealt with are problems confronting the farmer,
the influence of oil interest in politics, welfare spending, the metropolis and the suburb, and the influence
of psychology.

1567 Faulkner, Harold U. FROM VERSAILLES TO THE NEW DEAL: A CHRON-
ICLE OF THE HARDING-COOLIDGE-HOOVER ERA. New Haven, Conn.:
Yale University Press, 1950. 397 p. Illus., ports.

A general history of the period by an economic historian, who stresses political and economic developments, looking at successes as well as failures.

1568 Hicks, John D. REPUBLICAN ASCENDANCY, 1921-1933. New York: Harper & Row, 1960. 318 p. Illus.

This survey of the period, although dealing to a large extent with politics and foreign affairs, considers the impact of such developments as the automobile, the airplane, and radio on American society. The author does not think very highly of the political leadership of the period.

1569 Leighton, Isabel, ed. THE ASPIRIN AGE, 1919-1941. New York: Simon & Schuster, 1949. 500 p.

A collection of twenty-two articles written by leading writers, scholars, and public personalities, analyzing events between the two world wars. Ranges from a discussion of the "forgotten men of Versailles" to "Pearl Harbor Sunday," with plenty of social commentary in between.

1570 Leuchtenburg, William E. THE PERILS OF PROSPERITY, 1914-1932. Chicago: University of Chicago Press, 1958. 313 p.

A misleading title for what is a general survey of the period, dealing with political, economic, and social matters in a fresh interpretation.

Slosson, Preston W. THE GREAT CRUSADE AND AFTER. See no. 1528.

2. Topical

a. BLACK AMERICANS

1571 Cronon, Edmund D. BLACK MOSES: THE STORY OF MARCUS GARVEY AND THE UNIVERSAL NEGRO IMPROVEMENT ASSOCIATION. Madison: University of Wisconsin Press, 1955. 278 p. Illus.

An objective view of the Jamaican-born black leader whose controversial career in New York in the years 1920-25 ended in trial and conviction for fraud.

1572 Osofsky, Gilbert. HARLEM: THE MAKING OF A GHETTO: NEGRO NEW YORK, 1890-1930. New York: Harper & Row, 1966. 270 p. Illus., ports., facsims.

Traces the steps by which an "aristocratic upper-class white community" was transformed into a crowded black

ghetto. Osofsky investigated the business and real es-
tate transactions that accomplished the transformation
and the building of the black political structure. He
believes the pattern in Harlem has been replicated in
other northern cities.

1573 Vincent, Theodore G. BLACK POWER AND THE GARVEY MOVEMENT.
Berkeley, Calif.: Ramparts Press, 1971. 299 p. Illus., ports.

A study of the black nationalist Garveyism of the 1920s.
Vincent sets forth Marcus Garvey's ideas in detail, discusses the ideological struggle among blacks in the twenties and thirties, and seeks to establish a tie between
the radicalism of Garvey and the black power movement
of the present.

b. BUSINESS AND ECONOMICS

1574 Prothro, James W. DOLLAR DECADE: BUSINESS IDEAS IN THE 1920's.
Baton Rouge: Louisiana State University Press, 1954. 277 p.

The author depends heavily on the views of the National Association of Manufacturers and the Chamber of Commerce as representative of American business generally.
He is critical of those whose policies led toward the
economic catastrophe of the thirties.

1575 Soule, George H. PROSPERITY DECADE: FROM WAR TO DEPRESSION,
1917-1929. New York: Rinehart, 1947. 380 p. Ports., plates.

An economic history of the dozen years of prosperity
before the great collapse. Soule provides much information.

c. DIPLOMACY

1576 Ellis, L. Ethan. FRANK B. KELLOGG AND AMERICAN FOREIGN RE-
LATIONS, 1925-1929. New Brunswick, N.J.: Rutgers University Press,
1961. 303 p.

Politics and diplomacy in the administration of Coolidge,
when Kellogg served as secretary of state. A documented history that deals with such major issues as disarmament and the Kellogg-Briand Pact, and Chinese,
Mexican, and Nicaraguan relations.

1577 _____. REPUBLICAN FOREIGN POLICY, 1921-1933. New Brunswick,
N.J.: Rutgers University Press, 1968. 413 p. Illus., ports.

A study of the policies of Presidents Harding, Coolidge,

and Hoover, and their secretaries of state, Hughes, Kellogg, and Stimson. Ellis characterizes these officials as interested in foreign affairs but unwilling to commit the United States to serious action.

1578 Feis, Herbert. THE DIPLOMACY OF THE DOLLAR: FIRST ERA, 1919-1932. 1950. Reprint. Hamden, Conn.: Archon Books, 1965. 88 p.

A very brief outline of the government's involvement with private business in arranging foreign investment, by an economic adviser to the Department of State.

1579 Ferrell, Robert H. PEACE IN THEIR TIME: THE ORIGINS OF THE KELLOGG-BRIAND PACT. 1952. Reprint. New York: W.W. Norton, 1969. 293 p.

A study of the treaty of 1928, which was to outlaw war. Ferrell examines the politicians and diplomats who supported it and the public belief in its promises.

1580 Iriye, Akira. AFTER IMPERIALISM: THE SEARCH FOR A NEW ORDER IN THE FAR EAST, 1921-1931. Cambridge, Mass.: Harvard University Press, 1965. 383 p. Map.

Although concentrating on events in Asia, the book provides students of American history with an understanding of forces at work in the area that ultimately involved the United States. The author deals with developments from the Washington Conference of 1921-22 to the Manchurian Crisis of 1931.

1581 Nevins, Allan. THE UNITED STATES IN A CHAOTIC WORLD: CHRONICLE OF INTERNATIONAL AFFAIRS, 1918-1933. 1950. Reprint. New York: United States Publishers Association, 1970. 261 p. Illus.

A history of the political and diplomatic turmoil following the First World War and the role played by the United States in the attempt to stabilize international relations.

1582 Parrini, Carl P. HEIR TO EMPIRE: U.S. ECONOMIC DIPLOMACY, 1916-1923. Pittsburgh: University of Pittsburgh Press, 1969. 303 p. Tables.

A positive picture of American big business, which the author interprets as having the goal of world peace, to be achieved through an American guarantee of an open door for trade throughout the world. The policy was established during the administration of Wilson and was perpetuated during that of Harding.

d. FEMINISM

See relevant entries under Feminism in 2,B,10 and 8,A,2,e.

e. GOVERNMENT AND POLITICS

1583 Bagby, Wesley M. THE ROAD TO NORMALCY: THE PRESIDENTIAL CAMPAIGN AND ELECTION OF 1920. Baltimore: Johns Hopkins Press, 1962. 206 p.

A detailed analysis of the campaign that produced a Republican landslide. Bagby gives reasons why domestic and foreign policy considerations led to this.

1584 Burner, David. THE POLITICS OF PROVINCIALISM: THE DEMOCRATIC PARTY IN TRANSITION, 1918-1932. New York: Alfred A. Knopf, 1968. 306 p.

Examines the rural-agricultural and the urban wings of the Democratic party and the tensions between them. The former under Bryan gradually gave way to the latter, as was demonstrated by the nomination of Al Smith. Smith was unable to unite the fragments of the party, a feat later performed by F.D. Roosevelt.

Divine, Robert A. AMERICAN IMMIGRATION POLICY. See no. 358.

1585 Draper, Theodore. THE ROOTS OF AMERICAN COMMUNISM. New York: Viking Press, 1957. 508 p. Illus., ports., facsims.

A former Communist's objective account of the early years of the movement (1919-22). Draper delves deeply into the primary sources and utilizes interviews with former leaders of the party. He explains the ins and outs of party doctrine.

1586 Rice, Arnold S. THE KU KLUX KLAN IN AMERICAN POLITICS. Washington, D.C.: Public Affairs Press, 1962. 150 p.

Rice deals with the years from 1915, when the Klan was reborn, to the election of a Catholic to the presidency in 1960, which he considers an appropriate terminal date. He reviews the activities of a branch of the Klan in the various southern and border states.

1587 Schriftgiesser, Karl. THIS WAS NORMALCY: AN ACCOUNT OF PARTY POLITICS DURING TWELVE REPUBLICAN YEARS, 1920-1932. 1948. Reprint. New York: Oriole Editions, 1973. 335 p.

A study of politics during the administrations of Coolidge,

Harding and Hoover. The author is caustic in his evaluation of all three. His chapter title on the first sets
the tone: "A President Abdicates."

1588 Silva, Ruth C. RUM, RELIGION, AND VOTES: 1928 RE-EXAMINED.
University Park: Pennsylvania State University Press, 1962. 85 p.

A study largely based on quantification. The author
concludes that Smith's defeat cannot be explained on
religious grounds.

1589 Swain, Donald C. FEDERAL CONSERVATION POLICY, 1921-1933. Berkeley and Los Angeles: University of California Press, 1963. 221 p. Ports.

Swain sees the conservation policies that emerged under
Theodore Roosevelt, expanding and maturing under Harding, Coolidge, and Hoover--contrary to what others have
thought.

1590 Weinstein, James. THE DECLINE OF SOCIALISM IN AMERICA, 1912-
1925. New York: Monthly Review Press, 1967. 378 p.

Dates the beginning of the decline of socialism in 1919,
thus refuting the view that it occurred as early as 1912.
Weinstein has made heavy use of local labor newspapers
to prove his point.

1591 Zink, Harold. CITY BOSSES IN THE UNITED STATES: A STUDY OF
TWENTY MUNICIPAL BOSSES. 1930. Reprint. New York: AMS Press,
1968. 382 p. Port.

Zink brings together much material on leading bosses
and presents a scholarly, dispassionate comparison of how
they worked in the Boston, Brooklyn, New York, Philadelphia, Pittsburgh, Cincinnati, Chicago, Minneapolis,
St. Louis, New Orleans, and San Francisco of his day.

f. INTELLECTUAL AND SOCIAL LIFE

1592 Baritz, Loren, ed. THE CULTURE OF THE TWENTIES. Indianapolis:
Bobbs-Merrill, 1970. 497 p. Illus.

A collection of materials from the years 1920-29. The
sections deal with disillusionment, political and religious
fundamentalism, business, the younger generation, writers,
social critics, and technology.

Barnouw, Erik. HISTORY OF BROADCASTING. See no. 291.

1593 Case, Victoria, and Case, Robert O. WE CALLED IT CULTURE: THE

STORY OF CHAUTAUQUA. 1948. Reprint. Freeport, N.Y.: Books for Libraries Press, 1970. 282 p.

> The implementation of the ideal of "self-improvement" at the original camp by Lake Chautauqua, New York, and the development of similar ventures across the country where orators and performers of all types appeared.

1594 Chambers, Clarke A. SEEDTIME OF REFORM: AMERICAN SOCIAL SERVICE AND SOCIAL ACTION, 1918-1933. Minneapolis: University of Minnesota Press, 1963. 344 p.

> The rise of social welfare sentiment and activity. Chambers sees this movement as preparing the ground for much of what happened in the New Deal.

1595 Lynd, Robert S., and Lynd, Helen M. MIDDLETOWN: A STUDY IN CONTEMPORARY AMERICAN CULTURE. New York: Harcourt, Brace, 1929. 560 p. Tables.

> A pathbreaking anthropological and sociological case study of an American community in 1924. The Lynds studied the residents of Muncie, Indiana, to determine the pattern of their lives in work, play, family relations, education, religion, and community activities. The work has been widely used in writings on the twenties.

1596 _____. MIDDLETOWN IN TRANSITION: A STUDY IN CULTURAL CONFLICTS. New York: Harcourt, Brace, 1937. 662 p. Diagr.

> A sequel to the Lynds' MIDDLETOWN, q.v., no. 1595. This book analyzes what had happened to this "typical" midwestern American city (Muncie, Indiana) since 1925 and should be read with the earlier study.

g. LABOR

1597 Bernstein, Irving. THE LEAN YEARS: A HISTORY OF THE AMERICAN WORKER, 1920-1933. Boston: Houghton Mifflin, 1960. 577 p. Illus.

> Attempts to place labor--organized and unorganized--in the political, economic, and social context of the time. Bernstein deals with problems of organization, court contests, the slide into depression during the Hoover administration, and much more. A very full treatment.

h. LITERATURE

1598 Baker, Carlos. ERNEST HEMINGWAY: A LIFE STORY. New York:

Charles Scribner's Sons, 1969. 713 p. Illus., ports.

An objective, dispassionate account of a passionate writer. Baker's book is the result of much research.

1599 Cowley, Malcolm. EXILE'S RETURN: A LITERARY ODYSSEY OF THE 1920's. New ed. New York: Viking Press, 1951. 328 p.

An explanation of the ideas and writings of the "lost generation" of literary men of the 1920s. Autobiographical elements are included, with discussions of Hemingway, Fitzgerald, Dos Passos, Eliot, Cummings, and others.

1600 Geismar, Maxwell. WRITERS IN CRISIS: THE AMERICAN NOVEL, 1925-1940. 1942. Reprint. New York: E.P. Dutton, 1971. 318 p. Paperbound.

Places the contributions of leading writers in a cultural context, drawing out the sociological, psychological and ethical values in their works. Considers Ring Lardner, Ernest Hemingway, John Dos Passos, William Faulkner, Thomas Wolfe, John Steinbeck.

1601 Hoffman, Frederick J. THE TWENTIES: AMERICAN WRITING IN THE POSTWAR DECADE. New York: Viking Press, 1955. 480 p.

An analysis of the most important literary artists who flourished in the twenties. Hoffman sets the work of Cather, Cummings, Crane, Dos Passos, Faulkner, Fitzgerald, Hemingway, Mencken, Pound, and Williams, in the intellectual context of the times.

1602 Johnson, James Weldon. GOD'S TROMBONES: SEVEN NEGRO SERMONS IN VERSE. 1927. Reprint. New York: Viking Press, 1948. 56 p. Illus.

Johnson puts sermons by black preachers he heard as a child into verse form. Rich in emotion and expression.

1603 Krutch, Joseph Wood. THE MODERN TEMPER: A STUDY AND A CONFESSION. New York: Harcourt, Brace, 1929. 265 p.

An account of the author's intellectual quest for meaning in an age when science seemed to have undermined the basis of the Christian faith. A good reflection of the mood brought on by World War I and resultant disillusionment.

1604 Turnbull, Andrew. SCOTT FITZGERALD. New York: Charles Scribner's Sons, 1962. 364 p. Illus.

Based both on documentation and personal association. Turnbull deals more with the man than with his writings and attempts to get behind the myths that had grown up about him.

j. PROHIBITION

1605 Asbury, Herbert. THE GREAT ILLUSION: AN INFORMAL HISTORY OF PROHIBITION. Garden City, N.Y.: Doubleday, 1950. 352 p.

Asbury deals with the rise and development of ideas about temperance from the colonial period to the twentieth century and with the turbulent history of Prohibition under the Eighteenth Amendment, 1920-34. A social history with elements of humor.

1606 Krout, John A. THE ORIGINS OF PROHIBITION. 1925. Reprint. New York: Russell & Russell, 1967. 339 p.

Traces Prohibition back to its origins in the temperance movement and demonstrates that the Eighteenth Amendment was the result of an evolution of sentiment concerning hard liquor. A detailed study.

1607 Sinclair, Andrew. PROHIBITION: THE ERA OF EXCESS. Boston: Little, Brown, 1962. 493 p. Illus.

An examination of the social and psychological springs of the Prohibition movement and life under the Eighteenth Amendment, by a British historian and novelist. Sinclair stresses the presence of extremists on both sides of the issue.

k. RELIGION

1608 Carter, Paul H. THE DECLINE AND REVIVAL OF THE SOCIAL GOSPEL: SOCIAL AND POLITICAL LIBERALISM IN THE AMERICAN PROTESTANT CHURCHES, 1920-1940. Ithaca, N.Y.: Cornell University Press, 1954. 277 p.

Attempts to show that the Social Gospel did not expire in World War I. Carter, depending heavily on the church press, discusses the leaders and the issues of social Christianity in the generation before World War II.

1609 Furniss, Norman F. THE FUNDAMENTALIST CONTROVERSY, 1918-1931. 1954. Reprint. Hamden, Conn.: Archon Books, 1963. 207 p.

The challenge of Darwinian thought to Christian theology and the resultant rise of modernist and fundamentalist

camps is dealt with in an absorbing and balanced manner. The highlight of the period was the Scopes "mon-
key trial" in Tennessee.

1610 Gatewood, Willard B., Jr., ed. CONTROVERSY IN THE TWENTIES:
FUNDAMENTALISM, MODERNISM, AND EVOLUTION. Nashville, Tenn.:
Vanderbilt University Press, 1969. 468 p.

An anthology that combines documentary material from
the antagonists in the controversy and the interpretations
of later historians.

1611 Ginger, Ray. SIX DAYS OR FOREVER?: TENNESSEE V. JOHN THOM-
AS SCOPES. 1958. Reprint. Chicago: Quadrangle Books, 1969. 258
p.

An account of the legal battle which pitted William
Jennings Bryan and Clarence Darrow against each other
on the question of teaching Darwinian evolution in the
schools. Ginger gives a clear explanation of the issues and provides much local color.

I. THE SACCO-VANZETTI CASE

1612 Joughin, G. Louis, and Morgan, Edmund M. THE LEGACY OF SACCO
AND VANZETTI. 1948. Reprint. Chicago: Quadrangle Books, 1964.
615 p.

A thorough, critical review of the evidence presented
in the Sacco-Vanzetti case and an exposition of the impact the case has had in American law, society, and
literature.

1613 Russell, Francis. TRAGEDY IN DEDHAM: THE STORY OF THE SACCO-
VANZETTI CASE. "50th anniversary edition." New York: McGraw-Hill
Book Co., 1971. 503 p. Illus., ports., maps.

Recreates the trial in 1921 of the anarchists accused of
murder in a holdup in Massachusetts and the vehement
protests that arose over their conviction and execution
(which took place ten years later). Russell examines
the evidence in detail. The first edition of this book
appeared in 1962.

m. THE SOUTH

Cash, Wilbur J. MIND OF THE SOUTH. See no. 1064.

1614 Clark, Thomas D. THE EMERGING SOUTH. 2d ed. New York: Oxford University Press, 1968. 361 p.

> An analysis of the South since 1920. Clark notes the reluctance to part with established customs even under the impact of industrialization and urbanization.

Scott, Anne Fior. SOUTHERN LADY. See. no. 331.

1615 Tindall, George B. THE EMERGENCE OF THE NEW SOUTH, 1913-1945. Baton Rouge: Louisiana State University Press, 1967. 822 p. Illus., ports.

> Carries the story of the "New South" through two world wars and the period in between, stressing changing economic conditions, especially the rise of industry. Tindall also considers the literary renaissance and the relationship between the values of the South and those of the rest of the country. This is volume 10 of A HISTORY OF THE SOUTH, a joint venture of several historians.

n. THE TEAPOT DOME SCANDAL

1616 Bates, J. Leonard. THE ORIGINS OF TEAPOT DOME: PROGRESSIVES, PARTIES AND PETROLEUM, 1909-1921. Urbana: University of Illinois Press, 1963. 286 p.

> Traces the background of the great scandal of the Harding presidency. Bates shows there was no settled government policy regarding leasing of oil wells on government property. He examines the positions of the oil men, the Navy Department, the conservationists, and the political parties.

1617 Noggle, Burl. TEAPOT DOME: OIL AND POLITICS IN THE 1920's. Baton Rouge: Louisiana State University Press, 1962. 243 p. Illus., ports., cartoons.

> An attempt at an objective account of the famous scandal. Noggle covers government policy on oil leases, the part played by Secretary Albert B. Fall, etc., and arguments of the conservationists.

3. Prominent Individuals

WILLIAM JENNINGS BRYAN

1618 Levine, Lawrence W. DEFENDER OF THE FAITH: WILLIAM JENNINGS BRYAN: THE LAST DECADE, 1915-1925. New York: Oxford University

Press, 1965. 395 p. Front.

> The last period of Bryan's life, when he promoted fundamentalist religion, especially in the Scopes trial in Tennessee, and trumpeted the virtues of Prohibition. Levine attempts to show these positions as wholly consistent with his earlier political actions.

For other books on Bryan, see the section on Prominent Individuals, 7,B,3.

CALVIN COOLIDGE

1619 McCoy, Donald R. CALVIN COOLIDGE, THE QUIET PRESIDENT. New York: Macmillan, 1967. 480 p.

> A less than flattering portrait of a president. McCoy, using widely scattered materials, recreates Coolidge's life and analyzes his contributions as a leader. Coolidge, he believes, failed to look ahead in preparation for problems as they would arise.

1620 White, William Allen. A PURITAN IN BABYLON: THE STORY OF CALVIN COOLIDGE. 1938. Reprint. Gloucester, Mass.: Peter Smith, 1973. 476 p.

> A somewhat cynical appraisal of the president. White takes the view that Coolidge's outlook was appropriate to an earlier time and a rural, agricultural community. With his own time and national problems, he was unable to cope. Written with insight and wit.

CLARENCE DARROW

1621 Darrow, Clarence S. THE STORY OF MY LIFE. 1932. Reprint. New York: Grosset & Dunlap, 1957. 465 p. Paperbound.

> The famous criminal attorney's account of his own career, stressing his campaigns on behalf of the underdog. Gives his views on many issues of the time, including Prohibition, evolution and the Bible, death and immortality, and crime, criminals, and punishment.

1622 Stone, Irving. CLARENCE DARROW FOR THE DEFENSE: A BIOGRAPHY. Garden City, N.Y.: Doubleday, Doran, 1941. 584 p. Front.

> Concentrates on Darrow's turbulent public life and the humanitarian and legal causes he espoused. A sympathetic but not uncritical work, written in quite readable prose.

HENRY FORD

1623 Burlingame, Roger. HENRY FORD: A GREAT LIFE IN BRIEF. New York: Alfred A. Knopf, 1954. 201 p.

> A popular account in brief compass. Burlingame traces Ford's life from his beginnings on a Michigan farm to the development of his successful assembly line production techniques. He deals honestly with the unlikable aspects of Ford's personality.

1624 Nevins, Allan, and Hill, Frank Ernest. FORD. 3 vols. New York: Charles Scribner's Sons, 1954-63. Illus., ports., maps, facsim., geneal. table.

> This lengthy work deals with the man, the automobile and company he developed, and his various nonautomotive campaigns, in an objective and readable manner. The authors used the extensive Ford archives. Volume 1: THE TIMES, THE MAN, THE COMPANY; volume 2: EXPANSION AND CHALLENGE, 1915-1933; volume 3: DECLINE AND REBIRTH, 1933-1962.

WARREN HARDING

1625 Adams, Samuel Hopkins. INCREDIBLE ERA: THE LIFE AND TIMES OF WARREN GAMALIEL HARDING. Boston: Houghton Mifflin, 1939. 463 p. Front., ports., plates.

> The novelist and muckraking journalist's account of Harding's career, with full measure given on the scandals of his administration.

1626 Russell, Francis. THE SHADOW OF BLOOMING GROVE: WARREN G. HARDING IN HIS TIMES. New York: McGraw-Hill Book Co., 1968. 707 p.

> Carries Harding through his career in Ohio politics into the convention of 1920 and into the White House. Russell misses none of the squalidness of Harding's involvements, whether in politics or in love. A vivid portrait.

CHARLES EVANS HUGHES

1627 Perkins, Dexter. CHARLES EVANS HUGHES AND AMERICAN DEMOCRATIC STATESMANSHIP. Boston: Little, Brown, 1956. 224 p.

> This brief biography deals lucidly with the manifold aspects of Hughes's career; it does not dwell on personal qualities but stresses his thoughts and accomplishments.

1628 Pusey, Merlo J. CHARLES EVANS HUGHES. 2 vols. New York: Macmillan, 1951. Illus., ports., cartoons.

> A full-length portrait of the lawyer, professor, governor, secretary of state, and chief justice of the Supreme Court. Pusey utilizes not only documentation but notes of conversations he had with Hughes. A sympathetic presentation of the man and his views.

FIORELLA LA GUARDIA

1629 Mann, Arthur. La GUARDIA: A FIGHTER AGAINST HIS TIMES, 1882-1933. 1959. Reprint. Chicago: University of Chicago Press, 1969. 384 p. Illus. Paperbound.

> A scholarly, readable work, the high point of which is La Guardia's career in Congress. A revealing portrait of a many-sided personality.

1630 Zinn, Howard. La GUARDIA IN CONGRESS. Ithaca, N.Y.: Cornell University Press, 1959. 299 p.

> Zinn interprets La Guardia as a forerunner of the New Deal. In Congress "the Little Flower" found himself in opposition to restrictive quotas on immigration, in favor of the causes of the immigrant, labor, and the farmer. A well-documented study.

H.L. MENCKEN

1631 Manchester, William. DISTURBER OF THE PEACE: THE LIFE OF H.L. MENCKEN. New York: Harper & Brothers, 1951. 350 p. Ports.

> A biography written with an irreverent wit befitting the subject. Mencken opened his files to Manchester. The introduction is by Gerald W. Johnson.

AL SMITH

1632 Handlin, Oscar. AL SMITH AND HIS AMERICA. Boston: Little, Brown, 1958. 219 p.

> This balanced view of Smith places him in the political and social milieu of New York. Handlin treats Smith's failure to achieve the presidency because of his Catholicism as a tragedy.

1633 Josephson, Matthew, and Josephson, Hannah. AL SMITH: HERO OF THE CITIES: A POLITICAL PORTRAIT DRAWING ON THE PAPERS OF FRANCES PERKINS. Boston: Houghton Mifflin, 1969. 527 p. Ports.

A full biography of the governor of New York. The Josephsons have been able to draw on the papers of Frances Perkins, secretary of labor under F.D. Roosevelt. Perkins had earlier been an associate of Smith in New York government.

D. DEPRESSION AND THE NEW DEAL

1. General

1634 Allen, Frederick Lewis. SINCE YESTERDAY: THE NINETEEN-THIRTIES IN AMERICA, SEPTEMBER 3, 1929-SEPTEMBER 3, 1939. New York: Harper & Brothers, 1940. 376 p. Front., ports., plates, facsims.

A sequel to Allen's colorful account of the twenties, ONLY YESTERDAY, q.v., no. 1565. He begins with 1929 and carries the story to the outbreak of World War II. An informal review of the depression period.

1635 Freidel, Frank, ed. THE NEW DEAL AND THE AMERICAN PEOPLE. Englewood Cliffs, N.J.: Prentice-Hall, 1964. 160 p. Paperbound.

Selections from the period, with brief headnotes by the editor. Among the topics dealt with are relief, the drive for recovery, reform, businessmen and the New Deal, elections.

Goldman, Eric F. RENDEZVOUS WITH DESTINY. See no. 1447.

Hicks, John D. REPUBLICAN ASCENDANCY. See no. 1568.

Leighton, Isabel, ed. ASPIRIN AGE. See no. 1569.

1636 Leuchtenburg, William E. FRANKLIN D. ROOSEVELT AND THE NEW DEAL. 1932-1940. New York: Harper & Row, 1963. 391 p. Illus.

This overall view of the era of President F.D. Roosevelt is concise yet comprehensive. Leuchtenburg stresses Roosevelt's desire to enlist the Congress and the people in the campaign to achieve economic recovery at a time when other nations were turning to dictatorship. FDR, however, did expand the power of the presidency by the use of the executive order. The author traces the development of the various agencies created to contend with the economic and social ills of the time. He makes use of the Columbia University Oral History Collection as well as written documentary evidence.

1637 _____, ed. THE NEW DEAL: A DOCUMENTARY HISTORY. Columbia: University of South Carolina Press, 1968. 291 p.

A selection of pieces contemporary to the time of the New Deal. Leuchtenburg provides an introductory essay and a headnote to each selection. In addition to speeches and statements by Franklin D. Roosevelt and other political leaders, such as A.A. Berle, Jr., Hugh Johnson, and David Lilienthal, he includes writings of such literary men as Stephen Vincent Benet, Sherwood Anderson, John Steinbeck, H.L. Mencken, and Robinson Jeffers.

1638 Perkins, Dexter. THE NEW AGE OF FRANKLIN ROOSEVELT, 1932-1945. Chicago: University of Chicago Press, 1957. 193 p.

An overview of the period dealing with U.S. domestic politics and problems and with America's part in World War II. An impartial approach.

1639 Schlesinger, Arthur M., Jr. THE AGE OF ROOSEVELT. 3 vols. to date. Boston: Houghton Mifflin, 1957- .

A history of the New Deal years which is still in progress. Schlesinger begins his account with the 1920s, examining the attitudes of big business, the economic policies of government, and how these were contested by many in the intellectual community. He then traces the failure of the economy under Hoover and the development of Roosevelt's policies in the so-called first and second New Deals. Schlesinger so far has covered the years to Roosevelt's renomination in 1936. Volume 1: THE CRISIS OF THE OLD ORDER, 1919-1933; volume 2: THE COMING OF THE NEW DEAL; volume 3: THE POLITICS OF UPHEAVAL.

1640 Shannon, David A., ed. THE GREAT DEPRESSION. Englewood Cliffs, N.J.: Prentice-Hall, 1960. 188 p. Paperbound.

A collection of writings from the time with brief introductions by the editor. The sections deal with the stock market crash, the farmer, relief, vagrants and other nomads, bank failures and unemployment among the middle classes, and education in a depression.

1641 Sternsher, Bernard, ed. THE NEW DEAL: DOCTRINES AND DEMOCRACY. Boston: Allyn and Bacon, 1966. 232 p. Paperbound.

A collection of scholarly articles discussing aspects of the New Deal. The topics include laissez-faire, socialism, antitrustism, concentration and control, Keynesianism, and neomercantilism.

1642 Terkel, Studs. HARD TIMES: AN ORAL HISTORY OF THE GREAT DE-
PRESSION. New York: Pantheon Books, 1970. 475 p.

> The results of interviews by the noted Chicago radio
> broadcaster. Persons from all walks of life--charwomen
> to millionaires to politicians--share their memories of
> how the Great Depression affected them, their families,
> their society. A penetrating primary source.

1643 Wecter, Dixon. THE AGE OF THE GREAT DEPRESSION, 1929-1941.
New York: Macmillan, 1948. 448 p. Illus., ports.

> A general survey, from the 1929 stock market crash to
> America's entry into the Second World War. Wecter
> stresses social developments in an account that compres-
> ses much detail into little space.

2. Topical

a. AGRICULTURE

> Saloutos, Theodore, and Hicks, John D. AGRICULTURAL DISCONTENT
> IN THE MIDDLE WEST. See no. 235.

b. BLACK AMERICANS

1644 Frazier, E. Franklin. THE NEGRO FAMILY IN THE UNITED STATES.
Rev. and abr. ed. Chicago: University of Chicago Press, 1966. 394 p.

> This sociological study, originally published in 1939, is
> widely recognized for its importance. It deals with the
> structure of the family; the black in education, business,
> and industry; housing; and the class structure among
> blacks. This edition has a foreword by Nathan Glazer.

1645 Northrup, Herbert R. ORGANIZED LABOR AND THE NEGRO. New
York: Harper & Brothers, 1944. 330 p. Tables.

> The status of the black in American labor and industry.
> The author surveyed a number of industries to determine
> such matters as hiring practices, racial composition, and
> segregation.

1646 Wolters, Raymond. NEGROES AND THE GREAT DEPRESSION: THE PROB-
LEM OF ECONOMIC RECOVERY. Westport, Conn.: Greenwood Press,
1970. 415 p.

> The author is concerned with New Deal treatment of the
> black and the efforts of black leaders to see that their
> people benefited from government programs. Wolters

concentrates on programs established under the National
Industrial Recovery Act and the Agricultural Adjustment
Act.

c. BUSINESS AND ECONOMICS

1647 Arnold, Thurman. THE FOLKLORE OF CAPITALISM. 1937. Reprint.
New Haven, Conn.: Yale University Press, 1962. 427 p.

A dissection of the myths of capitalism, with a prescription for its improvement; includes many down-to-earth
examples and is written with humor.

1648 Berle, A.A., Jr., and Means, Gardiner C. THE MODERN CORPORA-
TION AND PRIVATE PROPERTY. Rev. ed. New York: Harcourt, Brace
& World, 1968. 426 p. Illus.

Originally appeared in 1932. The authors accept the
large corporation as a fact of modern industrial society,
examine its organization and effects, and set forth pre-
scriptions for controlling it.

1649 Fusfeld, Daniel R. THE ECONOMIC THOUGHT OF FRANKLIN D. ROOSE-
VELT AND THE ORIGINS OF THE NEW DEAL. 1956. Reprint. New
York: AMS Press, 1970. 337 p.

Seeks the roots of FDR's economic theory. Fusfeld looks
at his family, his education, and the influences on him
of Theodore Roosevelt and Woodrow Wilson, in an attempt to demonstrate the relation of his background to
the actions he took as president.

1650 Galbraith, John Kenneth. THE GREAT CRASH, 1929. 3d ed. Boston:
Houghton Mifflin, 1972. 235 p. Front.

Traces the onset of the 1929 financial collapse back to
the bull market of 1927 during the Coolidge administration. Galbraith believes that failure to control feverish
speculation made the crash inevitable. He describes the
Federal Reserve System, the stock market, and the banking system in operation at the time. This book is a good
example of Galbraith's winning prose style.

1651 Hansen, Alvin Harvey. FULL RECOVERY OR STAGNATION? New York:
W.W. Norton, 1938. 350 p. Diagr.

An economist's analysis of cyclical fluctuations in the
nation's economy, from 1918 to the depression years.
He deals with both domestic and international aspects.

1652 Hawley, Ellis W. THE NEW DEAL AND THE PROBLEM OF MONOPOLY:

A STUDY IN ECONOMIC AMBIVALENCE. Princeton, N.J.: Princeton University Press, 1966. 540 p.

> An examination of contending ideals concerning concentration of economic power in the depression years. In this exposition of the ideas of advocates of antitrust action and a return to competition, of those who sought a planned economy with controls on prices and profits, and of those who sought a system of self-governing trade associations, Hawley makes use of the papers of members of the FDR administration.

1653 Josephson, Matthew. THE MONEY LORDS: THE GREAT FINANCE CAPITALISTS, 1925-1950. New York: Weybright and Talley, 1972. 384 p.

> Based on his own experience in Wall Street as well as on research. Josephson characterizes many of the leading financiers of the period and discusses the economic impact of their doings. Among many touched on are Samuel Insull, Henry Kaiser, Joseph Kennedy, Stuart Symington, Wendell Willkie, and Robert R. Young.

1654 Mitchell, Broadus. DEPRESSION DECADE: FROM NEW ERA THROUGH NEW DEAL, 1929-1941. New York: Rinehart, 1947. 480 p. Illus.

> An economic history, from the great crash on Wall Street to the U.S. entry into World War II. Mitchell includes a wealth of detail.

1655 Rees, Goronwy. THE GREAT SLUMP: CAPITALISM IN CRISIS, 1929-33. New York: Harper & Row, 1970. 309 p. Ports., plates.

> A Welsh scholar's view of the Great Depression, written from an international perspective. He traces the spreading economic slump from one country to another, describing the resultant social and political results. He blames the upheaval on outmoded economic policies and the failure of leaders to abandon economic dogma.

1656 Romasco, Albert U. THE POVERTY OF ABUNDANCE: HOOVER, THE NATION, THE DEPRESSION. New York: Oxford University Press, 1965. 292 p.

> As the title indicates, the author examines the consequences of depression striking the richest nation in history. Romasco explains the actions President Hoover took to counteract the slump; he believes the effort educated American leaders to the necessity of abandoning rigid economic thinking and the need to seek new approaches.

d. DIPLOMACY

1657 Browder, Robert P. THE ORIGINS OF SOVIET-AMERICAN DIPLOMACY.
Princeton, N.J.: Princeton University Press, 1953. 267 p.

Covers the years 1917-35 and the question of whether
the United States should give diplomatic recognition to
the Soviet Union. Browder considers the views of leading segments of American society and explains the reasons for the positive decision of the government.

1658 DeConde, Alexander. HERBERT HOOVER'S LATIN-AMERICAN POLICY.
1951. Reprint. New York: Octagon Books, 1970. 167 p.

Traces the sympathetic policy of Hoover toward the Latin American nations. DeConde pictures Hoover as a
skilled negotiator.

1659 Dozer, Donald M. ARE WE GOOD NEIGHBORS? THREE DECADES OF
INTER-AMERICAN RELATIONS, 1930-1960. 1959. Reprint. New York:
Johnson Reprint Corp., 1972. 474 p.

Dozer makes an exposition of the "good neighbor policy"
of the United States towards Latin America as it originated in the administration of FDR and the effect World
War II and the Cold War have had on relations of the
two.

Ellis, L. Ethan. REPUBLICAN FOREIGN POLICY. See no. 1577.

1660 Ferrell, Robert H. AMERICAN DIPLOMACY IN THE GREAT DEPRESSION:
HOOVER-STIMSON FOREIGN POLICY, 1929-1933. 1957. Reprint. New
York: W.W. Norton, 1970. 328 p. Maps.

This study indicates a growing sentiment on the part of
Secretary of State Stimson for an increased American
role in international affairs. Ferrell includes considerable detail on the London Economic Conference.

e. GOVERNMENT AND POLITICS

1661 Bell, Daniel. MARXIAN SOCIALISM IN THE UNITED STATES. Princeton, N.J.: Princeton University Press, 1967. 228 p. Paperbound.

This brief history sets socialism in the context of American life and discusses specifically the Socialist Labor
party, the Socialist party, and the Communist party.

1662 Binkley, Wilfred W. PRESIDENT AND CONGRESS. 3d rev. ed. New
York: Alfred A. Knopf, 1962. 403 p. Paperbound.

Published in 1937 as THE POWERS OF THE PRESIDENT.
Binkley believes the two parties hold differing views of
the presidency, the Democrats looking on the chief executive as a tribune of the people, the Republicans believing he should be checked in his actions by Congress.

1663 Campbell, Christina McF. THE FARM BUREAU AND THE NEW DEAL: A
STUDY OF MAKING OF NATIONAL FARM POLICY, 1933-1940. Urbana: University of Illinois Press, 1962. 225 p. Tables.

Among other sources, the author has used the files of
the Farm Bureau Federation to determine what the farmers wanted and how they related to the government
under the New Deal.

1664 Graham, Otis L. AN ENCORE FOR REFORM: THE OLD PROGRESSIVES
AND THE NEW DEAL. New York: Oxford University Press, 1967. 264
p.

An exposition of the ideas of a selection of Progressives,
and of how they received the New Deal. Graham does
not see a continuity from the earlier movement to the
later.

1665 Holtzman, Abraham. THE TOWNSEND MOVEMENT: A POLITICAL
STUDY. New York: Bookman, 1963. 256 p. Ports., tables.

Analysis of the Townsend Plan and its promoter, Dr.
Francis Townsend. Holtzman looks at supporters of the
plan as a pressure group and as a third political party.

1666 McCoy, Donald R. ANGRY VOICES: LEFT-OF-CENTER POLITICS IN
THE NEW DEAL ERA. Lawrence: University of Kansas Press, 1958. 224
p.

An examination of third parties, other groups to the political left, and the New Deal. McCoy deals with the
unsuccessful efforts of such groups as the League for Independent Political Action, the Farmer-Labor or American Commonwealth Political Federation, the Union Party,
the National Progressives of America.

1667 Mann, Arthur. La GUARDIA COMES TO POWER: 1933. 1965. Reprint.
Chicago: University of Chicago Press, 1969. 199 p. Maps. Paperbound.

La Guardia's election, as a fusion candidate, to mayor
of New York in a time of political corruption and deepening depression. An excellent study of city politics.

See also works on La Guardia in the section on Prominent Individuals, 8,C,3.

1668 Moley, Raymond. THE FIRST NEW DEAL. New York: Harcourt, Brace
& World, 1966. 600 p.

The recollections of the organizer of Franklin Roosevelt's
"Brains Trust." Moley, who left the faculty of Columbia University in order to take on the job, became a
close advisor of the president. He gives an account of
Roosevelt as a leader and of the steps taken to fight
the depression. Moley later broke with Roosevelt and
took a conservative stance. This account is written
from this later perspective.

1669 Patterson, James T. CONGRESSIONAL CONSERVATISM AND THE NEW
DEAL: THE GROWTH OF THE CONSERVATIVE COALITION IN CON-
GRESS, 1933-1939. Lexington: University of Kentucky Press, 1967.
378 p. Illus., ports.

A study of FDR's critics in Congress and the development of a coalition against his policies. Patterson examines the attitudes and legislative actions of such men
as Josiah W. Bailey, Harry F. Byrd, Carter Glass,
Walter F. George, Millard E. Tydings, and Burton K.
Wheeler.

1670 Robinson, Edgar E. THE ROOSEVELT LEADERSHIP, 1933-1935. Philadelphia: Lippincott, 1955. 491 p.

Probably the most negative evaluation yet written of
the presidency of Franklin D. Roosevelt. Robinson does
not trace the history of the New Deal in detail but
rather gives a critique of Roosevelt's purpose and method
and an evaluation of him as a leader. In Robinson's
view Roosevelt was a demagogue.

1671 Sindler, Allan P. HUEY LONG'S LOUISIANA: STATE POLITICS, 1920-
1952. Baltimore: Johns Hopkins Press, 1956. 331 p. Maps, tables.

Attempts to achieve a balance between consideration of
Long and of the state politics from which he sprang.
The author briefly reviews ante- and post-bellum Louisiana and then concentrates on the years 1920-52, tracing
the career of the "Kingfish" and his successors.

1672 Swing, Raymond Gram. FORERUNNERS OF AMERICAN FASCISM. 1935.
Reprint. Freeport, N.Y.: Books for Libraries Press, 1969. 168 p.

The noted political commentator's analysis of conditions
in the United States which would open the possibility
of the introduction of fascism. He discusses five prominent individuals as demagogues who would lead to its
inception: Father Charles Coughlin, Senators Huey Long
and Theodore Bilbo, Charles Townsend, and William
Randolph Hearst.

1673 Tugwell, Rexford Guy. THE BRAINS TRUST. New York: Viking Press, 1968. 570 p.

> An inside view of the political process by a member of FDR's group of advisors. Tugwell, a professor of economics, joined the New Deal without prior political experience. He was particularly impressed by the election of 1932, an account of which he gives here. Although recognizing FDR's faults, Tugwell stresses his skill as a political leader.

1674 Wolfskill, George. THE REVOLT OF THE CONSERVATIVES: A HISTORY OF THE AMERICAN LIBERTY LEAGUE, 1934-1940. Boston: Houghton Mifflin, 1962. 303 p. Illus.

> The League was a leading opponent of the New Deal. Wolfskill describes the participants, the organization, and for what it stood.

f. THE JUDICIARY

1675 Corwin, Edward S. CONSTITUTIONAL REVOLUTION, LTD. Claremont, Calif.: Claremont Colleges, 1941. 130 p.

> Originally lectures by a legal scholar delivered at Pomona and the other Claremont colleges. Corwin explains what impact centralization of power in the federal government has had on business, the citizenry, the states, the Congress, and the judiciary.

1676 Jackson, Robert H. THE STRUGGLE FOR JUDICIAL SUPREMACY: A STUDY OF A CRISIS IN AMERICAN POWER POLITICS. New York: Alfred A. Knopf, 1941. 381 p.

> A general consideration of judicial power, followed by an exposition of the issues involved in the attempt of Roosevelt to enlarge the Supreme Court in 1936. Jackson, who was attorney general at the time of writing, justifies the New Deal's desire to stem the political power of the Court.

1677 Pritchett, C. Herman. THE ROOSEVELT COURT: A STUDY IN JUDICIAL POLITICS AND VALUES, 1937-1947. 1948. Reprint. Chicago: Quadrangle Books, 1969. 330 p. Diagrs. Paperbound.

> A study of the psychological and sociological values of the justices of the Supreme Court. The author analyzes the most important cases that came before them and explains their disagreements, which were pronounced.

g. LABOR

1678 Bernstein, Irving. NEW DEAL COLLECTIVE BARGAINING POLICY. Berkeley and Los Angeles: University of California Press, 1950. 189 p.

> Early New Deal policies (1933-35) on labor and unions.
> Bernstein is particularly concerned with the Wagner Act,
> the Railroad Labor Act, and the National Labor Relations Act.

1679 _____. TURBULENT YEARS: A HISTORY OF THE AMERICAN WORKER, 1933-1941. Boston: Houghton Mifflin, 1970. 887 p. Illus., ports.

> A sequel to the author's LEAN YEARS, q.v., no. 1597,
> filled with personalities, anecdotes, and accounts of the
> significant accomplishments of organized labor. Bernstein tries for objectivity; if anything he is more critical of certain labor leaders than of the businessmen with
> whom they dealt.

1680 Fine, Sidney. SIT-DOWN: THE GENERAL MOTORS STRIKE OF 1936-1937. Ann Arbor: University of Michigan Press, 1969. 457 p. Illus., ports.

> A full discussion of what the author believes to be the
> most significant strike of the twentieth century. Fine
> gives the background of General Motors, examines the
> working conditions in the plant at Flint, Michigan, the
> issues in the strike, and the rise of Walter and Victor
> Reuther and the United Automobile Workers.

Morris, James O. CONFLICT WITHIN THE AFL. See no. 401.

h. LITERATURE

1681 Aaron, Daniel. WRITERS ON THE LEFT: EPISODES IN AMERICAN LITERARY COMMUNISM. New York: Harcourt, Brace & World, 1961. 476 p.

> An analysis of writers who responded to the appeal of
> communism between 1912 and the early forties. Aaron
> blends history, biography, and literary criticism to create
> an objective account of the ills of American society and
> how some attempted to deal with them.

1682 Brooks, Van Wyck. AMERICA'S COMING-OF-AGE. Rev. ed. Garden City, N.Y.: Doubleday, 1958. 183 p. Paperbound.

> First published in 1934 as THREE ESSAYS ON AMERICA.
> The pieces had been written earlier. Brooks at this point

had a low opinion of the American mind because he
saw it as an expression of an impoverished American
spirit.

Geismar, Maxwell. WRITERS IN CRISIS. See. no. 1600.

1683 Swados, Harvey, ed. THE AMERICAN WRITERS AND THE GREAT DE-
PRESSION. Indianapolis: Bobbs-Merrill, 1966. 561 p. Illus.

An anthology of reactions to the depression, from fiction
and nonfiction of the time. Swados divides the collection topically (workers, farmers, women, the down-and-
out, etc.) and includes writings of Louis Adamic, James
Agee, Sherwood Anderson, e.e. cummings, John Dos
Passos, James T. Farrell, Ernest Hemingway, John Steinbeck, Richard Wright, et al.

j. NEW DEAL AGENCIES AND PROGRAMS

1684 Baldwin, Sidney. POVERTY AND POLITICS: THE RISE AND DECLINE
OF THE FARM SECURITY ADMINISTRATION. Chapel Hill: University
of North Carolina Press, 1968. 454 p. Illus.

The author sets forth the ideals and policies of FSA, the
New Deal agency designated to combat rural poverty,
and also describes the politics and internal struggles in
the Department of Agriculture, to which FSA was ultimately transferred.

1685 Charles, Searle F. MINISTER OF RELIEF: HARRY HOPKINS AND THE
DEPRESSION. Syracuse, N.Y.: Syracuse University Press, 1963. 297
p. Illus., port.

A detailed examination of the relief program of Roosevelt's New Deal, focusing on the work of its chief administrator. Charles sees Roosevelt and Hopkins as grop-
ing for answers to massive economic and social problems
by trial and error. He narrates in detail the operations
of the Federal Emergency Relief Administration, the Civil Works Administration, and the Works Progress Administration. His evaluation of their accomplishments is a
positive one.

1686 Conkin, Paul K. TOMORROW A NEW WORLD: THE NEW DEAL COM-
MUNITY PROGRAM. Ithaca, N.Y.: Cornell University Press, 1959. 359
p. Maps.

An impartial, detailed account of the Community Program. Conkin looks at the nature of the various experiments, at the leaders, at the confusion and failure that
plagued them.

1687 Douglas, Paul H. SOCIAL SECURITY IN THE UNITED STATES: AN ANALYSIS AND APPRAISAL OF THE FEDERAL SOCIAL SECURITY ACT. 2d ed. 1939. Reprint. New York: DaCapo Press, 1971. 507 p.

Douglas was, in his professorial years before election to the U.S. Senate, a leading advocate of social security. In this book he combines a legislative history of the Social Security Act with an analysis of its features and prospective problems.

1688 Howard, Donald S. THE WPA AND FEDERAL RELIEF POLICY. 1943. Reprint. New York: DaCapo Press, 1973. 879 p. Illus.

An exhaustive treatment of the Works Progress Administration. Howard deals with the internal structure, its relation to other relief efforts, and with all aspects of its operations in society: projects, wages, numbers employed, etc.

1689 Johnson, Hugh S. THE BLUE EAGLE, FROM EGG TO EARTH. Garden City, N.Y.: Doubleday, Doran, 1935. 473 p. Illus., ports., plates.

General Hugh Johnson, head of the National Recovery Administration, gives his account of its conception, inception, and demise as part of an autobiographical book. His passionate concern for social justice pervades the more polemical sections. Good picture of the controversies stirred up by the New Deal.

1690 Kirkendall, Richard S. SOCIAL SCIENTISTS AND FARM POLITICS IN THE AGE OF ROOSEVELT. Columbia: University of Missouri Press, 1966. 367 p. Ports.

The entrance of social scientists into politics and their accomplishments and frustrations, put in the context of agricultural politics. Kirkendall guides the reader through the maze of bureaucratic actions, political machinations, lobbying, etc., over a twenty-year period.

1691 Lilienthal, David E. TVA: DEMOCRACY ON THE MARCH. New York: Harper & Brothers, 1953. 318 p. Illus., map.

A revision of a work first published in 1944. Lilienthal reveals how the government and the people in the Tennessee Valley made the great public works project a success.

1692 Lubove, Roy. THE STRUGGLE FOR SOCIAL SECURITY, 1900-1935. Cambridge, Mass.: Harvard University Press, 1968. 284 p.

Lubove sets forth the attitudes of the voluntary social welfare organizations and the political debates involved

in the adoption of social welfare legislation. The specific measures dealt with are workmen's compensation,
unemployment insurance, old age assistance and insurance, widows' pensions, and health insurance (not yet
adopted).

1693 Lyon, Leverett S., et al. THE NATIONAL RECOVERY ADMINISTRATION:
AN ANALYSIS AND APPRAISAL. 1935. Reprint. New York: DaCapo
Press, 1972. 969 p.

A thorough study of the NRA and the role it played in
recovery from the depression, by former members of its
staff. It deals with the agency's administrative organization as well as with issues in the nation: industrial
relations, trade practices, employment, etc.

1694 Mathews, Jane DeHart. THE FEDERAL THEATRE, 1935-1939: PLAYS,
RELIEF AND POLITICS. Princeton, N.J.: Princeton University Press,
1967. 354 p. Illus., ports.

A history of the Works Progress Administration's Theatre
Project, which employed playwrights, directors, actors,
and other stage personnel in the depression years, 1935-
39. The author deals with politics, bureaucrats, unions,
theatre folk, artistic aspiration and experimentation, and
the conflicts that arose among all of these elements.

1695 Salmond, John A. THE CIVILIAN CONSERVATION CORPS, 1933-1942:
A NEW DEAL CASE STUDY. Durham, N.C.: Duke University Press,
1967. 246 p.

The nine-year history of the CCC in a study that concentrates on the administration of the program. Salmond
had access to the papers of Robert Fechner, director
of the program, and other primary sources.

1696 Selznick, Philip. TVA AND THE GRASS ROOTS: A STUDY IN THE
SOCIOLOGY OF FORMAL ORGANIZATION. 1949. Reprint. New York:
Harper & Row, 1966. 290 p. Paperbound.

A sociological analysis of the Tennessee Valley Authority. Selznick concerns himself with TVA's organization
and the attempts to accomplish its aims with the cooperation of local organizations. He draws theoretical conclusions on organization from the results.

1697 Witte, Edwin E. THE DEVELOPMENT OF THE SOCIAL SECURITY ACT:
A MEMORANDUM ON THE HISTORY OF THE COMMITTEE ON ECO-
NOMIC SECURITY AND DRAFTING AND LEGISLATIVE HISTORY OF
THE SOCIAL SECURITY ACT. Madison: University of Wisconsin Press,
1962. 220 p.

> The author was one of the drafters of the act. He gives
> the background and explains its provisions.

3. Prominent Individuals

FATHER COUGHLIN

1698 Tull, Charles J. FATHER COUGHLIN AND THE NEW DEAL. Syracuse,
N.Y.: Syracuse University Press, 1965. 292 p.

> The "radio priest" who broadcast from Royal Oak, Michi-
> gan, each Sunday and helped mold right-wing political
> thought. Tull examines Coughlin's ideas impartially.

ROBERT FROST

1699 Thompson, Lawrance. ROBERT FROST. 2 vols. New York: Holt, Rinehart and Winston, 1966-70. Illus., ports.

> An authorized biography based on careful culling of the
> records and many conversations with the poet. Thomp-
> son shows that Frost was not an easy man to relate to.
> He diligently traces the years of doubt and struggle be-
> fore Frost received recognition in his own land. Vol-
> ume 1: THE EARLY YEARS, 1874-1915; volume 2: THE
> YEARS OF TRIUMPH, 1915-1938.

HERBERT HOOVER

1700 Hoover, Herbert C. MEMOIRS. 3 vols. New York: Macmillan, 1951-
52. Illus., ports.

> Hoover's own view of his career as engineer, interna-
> tional relief administrator, and as president. Inevitably
> of most interest is his version of the economic collapse
> that occurred during his time in the White House. Hoover
> ties the domestic depression to international factors over
> which he had no control. He is highly critical of Frank-
> lin Roosevelt's New Deal, which he claims made use of
> features of socialism and fascism. Volume 1: YEARS
> OF ADVENTURE, 1874-1920; volume 2: THE CABINET
> AND PRESIDENCY, 1920-1933; volume 3: THE GREAT
> DEPRESSION, 1929-1941.

1701 Lyons, Eugene. THE HERBERT HOOVER STORY. Washington: Human
Events, 1959. 358 p.

> Originally published in 1948 as OUR UNKNOWN PRESI-
> DENT. Lyons attempts to refurbish Hoover's image. He

deals with his long and varied career before the presidency as well as with the misfortunes of the depression.

1702 Myers, William Starr, ed. THE STATE PAPERS AND OTHER PUBLIC WRITINGS OF HERBERT HOOVER. 2 vols. 1934. Reprint. New York: Kraus Reprint Co., 1970.

The president's messages to Congress, addresses, press statements, radio broadcasts, campaign speeches, etc. Volume 1: 4 MARCH 1929 TO OCTOBER 1931; volume 2: 1 OCTOBER 1931 TO 4 MARCH 1933.

1703 Warren, Harris G. HERBERT HOOVER AND THE GREAT DEPRESSION. New York: Oxford University Press, 1959. 372 p.

A sympathetic treatment of Hoover's career. Warren traces his development from childhood to his years of success in business and as relief administrator in World War I, but devotes most space to the problems Hoover confronted in the presidency. He contends that Hoover was often criticized unfairly and that he made possible much that was accomplished by the New Deal.

HAROLD L. ICKES

1704 Ickes, Harold L. THE SECRET DIARY OF HAROLD L. ICKES. 3 vols. New York: Simon & Schuster, 1953-54.

The daily jottings of the "Old Curmudgeon," commenting on the personalities and the events in cabinet meetings, and the government generally, under FDR. Bickering, backbiting, jostling for authority, etc., are revealed in a frank, often humorous, account. Volume 1: THE FIRST THOUSAND DAYS, 1933-1936; volume 2: THE INSIDE STRUGGLE, 1936-1939; volume 3: THE LOWERING CLOUDS, 1939-1941.

JOHN L. LEWIS

1705 Alinsky, Saul D. JOHN L. LEWIS: AN UNAUTHORIZED BIOGRAPHY. 1949. Reprint. New York: Alfred A. Knopf, 1970. 406 p. Illus. Paperbound.

Despite the title, a very favorable account of the president of the United Mine Workers; a lively biography making use of much information supplied by Lewis.

DAVID E. LILIENTHAL

1706 Lilienthal, David E. THE JOURNALS OF DAVID E. LILIENTHAL. 5

vols. New York: Harper & Row, 1964-71. Illus., ports.

A view of public life by the chief planner of the Tennessee Valley Authority, as contained in the journals
he kept, which provides glimpses into the workings and
personalities of the administrations of Roosevelt and
Truman. Volume 1: THE TVA YEARS, 1939-1945;
volume 2: THE ATOMIC ENERGY YEARS, 1945-1950;
volume 3: VENTURESOME YEARS, 1950-1955; volume
4: THE ROAD TO CHANGE, 1955-1959; volume 5:
THE HARVEST YEARS, 1959-1963.

HUEY LONG

1707 Williams, T. Harry. HUEY LONG. New York: Alfred A. Knopf, 1969.
920 p. Illus., ports., facsims.

A vivid biography of the Louisiana governor and U.S.
senator, by a noted historian of the South. Williams
traces Long's rise from humble beginnings to the point
when, as a competitor of the popular Franklin Roosevelt,
his career was cut short by an assassin's bullet in 1935.
Williams has made extensive use of primary documents
and pictures a colorful character in a colorful style.

HENRY MORGENTHAU

1708 Blum, John M. FROM THE MORGENTHAU DIARIES. 3 vols. Boston:
Houghton Mifflin, 1959-67. Illus., ports.

From many volumes of documents compiled by Henry
Morgenthau, who served as secretary of the treasury
(1934-45) in the administration of F.D. Roosevelt, Blum
presents a synthesis that contains elements of autobiography and biography as well as the history of the New
Deal years. The perspective is primarily that of Morgenthau, and thus the book provides primary source material. Volume 1: YEARS OF CRISIS, 1928-1938; volume 2: YEARS OF URGENCY, 1938-1941; volume 3:
YEARS OF WAR, 1941-1945.

1709 _____. ROOSEVELT AND MORGENTHAU: A REVISION AND CON-
DENSATION OF "FROM THE MORGENTHAU DIARIES." Boston: Houghton Mifflin, 1970. 686 p.

A shorter version of the three-volume work, q.v., no.
1708.

ELEANOR ROOSEVELT

1710 Roosevelt, Eleanor. THIS I REMEMBER. New York: Harper & Brothers,

1949. 397 p.

Along with the earlier THIS IS MY STORY, this work
forms the autobiography of Mrs. F.D. Roosevelt. She
deals here with the years between FDR's election as
governor of New York and his death. Many insights
into events and personalities are contained in unadorned,
yet moving, account.

FRANKLIN ROOSEVELT

1711 Burns, James MacGregor. ROOSEVELT: THE LION AND THE FOX.
New York: Harcourt, Brace, 1956. 569 p. Illus.

A study of Roosevelt the man and how his background
and the ideological environment of the era affected
his ability to lead. Burns sees Roosevelt as adept in
the art of compromise and as presiding as a mediator
or broker among the contending groups and forces of the
time. The gains of this approach, he believes, were
often short term and were made at the expense of long-
range advance.

1712 Freidel, Frank B. FRANKLIN D. ROOSEVELT. 4 vols. to date. Boston:
Little, Brown, 1952- . Illus., ports.

A work in progress, projected at six volumes. Freidel
makes thorough use of FDR papers. Volume 1: THE
APPRENTICESHIP; volume 2: THE ORDEAL; volume 3:
THE TRIUMPH; volume 4: LAUNCHING THE NEW
DEAL.

1713 Lash, Joseph. ELEANOR AND FRANKLIN: THE STORY OF THEIR RE-
LATIONSHIP, BASED ON ELEANOR ROOSEVELT'S PRIVATE PAPERS. New
York: W.W. Norton, 1971. 783 p. Illus., ports., geneal. table.

This biography of Eleanor Roosevelt, by an acquaintance,
tells of her relationship with her husband and family
and examines her various roles in public life; it is
based on personal interviews as well as extensive documentation. This volume ends with the president's death
in 1945. For a continuation see ELEANOR: THE YEARS
ALONE, q.v., no. 1933.

1714 Rosenman, Samuel I., ed. THE PUBLIC PAPERS AND ADDRESSES OF
FRANKLIN D. ROOSEVELT. 13 vols. Vols. 1-5. New York: Random
House, 1938. Vols. 6-9. New York: Macmillan, 1941. Vols. 10-13.
New York: Harper & Brothers, 1950.

Roosevelt's speeches, messages to Congress, radio ("fire-
side") chats, war messages to the Allies, press confer-

ences, etc. Rosenman supplies an introduction to each
volume, setting the materials in historical context, and
an extensive note on each item. Volumes 1-7 deal
with phases of the New Deal; volumes 8-13 with World
War II. A cumulative topical table is in the final
volume.

1715 Sherwood, Robert E. ROOSEVELT AND HOPKINS: AN INTIMATE HIS-
TORY. Rev. ed. New York: Harper & Brothers, 1950. 1,021 p. Illus., ports., map.

The playwright, a member of the Roosevelt administration and friend of FDR and Hopkins, bases his story on
the latter's papers. Truly revealing of their personalities and of the New Deal and World War II years.

1716 Tugwell, Rexford Guy. THE DEMOCRATIC ROOSEVELT: A BIOGRAPHY OF
FRANKLIN D. ROOSEVELT. 1957. Reprint. Baltimore: Penguin Books,
1969. 712 p. Illus., ports. Paperbound.

An evaluation by one who worked closely with Franklin
D. Roosevelt as a member of the "Brains Trust." Tugwell, who served as head of the Resettlement Administration, pays particular attention to the role a government agency can play in effecting change in society.

1717 _____. FDR: ARCHITECT OF AN ERA. New York: Macmillan, 1967.
287 p. Ports.

A warm biography of Franklin Roosevelt, by a co-worker
and friend, which concentrates on the substance and
style of his politics and his hopes for lasting accomplishments on behalf of the nation.

ROBERT F. WAGNER

1718 Huthmacher, J. Joseph. SENATOR ROBERT F. WAGNER AND THE RISE
OF URBAN LIBERALISM. New York: Atheneum, 1968. 373 p. Ports.

A biography of the senator responsible for much of the
significant social legislation of the New Deal period.
The Wagner Act and other projects are examined in detail.

E. WORLD WAR II

1. General

1719 Buchanan, A. Russell. THE UNITED STATES AND WORLD WAR II. 2

vols. New York: Harper & Row, 1964. 652 p. Illus., ports., maps.

This narrative history deals with the period of neutrality,
the increasing involvement in the war, and full-scale
participation. Buchanan considers all aspects of the
war at home and on the battlefield.

1720 Churchill, Winston. THE SECOND WORLD WAR. 6 vols. Boston:
Houghton Mifflin, 1948-53. Illus., ports., maps.

The prime minister's first-hand account, which gives insight into the problems faced by Britain during the bomb-
ings, progress of the war, politically and militarily, and
cooperation among the Allies to defeat the Axis. Written in Churchill's inimitable style. Volume 1: THE
GATHERING STORM; volume 2: THEIR FINEST HOUR;
volume 3: THE GRAND ALLIANCE; volume 4: THE
HINGE OF FATE; volume 5: CLOSING THE RING;
volume 6: TRIUMPH AND TRAGEDY.

1721 Davis, Kenneth S. EXPERIENCE OF WAR: THE UNITED STATES IN
WORLD WAR II. Garden City, N.Y.: Doubleday, 1965. 713 p. Maps.

A discussion of developments from the period of neutrality to the end of the war. The author writes in a vivid style and provides character sketches of the leading
participants.

1722 Goodman, Jack, ed. WHILE YOU WERE GONE: A REPORT ON WAR-
TIME LIFE IN THE UNITED STATES. New York: Simon & Schuster,
1946. 633 p.

A collection of articles by notable writers. Included
are Paul Gallico, Allan Nevins, Anna W.M. Wolf,
and many others.

2. Topical

a. THE ATOMIC BOMB

1723 Compton, Arthur H. ATOMIC QUEST: A PERSONAL NARRATIVE. New
York: Oxford University Press, 1956. 370 p. Illus.

Compton, a member of the Manhattan Project, recounts
the secret development of the atomic bomb. He trans-
lates scientific terminology into plain English and spices
his narrative with humorous anecdotes.

1724 Groves, Leslie R. NOW IT CAN BE TOLD: THE STORY OF THE MAN-
HATTAN PROJECT. New York: Harper & Row, 1962. 478 p.

The development of the atom bomb, in an account by
the man who directed the project between 1942 and
1946. Groves provides much information and candidly
admits mistakes made on the way to success.

b. DIPLOMACY

1725 Beard, Charles A. PRESIDENT ROOSEVELT AND THE COMING OF THE
WAR, 1941: A STUDY IN APPEARANCES AND REALITY. 1948. Reprint. Hamden, Conn.: Shoe String Press, 1968. 620 p.

The attack of a prominent American historian on FDR
for what he believed were actions designed to provoke
a Japanese attack. Beard makes heavy use of the materials compiled by the joint congressional committee.

1726 Chamberlain, William Henry. AMERICA'S SECOND CRUSADE. Chicago:
Henry Regnery, 1950. 372 p.

Very critical account of FDR and America's entrance
into the war. Chamberlain does not believe the country gained by this "second crusade" but rather, lost.

1727 Divine, Robert A. ROOSEVELT AND WORLD WAR II. Baltimore: Johns
Hopkins Press, 1969. 117 p.

Originally the Albert Shaw Lectures in Diplomatic History at Johns Hopkins University. Divine makes a critical appraisal of FDR's accomplishments in foreign affairs.

1728 Dunn, Frederick S. PEACE-MAKING AND THE SETTLEMENT WITH JA-
PAN. Princeton, N.J.: Princeton University Press, 1963. 210 p.

The negotiations that led to peace between the United
States and Japan. Dunn explains the provisions of the
treaty by tracing events during the war.

1729 Feis, Herbert. THE ATOMIC BOMB AND THE END OF WORLD WAR II.
Rev. ed. Princeton, N.J.: Princeton University Press, 1966. 219 p.

First published in 1961 as JAPAN SUBDUED. The author
continues the history where he left off in BETWEEN WAR
AND PEACE, q.v., no. 1730, tracing the steps in the
momentous decision to drop the bomb on Japan, along
with other actions of significance by the antagonists.

1730 _____. BETWEEN WAR AND PEACE: THE POTSDAM CONFERENCE.
Princeton, N.J.: Princeton University Press, 1960. 375 p. Maps.

Continues the history where the author left off in CHURCH-
ILL, ROOSEVELT, STALIN, q.v., no. 1732. Feis ex-

plains the negotiations at Potsdam and the resultant beginnings of the Cold War.

1731 _____. THE CHINA TANGLE: THE AMERICAN EFFORT IN CHINA
FROM PEARL HARBOR TO THE MARSHALL MISSION. 1953. Reprint.
New York: Atheneum, 1965. 454 p.

An account, based on official government diplomatic
records, of U.S. attempts from 1941 to 1946 to help
the Chinese government ward off communism.

1732 _____. CHURCHILL, ROOSEVELT, STALIN: THE WAR THEY WAGED
AND THE PEACE THEY SOUGHT. 2d ed. Princeton, N.J.: Princeton
University Press, 1967. 713 p. Maps.

A diplomatic specialist's telling of the joint war effort
that overcame the Axis. Feis covers the years 1940 to
1945 chronologically, explaining each wartime conference and agreement.

1733 _____. CONTEST OVER JAPAN. New York: W.W. Norton, 1967.
187 p.

An account of the rivalry between the United States
and the Soviet Union to control the future of Japan in
the years of occupation, 1945-52. Feis sets this contention in the context of developments in Europe and
the emerging Cold War.

1734 _____. THE ROAD TO PEARL HARBOR: THE COMING OF THE WAR
BETWEEN THE UNITED STATES AND JAPAN. Princeton, N.J.: Princeton University Press, 1950. 368 p. Map.

A step-by-step account of the sources of friction which
led to confrontation and war, by a former member of
the State Department. Feis uses American and Japanese
sources in this well-documented study.

1735 Griswold, A. Whitney. THE FAR EASTERN POLICY OF THE UNITED
STATES. 1938. Reprint. New Haven, Conn.: Yale University Press,
1962. 530 p.

A thorough review of U.S. policy in the area from the
occupation of the Philippines to the time of writing.

1736 Kimball, Warren F. THE MOST UNSORDID ACT: LEND-LEASE, 1939-
1941. Baltimore: Johns Hopkins Press, 1969. 292 p.

The process by which the United States came to the
decision to "lend or lease" war material to the British.
Kimball shows that the monetary crisis which Great Bri-

tain experienced spurred the Americans to devise a plan
by which vital supplies could be transferred to them.

1737 Kolko, Gabriel. THE POLITICS OF WAR: THE WORLD AND UNITED
STATES FOREIGN POLICY, 1943-1945. New York: Random House,
1968. 695 p.

A highly critical interpretation of American intentions
in World War II by a "New Left" historian. Kolko
believes American policy was designed to promote the
interests of capitalism even at the expense of great
suffering.

1738 Pratt, Julius W. CORDELL HULL, 1933-1944. 2 vols. New York:
Cooper Square, 1964.

Hull's service as secretary of state in the Roosevelt administration, analyzed by a diplomatic historian. Pratt
presents a balanced view of the man and his policies.
This work is part of S.F. Bemis et al., AMERICAN
SECRETARIES OF STATE AND THEIR DIPLOMACY. See
no. 302.

1739 Schroeder, Paul W. THE AXIS ALLIANCE AND JAPANESE-AMERICAN
RELATIONS, 1941. Ithaca, N.Y.: Cornell University Press, 1958. 255
p.

An evaluation of the influence of the Tripartite Pact of
Germany, Italy, and Japan upon the latter's decision to
attack the United States. The author does not believe
the American government was seeking a confrontation.

1740 Smith, Gaddis. AMERICAN DIPLOMACY DURING THE SECOND WORLD
WAR, 1941-1945. New York: Wiley, 1965. 203 p. Maps.

This brief account of American diplomacy evaluates the
strengths and weaknesses of FDR and other American leaders.
Scholarly and readable.

1741 Snell, John L. ILLUSION AND NECESSITY: THE DIPLOMACY OF GLO-
BAL WAR, 1939-1945. Boston: Houghton Mifflin, 1963. 240 p. Maps.
Paperbound.

Sets forth the "realism and illusion" that permeated the
diplomacy of both the Allies and the Axis. Snell attempts to show how the Cold War developed out of policies adopted in the hot war.

1742 Tansill, Charles C. BACK DOOR TO WAR: ROOSEVELT FOREIGN POLI-
CY, 1933-1941. Chicago: Henry Regnery, 1952. 711 p.

American foreign policy from the close of World War I

to U.S. entry into World War II. A well-documented
account. Tansill is quite critical of the actions of
F.D. Roosevelt and members of his administration.

1743 Tsou, Tang. AMERICA'S FAILURE IN CHINA, 1941-1950. Chicago: University of Chicago Press, 1963. 614 p.

A book critical of the American role in China, the
author believing that if the United States had exerted
more influence and power the course of developments
would have been different. A scholarly analysis.

1744 Tuchman, Barbara. STILWELL AND THE AMERICAN EXPERIENCE IN CHINA, 1911-45. New York: Macmillan, 1970. 636 p. Illus., ports., maps.

Joseph W. Stilwell (1883-1946) served on a number of
occasions in a number of capacities in China. The
author says that he was "quintessentially American" and,
therefore, his career is helpful in illuminating the
events that led to the ultimate success of the Chinese
Communists.

1745 Wilson, Theodore A. THE FIRST SUMMIT: ROOSEVELT AND CHURCHILL AT PLACENTIA BAY, 1941. Boston: Houghton Mifflin, 1969. 360 p. Illus., ports., facsims.

The meeting between the leaders of the Allies which
ironed out differences and resulted in the Atlantic Charter. Wilson covers the discussions in great detail.

c. GOVERNMENT AND POLITICS

1746 Corwin, Edward S. TOTAL WAR AND THE CONSTITUTION: FIVE LECTURES. New York: Alfred A. Knopf, 1947. 202 p.

The lectures were delivered under the sponsorship of the
William W. Cook Foundation at the University of Michigan in 1946. Corwin deals with how the Constitution
is stretched in total war (he deals with World War II,
with references to the Civil War and World War I) and
how power passes into the hands of the president, either
by delegation by Congress or because of the executive's
response to emergencies.

1747 Dawson, R.H. THE DECISION TO AID RUSSIA, 1941: FOREIGN POLICY AND DOMESTIC POLITICS. Chapel Hill: University of North Carolina Press, 1959. 330 p.

The politically difficult decision to aid the Soviet Union
once the Germans had attacked is described in detail.

Dawson explains the methods used by Roosevelt's administration to persuade Congress and the public that such an
action would be in the best interest of the United States.

1748 Divine, Robert A. SECOND CHANCE: THE TRIUMPH OF INTERNA-
TIONALISM IN AMERICA DURING WORLD WAR II. New York: Atheneum, 1967. 380 p.

A lucid account of the campaign to bring American public opinion to an internationalist position and to support
of U.S. participation in the United Nations. Divine
attributes the success of the campaign to pressure groups,
political leaders, and journalists and writers.

1749 Taylor, F. Jay. THE UNITED STATES AND THE SPANISH CIVIL WAR.
1956. Reprint. New York: Octagon Books, 1971. 288 p. Map.

A review of U.S. governmental and public opinion concerning a war which Taylor interprets as a prelude to
World War II. He uses many published and unpublished
sources.

1750 Young, Roland A. CONGRESSIONAL POLITICS IN THE SECOND WORLD
WAR. New York: Columbia University Press, 1956. 281 p. Illus.

Congress's role in conversion from a peace to a war
footing, in a work by an economist. Lucidly written.

d. GOVERNMENT WAR PROGRAMS

1751 Baxter, James Phinney III. SCIENTISTS AGAINST TIME. Boston: Little,
Brown, 1946. 494 p. Illus., front., ports., plates, diagrs.

An account of the role of scientists in developing new
weapons for the prosecution of World War II. Baxter
tells the story of the Office of Scientific Research and
Development and the relation of its members to the president, the military brass, the financial problems, etc.
He explains complicated scientific developments in the
language of the layman.

1752 Catton, Bruce. THE WAR LORDS OF WASHINGTON. New York: Harcourt, Brace, 1948. 313 p.

The personal reflections of a journalist who served as
director of information of the War Production Board.
Catton deals not only with the huge problems of mobilization of industry but with the petty backbiting and
rivalries within the bureaucracy.

1753 Clinard, Marshall B. THE BLACK MARKET: A STUDY OF WHITE COL-

LAR CRIME. New York: Rinehart, 1952. 409 p. Illus.

A former member of the enforcement unit of the Office of Price Administration (OPA) examines the black market in meat, rent, and gasoline, problems of enforcement of government regulations, and public attitudes.

1754 Janeway, Eliot. THE STRUGGLE FOR SURVIVAL: A CHRONICLE OF ECONOMIC MOBILIZATION IN WORLD WAR II. 1951. Reprint. New York: Weybright & Talley, 1968. 311 p.

An account of the effort to put the United States on a war footing. Janeway describes the various boards, commissions, and offices set up to accomplish the task and their dealings with industry, labor, farmers, and others.

1755 Nelson, Donald M. ARSENAL OF DEMOCRACY: THE STORY OF AMERICAN WAR PRODUCTION. New York: Harcourt, Brace, 1946. 457 p. Illus.

The chairman of the War Production Board gives his own account of its problems and accomplishments in mobilizing the country's industry for war. An informal and somewhat optimistic interpretation.

1756 Wilcox, Walter W. THE FARMER IN THE SECOND WORLD WAR. 1947. Reprint. New York: DaCapo Press, 1973. 422 p. Illus.

This study, based on congressional and other records, reveals details of the responsibility placed on farmers for increased production in wartime and the problems of organization and coordination by government.

e. ISOLATIONISM AND INTERVENTION

1757 Adler, Selig. THE ISOLATIONIST IMPULSE: ITS TWENTIETH CENTURY REACTION. New York: Abelard-Schuman, 1957. 538 p.

Adler sets forth the attitudes of those who sought to isolate the United States from the wars of the rest of the world in the period from World War I to the close of World War II. The Middle West, Charles Lindbergh's activities, and the America First Committee are given special attention.

1758 Cole, Wayne S. AMERICA FIRST: THE BATTLE AGAINST INTERVENTION, 1940-1941. Madison: University of Wisconsin Press, 1953. 316 p. Illus., ports.

A history of the America First Committee and its efforts

to keep the United States out of World War II. Cole's
dispassionate account includes such matters as membership, organization, finance, strategy, and how the Committee attempted to counteract charges that it was Nazi,
anti-Semitic, pacifist, and reactionary.

1759 _____. SENATOR GERALD P. NYE AND AMERICAN FOREIGN RELA-
TIONS. Minneapolis: University of Minnesota Press, 1962. 293 p. Illus.

An account of a leading isolationist who, as senator
from North Dakota, led the campaign for the enactment
of the neutrality laws and opposed FDR's internationalist
policies. Cole makes use of a great deal of documentary material as well as interviews with the senator and
his acquaintances.

1760 Divine, Robert A. THE ILLUSION OF NEUTRALITY. Chicago: University of Chicago Press, 1962. 381 p.

A study in foreign policy. Divine traces the evolution
of neutrality legislation in the years 1935-39. He sees
little but unreality in the world view held by those advocating such an approach.

1761 _____. THE RELUCTANT BELLIGERENT: AMERICAN ENTRY INTO
WORLD WAR II. New York: Wiley, 1965. 183 p. Maps.

The consequence of U.S. attempts to withdraw from the
world arena in the thirties was the expansion of power
of Germany, Italy, and Japan. Concentrating to a
great extent on FDR, Divine shows how the country
finally came to recognize the peril of its position.

1762 Drummond, Donald F. THE PASSING OF AMERICAN NEUTRALITY, 1937-
1941. Ann Arbor: University of Michigan Press, 1955. 415 p.

A factual, well-documented account of diplomacy in
the period from the passage of the Neutrality Act, 1
May 1937, to the Japanese attack on Pearl Harbor, 7
December 1941.

1763 Jonas, Manfred. ISOLATIONISM IN AMERICA, 1935-1941. Ithaca,
N.Y.: Cornell University Press, 1966. 326 p.

Jonas examines the position taken by those who advocated
U.S. isolation from world problems. He dissects the
legislation declaring American neutrality and isolationist
reactions to such international concerns as the Spanish
Civil War and Italy's conquest of Ethiopia.

1764 Langer, William L., and Gleason, S. Everett. THE CHALLENGE TO ISOLATION: THE WORLD CRISIS OF 1937-1940 AND AMERICAN FOREIGN POLICY. 2 vols. 1952-53. Reprint. New York: Harper & Row, 1964.

> An objective study. The authors had access to files of the Department of State and other official and private records in the writing of this detailed account.

f. JAPANESE-AMERICAN EVACUATION

1765 Girdner, Audrie, and Loftis, Anne. THE GREAT BETRAYAL: THE EVACUATION OF THE JAPANESE-AMERICANS DURING WORLD WAR II. New York: Macmillan, 1969. 572 p. Illus., ports., map.

> The story of the internment of the Americans of Japanese descent. The authors make extensive use of records available but also use the results of many interviews with those who experienced the removal.

1766 Grodzins, Morton M. AMERICANS BETRAYED: POLITICS AND THE JAPANESE EVACUATION. Chicago: University of Chicago, 1949. 461 p. Charts, graphs.

> A discussion of the constitutional issues that arose out of the herding of Americans of Japanese ancestry into concentration camps during World War II. Grodzins believes that, although the action was justified on grounds of national security, it was really motivated by political and economic considerations.

1767 ten Broek, Jacobus, et al. PREJUDICE, WAR AND THE CONSTITUTION: JAPANESE EVACUATION AND RESETTLEMENT. 1954. Reprint. Berkeley and Los Angeles: University of California Press, 1968. 424 p.

> The authors examine the removal of the Japanese Americans from legal, social, psychological, as well as historical points of view.

g. LABOR

1768 Seidman, Joel I. AMERICAN LABOR FROM DEFENSE TO RECONVERSION. Chicago: University of Chicago Press, 1953. 307 p.

> Seidman gives an account of the conduct of labor unions in the crisis of war during which time their ranks swelled because of war industries, as well as of the restraints placed on them by the Taft-Hartley Act of 1947.

1769 Weaver, Robert C. NEGRO LABOR: A NATIONAL PROBLEM. 1946. Reprint. Port Washington, N.Y.: Kennikat Press, 1969. 343 p.

> The problems of black labor in World War II and during peace-time reconversion. Weaver martials statistics to underline such problems as the inadequate vocational training available to blacks.

h. PACIFISM

Chatfield, C. FOR PEACE AND JUSTICE. See no. 1551.

1770 Sibley, Mulford Q., and Jacob, Philip E. CONSCRIPTION OF CON-SCIENCE: THE AMERICAN STATE AND THE CONSCIENTIOUS OBJEC-TOR, 1940-1947. Ithaca, N.Y.: Cornell University Press, 1952. 590 p. Charts.

> A detailed study that makes use of statistics. The authors, while sympathetic to conscientious objectors, maintain a balanced approach.

j. WARFARE

1771 Bradley, Omar N. A SOLDIER'S STORY. New York: Henry Holt, 1951. 638 p. Illus., ports., maps.

> Bradley's experiences in World War II, with all of the important battles and personalities crowding the book's pages. He is modest in regard to his own accomplishments and frank (but charitable) in regard to the actions of others.

1772 Chandler, Alfred D., Jr. THE PAPERS OF DWIGHT DAVID EISENHOW-ER: THE WAR YEARS. 5 vols. Baltimore: Johns Hopkins Press, 1970. Illus., fronts., ports., maps.

> General Eisenhower served as supreme commander of the Allied forces in Europe in World War II. The editor supplies notes on each item. Volume 5 is devoted to bibliography, maps, glossary, general index, and an essay on Eisenhower as a commander.

1773 Eisenhower, Dwight David. CRUSADE IN EUROPE. New York: Doubleday, 1948. 573 p. Illus., maps.

> The supreme commander's version of what happened in the European theatre in World War II. A simple, clear account which includes explanations of strategy and evaluations of the contributions of his military colleagues in the Allied forces.

1774 Greenfield, Kent R. AMERICAN STRATEGY IN WORLD WAR II: A RE-
CONSIDERATION. Baltimore: Johns Hopkins Press, 1963. 153 p.

In original form, the J.P. Young Lectures at Memphis
State University, 1962. The topics: Elements of Coalition Strategy, American and British Strategy: How
Much Did They Differ?, Franklin Roosevelt: Commander-
in-Chief, Air Power and Strategy.

1775 Hoyle, Martha Byrd. A WORLD IN FLAMES: A HISTORY OF WORLD
WAR II. New York: Atheneum, 1970. 377 p. Maps.

This popular history seeks to cover each significant battle
chronologically. The author includes a chronology,
and her narrative is complemented by the maps included.

1776 Morison, Samuel Eliot. HISTORY OF UNITED STATES NAVAL OPERA-
TIONS IN WORLD WAR II. 15 vols. Boston: Little, Brown, 1947-62.
Front., ports., plates, maps.

President Roosevelt agreed to Morison's suggestion that
he be allowed to witness naval actions with a view to
composition of this history. Roosevelt commissioned
Morison as a rear admiral and gave him a small staff.
This work covers every phase of the war and is in the
style for which Morison is noted.

1777 _____. THE TWO-OCEAN WAR: A SHORT HISTORY OF THE UNITED
STATES NAVY IN THE SECOND WORLD WAR. Boston: Little, Brown,
1963. 611 p. Illus.

A one-volume version of author's HISTORY OF UNITED
STATES NAVAL OPERATIONS IN WORLD WAR II,
q.v., no. 1776.

1778 Snyder, Louis L. THE WAR: A CONCISE HISTORY, 1939-1945. New
York: Julian Messner, 1960. 579 p. Illus., maps.

A popularly written chronicle of the war that traces
events on all fronts and gives lively sketches of the
leaders.

1779 Wilmot, Chester. THE STRUGGLE FOR EUROPE. New York: Harper &
Brothers, 1952. 766 p. Maps.

A book that presents both the political and military
strategies of the war. The author, an Australian with
personal experience in the war in Britain, presents a
full, well-written narrative of events from Dunkirk to
the surrender of Germany. Western Allies won the war,
but, he believes, the Soviet Union managed a political
victory in its dominance of eastern Europe.

1780 Wohlstetter, Roberta. PEARL HARBOR: WARNING AND DECISION. Stanford, Calif.: Stanford University Press, 1962. 426 p. Maps.

> The author believes that American officials had many signals that the Japanese planned to attack Pearl Harbor. She gives her analysis of why such intelligence did not lead to a correct interpretation of the situation.

3. Prominent Individuals

BERNARD BARUCH

1781 Baruch, Bernard M. BARUCH. 2 vols. New York: Holt, 1957-60. Illus., port.

> The autobiography of the financier, philanthropist, and public servant (chairman of the War Industries Board) which reveals a reasonable, considerate personality and contains insight on his contemporaries and the events through which he lived. Volume 1: MY OWN STORY; volume 2: THE PUBLIC YEARS.

1782 Coit, Margaret L. MR. BARUCH. Boston: Houghton Mifflin, 1957. 798 p. Port.

> A rich biography that reveals much of the man and of the period.

JAMES BYRNES

1783 Byrnes, James F. ALL IN ONE LIFETIME. New York: Harper & Brothers, 1958. 442 p. Illus.

> The personal reminiscences of a long-time public servant. Byrnes served in both branches of Congress, on the Supreme Court, in wartime positions in FDR's administration, as secretary of state under Truman, as governor of South Carolina. His book reveals much about the events and personalities of his time.

CORDELL HULL

1784 Hull, Cordell. MEMOIRS. 2 vols. New York: Macmillan, 1948. Port.

> A straightforward account by the congressman and senator from Tennessee and secretary of state from 1933 to 1944. He includes much detail. Particularly valuable for World War II years.

GEORGE C. MARSHALL

1785 Pogue, Forrest C. GEORGE C. MARSHALL. 3 vols. to date. New York: Viking Press, 1963- . Illus., ports., maps.

>   A series in progress. A biography of the general who served as both chief of staff during World War II and as secretary of state under Truman. Marshall emerges as a man of conscience and integrity. Volume 1: EDUCATION OF A GENERAL, 1880-1939; volume 2: ORDEAL AND HOPE, 1939-1942; volume 3: ORGANIZER OF VICTORY, 1943-1945.

FRANKLIN D. ROOSEVELT

1786 Burns, James MacGregor. ROOSEVELT: THE SOLDIER OF FREEDOM. New York: Harcourt Brace Jovanovich, 1970. 736 p. Illus., ports., plans.

>   A sequel to Burns's ROOSEVELT: THE LION AND THE FOX, q.v., no. 1711, this volume covers the period from the election of FDR to his third term in 1940 to his death in April 1945. Burns pictures Roosevelt as unwilling to relate long-term goals for peace to the immediate goals in war and is critical of his leadership in other ways as well. The book combines keen analysis of diplomatic issues with an appreciation of the human touches in FDR's life.

For other works on F.D. Roosevelt see the section on Prominent Individuals, 8,D,3.

HENRY L. STIMSON

1787 Morison, Elting E. TURMOIL AND TRADITION: A STUDY OF THE LIFE AND TIMES OF HENRY L. STIMSON. Boston: Houghton Mifflin, 1960. 686 p. Illus.

>   A study of the lawyer from New York who spent important years in service of the U.S. government as secretary of war in Taft's cabinet, as secretary of state under Hoover, and as secretary of war again under F.D. Roosevelt. A scholarly, appreciative biography that ties events in Stimson's life to the times in which he lived.

HENRY A. WALLACE

1788 Wallace, Henry A. THE PRICE OF VISION: THE DIARY OF HENRY A. WALLACE, 1942-1946. Edited by John M. Blum. Boston: Houghton

Mifflin, 1973. 717 p.

A frank account of Wallace's political experience in
the New and Fair Deal periods, with characterizations
of many leading personalities, including Franklin D.
Roosevelt and Harry S. Truman, and discussions of political machinations, war strategy, the Cold War, etc.
The editor provides a biographical sketch of Wallace.

Chapter 9

AMERICA SINCE THE SECOND WORLD WAR, 1945-75

A. DOMESTIC TURBULENCE AND CHANGE

1. General

1789 Brogan, D.W. AMERICA IN THE MODERN WORLD. New Brunswick, N.J.: Rutgers University Press, 1960. 117 p.

> A series of lectures delivered by the British historian of America at Rutgers University, 1959. Brogan deals with national character, American life, education--its pluses and minuses--and, especially, with U.S. competition with the Soviet Union.

1790 Brooks, John. GREAT LEAP: THE PAST TWENTY-FIVE YEARS IN AMERI-CA. New York: Harper & Row, 1966. 382 p. Illus.

> An extended essay analyzing the years 1939-64. Brooks considers 1939 as a watershed in American history, and he interprets the rapid change that has occurred nationally and internationally since then.

1791 Goldman, Eric F. THE CRUCIAL DECADE: AMERICA, 1945-1955. New York: Alfred A. Knopf, 1956. 298 p.

> Goldman, writing in a light manner, interprets a decade which he believes "crucial" because during that time Americans confirmed their intention to extend the welfare state and to continue the containment of the Communist nations. He often dwells on less important matters, however.

1792 Gunther, John. INSIDE U.S.A. New York: Harper & Brothers, 1947. 997 p. Maps, chart.

> An amazingly detailed account of the people and communities of the United States at the time of writing.

Gunther delves into state politics in depth, giving
sketches of the political leaders and descriptions of
problems facing the body politic. Lively, colorful
account.

1793 Lerner, Max. AMERICA AS A CIVILIZATION: LIFE AND THOUGHT IN
THE UNITED STATES TODAY. New York: Simon and Schuster, 1957.
1,051 p.

An attempt to capture the essence of America; an extensive work of interpretation dealing with history, government, economics, culture, etc.

2. Topical

a. BLACK AMERICANS AND CIVIL RIGHTS

1794 Boesel, David, and Rossi, Peter H., eds. CITIES UNDER SIEGE: AN
ANATOMY OF THE GHETTO RIOTS, 1964-1968. New York: Basic
Books, 1971. 447 p. Illus., tables.

A collection of articles. The editors have grouped the
material to present accounts of particular riots (such
as those in Newark and Los Angeles), reactions by public and government officials, and historical insight into
how the riots fit into a long-term pattern of violence in
America.

1795 Brink, William, and Harris, Louis. THE NEGRO REVOLUTION IN AMERI-
CA: WHAT NEGROES WANT, WHY AND HOW THEY ARE FIGHTING,
WHOM THEY SUPPORT, WHAT WHITES THINK OF THEM AND THEIR
DEMANDS. New York: Simon and Schuster, 1964. 250 p. Tables.

The authors summarize material gathered in a nationwide
survey conducted for NEWSWEEK magazine. The sample
consisted of a cross section of the population--12,000
blacks, 12,000 whites, from the North and the South.
Topics covered: education, housing, employment, voting, desegregation of facilities, etc.

1796 Broderick, Francis L., and Meier, August, eds. NEGRO PROTEST THOUGHT
IN THE TWENTIETH CENTURY. Indianapolis: Bobbs-Merrill, 1966. 486
p.

This selection of documents traces black thought through
its phases from accommodation to "the new militancy."

1797 Carmichael, Stokely, and Hamilton, Charles V. BLACK POWER: THE
POLITICS OF LIBERATION IN AMERICA. New York: Random House,
1967. 210 p.

Because the black man has been kept down by American whites, the authors insist that he must achieve a power base of his own, that only then can he stand on an equal footing with whites and cooperate with them. The book is strong on analysis of what is wrong, but weak on prescription for improvement.

1798 Drake, St. Clair, and Cayton, Horace R. BLACK METROPOLIS: A STUDY OF NEGRO LIFE IN A NORTHERN CITY. Rev. and enl. ed. 2 vols. New York: Harcourt, Brace & World, 1970. Illus., maps. Paperbound.

The life of the black man in south side Chicago, studied by a team of sociologists for a number of years. A keen, dispassionate analysis of the internal life of the "ghetto" and its external relations with the rest of the city. The original edition of this work appeared in 1945.

Handlin, Oscar. RACE AND NATIONALITY IN AMERICAN LIFE. See no. 359.

1799 Kesselman, Louis C. THE SOCIAL POLITICS OF FEPC: A STUDY IN REFORM PRESSURE MOVEMENTS. Chapel Hill: University of North Carolina Press, 1948. 270 p. Diagr.

A study of the Fair Employment Practices Commission, which played a pioneering role in increasing employment opportunities for blacks. Kesselman presents his work as a case study of what pressure groups can accomplish in a democratic society.

1800 King, Martin Luther, Jr. STRIDE TOWARD FREEDOM: THE MONTGOMERY STORY. New York: Harper & Brothers, 1958. 230 p. Illus.

The civil rights leader's account of the Alabama bus boycott by blacks over Jim Crow segregation practices in 1955-56. The event, an important milestone in black progress, is described in a relatively dispassionate narrative.

1801 _____. WHY WE CAN'T WAIT. New York: Harper & Row, 1964. 160 p. Illus., ports.

King recounts the story of the Birmingham demonstrations and the March on Washington and touches on such topics as racial discrimination, gradualism, the Black Muslims, and leadership of the civil rights movement.

1802 Lewis, Anthony, and the NEW YORK TIMES. PORTRAIT OF A DECADE: THE SECOND AMERICAN REVOLUTION. New York: Random House,

1964. 322 p.

The black struggle for civil rights from the Brown decision of the Supreme Court in 1954 to the Voting Rights
Act of 1964. An account by Anthony Lewis is supplemented with articles by twenty or so authors which appeared in the NEW YORK TIMES. Among the many
topics included: the Montgomery bus boycott, the
Meredith case at the University of Mississippi, and the
Little Rock public school problem.

1803 Lincoln, C. Eric. THE BLACK MUSLIMS IN AMERICA. Rev. ed. Boston: Beacon Press, 1973. 333 p.

An objective study by a black sociologist of the rise of
the black religious sect. Lincoln discusses the make-up
of the Muslim movement, its doctrine, leadership, and
goals. He believes their demand for a state separate
from whites is dangerous and that racial justice will
mitigate such tendencies.

1804 Lomax, Louis E. THE NEGRO REVOLT. New York: Harper & Row,
1962. 271 p.

Lomax places the civil rights protests and other manifestations of black discontent in historical context. He
explains those factors that brought about the change in
attitudes.

Miller, L. THE PETITIONERS. See no. 265.

1805 Myrdal, Gunnar, et al. AN AMERICAN DILEMMA: THE NEGRO PROB-
LEM AND MODERN DEMOCRACY. 1944. Reprint. New York: Harper
& Row, 1962. 1,483 p. Illus.

A study of the life of the black man in America by a
team of scholars headed by a Swedish social economist,
sponsored by the Carnegie Corporation. The treatment of
blacks in all areas of American life was measured against
the "American creed" in this objective work, which has
not been superseded. The original edition was in two
volumes.

1806 Silver, James W. MISSISSIPPI: THE CLOSED SOCIETY. Enl. ed. New
York: Harcourt, Brace & World, 1966. 404 p. Map, facsims.

A discussion of the explosive situation at the University
of Mississippi when, by court order, black James Meredith enrolled as a student. Silver, then a professor of
history at the university, described the rioting and the
nature of Mississippi society in this book, which was
first published in 1964.

1807 U.S. National Advisory Commission on Civil Disorders. REPORT OF THE
      NATIONAL ADVISORY COMMISSION ON CIVIL DISORDERS. New York:
      Bantam Books, 1968. 682 p. Illus., charts. Paperbound.

> The report of the commission appointed by President
> Johnson to study the causes of violent disruptions in
> urban areas includes descriptions of riots in a number
> of cities, traces development of racial ghettos, analyzes
> the condition of family life and the economics of the
> ghetto, and makes recommendations for a course of ac-
> tion. This edition has an introduction by Tom Wicker
> of the NEW YORK TIMES.

1808 Weaver, Robert C. THE NEGRO GHETTO. 1948. Reprint. New York:
      Russell & Russell, 1967. 422 p. Illus., maps.

> A sociological, analytical study of black segregation in
> northern housing. Weaver has amassed figures to prove
> his case.

b. BUSINESS AND ECONOMICS

1809 Chandler, Lester V. INFLATION IN THE UNITED STATES, 1940-1948.
      New York: Harper & Brothers, 1951. 413 p. Illus.

> Begins just before American entry into World War II and
> runs into the postwar years. Chandler observes the ef-
> fects of monetary, fiscal, and wage policies on the rate
> of inflation, as background to a consideration of public
> policy.

1810 Galbraith, John Kenneth. THE AFFLUENT SOCIETY. 2d rev. ed. Bos-
      ton: Houghton Mifflin, 1969. 365 p.

> An attack on the "conventional wisdom" in economics,
> which Galbraith believes out of place in today's world.
> The prevalence of these ideas has caused a concentra-
> tion on manufacture of goods and the creation of phoney
> demand instead of concentration on public services.

1811 _____. AMERICAN CAPITALISM: THE CONCEPT OF COUNTERVAILING
      POWER. Rev. ed. Boston: Houghton Mifflin, 1956. 208 p.

> In his usual clear and witty style the noted economist
> analyzes changes that have occurred since World War II
> to bring the United States in line with the economic
> views of John Maynard Keynes. Galbraith sees orga-
> nized labor as having gained the strength to countervail
> the influence of the large business corporation.

1812 Heller, Walter. NEW DIMENSIONS OF POLITICAL ECONOMY. Cambridge, Mass.: Harvard University Press, 1966. 212 p.

The Godkin Lectures at Harvard University, 1966. Heller, who had served as chairman of the Council of Economic Advisers, places great stress on the efficacy of fiscal policy in sustaining prosperity.

1813 Kolko, Gabriel. WEALTH AND POWER IN AMERICA: AN ANALYSIS OF SOCIAL CLASS AND INCOME DISTRIBUTION, 1962. Reprint. New York: Praeger, 1970. 192 p.

An attack on economists who have stated that income is more equally distributed than in past generations. Kolko gives evidence to show that the same disparities are present now as were in 1910. He discusses consequences in housing, health, education, etc.

1814 Vatter, Harold G. THE U.S. ECONOMY IN THE 1950'S: AN ECONOMIC HISTORY. New York: W.W. Norton, 1963. 308 p. Charts. Paperbound.

A study of the "economic contours" of what the author considers a significant decade. He sets the fifties into the context of American economic history and then examines its distinctive features, trying to isolate those factors, such as government spending, that stimulated economic growth.

c. ECOLOGY

1815 Commoner, Barry. THE CLOSING CIRCLE: NATURE, MAN, AND TECHNOLOGY. New York: Alfred A. Knopf, 1971. 336 p.

The pollution of the environment is explained in all of its aspects and ramifications. Commoner deals with poisoning of air, water, and earth. In addition, he spells out the consequences for genetics of atomic fallout. He calls for a reordering of industrial priorities.

d. FEMINISM

1816 Cassara, Beverly Benner, ed. AMERICAN WOMEN: THE CHANGING IMAGE. Boston: Beacon Press, 1962. 157 p.

An early contribution to the revived concern for women's position in American society, this collection brings together the views of prominent women professionals--including Pearl S. Buck, Agnes De Mille, Margaret Mead, and Agnes E. Meyer--who discuss the stresses, strains, and accomplishments possible for women in the male-dominated professional world.

1817 Firestone, Shulamith. THE DIALECTIC OF SEX: THE CASE FOR FEMI-
NIST REVOLUTION. New York: William Morrow, 1970. 274 p.

A radical critique of present-day society and a prescription for utopia. Firestone would replace the present
family, do away with labor, and free people to indulge
in all forms of sexuality. In the process of formulating
her own views, she disputes Marx and Freud, among
others.

1818 Friedan, Betty. THE FEMININE MYSTIQUE. New York: W.W. Norton,
1974. 410 p.

A significant book in the new feminist movement, first
published in 1963. The author, using popular women's
magazines of the 1950s, demonstrates that the ideal
woman has been pictured as a housewife whose major
concern is her children and making herself sexually at-
tractive to her husband. Friedan believes this insidious
image cut the ground from under the progress women had
made from the time of the suffrage movement and, instead of bringing personal fulfillment, has created mal-
aise.

1819 Millett, Kate. SEXUAL POLITICS. Garden City, N.Y.: Doubleday,
1970. 405 p.

An analysis of literature and other aspects of what the
author considers a male chauvinist society. She analyzes explicit sexual themes in literature to demonstrate
that women have been held in subjection by men.

1820 Morgan, Robin, ed. SISTERHOOD IS POWERFUL: AN ANTHOLOGY OF
WRITINGS FROM THE WOMEN'S LIBERATION MOVEMENT. New York:
Random House, 1970. 644 p. Illus.

This collection demonstrates wide-ranging concern for
the place of women in America. The authors come from
all areas of the society. Among the many topics is discrimination against women in the professions, such as
law, medicine, publishing, psychology, religion.

O'Neill, W.L. EVERYONE WAS BRAVE. See no. 330.

e. GOVERNMENT AND POLITICS

i. General

1821 Anderson, Patrick. THE PRESIDENT'S MEN: WHITE HOUSE ASSISTANTS
OF FRANKLIN D. ROOSEVELT, HARRY S. TRUMAN, DWIGHT D. EISEN-

HOWER, JOHN F. KENNEDY, AND LYNDON B. JOHNSON. Garden City, N.Y.: Doubleday, 1968. 428 p.

> Discusses the role of the men around the president in the executive branch, using many examples. Anderson, who was in a similar position, describes their relations with the chief executive, Congress, the press, and the bureaucracy. Based partly on interviews.

1822 Bell, Daniel. THE END OF IDEOLOGY: ON THE EXHAUSTION OF POLITICAL IDEAS IN THE FIFTIES. Glencoe, Ill.: Free Press, 1960. 416 p.

> A collection of articles by the sociologist and journalist, a former labor editor of FORTUNE, in which many of the pieces were first published, 1948-58. Topics include the ruling class, crime, socialism, ideology and the failure of Marxism.

1823 Burns, James MacGregor. THE DEADLOCK OF DEMOCRACY: FOUR-PARTY POLITICS IN AMERICA. Englewood Cliffs, N.J.: Prentice-Hall, 1963. 388 p.

> Diagnosis and prescription for U.S. political ills. Burns believes each of the two major parties is split into presidential and congressional wings, making, in fact, four parties. He traces the problem historically to its roots and gives advice as to how the two parties may be made whole.

_____. PRESIDENTIAL GOVERNMENT. See no. 334.

1824 Campbell, Angus, et al. THE AMERICAN VOTER. New York: Wiley, 1960. 581 p. Tables, diagrs.

> From the staff of the Survey Research Center, University of Michigan. The authors give a profile of the American voter and tell how he behaves and why, based on questionnaires and other statistical materials.

1825 Carr, Robert K. THE HOUSE COMMITTEE ON UN-AMERICAN ACTIVITIES, 1945-1950. Ithaca, N.Y.: Cornell University Press, 1952. 502 p.

> A dispassionate account of the very controversial committee, by a professor of law and political science. He uses the committee's records to substantiate his analysis.

1826 Key, V.O., Jr. POLITICS, PARTIES, AND PRESSURE GROUPS. 5th ed. New York: Crowell, 1964. 751 p. Illus., maps, diagrs.

> An examination of the interplay of interest groups, poli-

ticians, and citizens at the polls. Key looks at formal
party organization but stresses that this is only one of
many aspects of the political process.

1827 Mills, C. Wright. THE POWER ELITE. 1956. Reprint. New York: Oxford University Press, 1963. 423 p.

An argumentative analysis of American society by a
sociologist. Mills is highly critical of the power structure of the country. Among the groups with which he
deals are the politicians, the "warlords," and the very
wealthy.

1828 Neustadt, Richard E. PRESIDENTIAL POWER: THE POLITICS OF LEAD-
ERSHIP. New York: Wiley, 1960. 224 p. Illus.

Attempts to show how presidents gain and use power,
through a series of case studies. Neustadt uses the
F.D. Roosevelt, Truman, and Eisenhower administrations
as examples. He himself had served in the first two.

1829 Rossiter, Clinton L. PARTIES AND POLITICS IN AMERICA. Ithaca,
N.Y.: Cornell University Press, 1960. 212 p.

Originally a series of lectures at Cornell University in
1960. Rossiter examines the emergence of two parties
in U.S. history and then analyzes the Republicans and
the Democrats, showing what they stand for and trends
developing in each group. A lively account.

1830 Scammon, Richard M., and Wattenberg, Ben J. THE REAL MAJORITY.
New York: Coward-McCann, 1970. 348 p. Illus.

A discussion of recent elections, with a heavy accent
on the results of political polls. The authors try to
determine true concerns of American voters and give
advice to those who may be candidates in 1976.

1831 Shannon, David A. THE DECLINE OF AMERICAN COMMUNISM: A
HISTORY OF THE COMMUNIST PARTY OF THE UNITED STATES SINCE
1945. 1959. Reprint. Chatham, N.J.: Chatham, 1971. 438 p.

Shannon traces the declining fortunes of the Communist
party from its high point at the close of World War II.
His work is based on a thorough study of the sources.
Sponsored by the Fund for the Republic, it is designed
as a sequel to Theodore Draper's ROOTS OF AMERICAN
COMMUNISM, q.v., no. 1585.

1832 Sundquist, James L. POLITICS AND POLICY: THE EISENHOWER, KEN-
NEDY, AND JOHNSON YEARS. Washington, D.C.: Brookings Institution,

1968. 568 p. Illus.

A study of policy making and what Sundquist sees as an alternation of creative and relatively inactive phases in the operations of the U.S. government. He looks particularly at issues prominent in the years 1953-67: unemployment, poverty, civil rights, education, health care, and ecology.

1833 Tugwell, Rexford Guy. OFF COURSE: FROM TRUMAN TO NIXON. New York: Praeger, 1971. 336 p.

With the perspective of a member of FDR's "Brains Trust," Tugwell measures the performance of Truman, Eisenhower, Kennedy, and Nixon in the presidency; he holds that they all fail to measure up to Roosevelt. Tugwell is convinced, for instance, that FDR would have avoided the Cold War and pursued a policy of coexistence.

1834 Wagner, Susan. THE FEDERAL TRADE COMMISSION. New York: Praeger, 1971. 268 p. Illus., ports., charts.

The author examines the FTC to see how effective it has been. She covers the organization of the agency (established in 1914); certain specific problems with which it has had to contend, such as restraints of trade, mergers, deceptive practices, false advertising and the rise of "consumerism."

1835 Willoughby, William R. THE ST. LAWRENCE WATERWAY: A STUDY IN POLITICS AND DIPLOMACY. Madison: University of Wisconsin Press, 1961. 381 p. Illus.

The author traces the two-hundred-year-old debate as to the desirability of deepening the St. Lawrence to make it navigable to the Great Lakes, explaining the motivations of contending interest groups and obstructionists. The engineering problems proved easier to overcome than the opposition and the seaway was opened in 1959. Based on extensive archival research.

ii. Truman Administration

1836 Bernstein, Barton J., ed. POLITICS AND POLICIES OF THE TRUMAN ADMINISTRATION. Chicago: Quadrangle Books, 1970. 330 p.

A series of articles by revisionist historians of the "New Left" who are highly critical of Truman on domestic and foreign policies. For instance, he is saddled with responsibility for starting the Cold War. The authors are Lloyd Gardner, David Green, Thomas Paterson, Athan Theoharis, and the editor.

1837 Bernstein, Barton J., and Matusow, Allen J., eds. THE TRUMAN AD-
MINISTRATION: A DOCUMENTARY HISTORY. New York: Harper &
Row, 1966. 526 p. Illus., ports.

An excellent selection of documents illustrating problems
confronted by the Truman administration. The papers
range from excerpts from diaries and private papers of
prominent figures to official documents, with brief com-
mentaries by the editors.

1838 Freeland, Richard M. THE TRUMAN DOCTRINE AND THE ORIGINS OF
McCARTHYISM: FOREIGN POLICY, DOMESTIC POLITICS, AND INTER-
NAL SECURITY, 1946-1948. New York: Alfred A. Knopf, 1972. 444
p.

The author seeks to show that the Truman administration
fanned the fires of anticommunism in order to build support for economic aid to Europe under the Marshall Plan.
This set the scene for the emergence of McCarthyism.

1839 Phillips, Cabell. THE TRUMAN PRESIDENCY: THE HISTORY OF A TRI-
UMPHANT SUCCESSION. New York: Macmillan, 1966. 476 p.

An analysis of Truman that discusses both his strengths
and weaknesses as chief executive. Phillips touches on
the important problems he confronted and ranks him high
on the list of American presidents.

1840 Ross, Irwin. THE LONELIEST CAMPAIGN: THE TRUMAN VICTORY OF
1948. New York: New American Library, 1968. 312 p. Illus., ports.

An account of Truman's upset victory over Thomas Dewey. Ross traces the campaign strategy step by step and
gives reasons for the unexpected result.

1841 Schmidt, Karl M. HENRY A. WALLACE: QUIXOTIC CRUSADE, 1948.
Syracuse, N.Y.: Syracuse University Press, 1960. 362 p. Illus.

An analytical study of the presidential campaign of 1948
in which Henry Wallace ran as candidate of the short-
lived Progressive party. Schmidt discusses Wallace's
break with Truman and all aspects of his attempt to win
the presidency.

1842 Theoharis, Athan G. SEEDS OF REPRESSION: HARRY S. TRUMAN AND
THE ORIGINS OF McCARTHYISM. Chicago: Quadrangle Books, 1971.
249 p.

Theoharis sees President Truman's policies, which sought
total victory of the West over communism and total security against an internal Communist menace, as responsible
for the state of mind that led to McCarthyism. Examines.

in detail the Yalta agreements, the loyalty program, and other aspects of the period. Theoharis has made extensive use of the papers in the Truman Library.

iii. Eisenhower Administration

1843 Albertson, Dean, ed. EISENHOWER AS PRESIDENT. New York: Hill and Wang, 1963. 192 p.

A collection of articles by participants in, and observers of, the Eisenhower administration, dealing with politics, administration, atomic energy, the economy, etc. Eisenhower's "farewell address" is also included.

1844 Branyan, Robert L., and Larsen, Lawrence H., eds. THE EISENHOWER ADMINISTRATION, 1953-1961: A DOCUMENTARY HISTORY. 2 vols. New York: Random House, 1971.

A large collection of primary materials, many drawn from the Dwight D. Eisenhower Library. The editors have included documents on the major issues of the time, introducing each section with comments that place the materials in context.

1845 Eulau, Heinz. CLASS AND PARTY IN THE EISENHOWER YEARS: CLASS ROLES AND PERSPECTIVES IN THE 1952 AND 1956 ELECTIONS. New York: Free Press of Glencoe, 1962. 162 p.

The political behavior of voters in the two presidential races of Eisenhower and Stevenson. The interplay of class and party affiliation is analyzed on the basis of national samples.

1846 Hughes, Emmet J. THE ORDEAL OF POWER: A POLITICAL MEMOIR OF THE EISENHOWER YEARS. New York: Atheneum, 1963. 372 p.

Hughes spent over two years with Eisenhower as speech writer before disagreements over policy led him to resign. This is a very frank--some think indiscreet--account of that period. Among other complaints, he laments the fact that the president left foreign policy too much in the hands of Secretary Dulles and that he failed to make over the Republican party.

1847 Lubell, Samuel. THE REVOLT OF THE MODERATES. New York: Harper & Brothers, 1956. 308 p. Illus.

A political commentator's analysis of moderate views among the middle class electorate during the Eisenhower period. Lubell gathered his information by spending much time traveling across the country and visiting the people of whom he writes.

1848 Thomson, Charles A.H., and Shattuck, Frances M. THE 1956 PRESIDEN-TIAL CAMPAIGN. Washington, D.C.: Brookings Institution, 1960. 397 p. Tables.

A systematic analysis of the second presidential race between Eisenhower and Stevenson which also has value because it shows the process by which nominating con-ventions choose candidates and how campaigns are run.

iv. Kennedy Administration

1849 Manchester, William. THE DEATH OF A PRESIDENT, NOVEMBER 20-NOVEMBER 25, 1963. New York: Harper & Row, 1967. 726 p. Maps, plans.

An account of the assassination of President John F. Kennedy by a friend of the family. An emotional ac-count which depends on much oral material.

1850 Schlesinger, Arthur M., Jr. A THOUSAND DAYS: JOHN F. KENNEDY IN THE WHITE HOUSE. Boston: Houghton Mifflin, 1965. 1,102 p.

The account of a historian who served as a special as-sistant to the president. As such it is more a personal account than an objective history, but it gives informa-tion and insight on the main events of the time and the personalities who made up the administration.

1851 U.S. President's Commission on the Assassination of President Kennedy. INVESTIGATION OF THE ASSASSINATION OF PRESIDENT JOHN F. KENNEDY: HEARINGS BEFORE THE PRESIDENT'S COMMISSION ON THE ASSASSINATION OF PRESIDENT KENNEDY. 26 vols. Washington, D.C.: Government Printing Office, 1964. Illus., ports., maps, facsims.

A massive compilation of the hearings held by the War-ren Commission and the exhibits and evidence considered by it.

1852 _____. REPORT OF THE PRESIDENT'S COMMISSION ON THE ASSAS-SINATION OF PRESIDENT JOHN F. KENNEDY. WASHINGTON, D.C.: Government Printing Office, 1964. 912 p. Illus., ports., maps, facsims.

The official report of the commission headed by Chief Justice Earl Warren. It sets forth in detail analysis of evidence which led it to conclude that the assassin was Lee Harvey Oswald acting alone.

1853 _____. REPORT OF THE WARREN COMMISSION ON THE ASSASSINA-
TION OF PRESIDENT KENNEDY. New York: Bantam Books, 1964. 766
p. Illus., ports. Paperbound.

> This version of the Warren Commission report includes
> an introduction by Harrison E. Salisbury and materials
> by other reporters of the NEW YORK TIMES.

1854 White, Theodore H. THE MAKING OF THE PRESIDENT, 1960. New
York: Atheneum, 1961. 400 p.

> The author spent much time traveling with the entour-
> ages of Kennedy, Nixon, and five other presidential as-
> pirants, studying their campaign styles and organizations.
> White conveys the color of the campaign and gives his
> analysis of the meaning of the results.

v. Johnson Administration

1855 Goldman, Eric F. THE TRAGEDY OF LYNDON JOHNSON. New York:
Alfred A. Knopf, 1969. 564 p.

> The author served briefly (1963-66) in the Johnson ad-
> ministration as academic intellectual-in-residence. This
> book is partly concerned with his own experience and
> partly an evaluation of LBJ's record in office. Vanity
> and Vietnam, he believes to be among the causes for
> Johnson's loss of esteem among the people. He includes
> many anecdotes.

1856 Johnson, Lyndon B. THE VANTAGE POINT: PERSPECTIVES OF THE
PRESIDENCY, 1963-1969. New York: Holt, Rinehart and Winston, 1971.
646 p. Illus., ports., maps.

> Johnson's recounting of his years in the presidency,
> stressing the accomplishments he considered most impor-
> tant: civil rights legislation, the "War on Poverty" and
> other social programs, space exploration, and foreign
> affairs. He has kept his down-to-earth sense of humor
> in severe check in this account.

1857 White, Theodore H. THE MAKING OF THE PRESIDENT, 1964. New
York: Atheneum, 1965. 442 p.

> The Johnson-Goldwater campaign is recounted, beginning
> with the assassination of Kennedy. White explains how
> the Goldwater faction captured the Republican nomina-
> tion and then follows the campaign step by step, showing
> the importance of such questions as civil rights, and
> whose finger would be on the "nuclear button."

vi. Nixon Administration

1858 Bernstein, Carl, and Woodward, Bob. ALL THE PRESIDENT'S MEN. New York: Simon and Schuster, 1974. 349 p. Ports.

> The account of how the involvement of Nixon's staff and others in the Watergate cover-up was uncovered by the men who did it as reporters for the WASHINGTON POST. A revealing account of intrigue in the Federal City.

1859 Evans, Rowland, Jr., and Novak, Robert D. NIXON IN THE WHITE HOUSE: THE FRUSTRATION OF POWER. New York: Random House, 1971. 440 p.

> An appraisal of Nixon's presidency in the pre-Watergate period. The authors, a team of newspaper columnists, deal primarily with domestic matters, in which they see Nixon as not having performed very well, and less with foreign affairs, where they think he did better.

1860 McGinnis, Joe. SELLING THE PRESIDENT, 1968. New York: Trident Press, 1969. 254 p.

> McGinnis accompanied Nixon and his public relations firm as an observer and reports on how techniques designed to sell soap and other products on television were applied to the "selling" of the candidate. He includes examples of scripts used.

1861 U.S. House. IMPEACHMENT OF RICHARD M. NIXON, PRESIDENT OF THE UNITED STATES: THE FINAL REPORT OF THE COMMITTEE ON THE JUDICIARY, PETER W. RODINO, CHAIRMAN. New York: Viking Press, 1975. 783 p.

> The proceedings of the House Judiciary Committee that voted to recommend impeachment of President Nixon are reviewed in this report, which lists the impeachable offenses and gives evidence for the charges made. An introduction is supplied by R.W. Apple, Jr., of the NEW YORK TIMES.

1862 White, Theodore H. THE MAKING OF THE PRESIDENT, 1968. New York: Atheneum, 1969. 472 p. Maps.

> The contest between Richard Nixon and Hubert Humphrey, with George Wallace and his American Independent party and the Peace party also in the race. This was the year of violence in the streets of Chicago during the Democratic convention, the disaffection of the followers of Senator Eugene McCarthy, the assassination of Robert F.

Kennedy, a turbulent period put in perspective by a
noted political analyst.

1863 _____. THE MAKING OF THE PRESIDENT, 1972. New York: Atheneum, 1973. 411 p. Maps.

Another in the series of analyses of presidential elections
by a noted political commentator. White discusses the
campaigns of Nixon, McGovern, Humphrey, Wallace,
Lindsay, and Muskie, and touches on the first revela-
tions concerning the break-in at headquarters of the
Democratic party at the Watergate.

1864 Wills, Garry. NIXON AGONISTES: THE CRISIS OF THE SELF-MADE
MAN. Boston: Houghton Mifflin, 1970. 632 p.

Wills sees Nixon as the last product of the classical
liberalism which promoted the virtues of the self-made
man. Nixon is just one of many targets in this book
of unrelenting criticism of current politicians and their
rhetoric.

f. INDIANS

1865 Deloria, Vine, Jr. CUSTER DIED FOR YOUR SINS: AN INDIAN MANI-
FESTO. New York: Macmillan, 1969. 280 p.

A catalogue of the white man's sins of omission and
commission against the Indian. Deloria, with great wit,
tries to set the white straight on a number of the mis-
understandings he has concerning the red man.

g. INTELLECTUAL AND SOCIAL LIFE

Atkinson, Brooks. BROADWAY. See no. 248.

Barnouw, Erik. HISTORY OF BROADCASTING. Vol. 3. See no. 291.

1866 Berman, Ronald. AMERICA IN THE SIXTIES: AN INTELLECTUAL HIS-
TORY. New York: Free Press, 1968. 300 p.

Despite the title, the book is concerned only with certain aspects of intellectual history in the sixties. Using
many quotations, Berman concentrates primarily on the
attitudes and rhetoric of journals on the left of the political spectrum.

1867 Boorstin, Daniel J. THE IMAGE: OR, WHAT HAPPENED TO THE AMERI-
CAN DREAM. New York: Atheneum, 1962. 315 p.

A historian's criticism of the products of the "graphic revolution." Boorstin believes that Madison Avenue advertising men, television, and motion pictures have created an illusory world, a world of "pseudo-events," of which Americans have become captive. He concludes his jeremiad with some hints on how Americans may save themselves.

1868 Gordon, Milton M. ASSIMILATION IN AMERICAN LIFE: THE ROLE OF RACE, RELIGION AND NATIONAL ORIGINS. New York: Oxford University Press, 1964. 276 p.

An analysis of a culturally pluralistic society. Gordon denies that America is a melting pot; rather, he holds that it is made up of many "subsocieties" that have accommodated to the "core" society of Anglo-Saxon, Protestant, middle-class values while maintaining identities of their own.

1869 Herberg, Will. PROTESTANT, CATHOLIC, JEW: AN ESSAY IN AMERICAN RELIGIOUS SOCIOLOGY. Rev. ed. Garden City, N.Y.: Doubleday, 1960. 309 p. Paperbound.

Herberg sets forth his view that transcending the differences among the major religious faiths is a national faith to which all subscribe. He discusses the development of all three groups and their changing attitudes.

1870 Johnson, Walter, and Colligan, Francis J. THE FULBRIGHT PROGRAM: A HISTORY. Chicago: University of Chicago Press, 1965. 396 p.

The international exchange of scholars under the Fulbright-Hays Act is explained and evaluated. The authors give the legislative history of the program and show how it has been implemented in the various participating countries. (They served, respectively, as chairman and executive secretary of the board that initially implemented the program.) A foreword by Senator J. William Fulbright is included.

1871 King, Rufus. THE DRUG HANGUP: AMERICA'S FIFTY-YEAR FOLLY. New York: W.W. Norton, 1972. 396 p.

A thorough analysis of American attitudes toward narcotics and the government's increasingly repressive campaigns to cope with their use. King covers legislation, law enforcement, and agency organization. He believes the basic approach has been misguided.

1872 Mills, C. Wright. WHITE COLLAR: THE AMERICAN MIDDLE CLASSES. New York: Oxford University Press, 1951. 398 p.

In this sociological analysis dealing with the "new middle classes," Mills makes use of statistical data and his own observation and discusses in turn the place of managers, teachers, secretaries, nurses, salesgirls, insurance agents, receptionists, and lawyers in American society. His observations are often pungent, not to say biting.

1873 Packard, Vance O. THE HIDDEN PERSUADERS. New York: David McKay, 1957. 276 p.

Popular sociology. Packard is concerned with motivational research and how it is used, or misused, in advertising, and other methods used to persuade Americans to buy.

Richard, Jerry, ed. THE GOOD LIFE. See no. 970.

1874 Riesman, David, et al. THE LONELY CROWD: A STUDY OF THE CHANGING AMERICAN CHARACTER. Abr. ed. New Haven, Conn.: Yale University Press, 1961. 315 p. Paperbound.

A study of American character types. Riesman divides the population into inner-directed, other-directed, and autonomous individuals, seeing them as products of change in population, society, and technology. This edition contains a new foreword.

1875 Rosenberg, Bernard, and White, David M., eds. MASS CULTURE: THE POPULAR ARTS IN AMERICA. Glencoe, Ill.: Free Press, 1957. 561 p.

An anthology of pieces by social scientists, literary critics, journalists, and art critics viewing all phases of mass culture, from broadcasting to comic books.

1876 Tiedt, Sidney W. THE ROLE OF THE FEDERAL GOVERNMENT IN EDUCATION. New York: Oxford University Press, 1966. 253 p.

An analysis by an educator of the national government's increasing support of, and involvement in, education, and the problems posed to state and local governments as a result.

Weiss, Richard. AMERICAN MYTH OF SUCCESS. See no. 246.

1877 Whyte, William H. THE ORGANIZATION MAN. New York: Simon and Schuster, 1956. 429 p. Illus.

An analysis of the men and women who devote their careers to the organization and, after hours, drive or ride to suburbia. Whyte sees many areas of American

life taking on the form of the complex business organization, including education, medicine, the foundations,
and the church. He interprets such a development as
a threat to the quality of life.

h. LABOR

1878 Dayton, Eldorous L. WALTER REUTHER: THE AUTOCRAT OF THE BAR-
GAINING TABLE. New York: Devin-Adair, 1958. 280 p.

A journalist's highly critical account of the life of the
then President of the United Auto Workers and vice president of the AFL-CIO. Dayton analyzed Reuther's tendencies as socialistic and thought that he and his counterparts in Europe were capable of disrupting the economy of the West by strikes and inflation.

1879 Lee, R. Alton. TRUMAN AND TAFT-HARTLEY: A QUESTION OF MAN-
DATE. Lexington: University of Kentucky Press, 1966. 264 p.

A study of the Taft-Hartley labor law and the political
issue it became in the 1948 election. Despite Truman's
victory, he was unable to fulfill his pledge to organized
labor to repeal the law because of a conservative Republican and Southern Democratic coalition in Congress.
Lee analyzes these related problems.

1880 Millis, Harry A., and Brown, Emily C. FROM THE WAGNER ACT TO
TAFT-HARTLEY: A STUDY OF NATIONAL LABOR POLICY AND LABOR
RELATIONS. Chicago: University of Chicago Press, 1950. 734 p.

The evolution of U.S. labor legislation, with particular
emphasis on the Taft-Hartley Act (1947). The authors
give an exposition of its features in detail and outline
the impact it is expected to have on organized labor.

1881 Mills, C. Wright, and Schneider, Helen. THE NEW MEN OF POWER:
AMERICA'S LABOR LEADERS. New York: Harcourt, Brace, 1948. 323
p.

This account by sociologists provides a collective portrait, to a great extent based on statistical materials
(500 questionnaires). Deals with who made up labor
leadership, their patterns of thought, and their aspirations for labor and the country.

j. LITERATURE

1882 Baldwin, James. THE FIRE NEXT TIME. New York: Dial Press, 1963.
120 p.

A collection of essays which deals largely with the
relationship of blacks to whites in America. Baldwin
rejects the separation advocated by such groups as the
Black Muslims, contending the two groups need each
other.

1883 _____. NOTES OF A NATIVE SON. 1955. Reprint. Boston: Beacon
Press, 1968. 175 p. Paperbound.

A series of essays on the black man and Baldwin's own
life as an author, penetrating and at times bitter concerning the indignities heaped upon the Afro-American
by both friends and enemies.

1884 Brooks, Cleanth. WILLIAM FAULKNER: THE YOKNAPATAWPHA COUN-
TRY. New Haven, Conn.: Yale University Press, 1963. 513 p. Map.

A book of criticism and interpretation. Brooks examines
Faulkner's novels in light of the types of southerners who
inhabit his pages: yeoman farmers, sharecroppers, white
trash, et al. He deals both with Faulkner's major and
minor works.

1885 Eisinger, Chester E. FICTION IN THE FORTIES. Chicago: University
of Chicago Press, 1963. 392 p.

Places authors of the period in a political and intellectual framework. Eisinger covers the war novel, the
naturalistic novel, the search for identity, and liberal
and conservative approaches. Among the many persons
with whom he deals: Algren, Bellow, Capote, Cozzens,
Dos Passos, Faulkner, Hemingway, Mailer, McCarthy,
McCullers, Schulberg, Steinbeck, Warren, Welty.

k. McCARTHYISM

1886 Cooke, Alistair. A GENERATION ON TRIAL: U.S.A. V. ALGER HISS.
New York: A. Knopf, 1950. 370 p.

Cooke covered the Hiss trials for the GUARDIAN of
Manchester, England. This account depends heavily
on court transcripts. He also deals with Hiss's appear-
ance before the House Committee on Un-American Activities and is quite critical of its procedures. Cooke
writes with a humorous touch, although he does not make
light of the tragedy implicit in the confrontation of Hiss
and Whittaker Chambers.

Hyman, Harold M. TO TRY MEN'S SOULS. See no. 343.

1887 Latham, Earl. THE COMMUNIST CONTROVERSY IN WASHINGTON: FROM THE NEW DEAL TO McCARTHY. Cambridge, Mass.: Harvard University Press, 1966. 454 p.

> A clear, objective account of the debate over possible infiltration of the American government by Communists. Latham covers the early congressional hearings on the subject, Communist party activity in the government, and congressional attempts to determine whether Communists influenced American policy in China. Latham concludes that, while Communists were present in the government, their influence was insignificant.

Lipset, Seymour M., and Raab, Earl. POLITICS OF UNREASON. See no. 346.

1888 Rogin, Michael P. THE INTELLECTUALS AND MCCARTHY: THE RADICAL SPECTER. Cambridge, Mass.: MIT Press, 1967. 378 p. Illus., maps.

> Rogin attempts to dispute those interpreters who have seen McCarthyism as akin to populism and progressivism. He attempts to disprove the theory on the basis of voting patterns in the Midwest and other data. McCarthyism, he thinks, was fed by the right wing of the Republican party.

1889 Rorty, James, and Decter, Moshe. McCARTHY AND THE COMMUNISTS. Boston: Beacon Press, 1954. 172 p.

> An examination of the aims and methods of Senator Joseph R. McCarthy of Wisconsin in his campaign against alleged Communist infiltration of the State Department. The authors attempt to maintain a dispassionate tone.

1890 Rovere, Richard H. SENATOR JOE McCARTHY. New York: Harcourt, Brace, 1959. 280 p.

> This biography of the senator gives much insight into the workings of the American political structure and how McCarthy used it for his ends. Rovere concludes that McCarthy was an unprincipled demagogue.

I. MEXICAN-AMERICANS

1891 Grebler, Leo, et al. THE MEXICAN-AMERICAN PEOPLE: THE NATION'S SECOND LARGEST MINORITY. New York: Free Press, 1970. 795 p. Illus.

> An exhaustive sociological, economic, and political study of a "forgotten minority."

m. POVERTY

1892 Coles, Robert. CHILDREN OF CRISIS. 3 vols. to date. Boston: Little, Brown, 1967- . Illus.

> An intriguing and informative study of lower class blacks and whites in southern society by a research psychiatrist. Coles makes extensive use of tape-recorded interviews. Volume 1: A STUDY OF COURAGE AND FEAR; volume 2: MIGRANTS, SHARECROPPERS, MOUNTAINEERS; volume 3: THE SOUTH GOES NORTH.

1893 Donovan, John C. THE POLITICS OF POVERTY. New York: Pegasus, 1967. 172 p. Illus.

> A review of the drafting of the Economic Opportunity Act of 1964 and the widespread optimism and expectation created by the Johnson administration's rhetoric. Donovan points out that LBJ lost interest in the "War on Poverty" when he was prosecuting the war in Vietnam.

1894 Harrington, Michael. THE OTHER AMERICA: POVERTY IN THE UNITED STATES. New York: Macmillan, 1962. 192 p.

> A study of pockets of poverty in the midst of an affluent society. Harrington discusses in turn the dire plight of migrant workers, those who have failed as industrial workers, the aged, and others. He believes the problems so great that only the federal government can meet them. A progenitor of President Johnson's "War on Poverty."

1895 Levitan, Sar A. THE GREAT SOCIETY'S POOR LAW: A NEW APPROACH TO POVERTY. Baltimore: Johns Hopkins Press, 1969. 362 p. Illus.

> An analysis of the "War on Poverty" in its various forms under the Office of Economic Opportunity. Levitan shows the strengths and weaknesses of the Community Action Program, Head Start, Upward Bound, Vista, Neighborhood Youth Corps, and programs in community health, legal services, birth control, and aid to rural poor, migrant workers, and Indians.

1896 Wilcox, Clair. TOWARD SOCIAL WELFARE: AN ANALYSIS OF PROGRAMS AND PROPOSALS ATTACKING POVERTY, INSECURITY, AND INEQUALITY OF OPPORTUNITY. Homewood, Ill.: R.D. Irwin, 1969. 416 p.

> An economist's study of various efforts to eradicate poverty in the United States, a task he believes can be

accomplished. Wilcox discusses school desegregation,
open housing, fair employment practices, Medicare,
Social Security, aid to families with dependent children,
urban renewal, job programs, etc.

n. SPACE EXPLORATION

1897 Odishaw, Hugh, ed. THE EARTH IN SPACE. New York: Basic Books,
1967. 352 p.

Originally a series of lectures on the Voice of America.
Scientists touch on various aspects of their work in astro-
nomy, astrophysics, and geophysics. A glossary of technical terms is included.

1898 Sullivan, Walter, ed. AMERICA'S RACE FOR THE MOON: THE NEW
YORK TIMES STORY OF PROJECT APOLLO. New York: Random House,
1962. 164 p. Illus., front.

This collection of pieces on the Apollo Project, by
scientists and journalists, covers various aspects of the
venture. The volume is well illustrated.

1899 Von Braun, Wernher, and Ordway, Frederick. HISTORY OF ROCKETRY
AND SPACE TRAVEL. Rev. ed. New York: Crowell, 1969. Illus.,
ports., tables.

Places rocketry and space travel in the context of centuries of aspiration by mankind and then proceeds to
developments in this century, carrying the story to 1966.
Written in layman's language and profusely illustrated.

o. STUDENT PROTEST AND THE COUNTERCULTURE

1900 Cohen, Mitchell, and Hale, Dennis, eds. THE NEW STUDENT LEFT: AN
ANTHOLOGY. Boston: Beacon Press, 1966. 320 p.

Student writings, 1959-69, critical of the universities,
politics, the economic system. The articles originated
in the Student Nonviolent Coordinating Committee, Students for a Democratic Society, the Northern Student
Movement, and in magazines of the "movement."

1901 Lipset, Seymour M., and Wolin, Sheldon S., eds. THE BERKELEY STU-
DENT REVOLT: FACTS AND INTERPRETATIONS. Garden City, N.Y.:
Anchor Books, 1965. 599 p. Paperbound.

Articles and statements by students, academic administra-
tors, faculty members, and observers of the 1964 outbreak at the University of California at Berkeley. The

collection reveals the issues at stake and differences of outlook.

1902 Roszak, Theodore. THE MAKING OF A COUNTER CULTURE: REFLEC-TIONS ON THE TECHNOCRATIC SOCIETY AND ITS YOUTHFUL OPPO-SITION. Garden City, N.Y.: Doubleday, 1969. 318 p.

An exposition of the ideals of the counterculture and its mentors. Roszak sets forth the theories of Herbert Marcuse, Norman Brown, Allen Ginsburg, Alan Watts, Timothy Leary, and Paul Goodman, among others, and calls for the replacement of a society dominated by the disciplines of the natural and social sciences with one in which a visionary approach is given full sway.

p. THE SUPREME COURT UNDER WARREN

1903 Lewis, Anthony. GIDEON'S TRUMPET. New York: Random House, 1964. 262 p.

An account by the NEW YORK TIMES legal reporter of the case of Clarence Earl Gideon which, in 1963, the Supreme Court used as a vehicle to establish a person's right to legal counsel. Lewis describes Gideon's appeal to the Supreme Court, Abe Fortas's arguments in his behalf before the Court, and the implications of the decision for the legal system. In the process he provides a good account of procedures followed by the Court.

1904 Weaver, John D. WARREN: THE MAN, THE COURT, THE ERA. Boston: Little, Brown, 1967. 406 p. Port.

A highly favorable view of the governor of California and chief justice of the Supreme Court. Weaver describes the important cases that had come before Warren up to the time of writing.

q. URBAN RENEWAL

1905 Anderson, Martin. THE FEDERAL BULLDOZER: A CRITICAL ANALYSIS OF URBAN RENEWAL, 1949-1962. Cambridge, Mass.: MIT Press, 1964. 286 p. Illus.

A polemic against federal urban renewal policy. Anderson makes use of the files of the Urban Renewal Administration to show that it has failed in its goals. He is particularly critical of its failure to provide housing for low income groups.

Friedman, Lawrence M. GOVERNMENT AND SLUM HOUSING. See no. 452.

1906 Jacobs, Jane. THE DEATH AND LIFE OF GREAT AMERICAN CITIES.
New York: Random House, 1961. 458 p.

> An attack on urban renewal that proceeds by bull-
> dozing whole areas. The author contends that mixed
> neighborhoods--mixtures of residences, shops, small busi-
> nesses, etc.--are most conducive to pleasant and safe
> urban living. She gives specific examples from major
> cities.

1907 Lowe, Jeanne R. CITIES IN A RACE WITH TIME: PROGRESS AND POV-
ERTY IN AMERICA'S RENEWING CITIES. New York: Random House,
1967. 612 p. Illus., ports., maps.

> A discussion of the problems of urban renewal and the
> failure of cities, states, and the federal government to
> grapple with poverty, racial discrimination, economic
> development, and other problems that bear on urban re-
> newal. The author uses New York, New Haven, Phila-
> delphia, Pittsburgh, and Washington, D.C., as examples.

1908 Rae, John B. THE ROAD AND THE CAR IN AMERICAN LIFE. Cambridge,
Mass.: MIT Press, 1971. 404 p. Illus.

> How the face of the land and the lives of the people
> were radically changed by the introduction of the auto-
> mobile. Rae shows the relationship of road development
> to the development of vehicles, and deals with the im-
> pact on urban areas and the growth of suburbia. He is
> a partisan of the motor car.

3. Prominent Individuals

DEAN ACHESON

1909 Acheson, Dean. PRESENT AT THE CREATION: MY YEARS IN THE STATE
DEPARTMENT. New York: W.W. Norton, 1969. 812 p. Illus.

> Acheson was present at the creation of America's inter-
> national role (1941-53) as assistant secretary, undersecre-
> tary, and, for four years, secretary of state in the Tru-
> man administration. These memoirs are leisurely and
> filled with reflections on policy and personalities.

WHITTAKER CHAMBERS

1910 Chambers, Whittaker. WITNESS. New York: Random House, 1952. 808
p.

> An autobiographical account which deals with his years

as a Communist, his repudiation of the party, and his rise to fame as the accuser of Alger Hiss. Chambers has much to say about Stalinism and espionage in the United States.

JOHN FOSTER DULLES

1911 Beal, John R. JOHN FOSTER DULLES: A BIOGRAPHY. New York: Harper & Brothers, 1957. 331 p. Illus., ports.

A newsman's analysis of the secretary of state, based on his observations as a reporter assigned to Washington and on interviews with Dulles, his family, and friends. Beal deals with Dulles's earlier career as a corporation lawyer and his involvement in foreign affairs. An appreciative biography.

1912 Hoopes, Townsend. THE DEVIL AND JOHN FOSTER DULLES. Boston: Little, Brown, 1973. 576 p. Illus.

Seeks an understanding of Dulles's attitudes in his earlier life but concentrates on his career as secretary of state under Eisenhower, 1953-59. Hoopes believes Dulles's piety was out of step with the reality of the twentieth century and led him to take rigid positions where flexibility would have served the nation better.

DWIGHT D. EISENHOWER

1913 Eisenhower, Dwight D. THE WHITE HOUSE YEARS. 2 vols. Garden City, N.Y.: Doubleday, 1963-65. Illus., ports., maps.

A somewhat bland account by the ex-president of his experience as chief executive. Eisenhower tells the story in a simple, straightforward manner and conveys the patience that was obvious in his presidency. Volume 1: MANDATE FOR CHANGE, 1953-1956; volume 2: WAGING PEACE, 1956-1961.

1914 U.S. PUBLIC PAPERS OF THE PRESIDENTS OF THE UNITED STATES: DWIGHT D. EISENHOWER. 8 vols. Washington, D.C.: Government Printing Office, 1960-61. Fronts., ports.

Includes speeches, statements, press conference transcripts, etc.; one volume per year from 1953 to 1960 (actually January 1961).

J. WILLIAM FULBRIGHT

1915 Coffin, Tristram. SENATOR FULBRIGHT: PORTRAIT OF A PUBLIC PHI-

LOSOPHER. New York: E.P. Dutton, 1966. 378 p. Illus., ports.

> A highly favorable portrait of J. William Fulbright, who,
> as chairman of the Foreign Relations Committee, became
> a staunch opponent of American involvement in Vietnam.
> Coffin covers his years in law, business, and education
> as well.

ARTHUR J. GOLDBERG

1916 Moynihan, Daniel P., ed. THE DEFENSE OF FREEDOM: THE PUBLIC
PAPERS OF ARTHUR J. GOLDBERG. New York: Harper & Row, 1966.
360 p.

> Drawn from Goldberg's years as a labor lawyer, Supreme
> Court justice, and ambassador to the United Nations.
> The addresses deal with many aspects of domestic and
> international affairs and the need for each person to
> help widen the area of freedom. A good overview of
> Goldberg's social thought.

HUBERT H. HUMPHREY

1917 Sherrill, Robert, and Ernst, Harry W. DRUGSTORE LIBERAL. New York:
Grossman, 1968. 200 p.

> A barbed account of the political career of Hubert H.
> Humphrey published in the year he opposed Nixon for
> the presidency. The authors picture Humphrey as liberal
> for the sake of convenience, a man who is all things to
> all men, and a bumbler to boot.

LYNDON B. JOHNSON

1918 Evans, Rowland, Jr., and Novak, Robert D. LYNDON B. JOHNSON:
THE EXERCISE OF POWER: A POLITICAL BIOGRAPHY. New York:
New American Library, 1966. 606 p.

> A team of journalists scrutinizes the political career of
> LBJ from 1931 on. A keen analysis of the American
> political system, especially of the Senate, and how
> Johnson got on so well in it, with many lively anec-
> dotes.

1919 Geyelin, Philip L. LYNDON B. JOHNSON AND THE WORLD. New
York: Praeger, 1966. 318 p.

> An analysis of LBJ written while he was still in the presi-
> dency. Geyelin points to his strong points in foreign
> policy, but his over-all evaluation is quite critical. He

devotes much space to Johnson's intervention in the
Dominican Republic and in Vietnam.

1920 Sherrill, Robert. THE ACCIDENTAL PRESIDENT. New York: Grossman,
1967. 288 p.

A biting attack on LBJ. Sherrill attempts to demonstrate
that he is "treacherous, dishonest, manic-aggressive,
petty, [and] spoiled . . . ." He is particularly critical
of Johnson's actions in the Vietnam War.

1921 U.S. PUBLIC PAPERS OF THE PRESIDENTS OF THE UNITED STATES: LYN-
DON B. JOHNSON: CONTAINING THE PUBLIC MESSAGES, SPEECHES,
AND STATEMENTS OF THE PRESIDENT. 10 vols. Washington, D.C.:
Government Printing Office, 1965-70. Fronts.

Johnson's speeches, messages to Congress, press releases,
etc. Two volumes per year, from 1964 (actually 22
November 1963) to 1968 (actually 20 January 1969).

1922 White, William S. THE PROFESSIONAL: LYNDON B. JOHNSON:
Boston: Houghton Mifflin, 1964. 274 p.

Published during the Johnson-Goldwater campaign for
the presidency. A friend and fellow Texan looks at
LBJ as a person and a political leader. He is impressed
by what he sees.

GEORGE F. KENNAN

1923 Kennan, George F. MEMOIRS. 2 vols. Boston: Little, Brown, 1967-
72.

Kennan gives an evaluation of his years in the foreign
service and the part he played in determining American
policy. Since he was an architect of the policy of
"containment," his views on the Soviet Union are particularly worthy of note. Volume 1: 1925-1950; volume 2: 1950-1963.

JOHN F. KENNEDY

1924 Burns, James MacGregor. JOHN KENNEDY: A POLITICAL PROFILE.
New York: Harcourt, Brace & World, 1960. 309 p. Illus.

A campaign biography written for the presidential campaign, but one displaying thorough scholarship. Burns
analyzes Kennedy's political position as it emerged in
his legislative years.

1925 Gardner, John W., ed. TO TURN THE TIDE: A SELECTION FROM
PRESIDENT KENNEDY'S PUBLIC STATEMENTS, FROM HIS ELECTION
THROUGH THE 1961 ADJOURNMENT OF CONGRESS, SETTING FORTH
THE GOALS OF HIS FIRST LEGISLATIVE YEAR. New York: Harper &
Row, 1962. 235 p.

>Kennedy's speeches and statements in his early days in
>office. The foreword is by Carl Sandburg.

1926 Sorenson, Theodore. KENNEDY. New York: Harper & Row, 1965.
792 p. Port.

>An account by the president's speech writer which gives
>much detail about Kennedy's mode of operation and
>dramatically recounts such important events as the Cuban
>missile crisis. Much valuable information can be found
>here, although Sorensen has revealed little concerning
>the human frailities of his chief.

1927 U.S. PUBLIC PAPERS OF THE PRESIDENTS OF THE UNITED STATES: JOHN
F. KENNEDY: CONTAINING THE PUBLIC MESSAGES, SPEECHES, AND
STATEMENTS OF THE PRESIDENT. 3 vols. Washington, D.C.: Govern-
ment Printing Office, 1962-64. Fronts.

>Kennedy's speeches, remarks at various gatherings,
>transcripts of press conferences, messages to Congress,
>etc. One volume per year, 1961-63. The third vol-
>ume ends with a proclamation by President Lyndon B.
>Johnson of a national day of mourning following the as-
>sassination of President Kennedy.

MARTIN LUTHER KING

1928 Lewis, David L. KING: A CRITICAL BIOGRAPHY. New York: Praeger, 1970. 472 p. Illus., ports.

>The man, his thoughts, his failures, his accomplishments.
>Lewis shows how the demands of his time and race thrust
>Martin Luther King, Jr. into leadership and traces the ori-
>gins of his ideas on nonviolence and his opposition to
>the Vietnam War.

GEORGE McGOVERN

1929 Anson, Robert S. McGOVERN: A BIOGRAPHY. New York: Holt,
Rinehart and Winston, 1972. 316 p. Illus., ports.

>A favorable account of the senator from South Dakota,
>written in time for his campaign against Nixon for the
>presidency.

MALCOLM X

1930 Malcolm X, with the assistance of Alex Haley. THE AUTOBIOGRAPHY OF MALCOLM X. New York: Grove Press, 1965. 471 p. Illus., ports.

> The life of the black leader, from being a student in Detroit to Harlem pimp, to a Black Muslim, to his be- lief, shortly before he was assassinated, that American blacks are part of a world majority of dark-skinned peoples and should not resent whites. Malcolm's remi- niscences were recorded and are here transcribed by Haley. A moving account of a life of anguish and struggle.

RICHARD M. NIXON

1931 Nixon, Richard M. SIX CRISES. Garden City, N.Y.: Doubleday, 1962. 475 p.

> Publishing within two years of his defeat by Kennedy, Nixon discusses six crises in his political career. They are the Hiss case, the secret fund and the "Checkers speech," Eisenhower's heart attack, the mob attack on Nixon in Caracas, the "kitchen debate" with Khrush- chev in Russia, and the campaign of 1960.

1932 U.S. PUBLIC PAPERS OF THE PRESIDENTS: RICHARD NIXON: CON- TAINING THE PUBLIC MESSAGES, SPEECHES, AND STATEMENTS OF THE PRESIDENT. 3 vols. to date. Washington, D.C.: Government Printing Office, 1971- . Illus., fronts.

> Contains speeches, messages to Congress, transcripts of press conferences, remarks at various types of gather- ings, etc. One volume is devoted to each year, 1969- 1971.

ELEANOR ROOSEVELT

1933 Lash, Joseph P. ELEANOR: THE YEARS ALONE. New York: W.W. Norton, 1972. 368 p. Illus.

> A sequel to ELEANOR AND FRANKLIN, q.v., no. 1713. This volume picks up Mrs. Roosevelt's biography after the death of the president. A lucid narration of her service as delegate to the United Nations and as a determined participant in the affairs of the Democratic party, as well as her more private affairs.

ADLAI STEVENSON

1934 Davis, Kenneth S. THE POLITICS OF HONOR: A BIOGRAPHY OF AD-
LAI E. STEVENSON. New York: G.P. Putnam's Sons, 1967. 543 p.
Illus., ports.

> Originally published in 1957 as A PROPHET IN HIS
> OWN COUNTRY: THE TRIUMPHS AND DEFEATS OF
> ADLAI E. STEVENSON. A full biography, down to
> Stevenson's second try for the presidency in 1956.

1935 Johnson, Walter, and Evans, Carol. THE PAPERS OF ADLAI E. STEVEN-
SON. 4 vols. to date. Boston: Little, Brown, 1972- .

> Projected as a series of eight volumes. Letters, speeches,
> and documents that stemmed from Stevenson's position as
> assistant to the secretary of the navy, his role in the
> State Department in the formation of the United Nations,
> his years as governor of Illinois, and his first campaign
> for the presidency. Volume 1: THE BEGINNING OF
> EDUCATION, 1900-1941; volume 2: WASHINGTON
> TO SPRINGFIELD, 1941-1948; volume 3: GOVERNOR
> OF ILLINOIS, 1949-1953; volume 4: "LET'S TALK
> SENSE TO THE AMERICAN PEOPLE," 1952-1955.

1936 Stevenson, Adlai E. SPEECHES. New York: Random House, 1952. 128
p.

> Good examples of the lucid thought and expression of
> Stevenson as presidential candidate running on the Demo-
> cratic ticket against Dwight D. Eisenhower in 1952.
> The collection includes statements on political morality,
> international affairs, and domestic issues. Includes a
> foreword by novelist John Steinbeck and a brief biog-
> raphy of the candidate by Debs Myers and Ralph Martin.

ROBERT A. TAFT

1937 White, William S. THE TAFT STORY. New York: Harper & Brothers,
1954. 288 p. Illus., ports.

> A biographical essay that examines the role of Senator
> Robert A. Taft of Ohio in the Republican party and in
> relation to domestic and foreign policy. White is sym-
> pathetic but not uncritical.

HARRY S. TRUMAN

1938 Miller, Merle. PLAIN SPEAKING: AN ORAL BIOGRAPHY OF HARRY
S. TRUMAN. New York: Berkeley Publishing Corp.; distributed by

G.P. Putnam's Sons, 1974. 448 p.

A book derived from a series of television interviews of
ex-President Truman by Miller, which the network never
gained the courage to air. Truman is blunt and plain-
spoken in his evaluations of events and such persons as
General Douglas MacArthur.

1939 Truman, Harry S. MEMOIRS. 2 vols. Garden City, N.Y.: Doubleday,
1955-56.

Truman, in his usual plain-speaking manner, gives his
version of the challenging events of his presidency.
Volume 1: YEAR OF DECISIONS; volume 2: YEARS
OF TRIAL AND HOPE.

1940 U.S. PUBLIC PAPERS OF THE PRESIDENTS OF THE UNITED STATES:
HARRY S. TRUMAN: CONTAINING THE PUBLIC MESSAGES, SPEECHES
AND STATEMENTS OF THE PRESIDENT. 8 vols. Washington, D.C.:
Government Printing Office, 1961. Fronts.

Among the materials included: addresses and speeches,
messages to Congress, war messages, proclamations,
transcripts of press conferences. Volume 1 begins with
12 April 1945; volume 8 concludes with 20 January
1953. Each volume contains the papers for one year.

EARL WARREN

1941 Christman, Henry M. THE PUBLIC PAPERS OF CHIEF JUSTICE EARL
WARREN. New York: Simon and Schuster, 1959. 237 p.

Covers the years 1945-57, including Warren's service as
governor of California. Among the topics dealt with:
education, civil rights, public health, penal reform,
Justice Brandeis, and Senator La Follette.

B. THE UNITED STATES AS A WORLD POWER

1. General

1942 Agar, Herbert. THE PRICE OF POWER: AMERICA SINCE 1945. Chicago: University of Chicago Press, 1957. 199 p.

A treatment of the U.S. position in the world since
World War II. Agar analyzes events in light of the
American character and calls for a thoughtful approach
to the future in a world of Cold War.

1943 Kohn, Hans. AMERICAN NATIONALISM: AN INTERPRETIVE ESSAY.

New York: Macmillan, 1957. 272 p.

> Puts in the perspective of world affairs the development
> of American nationalism, which Kohn sees as having
> particular characteristics.

1944 Rostow, Walt W. THE UNITED STATES IN THE WORLD ARENA: AN
ESSAY IN RECENT HISTORY. New York: Harper & Brothers, 1960.
580 p. Tables, diagrs.

> An extended essay which deals with American develop-
> ments over a quarter century--with some looking back to
> earlier history--to determine how military and foreign
> policy has been affected by the nature of American
> life and how the nation can meet the demands made on
> it as a world power.

2. Topical

a. THE COLD WAR AND DIPLOMACY

1945 Baldwin, David A. ECONOMIC DEVELOPMENT AND AMERICAN FOR-
EIGN POLICY, 1943-1962. Chicago: University of Chicago Press, 1966.
292 p.

> A specialized work on economic policy. Baldwin at-
> tempts to show the reasoning by which the United States
> came to the decision to make "soft" rather than "hard"
> loans ("soft" being defined as long-term loans with low
> or no interest).

1946 Ball, George W. THE DISCIPLINE OF POWER: ESSENTIALS OF A MOD-
ERN WORLD STRUCTURE. Boston: Little, Brown, 1968. 364 p.

> Ball served as undersecretary of state under Kennedy and
> Johnson. This is a wide-ranging collection of his speeches,
> lectures, and articles on world problems facing the Uni-
> ted States; includes his prescription for future action.

1947 Brown, Seyom. THE FACES OF POWER: CONSTANCY AND CHANGE
IN UNITED STATES FOREIGN POLICY FROM TRUMAN TO JOHNSON.
New York: Columbia University Press, 1968. 410 p.

> Shows the basic continuity of foreign policy in the ad-
> ministrations of Truman, Eisenhower, Kennedy, and John-
> son, especially in those aspects having to do with the
> Cold War. The application of military and economic
> leverage by successive administrations is analyzed.

1948 Byrnes, James F. SPEAKING FRANKLY. New York: Harper & Brothers,
1947. 336 p. Ports.

A personal account of Byrnes's attendance as an observer
at the Yalta conference and of most of his time as secretary of state. He is highly critical of the Russians and
seems to call for a military confrontation. An important
document of the Cold War.

1949 Douglas, Paul H. AMERICA IN THE MARKET PLACE: TRADE, TARIFFS
AND THE BALANCE OF PAYMENTS. New York: Holt, Rinehart & Winston, 1966. 390 p.

A contemporary argument for free trade. Douglas believes that it would allow nations to specialize their
production. Furthermore, he takes the position that it
is morally as well as economically sound.

1950 Drummond, Roscoe, and Coblentz, Gaston. DUEL AT THE BRINK: JOHN
FOSTER DULLES' COMMAND OF AMERICAN POWER. Garden City,
N.Y.: Doubleday, 1960. 240 p. Illus.

An impartial appraisal of Dulles as secretary of state,
1953-59. Much of the material on which the book is
based was gathered by the two journalists from heads of
state, foreign ministers, and senior diplomats of other
nations with whom Dulles had dealings.

1951 Fleming, D.F. THE COLD WAR AND ITS ORIGINS, 1917-1960. 2 vols.
Garden City, N.Y.: Doubleday, 1961.

This study of the Cold War goes back to the beginnings
of the Soviet state and U.S. reaction to it and traces
the story to 1960. Fleming makes it clear that he does
not believe the Cold War was inevitable. It had its
origins in U.S. unwillingness to accept the idea that
the Soviets' major concern was with their own security
and the resultant domination of Eastern Europe.

1952 Fulbright, J. William. THE ARROGANCE OF POWER. New York: Random House, 1967. 280 p.

In original form the Christian A. Herter Lectures, Johns
Hopkins University, 1966; the chairman of the Senate
Foreign Relations Committee in a biting analysis of foreign policy in the Johnson administration. Fulbright
discusses American Cold War mentality and policy on
Russia, China, and Latin America, and gives a specific
plan for settlement of the Vietnam War.

1953 Graebner, Norman A. THE NEW ISOLATIONISM: A STUDY IN POLI-
TICS AND FOREIGN POLICY SINCE 1950. New York: Ronald Press,
1956. 289 p.

The impact of conservative political forces on the foreign

policies of the Truman and Eisenhower administrations,
in an analysis by a diplomatic historian.

1954 Halle, Louis. THE COLD WAR AS HISTORY. New York: Harper & Row,
1967. 448 p.

An analysis by a former member of the State Department.
Halle attempts to see the Cold War from the perspective
of both sides. He believes that both the Soviets and
the United States have misunderstood each other's intentions on numerous occasions.

1955 Herz, Martin F. BEGINNINGS OF THE COLD WAR. Bloomington: Indiana University Press, 1966. 224 p. Maps.

Primarily a narrative of the Yalta agreement and how
Poland was transformed into a Communist state under the
hegemony of the Soviet Union.

1956 Hilsman, Roger. TO MOVE A NATION: THE POLITICS OF FOREIGN
POLICY IN THE ADMINISTRATION OF JOHN F. KENNEDY. Garden
City, N.Y.: Doubleday, 1967. 624 p. Maps.

The foreign policy crises of the Kennedy administration,
from the perspective of a former member of the State
Department. Although critical of Kennedy in some things,
over-all he credits him with great successes. Among
the problems covered are the Bay of Pigs, the Cuban
missile crisis, Laos, the Congo, Indonesia, Malaysia,
China, and Vietnam.

1957 Horowitz, David. THE FREE WORLD COLOSSUS: A CRITIQUE OF AMERI-
CAN FOREIGN POLICY IN THE COLD WAR. Rev. ed. New York:
Hill and Wang, 1971. 466 p.

Horowitz measures U.S. actions by the ideals of liberty,
equality, and self-determination and finds them wanting.
America, because of possession of the atomic bomb, had
the power to settle differences with Russia and achieve
a world of peace, but instead followed a counter-
revolutionary policy.

1958 Kissinger, Henry A. NUCLEAR WEAPONS AND FOREIGN POLICY. New
York: Harper & Brothers, 1957. 455 p. Illus.

The product of three years of discussions by experts in
various fields assembled by the Council on Foreign Relations. It calls for a radical reappraisal of American
military and foreign policies in light of the development
of nuclear weapons.

1959 Kolko, Joyce, and Kolko, Gabriel. THE LIMITS OF POWER: THE WORLD AND UNITED STATES FOREIGN POLICY, 1945-1954. New York: Harper & Row, 1972. 832 p.

> The authors elaborate their thesis that U.S. actions in the international sphere in this century have been the result of a capitalist desire to dominate the world and insure stability at home. They have dug deeply into the record to substantiate their point of view. This study concerns itself with the Truman policy in Greece, Korea, and in the arms race.

1960 LaFeber, Walter. AMERICA, RUSSIA, AND THE COLD WAR, 1945-1966. 2d ed. New York: Wiley, 1972. 340 p. Maps.

> Looks at the springs of the Cold War in the domestic politics as well as the foreign policies of the two nations. LaFeber is critical of American policy, suggesting that an accommodation could be made with the Soviets.

1961 Spanier, John W. AMERICAN FOREIGN POLICY SINCE WORLD WAR II. 6th ed. New York: Praeger, 1973. 318 p.

> Spanier reviews American efforts from 1945 to the present to rebuild Europe through the Marshall Plan; the disruption of the alliance with the Soviet Union and the Cold War; the formation of NATO and other alliances around the world; the Korean War; and American intervention in places as diverse as Lebanon and the Dominican Republic. He attempts to show that the liberal, rational approach to power leaves the United States at a disadvantage in dealing with the Soviet Union.

1962 Stillman, Edmund, and Pfaff, William. POWER AND IMPOTENCE: THE FAILURE OF AMERICA'S FOREIGN POLICY. New York: Random House, 1966. 244 p.

> A critique of American foreign policy, which the authors believe is based on the assumption of American moral superiority to the rest of the world. They challenge the idea that the United States can impose its will everywhere and call for a policy in line with current realities.

1963 Trefousse, Hans L., ed. THE COLD WAR: A BOOK OF DOCUMENTS. New York: G.P. Putnam's Sons, 1965. 317 p.

> Covers the period 1 January 1942 (Declaration of the United Nations) to 7 August 1964 (U.S. Congressional Tonkin Gulf Resolution). Trefousse includes essential documents with brief comments.

1964 Ulam, Adam B. THE RIVALS: AMERICA AND RUSSIA SINCE WORLD WAR II. New York: Viking Press, 1971. 411 p.

> Takes what the author labels a realistic position toward the foreign policy of the United States, rejecting recent "New Left" scholarship. Ulam believes questions of morality concerning actions past and present are irrelevant in the conduct of international relations. He includes a detailed analysis of Soviet actions in the Cold War.

1965 Williams, William Appleman. THE TRAGEDY OF AMERICAN DIPLOMACY. 2d rev. and enl. ed. New York: Dell, 1972. 317 p. Paperbound.

> Williams is quite critical of American foreign policy, seeing continuity in the U.S. Open Door Policy and a type of economic imperialism practiced today.

b. THE CUBAN MISSILE CRISIS

1966 Abel, Elie. THE MISSILE CRISIS. Philadelphia: Lippincott, 1966. 220 p. Illus., ports., map, facsim.

> A journalist's account of the American-Soviet confrontation over the placing of missiles by the latter in Cuba. Abel follows events a step at a time from 14 to 28 October 1962.

1967 Divine, Robert A., ed. THE CUBAN MISSILE CRISIS. Chicago: Quadrangle Books, 1971. 248 p.

> A collection of pieces by political scientists, journalists, and others, interpreting the event as well as the statements and exchanges of Nikita Khruschev and John F. Kennedy.

1968 Kennedy, Robert F. THIRTEEN DAYS: A MEMOIR OF THE CUBAN MISSILE CRISIS. New York: W.W. Norton, 1969. 224 p. Illus., ports., facsim.

> The president's brother and close advisor at the time of the crisis, and attorney general in his administration, gives his view of the crisis as seen from the center of government. The manuscript was unfinished at the time of Senator Kennedy's assassination. Documents are appended.

c. EUROPE AND NATO

1969 Davison, Walter P. THE .BERLIN BLOCKADE: A STUDY IN COLD WAR

POLITICS. Princeton, N.J.: Princeton University Press, 1958. 423 p. Illus., ports., maps.

A product of the RAND Corporation. Davison describes the political situation in the few years preceding the 1948 blockade and analyzes that event. Much of his material is derived from witnesses.

1970 Osgood, Robert E. NATO: ENTANGLING ALLIANCE. Chicago: University of Chicago Press, 1962. 416 p.

A discussion of the formation and operation of the North Atlantic Treaty Organization, with concentration on its military aspects and political implications. Osgood firmly supports the organization.

1971 Schmitt, Hans A. THE PATH TO EUROPEAN UNION, FROM THE MARSHALL PLAN TO THE COMMON MARKET. Baton Rouge: Louisiana State University Press, 1962. 284 p. Tables, diagrs.

The forces working for unification of Europe are analyzed. Schmitt examines the Schuman Plan, the European Coal and Steel Community, and the Treaty of Rome (1957), and discusses prospects for the future.

1972 Zink, Harold. THE UNITED STATES IN GERMANY, 1944-1955. Princeton, N.J.: Van Nostrand, 1957. 384 p. Illus., ports., maps.

The U.S. occupation of Germany following World War II. Although the author was chief historian of the office of the U.S. High Commission, he is quite critical of certain phases of the military occupation and its personnel.

d. THE FAR EAST

1973 Fairbank, John K. THE UNITED STATES AND CHINA. 3d ed. Cambridge, Mass.: Harvard University Press, 1971. 516 p. Maps.

Places recent developments in China in the broad context of her long history. Fairbank is concerned with cultural as well as political matters. He reviews American involvement in Chinese affairs since the nineteenth century.

1974 Kawai, Kazuo. JAPAN'S AMERICAN INTERLUDE. Chicago: University of Chicago Press, 1960. 257 p.

U.S. occupation of Japan following World War II in an interpretation by a former Tokyo editor. Kawai deals with education, economics, the constitution, the place of the emperor, etc.

1975 Reischauer, Edwin O. THE UNITED STATES AND JAPAN. 3d ed. Cambridge, Mass.: Harvard University Press, 1965. 422 p. Maps.

> The diplomatic relations of the two nations, by the noted scholar of Japanese life, first published in 1950. This edition includes a revised chapter on postwar trends and the text of the treaty between the two nations.

e. THE KOREAN WAR

1976 Berger, Carl. THE KOREA KNOT: A MILITARY-POLITICAL HISTORY. Rev. ed. Philadelphia: University of Pennsylvania Press, 1965. 255 p. Map.

> The background of the Korean War and how the United States became embroiled in it. The author manages to maintain his objective stance in such emotion-producing developments as the recall of General MacArthur by President Truman.

1977 Higgins, Trumbull. KOREA AND THE FALL OF MACARTHUR: A PRECIS IN LIMITED WAR. New York: Oxford University Press, 1960. 230 p. Illus.

> A military historian's analysis of the recall of General MacArthur. Higgins relates domestic politics and the military situation in Korea and is critical of MacArthur for failing to follow civilian directives.

1978 Rees, David. KOREA: THE LIMITED WAR. New York: St. Martin's Press, 1964. 525 p. Illus., ports., maps.

> A Welsh historian's analysis of the implications of U.S. policy of containment of communism in the context of Korea. The author believes Truman's decision to pursue a limited war followed from the containment policy. He deals with all aspects of the struggle.

1979 Rovere, Richard H., and Schlesinger, Arthur M., Jr. THE GENERAL AND THE PRESIDENT AND THE FUTURE OF AMERICAN FOREIGN POLICY. New York: Farrar, Straus and Young, 1951. 336 p. Illus., map.

> The collaboration of a journalist and a historian on the conflict between President Truman and General MacArthur as to whose policy would prevail in the Korean War. The authors dissect MacArthur's career and personality and the implications of his recall and dismissal by Truman. They also look at American foreign policy as implemented by the president.

1980 Spanier, John W. THE TRUMAN-MacARTHUR CONTROVERSY AND THE

KOREAN WAR. Cambridge, Mass.: Harvard University Press, 1959. 323 p. Illus.

Uses the Truman–MacArthur disagreement on policy as a vehicle for an examination of the relations of civil authority and the military in context of a limited war. In the process, he discusses thoroughly the issues involved in the Korean War.

f. LATIN AMERICA

1981 Levinson, Jerome, and Onis, Juan de. THE ALLIANCE THAT LOST ITS WAY: A CRITICAL REPORT ON THE ALLIANCE FOR PROGRESS. Chicago: Quadrangle Books, 1970. 392 p.

This evaluation concludes that the Alliance was a failure, creating expectations followed by disillusionment. Levinson, earlier an official of the U.S. Agency for International Development, and Onis, a Latin American correspondent of the NEW YORK TIMES, set forth the origins of the Alliance and show how it worked in specific countries.

1982 Martin, John B. OVERTAKEN BY EVENTS: THE DOMINICAN CRISIS FROM THE FALL OF TRUJILLO TO THE CIVIL WAR. Garden City, N.Y.: Doubleday, 1966. 836 p. Illus., ports., maps.

The former U.S. ambassador to the Dominican Republic gives a first-hand account of the American intervention in 1965. In dramatic terms, he describes the complexities of the political situation and the embassy staff's attempt to deal with the chaos.

1983 Smith, Robert F. THE UNITED STATES AND CUBA: BUSINESS AND DIPLOMACY, 1917–1960. New York: Bookman, 1961. 256 p.

Smith takes the view that, although the United States has claimed an interest in self-determination, in the case of Cuba it has been on the side of the status quo. Government and business were interested in protecting American financial interests. Heavily documented.

g. THE MILITARY

1984 Hammond, Paul Y. ORGANIZING FOR DEFENSE: THE AMERICAN MILITARY ESTABLISHMENT IN THE TWENTIETH CENTURY. Princeton, N.J.: Princeton University Press, 1961. 414 p.

Hammond traces back to 1903 the origins of the present American military organization. He relates the organizational structure of the armed forces to the U.S. political system.

1985 Roberts, Chalmers M. THE NUCLEAR YEARS: THE ARMS RACE AND
ARMS CONTROL, 1945-1970. New York: Praeger, 1970. 170 p. Illus.

A history of disarmament negotiations from the close of
World War II to the Strategic Arms Limitation Talks
(SALT). Roberts includes valuable appendices: the
Baruch Plan; aerial inspection proposals ("open skies")
by the countries of the West and the Soviets; the treaty
banning tests of nuclear weapons in the atmosphere, in
outer space, and underwater; and the treaty on the non-
proliferation of nuclear weapons, 1 July 1968.

1986 Schwarz, Urs. AMERICAN STRATEGY: A NEW PERSPECTIVE: THE
GROWTH OF POLITICO-MILITARY THINKING IN THE UNITED STATES.
Garden City, N.Y.: Doubleday, 1966. 192 p.

A Swiss journalist sketches the history of American strategy but devotes most of the book to an analysis of developments since World War II.

h. UNITED NATIONS AND COLLECTIVE SECURITY

1987 Coyle, David Cushman. THE UNITED NATIONS AND HOW IT WORKS.
New ed. New York: Columbia University Press, 1966. 222 p.

A practical guide to the United Nations and how its
various functions are carried out. Among the topics
dealt with are: education, science, and culture; money
and trade; technical services; human rights; non-self-
governing peoples; international disputes; regional arrangements; disarmament; outer space and the atom; organization of the UN; and philosophy of the UN.

1988 Stromberg, Roland N. COLLECTIVE SECURITY AND AMERICAN FOREIGN
POLICY: FROM THE LEAGUE OF NATIONS TO NATO. New York:
Praeger, 1963. 301 p.

A critical appraisal of the American view of collective
security, which Stromberg sees as passe. He demonstrates that the concern for maintenance of a national sovereignty and inability of participants in a pact to agree
on a definition of aggression have severely limited the
concept.

j. THE VIETNAM WAR

1989 Cooper, Chester L. THE LOST CRUSADE: AMERICA IN VIETNAM. New
York: Dodd, Mead, 1970. 570 p.

A dispassionate, thorough account of U.S. involvement,

with concentration on the 1960s, the "Decade of Viet-nam." The author, who witnessed the events from within the government bureaucracy, attempts to tell the story as it was seen by participants with the same vantage point.

1990 Fall, Bernard B. THE TWO VIET-NAMS: A POLITICAL AND MILITARY ANALYSIS. 2d rev. ed. New York: Praeger, 1967. 520 p. Maps.

Sets Vietnam into the frame of Southeast Asia and French colonialism and traces its history to the division between North and South. Fall describes the careers of Ho Chi Minh and other prominent leaders and traces the political fragmentation of the country and the resultant war.

1991 Gravel, Mike, ed. THE PENTAGON PAPERS. The Senator Gravel Edition. 5 vols. Boston: Beacon Press, 1972.

The secret history of the U.S. involvement in Vietnam, written by staff members of the Department of Defense, parts of which were leaked to the newspapers by Daniel Ellsberg. This edition, supplied by Senator Gravel for publication, includes critical essays by Noam Chomsky and Howard Zinn.

1992 Halberstam, David. THE BEST AND THE BRIGHTEST. New York: Random House, 1972. 688 p.

Halberstam sets out to demonstrate how the "best and the brightest," earnest men and intellectuals in the Kennedy-Johnson administrations, dragged the country into the mire of Vietnam. The book is a combination of narrative and analysis of why the tragedy occurred.

1993 Hoopes, Townsend. THE LIMITS OF INTERVENTION: AN INSIDE AC-COUNT OF HOW THE JOHNSON POLICY OF ESCALATION IN VIET-NAM WAS REVERSED. Rev. ed. New York: David McKay, 1973. 270 p.

Hoopes, under secretary of the air force in the Johnson administration, gives an account of the maneuvering that led to LBJ's decision to withdraw from the presidential race (31 March 1968) and to link it with a de-escalation of American participation in the Vietnam War.

1994 Kahin, George McT., and Lewis, John W. THE UNITED STATES IN VIETNAM. Rev. ed. New York: Dial Press, 1969. 560 p. Maps.

Sketches the ancient history of Vietnam in order to provide understanding for the modern period, coverage of which comprises most of the book. The authors describe the various nationalistic attempts to overthrow the French

until success was achieved by the Vietminh at Dien
Bien Phu in 1954. They are very critical of the Americans as successors of the French.

1995 Shaplen, Robert. THE LOST REVOLUTION: THE U.S. IN VIETNAM,
1946-1966. Rev. ed. New York: Harper & Row, 1966. 428 p. Paperbound.

Concentrates on U.S. mistakes in Vietnam, both political and military. Shaplen compares the North and the
South, usually to the former's advantage. Although he
writes that the South Vietnamese and the Americans
have done badly in guerilla war, he does not recom-
mend withdrawal but persistence until an accommodation
can be reached with China.

C. PROMINENT INDIVIDUALS

For Prominent Individuals in this period, see 9,A,3.

AUTHOR AND SHORT TITLE INDEX

In addition to authors and short titles, this index includes editors, compilers, translators, and those who have contributed introductions and forewords to works cited in the text.

Index entries refer to entry numbers rather than page numbers.

Author and Short Title Index

1711, 1786

Burr, George Lincoln, (ed.) NARRA-
TIVES OF WITCHCRAFT CASES
597

Burr, Nelson, CRITICAL BIBLIOGRAPHY
OF RELIGION IN AMERICA 62;
RELIGION IN AMERICAN LIFE 91

Bush-Brown, Albert, ARCHITECTURE
OF AMERICA 249

BUSINESS HISTORY REVIEW 165

Butterfield, Lyman H., (ed.) ADAMS
FAMILY CORRESPONDENCE 727;
(ed.) DIARY AND AUTOBIOGRA-
PHY OF JOHN ADAMS 728; (ed.)
EARLIEST DIARY OF JOHN ADAMS
729; (ed.) LETTERS OF BENJAMIN
RUSH 787

Byrnes, James F., ALL IN ONE LIFE-
TIME 1783; SPEAKING FRANKLY
1948

C

Calef, Robert, (selection) 597

Calhoun, John, PAPERS 1088; (selection) 937

Callcott, Wilfrid H., CARIBBEAN
POLICY OF U.S. 1423

Callow, Alexander B., Jr., TWEED
RING 1365

Campbell, Angus, AMERICAN VOTER
1824

Campbell, Charles S., Jr., ANGLO-
AMERICAN UNDERSTANDING
1428; SPECIAL BUSINESS INTER-
ESTS AND OPEN DOOR POLICY
1432

Campbell, Christina McF., FARM
BUREAU AND NEW DEAL 1663

Campbell, E.G., REORGANIZATION
OF AMERICAN RAILROAD SYS-
TEM 1356

Campbell, Stanley W., SLAVE CATCH-
ERS 1037

CANADIAN REVIEW OF AMERICAN
STUDIES 148

Canby, Henry Seidel, THOREAU 1012

Capers, Gerald M., STEPHEN A.
DOUGLAS 1095

Cappon, Lester J., (ed.) ADAMS-
JEFFERSON LETTERS 730

Carmichael, Stokely, BLACK POWER
1797

Carnegie, Andrew, GOSPEL OF
WEALTH 1283

Carpenter, Jesse T., SOUTH AS A
CONSCIOUS MINORITY 1063

Carr, Robert K., HOUSE COMMITTEE
ON UN-AMERICAN ACTIVITIES
1825

Carroll, E. Malcolm, ORIGINS OF
WHIG PARTY 921

Carter, Everett, HOWELLS AND AGE
OF REALISM 1345

Carter, Harvey L., FAR WESTERN
FRONTIERS 69

Carter, Hodding, ANGRY SCAR 1221

Carter, Paul H., DECLINE AND RE-
VIVAL OF SOCIAL GOSPEL 1608

Case, Robert O., WE CALLED IT CUL-
TURE 1593

Case, Victoria, WE CALLED IT CUL-
TURE 1593

Cash, Wilbur J., MIND OF SOUTH
1064

Cassara, Beverly Benner, (ed.) AMERI-
CAN WOMEN 1816

Cassidy, Vincent H., SEA AROUND
THEM: ATLANTIC OCEAN, A.D.
1250 459

CATHOLIC HISTORICAL REVIEW 166

Catterall, Ralph C.H., SECOND
BANK OF U.S. 915

Catton, Bruce, CENTENNIAL HISTORY
OF CIVIL WAR 1110; GLORY
ROAD 1167; U.S. GRANT AND
AMERICAN MILITARY TRADITION
1234; MR. LINCOLN'S ARMY
1168; STILLNESS AT APPOMATTOX
1169; THIS HALLOWED GROUND
1170; WAR LORDS OF WASHING-
TON 1752

Cayton, Horace R., BLACK METROPO-
LIS 1798

Chafee, Zechariah, FREE SPEECH IN
U.S. 406

Chalmers, David M., HOODED AMERI-
CANISM 1222; SOCIAL AND PO-
LITICAL IDEAS OF MUCKRAKERS
1489; (ed.) I.M. Tarbell, HISTORY
OF STANDARD OIL COMPANY
1456

Chamberlain, John, FAREWELL TO RE-
FORM 1445

Chamberlain, William Henry, AMERI-

Author and Short Title Index

M

Author and Short Title Index

O

Y

Yearns, Wilfred B., CONFEDERATE CONGRESS 1129

Young, George B., POLITICS, STRATEGY, AND AMERICAN DIPLOMACY 1429

Young, James S., WASHINGTON COMMUNITY, 1800-1828 857

Young, Margaret Labash, (ed.) DIRECTORY OF SPECIAL LIBRARIES 114

Young, Roland A., CONGRESSIONAL POLITICS IN SECOND WORLD WAR 1750

Z

Zabriskie, Edward H., AMERICAN-RUSSIAN RIVALRY IN THE FAR EAST 1431

Zangrando, Robert L., (ed.) CIVIL RIGHTS AND AMERICAN NEGRO 260

Ziff, Larzer, AMERICAN 1890'S 1347; CAREER OF JOHN COTTON 602; (ed.) LITERATURE OF AMERICA: COLONIAL PERIOD 577

Zilversmit, Arthur, FIRST EMANCIPATION: ABOLITION OF SLAVERY IN NORTH 1049

Zink, Harold, CITY BOSSES IN U.S. 1591; U.S. IN GERMANY 1972

Zinn, Howard, LA GUARDIA IN CONGRESS 1630; (selection) 1991

Zobel, Hiller B., (ed.) LEGAL PAPERS OF JOHN ADAMS 734

Zuckerman, Michael, PEACEABLE KINGDOMS: NEW ENGLAND TOWNS IN EIGHTEENTH CENTURY 531

SUBJECT INDEX

Index entries refer to entry numbers rather than page numbers.

Subject Index